Teaching Mathematics

Critical Education Practice
(Vol. 7)
Garland Reference Library of Social Science
(Vol. 1097)

Critical Education Practice

Shirley R. Steinberg and Joe L. Kincheloe, Series Editors

Curriculum Development in the Postmodern Era
by Patrick Slattery

Occupied Reading
Critical Foundations for an Ecological Theory
by Alan A. Block

Anatomy of a Collaboration
Study of a College of Education/Public School Partnership
by Judith J. Slater

Becoming a Student of Teaching
Methodologies for Exploring Self and School Context
by Robert V. Bullough, Jr. and Andrew D. Gitlin

Democracy, Multiculturalism, and the Community College
A Critical Perspective
by Robert A. Rhoads and James R. Valadez

Teaching Mathematics
Toward a Sound Alternative
by Brent Davis

Teaching Mathematics

Toward a Sound Alternative

Brent Davis

GARLAND PUBLISHING, INC.
New York & London
1996

Library of Congress Cataloging-in-Publication Data

Davis, Brent.
Teaching mathematics : toward a sound alternative / Brent Davis.
p. cm. — (Garland reference library of social science ; vol. 1097. Critical education practice ; vol. 7)
Includes bibliographical references and index.
ISBN 0-8153-2297-6 (hardcover) ; (alk. paper)
ISBN 0-8153-2298-4 (paperback) ; (alk. paper)
1. Mathematics—Study and teaching. I. Title. II. Series: Garland reference library of social science ; v. 1097. III. Series: Garland reference library of social science. Critical education practice ; vol. 7.
QA11.D3468 1996
510'.71—dc20 96–1697
CIP

Cover drawing by the author.
Paperback cover design by Karin Badger.

Printed on acid-free, 250-year-life paper
Manufactured in the United States of America

This work is dedicated to my parents,
Ruby Kathleen Davis and Gordon Robert Davis

Contents

Series Editor's Preface

Who Would Have Ever Thought?

Shirley R. Steinberg

If I could have peered into my future twenty years ago and had seen that I would be writing a preface for a book on teaching mathematics, I would have stated firmly that my vision had been flawed and I was having someone else's screened in front of me. However, here I am, and here is Brent's book, *Teaching Mathematics: Toward a Sound Alternative.* Maybe if I had had a teacher like Brent for arithmetic and mathematics, I would not have found the vision so ludicrous.

However, it is precisely my fear and hatred of mathematics and repulsion toward it that drew Joe Kincheloe and myself to search for an author, a scholar, a teacher who could contextualize mathematics, make meaning from the meaning of mathematics and somehow make the "hurt" go away. We believe firmly that Brent has accomplished this fete/feat with this new book. Hopefully, both new and seasoned teachers will read this book and reinforce desires to "see": within the teaching and, more importantly, within the learning of mathematics.

In his search for definition and meaning, Brent has called for the integration—a symbiosis with the senses, more specifically, the hermeneutic act of "listening" to uncover and develop the talent (I mean talent, not act or process) of becoming a teacher and a student in arithmetic and mathematics. He does this both lyrically and theoretically, giving the *Critical Education Practice* series a book meant for both those who love and those (like myself) who hate numbers and making sense of them.

Enjoy this volume. I did, to my pleasant surprise. Would I could turn back the clock to those days when all I heard was:

Don't worry about it; math isn't important for girls.

I'm sick and tired of hearing that math is hard; you are just not applying yourself. How many times do I have to go over this?

Maybe you should look for a college that uses alternative admittance exams.

Shirley, I have told you over and over again: you must follow the formula exactly. It doesn't matter if you just come up with the right answer.

And finally:

This class is *essential to your education. Of course you will use it; someday you will be grateful that we made you take math.*

OK, maybe that last one was right: at least I had something to relate to in order to introduce Brent's book.

Foreword

Susan E.B. Pirie

"This simple question . . . goes way beyond our power of imagination. I mean I cannot explain this to you in visual terms. Of course I can do it in mathematical equations, but there's no metaphor for it."

"How can you live in a world that's unmetaphorical? I mean you have to perceive reality in one way."

—From *Mindwalk: A Film for Passionate Thinkers.* Paramount, 1990

Look at the cover of this book. What do you see? An ear, alert to the whisperings of understanding filtered from the reverberating clamor that plays around the nautilus shell? When you know what you are intended to perceive, it is hard to see otherwise, especially when the interpretation, as in this case, is such a sound one. Ignorant of the intended contextualizing title for the book when first shown the picture, I was drawn to a different "seeing." My first construal focused on the fetus curled at the heart of a recursively growing world, a new life connected to, developing from, and feeding on the richness of its past, but emerging from the many chambers of its history to display the art of teaching afresh. I dwell a little on this event because it exemplifies precisely what Davis would have us do: he would have us reconceptualize the notion of teaching through other metaphors. His thesis is that the listening ear can offer a new life to classroom mathematics. He takes on the tremendous task of integrating both the theoretical exploration of the roots of our mathematics and our learning, and the pragmatic practicalities of the teaching of mathematics. My task in these few pages is to provide a "foreword" to his work. What might this invitation mean? Clearly the writing of this foreword comes after the birth of the book, after I have engaged with the ideas and arguments it proposes, and in this sense it might be more appropriately termed an "afterword," influenced as it so obviously must be by what I have read. Its purpose is not to signpost the ways through the text; this Davis does himself in his own Front Word and I shall not be so presumptuous as to suggest that it is the "key to his communication." Wondering, then, I turned to Webster: "Front matter likely to be of interest but not necessarily essential for the understanding of the text of a book." I can live with that.

So, what of the book itself? It first came to me as a fat ringbinder of some four hundred pages. Hardly the stuff of armchair reading, and yet I was caught by the seditious play with words and the seductive patterning of ideas. I was held, in the way that any good novel can hold the reader, by the braiding of plot and theme, of issues for teaching and theoretical foundations, of characters and contexts. Here the players are learners, teachers, and mathematics itself. Their evolving and complex relationships form the fabric of his story. This is not a scientifically presented research report; it makes no more sense to read the introduction and then turn to the end to look for the conclusions than it does to read the opening lines of a mystery story to discover the protagonists and then to turn to the last page to see "who dunnit." Nor is it a "how to do it" recipe—there are no activities to take into the classroom on Monday, although looked at in another light its central message is mooting a way of doing and being in the classroom. What we have been given is a provocatively unfolding story of what it might mean to teach mathematics.

The insistence, especially within the social and cultural environment of an academic community, on the production of fossilizing, written artifacts, on the laying out, in concrete form, of our thinking, denies the possibilities inherent in an oral tradition of storytelling, a tradition which served to bind rather than to fragment communities, which through the exchange of transient sounds involved both the teller and the listener in the evolutionary enacting of ideas. Would Davis have preferred to tell his story this way? I like to think so. Certainly his plea for conceiving the classroom as a conversation is at odds with a convention that prescribes textbooks to be systematically worked through, thus inhibiting the natural unfolding and folding back that are so essential to the real growth of understanding.

This is not necessarily a comfortable book. No sooner have we been enticed into commitment to his redefining of the notions of the nature of both the knowledge and the knower of mathematics than we are brought suddenly and starkly face to face with accepted notions of curriculum. Davis is attempting to communicate to us, deeply and seriously, an altered way of enacting the world of teaching. His approach is not through challenging and attacking taken-for-granted preconceptions, although these are exposed for what they are—our conceptions only. Rather he invites us to inventise,* to take the status quo, the classroom as we know it, and render the familiar strange, with a view to exploring possibilities thus revealed. To this end we are presented with a framing through the metaphor of listening.

If we are looking to inventise the field of teaching, then mathematics itself also needs to be reconceptualized. The power of metaphorical framings is evident, and at one level I see mathematics as a connected collection of interdependent and related metaphors within which the learner lives. Metaphors, which begin as analogies to the world around us, are expanded, distorted, exploited, but rarely totally discarded, until eventually they are distilled for their pure abstracted essence. This essence is not the mathematics, however, but its simple enactment. What mathematics is comes out of who I am, and yet I cannot come to understand mathematics in any other way than through the fabric of my metaphorical understanding. One of the concerns of enactivism is a redefining of self and I wish to pause here for a moment and play with the notion of *mathematics* as "a self," a self that is a "nexus of meaning rather than an unchanging entity." This digression is not intended as an indulgent conceit but as an exploration offering insight to

* "Inventising" is a descriptor invented for the outermost layer of the Pirie-Kieren model for the growth of understanding: ". . . a person at this level has a full structured understanding and may therefore be able to break away from the preconceptions which brought about this understanding and create new questions which might grow into a totally new concept" (Pirie & Kieren, 1994, p. 171).

teaching. Let us construe mathematics not as a human endeavor, but as itself a living being. It breathes—it can inspire. It is one who plays rather than the play itself. It paints pictures of the world in which we live. We can engage it in conversation, but when it speaks we must remember that it is our choice whether to heed what it is saying or not. As with any persuasive orator, it speaks eloquently, but from a personal perspective that we can decide to ignore. Its world view does not have to be ours. It is saying "here is a way of being, and in this being lies *a* (but not *the*) potential for growth and change." How might such a re-envisioning of mathematics affect the classroom? How much less frightening might it seem to children? What if they were encouraged to resist its bullying and to see its problems as living possibilities and not as mandated chores? What if mathematics were seen as having wings to fly them to an enchanted isle? I invite you to explore and exploit this metaphor of mathematics as living and being. Feel and listen to the altered emotions and comprehensions that it offers to mathematics. More than merely representational, the language we use is a powerful determinant of what we are and how we view the environment that contains us.

One might be tempted to argue that alternative framings in human terms are inappropriate when it comes to thinking of the nature of mathematics. Mathematics is communicated via unique, unambiguous, silent, written symbols and thus cannot but be en'vision'ed. This, however, is to miss the fundamental nature of mathematical understanding. When we see symbols we "see" nothing. To gain understanding we need to listen to the personal inner echoes these symbols recall, the underlying metaphors they evoke. The symbols are not the mathematics, nor do they communicate "mathematics" in any holistic sense. They can only resonate with whatever understandings we have constructed so far. The child learning to count cannot dream of the meaning of number. We may look at "universal" symbols but we can only hear their message for us as individuals. To learn we have to engage in a dialogue between ourselves and our existing mathematical understanding.

There appears to be an increasing trend, within our ever growing and changing language, to coin new verbs from existing nouns—to "verb" one might say—and this leads directly to a plethora of "gerunding." This creative activity is allowing the expressing of new subtleties of meaning and the giving of dynamism to otherwise static notions. "Knowing" is not synonymous with "knowledge." In the English language the teacher and the craft of teaching have always been linked thus—teachers engage in teaching—but the subtle difference between "I teach" and "I am teaching" gives the craft of "teaching" a continuing, active quality, directly linked to the enactor, the teacher. And that is what mathematics teaching should be, an enacting (not an enactment) for the learner, a living through, a being with mathematics.

For Tom Kieren, with whom I have worked for many years, and for me this shift from the done to the doing has been vital. We are ourselves less concerned with the knowledge that a child possesses at any given instant; our focus is on the "coming to know," the dynamic "knowing" that portrays the growth of understanding. Our emphasis on this notion is reflected in the labels given to the layers of understanding within our model. All are in terms of gerunds: "image making," "property noticing," "structuring," and the all-important "primitive knowing," which forms the originating, the prime understanding on which all that is to follow will depend. It is attending to our past that underscores present sense making. It is the previously created understandings which will form the base out of which all future understanding will be built.

That "society tests what it values" is a belief long held by many learners. When the testing of the "done" is far easier than the assessing and evaluating of the "doing," the temptation is for teachers, too, to focus on the learnt rather than the learning. We can assess with ease the "what" but not the "how" of the learning taking place as students struggle to construct a path to understanding. We have standardized and accepted ways to photograph their arrival, but not the means to film their journey. Yet if we seek effective teaching we need ways of recognizing the paths that the students are laying down and a willingness to explore with them and to implicate ourselves in their constructing. Davis's deliberate change from the predominant metaphor of seeing to that of listening perhaps offers what we seek because it provides us with a power and a way to re-cognize.

I can only end by saying that this is a book I would have wished to write. Enjoy it!

More than we know, we are forced to live by symbols because the total reality of this wonderful, dangerous world we live in is too complex for us.

—*Source of the Thunder.* R.A. Caras

Acknowledgments

The term "complexification" is a recent addition to the English language, and one that I find appealing for at least two reasons. First, it points to what I perceive to be a general movement across a range of academic disciplines—away from attempts to impose linear and causal models onto phenomena and toward embracing the difficulty and ambiguity of existence. Second, it is a new word—a new pattern of acting. Its creation represents a deliberate attempt to affect the way we stand in the world. As Richard Rorty argues, it is by making up new words (or by using old ones in new ways) that we interrupt the *commonsense* notions that frame our actions. We enable ourselves to act differently.

Such is the spirit of this study: it is an attempt to complexify the phenomenon that we call "mathematics teaching" through suggesting a different way of speaking about it. A realization that goes along with this sort of project is that most phenomena are not only more complex than we might have believed; they are tied up in one another in ways that belie unraveling. Nothing is isolated; each thing affects every other thing. The task, then, of identifying those persons who and those events that contributed most significantly to the outcome that is this book is something of a guessing game. I, therefore, apologize to anyone who is not appropriately acknowledged here or in the text that follows. I readily confess that there are many persons whose contributions to this particular piece of work have been undeservedly overlooked. But there are those to whom I can point in confidence.

In particular, Tom Kieren, Max van Manen, Sol Sigurdson, Daiyo Sawada, Heidi Kass, Sandra Frid, Yatta Kanu, and Elaine Simmt have all participated significantly in my thinking in one way or another—and, in general, more through their lived examples than by what they've said or written. Similarly, the teachers who welcomed me into their classrooms and with whom I engaged in conversation were instrumental in the completion of this project. Debts are also owed to Susan Pirie and to Les Steffe, whose readings of the text contributed to it in important ways. On a more collective level, I would like to express my appreciation for the healthy, generative, and supportive environments provided by the communities of the University of Alberta's Department of Secondary Education (where the first draft of this text was written) and of the University of British Columbia's Department of Curriculum Studies (where it was completed).

I must also note the contribution made by Dennis Sumara. Much of what is written here is traceable to one of our many discussions and conversations. In addition to talking at length about the issues of schooling and teaching, Dennis has taught me about reading, about writing, and about becoming part of what I do . . . and, in many ways, this book is about that last point: (re-)integrating what I know, how I act, and who I am.

In addition, I would like to express my appreciation for the financial support provided for this project by the Social Sciences and Humanities Research Council of Canada, the University of Alberta, the Alberta Teachers' Association, and the Grande Prairie School District.

Finally, I would like to thank Shirley Steinberg and Joe Kincheloe for their generous invitation to complete the project that has become this book.

Front Word

The ironist's preferred form of argument is dialectical in the sense that she takes the unit of persuasion to be a vocabulary rather than a proposition. Her method is redescription rather than inference. Ironists specialize in redescribing ranges of objects or events in partially neologistic jargon, in the hopes that by the time she is finished using old words in new senses, not to mention introducing brand new words, people will no longer ask questions phrased in the old words. So the ironist thinks of logic as ancillary to dialectic.[1]

The opposite of irony is common sense.[2]

—*Richard Rorty*

Logic is an element within reason. Both love straight lines. That is why they are a favorite playground for the eye person. The straight line has an impelling and simplifying quality. Ana*-logic is linked with the ear. It moves, cautiously and carefully, along curves and spirals—like the spirals found in the human ear. Human thinking was originally founded on analogies—and analogical "thinking" is still more flexible, creative, revolutionary, intuitive, free, spontaneous, and less rigid, fixed, and violent than logical thought.*

—*Joachim-Ernst Berendt*[3]

Setting the Tone

Introduction

To get outside of the imprisoning framework of assumptions learned within a single tradition, habits of attention and interpretation need to be stretched and pulled and folded back upon themselves, life lived along a Möbius strip.

—Mary Catherine Bateson[4]

It is common practice, before embarking on the recital of a long journey, to give one's listeners an overview of the territory to be covered. This is especially valuable when the itinerary involves twists and turns, detours, and steps retraced. It makes it possible, at any moment to get a feeling for the overall picture.

—Hubert Reeves[5]

Seeing Through Arithmetic[6] was the title of the textbook series through which much of my generation was introduced to formal mathematics. That phrase came back to me in the midst of this writing and, for reasons that will become clear, the memory prompted me to wonder about the authors' reasons for choosing that name for their books. Was "seeing through" intended to provoke a sense of transparency, thus implying that the mathematics that lay ahead was simple, straightforward, obvious—that is, easily seen through? Or was the "seeing through" suggestive of the capacity to separate truths from lies, thus hinting that arithmetic involved some manner of deception that students must learn to see through? Perhaps the implication was that mathematics was going to be an ordeal, and that these texts were designed to help see us through arithmetic. Or, was the implication that arithmetic equips us with a sort of conceptual tool through which to examine the world? The purpose of our learning this subject was thus to foster abilities to see through (the lens of) arithmetic.

Whatever the case, from the beginning, my experiences with formal mathematics were framed in terms of the ocular: of seeing and observing, of clarity and illumination, of distinct boundaries and solid objects. This mathematics was embodied in rigidly structured curricula, in prescriptive teaching methods, in fill-in-the-blanks exercises—all of which contributed to a parsing of the subject matter into singular, sequential, unambiguous, inert, and obvious tidbits. Correspondingly, the role of the teacher was cast in terms of overseeing, projecting, supervising—of tidy and unproblematic separations of educator from learner, master from novice, authority from subject, teller from listener.

These dichotomies I know intimately, having lived both sides . . . but mostly from having participated in the well-meaning project of subjecting learners to an ocular-centric, di*vision*ary mathematics—a mathematics that powerfully enabled those who were capable of seeing through it, but that seemed a painful and demeaning experience for those who could not. Throughout my years as a mathematics teacher, I found myself uncomfortable with such consequences of my efforts to educate—so much so that I eventually had to step away from it. This text represents a sort of report of my efforts to re-cognize what it was I might have been doing in my classroom and to reformulate some sort of *sound* alternative.

The Setting

First and foremost, then, this is a book about mathematics teaching: about what it means to do mathematics and to educate in a climate of rapid change, uncertainty, and occasional hostility. It is a book about making sense of emerging mind-sets and shifting needs; a book through which I struggle with the questions: How might school mathematics have come to be about seeing through (or being seen through) the subject matter? and, How might we go about enacting a sound alternative to what is now occurring in mathematics classrooms?

This project is prompted in large part by a revolution of sorts that is occurring within our institutions of higher education. Over the past few decades, "critical," "postmodern," and "ecological" sensibilities have helped to bring about widespread interrogations of what were once considered indubitable facts, unproblematic distinctions, solid foundations, natural orders. Virtually every area of academic inquiry has been "exposed" for its cultural biases, its contribution to social stratification, and its complicity in projecting pervasive and fraudulent conceptions of reality. Among the primary targets of such analyses are formal education (as a key mechanism of enculturation) and mathematics (as a subtext of most modern scholarly activity).

The discipline of mathematics has suffered multiple blows in the current academic climate, and some are self-inflicted. Resulting largely from its own conclusions, mathematics has lost its status as the epitome of fixed and truthful knowledge. But the subject matter has also been identified as a key contributor to a plethora of modern crises. An enabler of scientific "advances," of military technologies, of normalizing statistical reductions, mathematics has been associated with the establishment and maintenance of power imbalances; contributing to wide-scale destruction of the planet; and disenfranchizing and depersonalizing the citizenry of Western cultures . . . all in the name of "progress." Once thought objective and neutral, mathematical knowledge has, in some discourse fields, become coterminous with masculinist, Western, bourgeois, and modernist regimes of power.

Formal education has faced similar and equally devastating criticisms. Accused of (and demonstrated as) having accomplished the exact opposite of its stated goals, our schooling system can no longer robe itself in the rhetoric of benevolence and hope. Far from making it possible for individuals to transcend their contexts, far from bettering the collective situation, the institution of formal education has been implicated in supporting (and, in some ways, creating) the very social, political, and bureaucratic circumstances it has claimed to interrupt.

Recent studies into learning have served to further problematize the project of formal education. With offerings that differ radically from the commonsense and cognitivist models on which much of modern schooling practice is founded, emerging accounts of cognition have pushed the mind out of the head and into social settings; linked thought to active and interactive bodies; and dissolved objective knowledge into fluid and co-specifying behaviors of dynamic agents. Such developments clearly run against the grain of traditional mathematics teaching—although they have not as yet had any sort of significant or sustained impact on conventional classroom practice.

Nevertheless, attentive to such transitions, mathematics educators are beginning to ask very different sorts of questions of themselves. Located as they are in the interstices of mathematical study, educational discourse, and cognitive theory, questions are being raised anew that—in the not too distant past—were generally considered settled: What is mathematics? Why do we teach it? What does it mean to think mathematically? What is teaching? Such are the issues that I address here.

From the Visual to the Auditory

My strategy in this inquiry into mathematics pedagogy is to focus on the language that we use to frame mathematics teaching—and, in particular, on those figures of speech and turns of phrase that are founded on the ocular.

We live, it seems, in an era that seeks constancy, uniformity, totality, clarity, and distinctness,[7] and so, while the visual is valued, the auditory tends to be held in contempt: *Seeing is believing,* but *you can't believe everything you hear; A picture* (i.e., an event of vision) *is worth a thousand words* (i.e., events of hearing). Nowhere is this mind-set more audible than in the discourse that surrounds the teaching of mathematics. Education has become a matter of *enlightenment,* where understandings are *insights* and teaching is a process of *illumination.* The *ideas* and *theorems*[8] of mathematics, situated at the core of a modern education, have come to be *seen* as certain knowledge, as pure reason. The popular belief is that mathematics provides us with a *lens* to *uncover* the hidden, to *clarify* the obscure, to *revise* the mistaken, and to *expose* the false.[9]

It thus seems that our desire for clearer vision—and for the absolutes that it promises—has brought on a sort of cultural deafness. Notions of harmony and attunement have been pushed into the realms of the quaint and the romantic in a quest for monotonic truth. In terms of mathematics teaching, a principal consequence of this loss of hearing is that learners—those we are to teach—have been reduced to silence; they are objects to be *seen and not heard.*

My basic argument is thus that there is much to be gained by exploring sonorous alternatives to the visual metaphors that frame our teaching of mathematics, for, as Erwin Straus explains, "Sound is somewhere *between* thing and no-thing. . . . [Sound] *is* something, yet it is not a thing one can manipulate; . . . it is not a thing, but neither is it no-thing."[10] Sound—in its multilayered richness, in its capacity for formless confusion, in its necessary proximity, in its inevitable transience, in the insubstantialness that makes it impossible to be grasped by our listening in the way objects of vision are halted, distinguished, and possessed by our sight—reminds us of the temporality of every part of our existence. The realm of the sonorous might thus provide us with better starting places for developing *senses* of knowledge, of human interaction, and of personal identity. And listening, the sound sense (which might be said to occur in fractional dimension between thing-ness and no-thing-ness), could help us to rethink what it means to teach. Occurring somewhere between the surety of the known and the uncertainty of the not-yet-known, the act of listening is similar to the project of education. It is, after all, when we are not certain that we are compelled to listen. Our listening is always and already in the transformative space of learning.

However, in seeking to develop the notion of mathematics teaching as a process of listening, I do not mean to dichotomize the sensory modalities of hearing and sight. Rather, the intention is to exaggerate the former in an effort to disrupt the privileged (and largely uninterrogated) status of the latter—a project that involves a risk of overstating their differences. A key instance of such overstatement is the repeated suggestion that vision is implicitly divisive whereas hearing is more encompassing and healing—a notion that has particular utility when it comes to discussing relationships, but one that is somewhat facile. One need only consider the ease and frequency with which joggers and rude neighbors cut themselves apart from their sonorous environments through personal and hi-fi stereos. And so I must forewarn readers that the point is not that such distinctions are absolute—for they are not—but that they are useful.

The intention then is to present our capacity to listen as an important—and, at the moment, largely overlooked—element of teaching. I do not seek a blind pedagogy, nor do I believe that teaching is currently deaf. Rather, the quest is for a middle way.

Enactivism and Hermeneutics

I thus approach this inquiry into mathematics teaching through the interpretive framework of *enactivism.* Drawn from, influenced by, and aligned with continental and pragmatic philosophy, Eastern thought, and ecological theory, enactivism is founded on a manner of thinking that seeks out "middle ways" amid disparate perspectives. But such middle ways should not be thought of as compromises. Rather, they represent attempts to sidestep seemingly irresolvable tensions by drawing attention to and offering alternatives for the assumptions that underlie varied opinions.

In the process, enactivism often demonstrates that diverse perspectives have more in common than surface appearances would suggest. As such, an inquiry oriented by enactivism relies on a different elocutionary style than most conventional scholarly reporting. Rather than employing the predominant mode of argumentation (i.e., the one that is modeled after the geometric proof), I draw from a manner of reasoning that favors analogy over logic, that embraces complexity but does not reject simplicity, that calls for a wise use of what we know over an unrelenting pursuit of further knowledge, and that, most importantly, values language for its capacity to transform reality over its ability to capture it.

This is not to say that this alternative way of presenting and developing ideas contradicts or rejects those traditions that employ deductive methodologies—among them, analytic philosophy, mathematics, and the sciences. On the contrary, there is an explicit acknowledgment that we are thoroughly inscribed by such traditions. Rather than attempting to negate the logical argument, then, the intent here is to complement it, based on the conviction that formal logic represents only one of many modes of reasoning. I see my project as adding to an already diverse discussion—and one of my principal strategies for doing so is to make use of an emerging literature that highlights the centrality of metaphor and other figurative devices in shaping our thinking and acting.

And so, my goal here is not to contribute to a mounting literature on the problems associated with mathematics teaching. Such discussions have been well-articulated, both in the multifaceted critiques offered by social commentators (who have alerted us to the unannounced agendas of mathematics education) and within the popular media (where the myths of school mathematics have been thoroughly challenged). Rather, my intention is to explore in detail an alternative manner of framing the task of mathematics pedagogy. I thus endeavor to bring together current discussions on a range of matters germane to the project of teaching mathematics for the purposes of interrogating and of reformulating current practices.

The research tradition I draw from is *hermeneutics.* Concerned both with what it is that we believe and how it might be that we have come to think and act in the ways we do, hermeneutics is attentive to the tensions, the breeches that punctuate our collective action. I have thus developed this writing around an exploration of the dichotomous landscape of mathematics education, guided by Rorty's admonition:

> *We can only hope to transcend our acculturation if our culture contains . . . splits which supply toeholds for new initiatives. Without such splits—without tensions which make people* listen *to new ideas in the hope of finding means of overcoming those tensions—there is no such hope.*[11]

Again, I do not strive to resolve the current tensions, but to explore alternatives to the systems of thought on which they are founded. In this project, the notion of *listening* is used both as a starting place for the inquiry and as a sort of collecting point for the various strands of thought that challenge our modern ways of *seeing* things. Listening, I argue, offers a more generous, more compassionate, more encompassing alternative to the divisiveness and violence of watching: whereas we *steal* a glance and *take* a look, we *lend* an ear and *give* a listen.

Indeed, an important part of this text is a hermeneutic and phenomenological investigation of listening itself, through which I suggest that listening involves far more than the "taking in" of sound. Listening, rather, is more toward an imaginative and conscientious participation in the unfolding of the world. Immediate, intimate, implicating, and interactive, listening is more an interrogation of one's perceptions than the mere sensory capacity.

What Might Mathematics Teaching Be?

Listening thus implies a wariness of certainty, a tentativeness of interpretation. It also engenders an attentiveness and responsiveness to ever-evolving circumstances and conceptions—that is, listening involves an attitude of (personal and collective) transformation.

These are the qualities I have attempted to bring to this "essay,"[12] this "bricolage."[13] Both of these words were coined by the French, and both are attuned to the intentions and the approach to research underlying this book. *Essay* derives from the verb *essayer* (to try), and so it announces a spirit of *trying on* and *testing for fit.* The goal of the essayist is thus explorative—sounding out new patterns of living rather than seeking greater degrees of Truth. A *bricolage* is a tinkering, a delving into possibilities, a playing with an emergent form. In terms of this research, the bricolage is a quest for a "good enough" sense of mathematics teaching, setting aside the popular and unending pursuits of optimal teaching methods. *Bricolage* also implies an attitude of eclecticism, an embracing of diversity.

In bringing the notions of listening, essay, and bricolage to this inquiry into mathematics teaching, I am pushing against the current tendencies to regard the roles of both teacher and researcher in terms of "specializations." I believe that the movement toward specialties within the context of public education (and in our studies of it) has contributed to a range of problems. As Wendell Berry asserts:

> *What happens under the rule of specialization is that . . . [the] community disintegrates because it loses the necessary understandings, forms, and enactments of the relations among materials and processes, principles and actions, ideals and realities, past and present, present and future, men and women, body and spirit, city and country, civilization and wilderness, growth and decay, life and death—just as the individual character loses the sense of a responsible involvement in these relations.*[14]

Among the consequences of my embracing an attitude of eclecticism is that, in spite of my announced intention to investigate mathematics teaching, I deliberately avoid trying to say what it *is.* That is, I do not try to fix it, to determine it, to convert it into something that might be specialized. Rather, I endeavor to locate it, in the manner of sound, in the ever-evolving realm of personal and collective action.

Consonant with this effort, the text is incomplete. It has gaps, discontinuities, inconsistencies, and loose ends. It lacks the structure and conclusive certainty of a deductive (and seductive) logical argument, for my goal was not to generate a text whose validity is principally derived from its internal consistency. Rather, I have attempted to weave the philosophical with the lived. I have thus written not in terms of actuality, constraint, and validity, but of possibility, necessity, and viability.

The Structure of the Writing

An immediate consequence of the fact that this text is more an essay than a report or an argument is that a particular sort of reading is required. One cannot get much of a "feel" for what is written by going through this introduction, glancing over the gathered "data," and examining the final chapter. What conclusions there are have been distributed throughout the text and, rather than attempting to corral the educational implications into some sort of closing summary, I have conceived of this entire project as being educational. As a teacher, who is guided by a conviction that the place of the educator is not simply to re-present others' ideas, but also to present possibilities, I have attempted to make this text educational.

The writing thus moves back and forth between what might be grossly described as theoretical and practical considerations. Each chapter begins with a discussion of the more abstract or general and moves toward the lived and particular as I endeavor to locate ideas and assertions within the actual teaching of mathematics. The latter parts of the chapters are, in fact, based on an extended collaborative effort between myself and a middle school mathematics teacher. Through anecdotes, quotes, and vignettes, I attempt to show how the ideas presented might be enacted—in effect, how a listening alternative to mathematics teaching might sound.

In this movement between the general and the particular, the abstract and the lived, I have struggled to push against the linear limitation of written language by taking the single thread of text and weaving it in both vertical and horizontal directions. That is, I have given each chapter a parallel structure in an attempt to develop two sets of simultaneous dialogues—one of which moves through a series of issues surrounding mathematics teaching, the other of which involves an exploration of the theoretical foundations of this text at various organizational and organismic levels. The issues that serve as gathering points for the discussions (and as the themes for the chapters) are: the theoretical and methodological orientations, the nature of mathematical knowledge, the place of formal education, the processes of cognition, and the possibilities for mathematics teaching. Similarly, the layers of the discussions contained in each chapter range from the global cultural/collective, through the institutional/interpersonal, to the more particular and immediate personal/individual considerations that are relevant to any discussion of mathematics teaching.

The text is thus divided into five chapters, and each of these chapters is comprised of three sections. Schematically, the structure might be represented by a rectangular grid in which the issues and levels are identified, respectively, on vertical and horizontal axes. (See Table 1, on which key words from each of the resulting "cells" are also identified.)

The text might just as easily have been divided into three chapters, each with five sections—and I would, in fact, recommend for anyone who cares to go through the document a second time to follow a sequence of corresponding sections rather than successive chapters.

One of my reasons for developing this structure was to avoid having to provide extensive elaboration of isolated points. Some of the topics that are dealt with have been difficult for me—difficult

Table 1. *A Conceptual Framework for the Structure of the Book*

SECTION → **CHAPTER ↓**	A. *Cultural*	B. *Institutional*	C. *(Inter)Personal*
1. *Conceptual Underpinnings*	Enactivism	Hermeneutics	Listening
2. *Subject Matter*	Mathematical Knowledge	Curriculum	Planning for Teaching
3. *Formal Education*	Culture Making	The Artistry of Teaching	Pedagogy
4. *Cognition*	Knowledge and Knowing	Understanding and Meaning	Play
5. *Teaching*	Backward Teaching	Assessment	Mathematics Teaching as Listening

not because they are conceptually complex, but because they tend to move against the current of *commonsense*; they resist being framed in conventional terms. In writing, I was thus faced with either attempting to provide detailed explications of issues as they came up or with presenting pivotal ideas as I went along and postponing elaboration until need or opportunity arose. I chose the latter.

As such, I might characterize the structure as *web-like* and *layered*. Each chapter (and section) picks up on the ideas of the preceding chapters (and sections), thus adding to the conceptual depth. In this way, the document has taken on a sort of recursive structure that might be interpreted visually as a series of concurrent circles (see Figure 1). Each successive layer encompasses and expands on that which has preceded it and, in this elaboration, effectively transforms the meaning and significance of what has come before. The process is, therefore, somewhat circular, multidimensional, and unending.

As these two sets of dialogue are laid atop one another (see Figure 2), a perhaps more representative (and certainly more descriptive) scheme than that suggested by a rectangular grid (as in Table 1) is created.

This layered approach highlights two features of this writing that reflect important aspects of the experienced world to which it points. The first is that the complexity of phenomena at various levels is not a function of scale. Rather, as one moves in on or away from an object or event, one inevitably finds the same order of com-

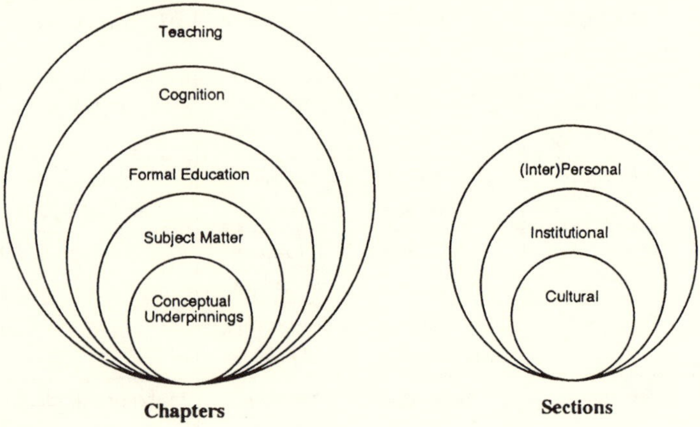

Figure 1. The Layered and Self-Similar Structures of the Chapters and Sections[15]

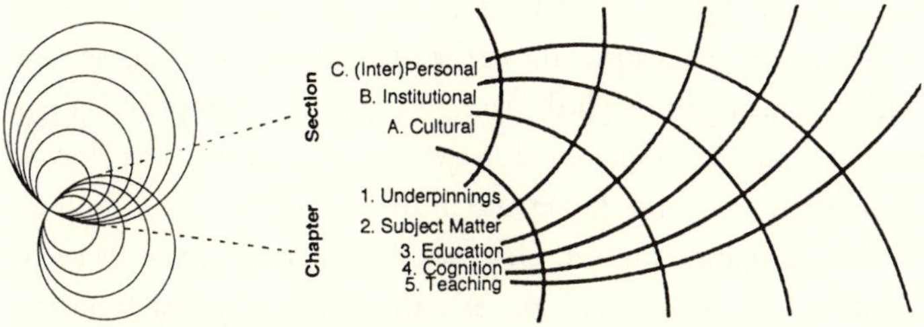

Figure 2. The Recursive Structure of the Book

plexity. The second feature is revealed as the exploration moves between cultural, institutional, and personal layers of the discussion. A certain self-similarity emerges as the same issues, the same images, and the same metaphors seem to arise on very different topics and conceptual levels. My project here is thus to arrive at a different sense of how, just as the parts are spread throughout the whole, the whole is enfolded in each of the parts.

As a reminder of this relationship between the general and the particular, I have adorned the title pages of each chapter with an image of a *fractal tree* at some stage of its growth. Briefly, a fractal tree is generated by repeatedly grafting a single shape—in this case, a simple two-pronged fork (see Figure 3), the tines of which are approximately two thirds the length of the handle—onto a larger image of itself. With each iteration, the tines of the preceding level become the handles of the new fork; one might say, in terms of a tree's growth, that last season's shoots become this year's branches.

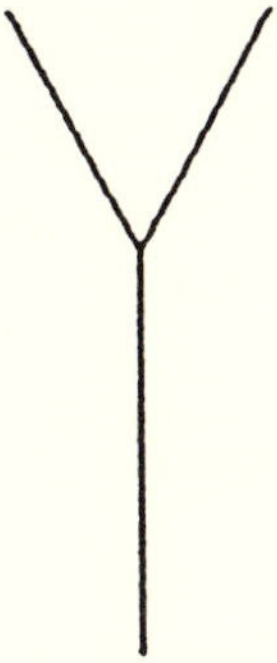

Figure 3. The Generator for the Fractal Tree

The fork-shape thus serves as a "fundamental particle" of sorts—the basic building block or the generator—of the tree. The information required to construct the entire figure is contained in each tiny fractal element, although the complexity of the "completed" figure may obscure the simplicity of its generative subunits. The "fractal" thus differs from the "fragment" in that it not only contributes to the whole, it announces it. However, in this simplicity, it belies the complex and unpredictable patterns that begin to appear as the iterated and reiterated elements start to play on themselves.[16]

The introductory understanding of fractal geometry that enabled the drawing of this figure has profoundly affected the way I see trees. It has also affected the way I understand a host of other phenomena, including the emergence of a new idea. It is thus that I have attempted to imbue each of the fifteen subsections of this document with a certain fractal-like integrity. That is, rather than permitting each piece to serve merely as a fragment of the whole—something virtually meaningless on its own—I have striven to hint at the greater richness of the more fully articulated document by exploring in depth a specific topic in each section. Considered separately, however, none of these sections is likely to provoke a different way of thinking about mathematics teaching. It is in the fabric of their interrelations that that possibility is presented.

Chapter 1

Close Your Eyes and Listen

Conceptual Underpinnings

Just as nature finds its way to the core of my personal life and becomes inextricably linked with it, so behavior patterns settle into that nature, being deposited in the form of a cultural world. Not only have I a physical world, not only do I live in the midst of earth, air and water, I have around me roads, plantations, villages, streets, churches, implements, a bell, a spoon, a pipe. Each of these objects is molded to the human action which it serves. Each one spreads round it an atmosphere of humanity.

—*Maurice Merleau-Ponty*[1]

I close my eyes, and the planet is auditory only: tree branches twist into tubas and saxes, are caught by large hands that press down valves, and everywhere on this ranch I hear feral music—ghostly tunes made not by animals gone wild but by grasses, sagebrush, and fence wire singing.

—*Gretel Ehrlich*[2]

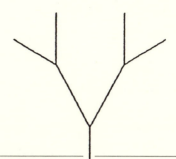

Section A
Enactivism

[O]rganism and environment enfold into each other
and unfold from one another
in the fundamental circularity that is life itself.
—Francisco Varela, Evan Thompson, and Eleanor Rosch[3]

I listen, because it reminds me again and again
that the whole world runs by rhythms
I have not yet learned to recognize.
—Thomas Merton[4]

Much of the recent activity in the field of mathematics education has consisted in efforts to negotiate a series of impassable dichotomies—dichotomies that seem to be the direct and inevitable consequences of a collision between traditional objectivist perspectives and more recent subjectivist proposals. In this section, I examine the origins of the mode of bipolar thinking that has given rise to these tensions, seeking not to resolve them but to understand them more deeply. It is by endeavoring to develop such understandings, I suggest, that we open up possibilities for not merely healing the "gaps," but for side-stepping the mode of thinking (and acting) out of which they arise.

In beginning the discussion in this manner, I do not wish to suggest that the dichotomies that we construct and through which we make sense of the world are unhelpful, but that they should not be regarded as absolute. Thought and language, it can easily be argued, are founded on our capacity to separate "this" from "that"—and so, to deny the possibility of such distinctions is to render human experience completely incomprehensible. It is thus that, rather than suggesting that mind/body, self/other, fact/faction, knower/known and other binaries are *false*—a move which is, in itself, dichotomizing—I invoke the pragmatist measure of truth and argue that such constructions are valid insofar as they are useful.

The point I attempt to make in this section, then, is that, in terms of mathematics teaching, many dichotomies have outlived their utility, having locked us in a modern mind-set which posits us as essentially autonomous entities: Not only are we isolated from one another, but we are set apart from the universe. The foundation of this sort of dualistic thought is the topic I turn to presently. That discussion serves as a precursor to a brief introduction of an alternative orientation to issues of identity and cognition which, for the moment, I will describe as embracing complex and unpredictable evolutionary dynamics rather than imposing orderly and calculable mechanical processes.

Of all the parts of this book, this section is perhaps the most densely written. As such, I must ask for the indulgence and patience of those for whom some of the ideas are new. Once again, I have structured the writing so that each of these notions will be further developed in a context where they are applied to an issue of mathematics teaching. My main purpose here, in addition to situating some of the ideas philosophically, is to announce some of the central principles that will be used in the subsequent discussions.

Our Modern Heritage

The predominant epistemological perspective of the "modern" era was first announced by mathematician and philosopher René Descartes in the seventeenth century. Descartes, a contemporary of Galileo, Bacon, and Locke, and a predecessor of Newton, articulated two breaks from earlier perspectives on knowledge and modes of inquiry—perspectives which he rejected as inconsistent and unreliable mixtures of fact and fancy.

The first point of departure was on the issue of method, whereby Descartes denounced tradition, hearsay, mysticism, and religion as he called for the pre-eminence of the "natural light" of (mathematical) reason. Voicing a disdain for all other intellectual authorities, Descartes argued that all previous speculation should be rejected until indubitable principles, against which all other knowledge claims could be measured, were derived. In calling for this shift to a particular and narrow conception of *reason,* Descartes introduced many concepts and arguments which are foundational to modern science and analytic philosophy.

In this regard, perhaps his most noted contribution is his *cogito*—"I think"—which also marks his second break with tradition. Briefly, in his quest for a certain foundation for his epistemological system, Descartes arrived at the self-evident and self-verifying truth of the statement, "I think," and this axiom became the solid ground on which he sought to verify or refute all other knowledge.

It is important to note that Descartes' project was built upon a distrust of the evidence of the senses—a suspicion that was inherited from the ancient Greeks.[5] Because one's knowledge of the world was always and inevitably filtered through untrustworthy sensory organs, one could never know—in any absolute way—the "truth" of the (external) universe. At best, one could build better and better mental representations of the physical world, and the process of assembling those representations demanded a persistent attitude of questioning—an attitude that Descartes introduced as foundational to scientific inquiry. This "method of doubt" was offered as a screen to sift out *truths* from those knowledge claims that could not be validated. Rational thought was thus offered as a way of knowing that was both superior to and independent of a reliance on the senses. Descartes' model of reason—and the one that was to become *the* model of rationality in the modern world—was found in geometry, a discipline that offered a process of verification that Descartes regarded as the only route to unimpeachable fact.[6] For him, geometric reasoning offered a means of deducing the nature of the entire universe from foundational principles, with each deductive step bound to preceding steps in an irrefutable sequence of logical moves. It was thus that, according to Palmer, truth for Descartes was "more than merely the conformity between knower and known, it [was] the *subject's rational certainty* of this conformity."[7] Rational reflection ("rationalism") rather than empirical observation ("empiricism") was the key to knowledge.

In establishing the *cogito* as the foundation and geometric reason as the means of construction—that is, in specifying both the axioms and the logic of this manner of determining truth—Descartes advanced a mode of dualistic thought that permeates modern perspectives of the universe.[8] Positioning the radical subject (i.e., the modern ideal of "self" or identity as solitary, coherent, and independent of context) as the reference point for all that is known, for example, compelled him to propose the existence of at least one object—an Other—that was independent of himself and relative to whom he could situate himself as part of an objective world. Stated in different terms, in distinguishing the figure of the "self," Descartes also distinguished the background of the "not-self" which was collected under such names as "other" and "world." Thus arose the fundamental subject-object dichotomy. Paradoxically, this dichotomy also provided the impetus for the empiricist tradition which, contra Descartes' rationalist proposal, relies on observation and experiment as the basis of knowledge production.

Another split initiated by Descartes' thought was the dichotomizing of mind and body. In arguing that thinking is the basis for all truth, and hence of existence, Descartes was suggesting that a person is essentially a thinking thing—one that is capable of conceiving of itself as existing without a body. Put differently, it is not essential in Descartes' formulation that we have a corporeal existence. Of course, this mind/body separation finds its roots in earlier philosophical and religious thought. However, in giving it a rational "scientific" basis, Descartes set the stage for a series of tensions that now, collectively, serve as a pervasive and resilient backdrop to much, and perhaps most, of Western academic thought.

To elaborate, in constructing the world on the foundation of the *cogito,* Descartes articulated more than the separations of mind from body, self from other, and representation from reality—all of which might be described as manifestations of a mind/body dualism. In addition to the essential distinction between mental and physical objects (with the consequent priority being assigned to the former), Descartes also contributed to the foundation of a host of other dichotomies, including knower versus known, organism versus environment, human versus nature. Further, the Cartesian orientation contributed to a view of the Self as a unified coherent subject: an autonomous entity that is isolated from others, independently constituted, essentially static, and able to maintain its integrity through diverse experience.

Other consequences of this perspective, which I shall heretofore refer to as "modernist," included an empirical emphasis on the trustworthiness of methods used to develop knowledge (i.e., more accurate representations of reality). As such, method came to be seen in increasingly mechanical and technological terms; the universe, correspondingly, was reduced to a similarly technical form. Today, machine metaphors frame and reveal Western perspectives on the universe, the earth, nature, our bodies, and—ultimately, with the development of the computer—our minds. With this technical mind-set, the aim of inquiry has grown beyond the desire to better our understandings. The primary goal is now to control the objects of our inquiry. As Palmer elaborates, with the widespread acceptance of Descartes' conclusion that "the world has meaning only with respect to man," our relationship to the world is no longer cast in terms of open responsiveness, but in "restless efforts to master it."[9]

And, perhaps most significantly, with thought being afforded priority over *being* in Descartes' *cogito*, epistemic issues began to overshadow ontological concerns—a reversal that has had profound implications for our modern conceptions of both knowledge and education. I will return to a further exploration of the consequences of modernist philosophies in later chapters that deal more specifically with these topics.

Before moving on, though, an important point of clarification should be made. In this analysis of Descartes' work and the manner in which it figures into current thinking, my intention is not to denigrate his conclusions. Rather, I believe that he was a luminary, a critical figure in our cultural heritage. His contributions to our philosophical, mathematical, and scientific thought—not to mention our commonsense—have greatly enabled the technologies that permit our current standards of living. However, as I develop in this text, the truths of Descartes, while well-suited to the circumstances of the seventeenth century, do not fit well with the situations in which we find ourselves today. It is thus time to interrogate his legacy, asking ourselves about what we have been taking for granted and how our assumptions have shaped our perceptions and actions. Prompted by a host of crises, ranging from the personal to the planetary, we are coming to the slow realization that we must behave differently—

and the capacity to alter our action, I believe, rests on a willingness to explore different ways of thinking.

Foundations of an Alternative

It is interesting to note the prevalence in research reports of the claim that particular methodologies or perspectives are "anti-dualist." Reacting to a philosophical backlash against Cartesian (modernist or analytic) bipolar thinking, researchers and theorists are quick to point out that they have not succumbed to a "this-or-that" way of thinking. Nevertheless, within mathematics education at least, there seems to be an irresistible tendency to grant priority to one or the other of the "real" *known* (material or abstract) or the ideal *knower*—tendencies which, like the favoring of either empirical or rational modes of inquiry, find their origins in the same system of beliefs.

And so, in spite of their apparent diametric opposition, these modernist perspectives can quite easily be shown to be on the same rational loop—a loop which begins with the epistemic primacy of "I think." The consequences of dualistic ways of thinking, along with extensive critique of such thought, are offered by a group of theorists who tend to be gathered under the title of "postmodernism" (although not always by their own choosing). Unfortunately, while postmodern discourses have offered valuable critiques of Descartes' legacy, it seems that one of the precepts of postmodernism—that is, that the quest for new groundings is doomed to failure—has been profoundly misinterpreted as suggesting that we can say very little about anything. Not surprisingly, this conclusion has prompted numerous and zealous attempts to destroy the foundations of existing structures—thus demonstrating the temporal and contextual nature of all knowledge—while offering in their place the unsteady (and unsatisfactory) ground of fallibilist, relativist, and individualist accounts of knowing.

The new challenge thus seems to be the development of alternatives which abandon Cartesian assumptions but which do not give in to the temptation of establishing a new and irrefutable foundation. In this writing, I would like to explore one possibility that seems to be emerging from some convergent streams of thought that flow from such diverse disciplines and discourse fields as continental and pragmatist philosophy,[10] cognitive psychology,[11] ecological thought,[12] biology,[13] and mathematics. Growing numbers of theorists in these areas are starting from the evolutionary metaphors of Darwin rather than the analytic and reductionist model of Descartes. Their focus is thus on the dynamic interdependence of individual and environment, of knowledge and identity, and of self and other, rather than on their autonomous constitution. Variously referred to as "pragmatism," "enactivism," and "(deep or social) ecology," these strands of thought join with postmodern discourses to offer a critique of modern dichotomous thinking, calling for a remembering of our past and an embracing of the complexities of existence. Enactivist[14] theorists thus offer descriptions of knowledge and communication and models of cognition and learning which are historical, situational, dynamic, intersubjective, and consensual. More importantly, perhaps, and in sharp contrast to the modernist foci, they acknowledge the centrality of the phenomenal and experiential rather than fixating narrowly on the formulated.

In brief, then, my project is to explore an alternative way of interpreting ourselves in the universe—in the process seeking to displace both the *I* (as the starting point for any systematic knowledge of the world) and the *eye* (as the primary sensory modality in assembling such knowledge). In problematizing the disembodied-I of Descartes and the disembodied-eye of modern science, I argue for a movement toward a conception of our participation in the universe that is founded on the shifting boundaries of *us* within the negotiated and evolving space of *listening.*

The remainder of this section consists of an introduction to a few of the important elements of enactivist theories. Because these points will be elaborated upon in subsequent sections and chapters as they are applied to various issues related to the teaching of mathematics, this introduction is deliberately brief.

Searching for a Middle Way

Maurice Merleau-Ponty, a preeminent postwar French philosopher, has provided us with a radical reinterpretation of Descartes' *cogito.* Merleau-Ponty's goal in this project was to find an alternative to the bipolar divisive way of thinking that dominates Western scholarly thought.

In *Phenomenology of Perception*, Merleau-Ponty rejects both rationalist and empiricist accounts of perception—the former because it focuses too narrowly on the cognizing agent (thus failing to provide an adequate account of the "world"); the latter because it demands too great a correspondence between a real world object and the resulting perception. Seeking a middle ground between the mental and the physical (the inner and the outer), Merleau-Ponty suggests that the body is that which renders the mind and the world inseparable. Far from representing a discrete demarcation between subject and object, one's body is simultaneously of oneself and of the world. For Merleau-Ponty, then, the body is our means of belonging to our world—a world that shapes us and a world that we participate in shaping.

Taking up this notion, Varela, Thompson, and Rosch (who bring together biology, continental philosophy, and Buddhist thought) have endeavored to elaborate upon Merleau-Ponty's "fundamental intuition of double embodiment."[15] In this conception, the body is understood both as an outer (physical-biological) and as an inner (lived experiential-phenomenological) structure. These structures are not opposed; rather we "continuously circulate back and forth between them."[16]

An understanding of their use of the term "structure" is critical here. Briefly, one's structure comes about from the combined influences of biological constitution and one's history of interaction in the world—a notion that recalls Vygotsky's contention that human identity is subject to the dialectical play between biology and history.[17] For the current purposes, a person's structure may be thought of as being loosely synonymous with his or her personality or *self*. For the time being, however, I will be avoiding these terms because of the inflexibility and the permanence they connote when used in a modern context. One's structure, in contrast, is thought to be fluid, temporal, and necessarily undergoing change. As Maturana and Varela put it, "Ongoing structural change of living beings . . . is occurring at every moment, continuously, in many ways at the same time. It is the throbbing of all life."[18] Unlike modern conceptions of identity whereby one's *self* is regarded as a product, then, one's structure is product, producer, and process. *Structure* is thus a fluid notion that is analogous to our experience of the object/event of sound—

an idea that might be reflected in the presence of *sona* in the word "person."[19]

To foreshadow one of the principal implications of this text, a person's range of possible action is determined by his or her structure. Hence, in an interaction with another person, how he or she acts is not primarily a function of the other person's actions (as is presumed in transmission models of communication and teaching), but a consequence of his or her own structural dynamic. As Maturana and Varela explain:

> *[The] perturbations of the environment do not determine what happens to the living being; rather it is the structure of the living being that determine what change occurs in it. This interaction is not instructive, for it does not determine what its effects are going to be. . . . [The] changes that result from the interaction between the living being and its environment are brought about by the disturbing agent but* determined by the structure of the disturbed system.[20]

To the observer, however, it may appear that one person is functioning according to the directions given to him or her by another person. Nevertheless, it is more appropriate to think of the interaction as a choreography in which one influences and is complicit in, but cannot determine, the other's actions. Put differently, one does not "pick up information" from the environment; rather, one's structure specifies which environmental patterns will trigger action. Furthermore, these environmental patterns (or, in Maturana and Varela's terms, "perturbations") do not *cause* the person's actions. Rather, they present an occasion for the person to act according to his or her structure.

In such interactions, one's structure is necessarily affected, although not always visibly, and he or she thus emerges a "different person." The other person involved in the interaction is similarly affected, and so the two "co-emerge." Varela, Thompson, and Rosch use the term *co-emergence* to call attention to the manner in which organism and environment, self and other are "bound together in reciprocal specification and selection."[21] That is, the world's relationship to the organism is not merely uni-directional and constraining; the organism also initiates or contributes to the enactment of its environment. They *specify* one another. In this *mutual specification*, they *co-emerge*. The "subject," in this conception, is not and cannot be considered as disembodied or as objectively separated from the world. Both are entwined in the "fundamental circularity" of existence.

The full import of this notion is found in Varela, Thompson, and Rosch's interpretation of the word "embodied," which is used to highlight two points. First, as is more commonly acknowledged, "cognition depends on the kinds of experience that comes from having a body with various sensorimotor capacities."[22] On this point, Mark Johnson goes so far as to suggest that words and concepts are metaphorical extensions of originary bodily experiences.[23] The second and, perhaps, more critical point is that our sensorimotor capacities are embedded in and continuously shaped by broad biological, social, and historical contexts. Our knowledge and our identities—our structures or our embodiments—are thus dependent on "being in a world that is inseparable from our bodies, our language, and our social history."[24]

A more naive form of these ideas is found in current debates on the relative influence of nature and nurture on personality, intelligence, and other (ostensibly fixable) traits. Viewed through the lens of enactivist theory, these debates miss two essential points: First, they tend to separate biological from social or historical factors, thus implying that the contribution of "nature" is fixed from birth. The separation of the terms "nature" and "nurture" suggests that they can somehow be held distinct—that nurturance is not natural and that what is natural is singularly and automatically constituted. Second, the debates presume a passive cognizing agent who is shaped by various forces, but who plays no role in selecting or affecting those forces. Enactivist theory denies the possibility for these easy separations, arguing that such distinctions are both impossible and unnecessary.

With regard to the nature of the individual knower, Varela, Thompson, and Rosch suggest that the basis of cognition is not to be found in the Rationalist "I think" nor in the Empiricist "I observe"—both of which are founded on the premise of the detached knower (or disembodied I/eye)—but in the enactivist "I act." Acting encompasses both thought and observation; acting presumes both actor (subject) and acted upon (object). In brief, acting demands re-unions of mind and body and subject and object. It is this notion of embodied action that allows us to bypass the extreme positions of cognition as either recovering what is outer or projecting what is inner without seeking recourse in the supernatural or in metaphysics. The upshot is that cognition cannot be a matter of internalizing or forming accurate representations of things of the world. Rather, cognition is inseparable from and fundamental to perception and action. Perceptions guide actions; actions enable perceptions. This inseparability is expressed in Maturana and Varela's aphorism, *All doing is knowing, and all knowing is doing*,[25] and the term "enaction" is intended to remind us of the primacy of action in shaping our experiences, our perceptions, and our world.

The individual's cognition, in this conception, is analogous to the evolution of a species, whereby an idea or an action comes about not because it is "correct" or optimal, but because it is possible in the given context. In making this provocative association between cognition and evolution (and their use of this comparison does appear to be more than metaphorical), Varela, Thompson, and Rosch are also indicating that enactivist notions can be applied at levels other than the organismic. Stated otherwise, the "cognizing organism" of their discussion need not be a single self-contained and visibly-bounded unit. Although the time scale varies, the developmental processes of the species and the individual are, in essence, the same: the cognizing agent (i.e., species or person) is engaged in a perpetual process of adapting itself to a similarly dynamic and responsive environment.

The re-unification of the mind and body in contemporary discourses carries with it another important consequence: just as mind and body are inseparable, the distinctions we draw between ourselves are problematic. Our bodies serve to separate our individual selves from one another at the same time that they come together in complex action—in effect establishing a collective corpus which can be thought of as a body with its own integrity. This notion is often difficult for those in modern and Western societies where the notion of an autonomous and independent self is idolized (no doubt partly because of Descartes' philosophy). But it is an idea that is implicit in many parts of our language and, in particular, in our (metaphorical or literal?) uses the same sorts of terms to describe both individual and collective action.

Natural Selection *versus* Natural Drift

Enactivism draws upon various principles of a theory of neo-Darwinian evolution that Varela, Thompson, and Rosch refer to as "Natural Drift"—an interpretation of evolution that might be contrasted with the more prominent and popularly accepted "Natural Selection."

The commonsensical Natural Selection is founded on a conception of the environment as a *monological* authority. Species are thought to adapt to their essentially fixed contexts and, in the process, those organisms that are the best suited to the circumstances—the *fittest*—will inevitably prevail over their competitors. Evolution is thus thought to be a more or less linear progression toward increasingly sophisticated and complex life forms.

Natural Drift begins by rejecting the simple separation of organism and surroundings that is implicit in the notion of a fixed environment. Noting that species not only adapt to but participate in the altering of their contexts, those taking a Natural Drift perspective on evolution argue for an *ecological*—that is, a collective and mutually specifying—process of determination, rather than a monological authority. So framed, evolution is more a complex choreography than a linear progression, with the criterion for survival being an adequate *fit* with a dynamic setting rather than an optimal fitness to a fixed setting. In other words, it is not competition with fitter species that leads to extinction; it is the inability to keep pace (i.e., maintain fitness) with a changing environment—a logic of "good enough" that is in accord with current (constructivist and social constructivist) orientations toward the emergence of personal conceptions and collective knowledge. Natural Drift thus emphasizes cooperation over competition, ecologies over monologues, adequacy over optimality, movement over progress, and complexity over linearity.

An important upshot of this move from "the world as given" to "the world as unfolding through a choreography of action" is that the modern Cartesian desire to know the world *as it is* is thoroughly frustrated. The universe is constantly evolving, forever eluding any attempt to fix and to know it. It is thus that, for the enactivist, the world is *not preformed*, but *performed*. We are constantly enacting our sense of the world—in the process, because we are part of it, altering it. Varela, Thompson, and Rosch refer to this phenomenon as the "fundamental circularity," whereby they suggest that the universe changes when something as minuscule as a thought changes—because that thought is not merely in the universe; it is part of the universe. Hence, our efforts to understand the world are perhaps better thought of in terms of interpreting our own perceptions and patterns of acting within a dynamic context than in terms of coming to know that context as somehow independent of our participation.

The Contribution of Mathematics

Just as the mathematics of the seventeenth century was integral to the formulation of Descartes' philosophy, so the mathematics of today is making a vital contribution to the reformulation of our understanding of the universe. Three branches of inquiry, in particular, are worthy of note: fuzzy logic, non-linear dynamics, and complexity theory.

Fuzzy logic—which is not a system of logic that is fuzzy but one which embraces that *fuzziness* of our experiences and perceptions—challenges the 1-0, true-false, all-or-nothing manner of thinking that is implicit in modern world views. Fuzzy logicians have alerted us to the rough edges of our crisp categories and to the gaps in our precise definitions, in the process reminding us that the clear-cut boundaries we perceive tell us more about the observer than the observed. Even the primary category—the *I*—is regarded hazily bounded, as we are called to recognize the dynamic and fluid natures of our individual identities. In challenging the most fundamental of principles underlying our mathematics, the possibility of crisp categories, fuzzy logic is in harmony with the cross-disciplinary movement toward problematizing simplistic distinctions.

It is thus that the imagery offered by non-linear dynamics—or chaos theory—is displacing that of the linear equation to serve as a visual metaphor for our understanding of phenomena and relationships. As one closes in on the "edges" of a fractal figure, one does not find simple—or even simpler—boundaries. Rather, in our analysis of such boundaries, it becomes clear that their complicatedness is more a matter of how we choose to regard them than of their particular qualities, thus placing "observation" into the dialogical space of observer-observed rather than in the monological space of either.

Fractal geometry can also be used as a model to better understand enactivist theory. There is a certain fractal quality to this framework, as suggested by this self-similarity of processes across such conceptual levels as organism, collective, and species—a self-similarity that some have extended in both directions, from the subcellular to the biosphere. Of note are James Lovelock's[26] "Gaia hypothesis" in which the ideas are applied on a planetary scale and Varela's seminal work with Maturana,[27] which focuses on the interdependent and subordinate elements comprising our own biological structures.

It is this sort of layered self-similarity among phenomena that has become the focus of those investigating complexity theory. Concerned with those systems that exist on *the edge of chaos*—"where the components of a system never quite lock into place, and yet never quite dissolve into turbulence"[28]—complexivists have begun to forge a rigorous alternative to the linear and reductionist thinking that has dominated academic thought since the time of Descartes. Significantly, complexity theorists distinguish between systems that are *complex* (i.e., which are self-organizing, adaptive, and spontaneously evolving) and those that are merely *complicated* (e.g., mechanical devices), in the process dislodging the "clockwork universe" metaphor that was initiated by Descartes and his contemporaries and replacing it with a more holistic, organic model of the cosmos that hearkens back to premodern conceptions.

These sorts of ideas, all of which will be further developed in subsequent sections and chapters, point to a certain *synchronicity* across academic disciplines—and, indeed, throughout Western culture. (This sort of "grand coincidence," it might be noted, is one of the phenomena under study by complexity theorists.) Framed by some of the central principles of enactivism, I will be applying several of these ideas and exploring some of their implications for the teaching and learning of mathematics. (To this end, it is worth noting at this point that, with these sorts of developments, a new status to the discipline has been established. No longer believed to be the foundations to or the building blocks of reality, mathematical objects are now offered as possible models of or metaphors for varied phenomena.[29])

Section B
Hermeneutics

We are, as Proust declared, perched on a pyramid of past life, and if we do not see this, it is because we are obsessed by objective thought.

— *Maurice Merleau-Ponty*[1]

Harmony and melody result from the influence exerted by what is past on an ever-new present.

—*Joachim-Ernst Berendt*[2]

I recently went for a walk along a gravel path in the river valley. The trail had been one of my favorites in the summer when it was enclosed by trees and filled with life, but now, at the end of October, it had lost its vibrancy. The green denseness of life was gone and the busyness of squirrels and insects had ceased. All that was left were the skeletons of trees and drifts of decaying leaves. It was a place of colorlessness, of disarray, of *not* life. Where once I felt embraced, I now felt isolated and exposed.

Until I heard a sound: a soft rustling of leaves. I listened. More rustling. Then a bird. Two birds. Many birds, layered on crickets and piled on top of the leaves—the leaves that moved with something living.

A simple story, really. But for me, it was a moment that powerfully announced something about listening. Caught in a moment of modern angst—relying strictly on vision to guide me—I felt lonely and separated. But, in listening, I found myself again entangled in the complex web of existence.

But the event was not just a moment of listening, for I was reminded of more than the ecologies of being. I was also recalled to my status as a listener (and as a non-listener), to my awareness of what I know (and did not know), to my role as a learner (and educator). It was a moment of locating order in ambiguity, of finding integrity and harmony amid the chaotic. It was a particular event, but an event that in its particularity revealed the general. As an event of being, it altered the tone of every walk along that path that preceded it and every walk that would follow.

And it was an event that, at the instant of living through it, I felt might serve as a means of introducing a discussion of how I have approached this investigation of learning and teaching. It has been a study of moving back and forth between the particular and the general, investigating how the former reveals the latter, how the latter is contained in the former, and how a change in understanding of one affects the other. In effect, this study of listening has itself been an act of listening: of tuning, of becoming attuned.

Put differently, the research reported herein was a hermeneutic investigation. In this section I present some of the guiding principles of hermeneutics, in the process attempting to demonstrate how this orientation to inquiry is in harmony with the announced principles of enactivism and, as such, is essential to the project I have undertaken. My secondary purpose is to call for an increased attention to hermeneutics as an important interpretive framework for those involved in mathematics education research.

Some Background to Hermeneutics

A recent trend among those interested in developments in philosophical discourse is to discuss various shifts in thinking in terms of "turns." The modern or Cartesian era, for example, began with an "epistemological turn" whereby philosophy turned away from a concern with metaphysics and began to take up questions surrounding the possibility (and nature) of knowledge.

An "ontological turn" was announced in the work of the philosopher Martin Heidegger as he called into question the varied assumptions underpinning modernist discussions of knowledge and knowing subjects. Heidegger's project involved alerting us to the dangers of separating our analyses of what we know (the realm of epistemology) from the broader considerations of who we are—historically, biologically, and contextually (the realm of ontology). His work has been seminal in prompting another, more broadly embraced, transition: an "interpretive turn."

Benefiting from the interpretive practices of literary criticism, cultural anthropology, feminist theory, and ecological thought—to name a few—studies of interpretation, or hermeneutical inquiries, have now risen to prominence in a range of disciplines. Aware that all understanding is contextual, historical, social—and, hence, inherently biased—hermeneutic inquiry has been embraced by those who are concerned with better understanding various cultural phenomena.

In brief, then, hermeneutics is the art of interpretation. It is interested in meaning, in understanding, and in application. More particularly, hermeneutics is concerned with investigating the conditions that make certain understandings possible. It asks not only, What is it that we think? but also, How is it that we have come to think this way?—all with a view toward affecting how we act in the world. Hermeneutics is thus concerned with past, present, and projected understandings.

Hermeneutic research is a sort of philosophy of the "middle way"—which should not be taken to suggest that hermeneutics seeks to determine some mathematical average or to offer some sort of compromise in the face of apparent contradiction. Rather, there is a twofold sense of "middle way": First, there is a recognition that we are always thrown into the middle of things; we cannot extricate ourselves to gaze upon the objects of our inquiry. Second, against the background of the 1-0, this-or-that logic that serves as the foundation of much of modern knowledge, hermeneutics seeks a middle way that is neither this nor that—that acknowledges the inevitability of thinking in dichotomous terms but seeks the richer understanding that comes through problematizing the distinctions and boundaries that tend to be drawn.

And so, hermeneutics seeks to illuminate the moments at which we move to a greater understanding of our uniquely human situation as it is relationally shared with others in the world. It understands that there is no truth that is fixed once and for all, no method that can predetermine the location of truth, no authority who can say the way things "really are." As Joel Weinsheimer suggests, a motto for hermeneutics might be that "truth keeps happening."[3]

It is a field with a rich and a long history—a history that, because it has been thoroughly developed elsewhere,[4] I will address only briefly. Etymologically, *hermeneutics* is derived from the name and character of the Greek god Hermes, the messenger of the gods—and, not insignificantly, a trickster. The term thus echoes with senses of revelation, of coming to more profound understandings of the previously perplexing or paradoxical, and of a wariness of being overly certain.

With regard to its modern use, hermeneutics was originally a discipline of biblical interpretation, the goal of which was to excavate the truth of the sacred text. This task demanded not just an ability to translate or comprehend particular words, but a talent to locate the writings historically and contextually. As such, from its inception as a discipline, hermeneutics has been concerned with the evolution of ideas and meanings, and it has been aware of the situational nature of such understandings.

Hermeneutics, then, has historically been concerned with textual interpretation, and its evolution is thus perhaps most easily outlined by tracing the development of the term "text." Initially, to the hermeneut, the text was a sacred writing. Later the notion of text was expanded to encompass literary and legal documents. More recently, the hermeneutic text has come to be life itself—an evolutionary development that reveals the shift from an original epistemological focus (i.e., biblical and literary hermeneutics were concerned with uncovering the truth in written texts) to the more ontological concerns of recent branches of hermeneutic thought. ("Philosophical" and "radical" hermeneutics address questions of the meaning of human existence as revealed through the rich and varied texture of particular experiences.) Implicit in this shift of the meaning of "text" is Heidegger's conviction that Being and interpretation are inseparable. As Crusius phrases this idea, "interpretation . . . is human being, our mode of existence in the world."[5]

An etymology of "text" is helpful here, in part because the term is conventionally understood to refer strictly to written works. Originally, however, "text," like "web," was used to describe things woven, and so the metaphor of "life as text" does have a particular richness. Considered alongside the more popular "literature as text" metaphor, for example, the image of intertwined linguistic threads forming a tightly woven narrative fabric foregrounds the roles of language, of storytelling, and of rereading in the construction of our respective understandings and identities. The textual metaphor also offers an image of the interweaving of our selves in the fabric of our culture. Like the microscope and the telescope, which demonstrate that complexity is not a function of scale, the metaphor of text applied at different conceptual planes reveals that the web of existence is as tangled at the individual level as it is on a planetary level. And, perhaps more importantly, the references to text, textuality, and texture remind us that we ourselves are woven into the fabric that we seek to understand. It is from inside our traditions that we interrogate them. We cannot view them from the outside or above; there can be no metaphysical (i.e., above or beyond the experiential) truth. Truth, from within this web, is more something to be listened for from within than something be looked at from without.

We are, then, caught up in "a finite existence prestructured by the tremendous inertial force of the past,"[6] an existence that is, in effect, pre-interpreted for us. The promise of hermeneutics is not to unburden ourselves of this historical mass in a (modernist) quest to determine the one Truth; nor is its goal, through more profound understandings of the world, to control the future or to better manage the objects that surround us. Rather, the place of hermeneutics is to interrupt our unquestioned patterns of acting. "All philosophical hermeneutics can hope to do . . . is hold open an alternative, constantly pointing to ways of living and thinking less destructive of the earth and the human spirit."[7]

To engage in hermeneutics—to interpret—then, is to tug at the threads of this existential text, realizing that, in tugging, the texture of the entire fabric is altered. Put differently, hermeneutics does not reduce us to powerless victims of historical forces. Rather, it offers hope for the future in the recognition that our lives are shaped not just by the events of the past, but also by our projects and our projections. This phenomenon is an element of what Varela, Thompson, and Rosch call the "fundamental circularity" of existence. In their words:

We did not design our world. We simply found ourselves in it; we awoke both to ourselves and to the world we inhabit. We come to reflect on that world as we grow and live. We reflect on a world that is not made, but found, and yet it is also our structure that enables us to reflect upon this world. Thus, in reflection we find ourselves in a circle*: we are in a world that seems to be there before reflection begins, but that world is not separate from us.*[8]

Varela, Thompson, and Rosch are using the notion of circularity to illustrate that, while we are "thrown" (to borrow Heidegger's term) into a world that is not of our own making, once located, that world evolves with us. An event as mundane as a shifting thought, then, alters the whole universe, for that thought—that thread—like the thinker and the context in which it occurred, is part of the universe.

The Hermeneutic Circle

David Smith notes that, beginning with the contribution of Schleiermacher, the three common themes in hermeneutic inquiry have been "the inherent creativity of interpretation, the pivotal role of language in human understanding, and the interplay of part and whole in the process of interpretation."[9] This third theme, the back-and-forth movement between the particular and general, is more popularly referred to as the "hermeneutic circle." As one moves between the specific and the broad, one's understandings of both are deepened, and all other understandings are also affected.

The embeddedness of the particular in the general and the enactment of the general through the particular was first articulated by Schleiermacher who stated, "Every discourse depends on earlier thought . . . [and] it follows that every person is on the one hand a locus in which a given language is formed after an individual fashion, and on the other, a speaker who is only able to understand within the totality of language."[10] More grossly stated, in the study of interpretation, one's focus cannot be fixed on either the narrow or the broad, for fixing on an extreme denies the dialogic complexity of their fundamental circularity.

The notion is not unrelated to the circularity discussed by Varela, Thompson, and Rosch (noted earlier). Gadamer articulates a similar notion in his extension of the concept of the hermeneutic circle in which he more explicitly brings in the interpretive consciousness. For him, an interpretation involves first an appropriation of an event and, as one comes to meaning (interprets), a transformation of that event. The hermeneutic inquirer, in contrast to the social scientist,[11] thus cannot attempt to maintain the attitude of a detached observer whose goal is to provide an objective account of some phenomenon. Quite the contrary, the hermeneut recognizes his or her complicity in shaping the phenomenon, simultaneously affecting and affected by both the particular and the general, thus wholly embedded in the situation. In other words, the "object" of the hermeneutic inquiry is a moving target. As we study our conception of mathematics teaching, for example, our understanding of teaching—that is, the very "object" of our inquiry—changes . . . in part because of our efforts to understand it.[12] One of the central concerns of hermeneutics, and one of the reasons for a cyclical mode of inquiry, is the question of how one might go about inquiring into a phenomenon in which one is immersed, entangled, and complicit.

And so, hermeneutic inquiry cannot be conceived of as a linear process. While we as yet lack a word to describe the sort of path that might be taken through the research, terms such as recursive, circular, and reflective provide some sense of the process. Hermeneutics, then, seeks to undo our habit of "writing backward"—that is, of weaving narrative strands that serve to impose structure on and that enable us to extract meaning from an amorphous mass of, at the time of living through it, largely unformulated experience.

It is easy to see why hermeneutics is often perceived of as "philosophical" (in the derogatory sense). This description, while on one level appropriate (its purpose is to interrogate "commonsense"), is unfortunate. As Smith states, "We never think or interpret 'in general' as a rhetorical activity that bears no necessary connection to the world at large."[13] We cannot extract or abstract our thinking (or our selves) out of the world we are thinking about. In consequence, a "clear split between subjective thinking and objective thinking is ridiculous because my subjectivity gets its bearing from the very world I take as my object"[14] and with which, to recall an enactivist notion, I co-emerge.

In this writing, I have attempted to re-present this subject to object interplay and the general to particular movement in the structure on the document. Each chapter presents a cycle from the broad (the cultural) to the specific (the classroom); in each I have endeavored to enact the dialogical and circular nature of my and my co-researchers current understandings. I have also attempted to include a trace of the emergence of those understandings, but these traces are more often implicitly than blatantly stated. As such, at the outset, I provide an orienting statement as to the manner in which the guiding questions were developed and posed and the ways in which the research settings were "structured." Specific details of these elements are distributed throughout the text. The more general considerations follow.

The Hermeneutic Question

A theme running through this document is that, fundamentally, the nature of human experience is dialogical; my world is neither objectively fixed nor subjectively constituted, but negotiated with others with whom I find myself in communicative interaction. Correspondingly, as Silverman puts it, the stress in a hermeneutic inquiry "is not upon the subjective interests of the interpreter nor upon the objective features of the work itself, but on the act of interpreting and the significance of the interpretation that is produced."[15] These notions are critical to an understanding of hermeneutics and its concern for avoiding the unnecessary dichotomizing of subject and object and of self and other. Within a focus on the deliberate act of interpretation, the interpreter, the interpreted, and the interpretive community are simultaneously presented.

Within this frame, then, truth and knowledge are not static forms which, after discovery or creation, take on autonomous existences; truth and knowledge are always contingent, existing not in a single authority, but amid dynamic interaction and engagement. Truth and knowledge are dialogical. As such, the method used to investigate (interpret) a phenomenon needs to be similarly conversational—an idea that has implications not just for the style of the research, but for the questions that orient it.

Hans-Georg Gadamer[16] has provided us with a provocative exploration of this issue, arguing that the relationship between the research question and the phenomenon under study is not uni-directional, but reciprocal. Briefly, his suggestion is that the topic of investigation, at least in part, reveals the manner in which it should be investigated. Further, the phenomenon is shaped by the way we inquire into it—that is, by how we structure our question. Physicist Werner Heisenberg made essentially this same point in his famous statement, "What we observe is not nature itself but nature exposed to our method of questioning."

By calling into question our mode of questioning in this scientific age, hermeneuts like Gadamer have often been accused of being anti-methodological. The accusation is unjustified. The hermeneutic critique of conventional scientized approaches to research is *not* that those methods are wrong or inappropriate, but that they are narrow and inevitably lead to a particular (i.e., abstracted and ostensibly objective) sort of truth; they do not allow the researcher to be aware of, let alone to move outside of, a particular interpretive frame. Such research, we might say, is guided by the reductive question, "What is . . . ?" rather than the expansive, "What might be . . . ?" In contrast, successful hermeneutic research does not seek to close the doors of inquiry by arriving at some "answer" or uncovering some Truth. Rather, it seeks to open the doors wider, permitting both writer and reader to see their positions in a more open way. As Silverman puts it, the task of hermeneutics "is to raise questions rather than to answer them, to ask about rather than to conclude for, and to make a place where positions *can occur* rather than speak *from* positions."[17]

Another way of saying this is that all modes of research and inquiry are concerned with interpretation on some level. The sorts of interpretations that were generated from within the positivist tradition, along with the raw data of any study, might be called "first order." The inquirer is often completely unaware of the biases that he or she brought to the study while gathering and compiling such information; unaware that the *simple* acts of noticing and selecting are already interpretations. More recently, particularly among those engaged in research in the humanities, there has been a movement to announce one's positionings and theoretical framings—a movement that prompts us toward "second order" interpretations. An awareness (and formulated account) of the biases that help to shape one's conclusions is implicit at this level, and readers should have a sense of the author through his or her writing. Hermeneutics concerns itself with what might be called "third order" interpretations. Not only is there a deliberate attempt to participate in the generation of new ideas (first order), not only is the researcher compelled to be clear about his or her commitments and how those commitments might impinge on his or her interpretations (second order), there must also be an active interrogation of those commitments. As well, the interpretations should be brought to bear on the researcher's own circumstances. It is this obligation that places the researcher in the hermeneutic circle, constantly reading the particular against the general, the past, present, and projected against one another, and open to the transformative demands of dedicated inquiry. In this way, the hermeneut is inevitably incorporated—embodied—in his or her research and complicit in the phenomenon under investigation.

This point is made clearer in Gadamer's analysis of the nature of the hermeneutic question in which he develops the notion of "prejudice." Divesting it of its negative connotations, Gadamer uses prejudice to draw attention to the fact that what we hear and see is what we have been biologically and culturally predisposed to perceive. With regard to research, then, what we come to understand is very much determined by the manner in which our orienting question is posed, because the statement of the question can be understood only through our established prejudices. Of course, in articulating the notion of prejudice, Gadamer is not recommending that we avoid prejudgments, but that we seek them out and interrogate them and the conditions that underlie them—that is, to move to what I am calling a third order interpretation. Since perceptions are enabled (just as they are limited) by such prejudices, the goal is not to negate but to transform—that is, to perceive differently. Such transformational demands apply not only personal conceptions: the very identity of the researcher is subject to the same sort of evolutions.

This movement toward perceiving differently is possible (and necessary) only when the orienting question is permitted to be similarly negotiated or interrogated. In the hermeneutic investigation, therefore, the questions are never fixed. Indeed, the hermeneutic question might better be thought of as an issue or a topic of wonder. It is an entry point for excavation, not an arrow for answer seeking. It presents an opportunity to unearth the heretofore hidden "truths" of how we arrived at our current place. The hermeneutic question is an idea, for as Gadamer explains, "Every sudden idea has the structure of a question."[18] Moreover, "the sudden occurrence of the question is already a breach in the smooth front of popular opinion. Hence we say that a question 'occurs' to us, that it 'arises' or 'presents itself' more than we raise or present it."[19] Such is the question that oriented this research: the possibility of reconceiving of mathematics teaching as a process of listening. I hope to illustrate in the following pages the sort of exploration and play that this notion has invited. I also hope to give a deep sense of how, in the process of investigation, the orienting issue itself evolved through the dedicated, and oftentimes uncomfortable, interactions of the research participants (included among whom were fellow students, practicing teachers, professors, and unsuspecting acquaintances).

Such discomfort was to be expected because, as mentioned earlier, a hermeneutic investigation makes particular transformative demands on those involved. In seeking to interpret and to re-interpret experience, we are also seeking to affect how we stand in the world. A hermeneutic study, then, is fundamentally a moral undertaking. It makes no claims to the scientistic ideals of neutrality, objectivity, and generalizability. Rather, its goals are realized in deepened, practical, nondogmatic, and consensual understandings among its participants: viable understandings rather than verifiable facts, relevant interpretations rather than generalizable conclusions.

The Hermeneutic Conversation

"Hermeneutics" refers neither to a particular (instrumental) approach to research nor to a unified field of inquiry. Rather, it addresses a broad range of topics and issues. The unifying theme in hermeneutics is a persistent questioning of our taken-for-granted modes of speaking and acting.

It is thus that hermeneutics falls outside the conventional bounds of research methods—where the term "method" is understood to refer to a more-or-less static and rigorous procedure for attaining a prespecified end. It is interesting to note that, according to the *Oxford English Dictionary*, this definition of "method" arose in the seventeenth century (that is, in the same era as Descartes, Galileo, and Bacon). Prior to that time, a method was "a shared (*meta-*) way (*-odos*)." That is, a method was an approach to knowledge that foregrounded the place of common action and accord rather than the questing to erect an autonomous truth—the process rather than the goal. Hermeneutics is a method in this premodern sense.

It is thus that the conversation—that is, reciprocal engagement in a topic of mutual concern—is generally identified as the site in which this sort of inquiry happens, for it is in dialogue with one another that our conflicting prejudices are uncovered and transformed. Subjectivity dissolves into participation in dialogue, the point of which, as Crusius explains, "is not to hold a position against all challengers, but to listen, to allow one's opinions to be matured by opening oneself to partners in the dialogue whose horizons differ from our own."[20] Gadamer describes this process as a "fusion of horizons," where one's horizon is the ever-changing, historically- and situationally-shaped starting place of our thoughts and actions. In the conversation, Gadamer suggests, there is potential for such fusion as participants come to new understandings which are, at that moment of interactive unity, commonly held. A fusion of horizons is "an event of truth, a revealing-concealing that goes beyond the spontaneous, unscrutinized projections of preunderstanding."[21]

It is important to draw an initial distinction between a conversation and a discussion at this point. (The distinction is elaborated upon in the next section.) In the conversation, all of the participants are oriented toward deepening their understanding of the issue at hand. In a sense, then, the subject matter conducts the participants and there is a quality of self-forgetfulness as all concerned come to understand that they share in the truth of the interaction. The goal of the discussion, in contrast, is more toward the articulation of preformulated ideas, and so the subjects endeavor to exert some measure of control over the subject matter. The emphasis in the discussion is placed on the subjects' conceptual differences rather than on achieving a consensus. Rather than a forgetting of selves, there is a concretizing of subjective positions; horizons are not placed at hazard in the discussion.

Quite unlike the discussion, then, the conversation is fluid, meandering its way toward a destination that is not specific, but that will be commonly known. That the destination is unspecified and unanticipated is the strength of the conversation for, by being unconcerned with reaching a particular point (i.e., relinquishing the modernist desire for control)—by allowing the path to be laid down in walking—the participants are able to listen to the particularities that shape that path. The goal of the participants in a discussion, much in contrast, is often to remain rigidly in place, to be unswayed.

A distinction might also be drawn between the conversation and the interview as a foundation of research. The latter, which literally means "between views," might be regarded as an even more radical version of the discussion, where the agenda might be rigidly preset (through the selection of questions, settings, etc.) and, very often, where the interpretive framework is laid out well in advance of any sort of interaction. There is little or no intention of having one's own views affected—and, with the usually impersonal and undemanding protocols, there is little danger of this occurring. The conversation is quite the opposite, both in spirit and in consequence.

There are, of course, dangers in suggesting that a hermeneutic investigation relies so fundamentally on the conversation. First, for example, in our modern setting, there is always a temptation to methodologize—a proclivity that can serve only to prevent rather than provoke conversation. Second, in a related vein, while one might avoid such attempts to induce conversation, there often remains a compulsion to explain how one comes to be aware that a conversation is taking place. In my own research, this particular compulsion has proven very troublesome, and has led to the dissolution of potentially fruitful interactions rather than to their promotion. This consequence should not be surprising, for the idea that one can be aware that one is in a conversation is in some ways self-contradictory; it presumes an awareness of one's self and one's subjectivity. It is precisely this detached, observer-like awareness that must be set aside in order to allow a conversation in the first place.[22]

In other words, we can never be aware that a conversation *is taking place*. We can, however, be aware that one *has taken place*. When understandings have changed, when a new commonsense has been established—when self and other have been altered—it has happened.

A third difficulty with the apparent reliance on the conversation is that the emphasis might suggest a disregard for other forms of research. A friend's reaction to my explication of hermeneutic inquiry illustrates this point: "So, you just have to go around talking to people and trying to come to some kind of common understanding."

Quite the opposite, hermeneutic inquiry relies on the planned as well as the unplanned, the expected as well as the fortuitous. Essential features of my own research included etymological searches of key terms, observation of mathematics classes, planning units and lessons, discussions of theoretical and practical issues in teaching, participation in academic conferences, broad and deep readings in a range of disciplines—not to mention extensive writing and re-writing—all consistent with the sort of eclectic "puttering about" that is implicit in the notion of *bricolage* announced in the introduction. In particular, the exploration of historical accounts of various topics was of critical importance. Lacking a broad familiarity with the events and the perspectives that have shaped current practices and awarenesses, one's attempts to explore alternatives would probably be seriously constrained.

Further, day-to-day experiences, such as the one that I used to open this section, had "fuzzy" influences on the course of my life and, hence, and on the shape of this project. The extent and precise natures of these influences could never be determined. Nor would we want to do so in a hermeneutic inquiry. The goal is not to give a blow-by-blow account of how an understanding was reached, but to investigate how one's understandings might affect how one stands in the world.

The point here is not that this project was multifaceted; all research projects are. Nor is it that some aspects were orchestrated while others were improvised; the same is true of the most rigorously controlled scientific experiment. The point is that, in order for the conversations to occur at all, there had to be considerable advance preparation and learning. In other words, I had a responsibility to ensure that I was capable of engaging in conversation—a responsibility that demanded not just that I have an interest in the topic, but that I have an adequate conceptual background to think of things differently. There was little potential for engaging others without the possibility of challenging their thinking. And there was little likelihood that I would be able to listen for the "watershed moments" that constantly, but quietly, presented themselves. In contrast to those more rigidly controlled modes of research, the goals of which are replicability, generalizability, and verifiability, the hermeneutic investigation seeks to understand the rich textuality of the unique amid the immediately present. The goal is thus to embrace happenstance rather than to "explain it away."

From the Visual to the Auditory (Revisited)

The movement away from culturally privileged research methodologies toward a hermeneutic inquiry might be described as a shift from looking to listening.

We tend to use visual metaphors in our descriptions of scientific and scientized approaches. (A *glance* in a thesaurus for synonyms of such terms as "understanding" and "investigation" is most *revealing.*) Many science texts use the image of a disembodied eye to represent the scientific attitude, reinforcing the notion that, through vision, the subjective observer is separated from objective reality. The necessity of such separation is hardly surprising since the word "science" is derived from a term that meant "to cut apart." This scientific gaze, insofar as it is applied to issues in a social context, also tends to "freeze" phenomena. (This tendency is powerfully revealed in the pervasive use of statistics—derived from the Greek *states,* one that stops or steadies—as a basis of interpretation.)[23]

In contrast, the hermeneutic text endeavors to avoid these distancing and fixing activities, and this is why explications of hermeneutics tend to employ auditory metaphors. The notion that conversation is foundational to the hermeneutic inquiry, for example, has a figurative as well as a literal relevance as we seek to locate ourselves in the wider conversations of history and context. Further, the goals of hermeneutic research are toward *attunement* and *harmony* amid the *noise* of existence. One is concerned with *theme,* with *tone,* with *rhythm,* with *resonance.* As such, one is constantly reminded that understanding, like sound, is fleeting and unfixable.

Further, unlike the isolating tendencies of vision, sound incorporates. Sound pours into the listener, whereas the object of sight exists outside the observer. Walter Ong elaborates on this point:

> *Vision comes to a human being from one direction at a time: to look at a room or a landscape, I must move my eyes around from one part to another. When I hear, however, I gather sound simultaneously from every direction at once. . . . You can immerse yourself in hearing, in sound. There is no way to immerse yourself similarly in sight.*

By contrast with vision, the dissecting sense, sound is thus a unifying sense. A typical visual ideal is clarity and distinctness, a taking apart. . . . The auditory ideal, by contrast, is harmony, a putting together.

. . . Knowledge is ultimately not a fractioning but a unifying phenomenon, a striving for harmony.[24]

It is thus hardly accidental that, in my initial explorations of how mathematics teaching might be recast in terms of listening, I felt a particular resonance with the *sound* foundations of hermeneutics. There is a certain harmony implicit in the statement that this project—this quest into teachers' listening—is hermeneutic, for the hermeneutic attitude is a listening attitude.

But, what is the nature of listening? Or, more fundamentally, how might we investigate the phenomenon of listening?

(Hermeneutic) Phenomenology

Hermeneutics reveals that our understandings, our perceptions, our actions, our experiences are objects that are always and already interpreted; they are constituted within our common language, they are enacted in certain settings, they are framed by particular webs of relationships. By questioning the terms, the traditions, and the texts that shape our understandings, hermeneutics raises the hope that we might begin to think differently about our selves and our situations.

Hermeneutics, then, holds as its focus the reinterpretation of already interpreted phenomena, asking both, "What does this mean?" and "How has this meaning arisen?" But what of those phenomena that precede and invite interpretation—such as that which enables (or comes to be referred to as) our listening?

These sorts of questions demand a descriptive rather than a strictly interpretive methodology, and this is the realm of phenomenology—the study of experiences—which concentrates its efforts "upon re-achieving a direct and primitive contact with the world."[25] Phenomenology investigates the nature of things and events, seeking to undercut our theoretically-sedimented and linguistically-constituted preconceptions; phenomenology "demands of us a re-learning to look at the world as we meet it in immediate experience."[26]

The purpose is not to explain or control, but to bring us in closer contact with the world, in the process, fostering human responsibility in the construction of realities. Phenomenology thus asks, What is this experience like?

Historically, scientists have attempted to adopt positions of disembodied observers or disworlded minds that are parachuted into uncharted objective reality. Critiquing such positionings, Merleau-Ponty wrote, "The world is inseparable from the subject, but from a subject which is nothing but a project of the world, and the subject is inseparable from the world, but from a world which the subject itself projects."[27] We are complicit in the world, and so we can never really speak of it as removed from our selves. Phenomenology, then, "does not produce empirical or theoretical observations or accounts. Instead, it offers accounts of experienced space, time, body, and human relations as we live them."[28]

Of course, such description must occur within language. Phenomenological accounts are, therefore, interpretive (hermeneutic) accounts as well, aiming to tighten (rather than loosen) the bond between experiences and the theories or concepts we use to explain them. In attempting to (re)interpret experiences in this manner, phenomenology inevitably faces the paradox of using language to push language aside. The text of the phenomenological account, then, is not used primarily to offer descriptions but to point at or to disclose experiences that underlie those descriptions as they unfold relatively naively.

Invariably, this sort of investigation involves extensive writing and rewriting as one endeavors to pull away from what has long been taken-for-granted in our hurried and unreflective ways of living. Such undertakings demand attitudes of patient attentiveness and persistent questioning, never allowing one's conceptions to be fixed or settled. An inevitable consequence of a phenomenological investigation is thus a renewed appreciation of the complexity that permeates the simplest, most straightforward experience.

Because phenomenology is the study of the intersections of human experience in consciousness, it can be understood only by participating in the phenomenological method. The next section, on the nature of listening, represents my attempt to do just that.

Section C
Listening

It seems so simple . . . we have languages with
nuances that create fatter and fatter dictionaries . . .
We have perception that allows us to touch the moon . . .
Yet we cannot touch each other or the world around us . . .
We have forgotten how to listen.

—*Hannah Merker*[1]

Our listening needs to learn receptiveness, responsiveness, and care. Our listening needs to return to the intertwining of self and other, subject and object; for it is there that the roots of its communicativeness take hold and thrive.

—*David Levin*[2]

It is interesting to note how often the term "listening" arises in the current social, political, and economic contexts. Over the course of a typical news broadcast, it is not unusual to hear political candidates promising to listen to their prospective constituents or warring factions demanding that their opponents listen to their claims. In a school staffroom, teachers comment that they are no longer listened to: pupils seem to have lost the capacity; parents and the government seem to have lost the interest. In the hallways of the same school, students offer a similar lament: no one seems to be listening to them.

In each of these cases, one of the concerned parties feels distanced from the other and each believes that this distance might be reduced by listening. Unfortunately, demands for such listening are usually made of others; the concern is with someone else's inattention. It seems that we are wont to regard ourselves as capable listeners, and others simply as lacking this capacity. Consider, for example, how often one hears exchanges of the following form in the context of an argument or a heated discussion:

"If you would only listen!"

"No, you're the one who needs to listen!"

It is at first tempting to suggest that such exchanges indicate incompatible understandings of listening. In this section, I wish to argue against that idea: such understandings are not *incompatible*; they are *incomplete*, for they are founded on inaction rather than enaction. I approach the topic by developing a phenomenological account of listening, focusing not so much on what listening *is* but on what it might mean to think of ourselves as beings with the capacity to listen.

Underlying this exploration is the belief that the modernist notions which are implicit in most conventional conceptions of interpersonal communication are, simply put, false. We tend to take for granted, for instance, that we are insulated and autonomous individuals, that a mysterious substance called "information" can flow between us as we interact, that we are somehow in control of what is said and what is heard. In some current educational discourses, these ideas have coalesced into such notions as *voice* and *empowerment*—notions that acknowledge the ineffectiveness of communication in today's settings, but which reify instead of dismantle the modernist separations that underlie this ineffectiveness. Rather than seeking to promote conversation, we are compelled to perpetuate the model of competing monologues. The goal of such emancipatory discourse, it appears, is to promote listening—but by force. The reasoning seems to be that by developing more powerful voices, we will be able to reach across separations and we will be able to compel others to *see* things from our perspective. In brief, we want people to think the way we think.

In essence, this project is directed at proposing an alternative to this ideal. I contend that we do not need to amplify our voices in an effort to overcome chasms and walls. Rather, we need to realize that those barriers are not really there, and a deeper understanding of listening will enable us to dispel those pervasive illusions. The purpose of this section, then, is to come to deeper understandings of human communication and collective action—and I seek to accomplish these through a phenomenology of listening. In terms of the subsequent discussions of classroom phenomena, this section is of critical importance. In it I attempt both to translate some of the ideas from the preceding discussions into the context of interpersonal relationships and to introduce the interpretive framework that is later used to examine classroom events.

Our Collective Loss of Hearing

During the 1970s, a colleague and friend spent several years teaching in a remote village in Canada's far North. Early in her stay, several of the local Inuit women arrived at her door for an unannounced after-school visit.

Laura welcomed them into her home and, in true Western fashion, attempted to be a good host by serving tea and making light, but pleasant, conversation. To her frustration and concern, however, the collective response was one of prolonged and almost total silence. They sat in her living room, each quietly knitting or sewing. Not surprisingly, it was with considerable relief that Laura bade them a good evening some time later.

Months after, when relationships were better established and Laura felt herself more a part of the community, she asked some of her new friends about that first encounter—in the process inadvertently revealing her belief that her visitors had been suspicious of her intentions and had thus dropped by to place her under scrutiny. Laughing at this suggestion, the women assured her that their actions had nothing to do with any sort of initial apprehension. Rather, they explained, they had visited to get to know her better. Further, they had not thought of their collective action as being intrusive. Holding different conceptions of what it means to live together, they did not go to Laura's home to "visit" (in the Western sense of "dropping in" and departing without leaving a trace), but to dwell.[3]

My own interpretation of this story is that these Inuit women held a certain disdain for the Western uses of discussion and surveillance as a means of introduction (if they were even aware of them). Far from helping us to get to know one another, in such necessarily shallow interactions we mask ourselves with convention. The resulting "conversations" are more concealing than revealing, serving to underscore our respective subjectivities rather than helping to dissolve them in communicative action. It is by listening—by attending to the person's action and situation, and not just to his or her voice—that one comes to know the other.

It is toward a similar sense of listening that this section is directed, a listening that is neither limited in focus to the verbal nor itself held silent. And a listening that seems all but lost—over*look*ed—in our society.

For, as argued in the preceding section, ours is a culture that favors the visual over the auditory, and this characteristic of modernist societies represents a dramatic departure from earlier traditions. Walter Ong,[4] for example, in his account of the recent movement away from spoken (oral) traditions toward written (visual) ones—a shift that accompanied the "scientific revolution"—suggests that, not only has there been a loss of status for the auditory, there has emerged a contempt for the spoken, the heard, and the listened to.

Belenky, Clinchy, Goldberger, and Tarule, in a similar vein, point to the "allocation of listening to women,"[5] contending that our privileging of looking over hearing is tied inextricably to our modernist favoring of the masculine over the feminine. Consequently, within our culture, there is a pervasive use of visual metaphors to describe the many *facets* of education. We *see* learning as gaining *insight*, intelligence as *brightness*, investigation as *looking*, understanding as *seeing*, opinions as *perspectives* or *views*, hopes as *visions*, and (very often) teaching as super*vision*. More broadly, tendencies to associate truth with *light*, believing with *seeing*, and objectivity with the distance afforded only to the observer, point to the overwhelming domination of vision over the other senses. Contrasting visual with auditory metaphors, Belenky and her associates write:

> *Visual metaphors encourage standing at a distance to get a proper view, removing—it is believed—subject and object from a sphere of possible intercourse. Unlike the eye, the ear operates by registering nearby subtle change. Unlike the eye, the ear requires closeness between subject and object. Unlike seeing, speaking and listening suggest dialogue and interaction.*[6]

We tend to stand back in order to see and to move nearer in order to hear. Correspondingly, there is an element of discomfort associated with being watched, but we generally want to be listened to—in part, at least, because of the interaction afforded by listening. Whether I am the "listener" or the "listened to," I participate in a very different way than when I am the "watcher" or the "watched." In particular, because we are unable to shut off our hearing with the ease that we can close off our seeing, attempts to *not* hear often result in being compelled to listen more attentively. As suggested by the imperative, "Close your eyes and listen," we can easily cut ourselves apart from the objects of our vision, but we are inevitably immersed in the sonorous field of the situation.

Given the different manners in which hearing and sight situate us in relationships with others, it is perhaps not surprising to note that relationships among those who are hearing-impaired are often more strained that among those who are visually impaired. Berendt,[7] for example, comments on the very different sorts of interactions that occur among residents of homes for the deaf relative to those among residents of homes for the blind. The former tend more toward aggression and discord, the latter toward caution and compromise. And Helen Keller, in her letters and journals, frequently commented that the problems of deafness are "more complex" than the problems of blindness, for the deaf person is cut off from others in a much more profound way.[8]

Perhaps, then, the idea that Laura had missed during the first visits of her Inuit neighbors is that they had not come to hold her at a distance in their gaze, but to draw her into their circle in their listening.

Looking **for Listening**

Since beginning this study of listening, a favorite activity has been to "eavesdrop" on various sorts of interactions. These covert activities have not been limited to classrooms; settings have included offices, restaurants, airplanes, and conference halls. What has come as a surprise, and what may be more an indication of my own inability to escape the privileging of vision, is how easy it is to *see* listening.[9]

There is a particular bodily aspect to listening, a visible orienting to the subject of the discussion. When two persons converse, for example, it can be *seen* that they are listening to one another as the actions of their bodies become bodily *inter*actions. They lean into and reach out for one another, momentarily unaware that they are violating the Western taboos on proximity, touch, and extended eye contact. They seem to focus in a way that suggests they are oblivious to the noise around them; they attend to each word and to each action as though nothing of importance occurred prior to the discussion and nothing of importance awaits them at its end. They are unconcerned that their voices are perhaps too loud, that their bodies are too animated.

Listening, then, need be neither motionless nor silent (although more often than not, it seems, it is precisely this sort of inactive attention that is demanded of students by teachers). Of course, the listener may assume this posture, but it is something other than an audience's lack of motion or their silence that makes us aware that they are listening. In the classroom, for example, as the novel is read or the mathematical principle emerges, the teacher knows the students are listening not because they have ceased to move but because a certain rhythm or harmony is established—there is an awareness that each is immersed in and conducted by the same subject matter. The gazes are fixed not on the teacher nor on one another, but on that which is among them.

That the listener should not be thought of as the quiet partner in an interaction is suggested by our use of the term "sounding board." Just as the sounding board in a musical instrument is intended to resonate with, echo, and amplify the sounds generated by other parts of the instrument—that is, the sounding board participates in the music generated—so the listener who acts as a sounding board participates in the emerging conversation.

Important qualities of listening, then, are that it be active and participatory, and an immediate implication is that the listener cannot be held silent. (He or she may choose not to speak, however.) In the process of listening, one questions, challenges, smiles, frowns. We often characterize such interactive action as a "forgetting of self"—an intriguing notion, but one that I believe misdirects our attention. Listening more involves a dissolution of static notions of the self, permitting a re-membering of intersubjective awarenesses—a "joining of minds."

The Conversation

In my listening to listening, I have also begun to notice a clear distinction between two sorts of interactions which have a similar appearance but a very different texture: the discussion and the conversation. The distinction between these communicative forms is not so much evident in the words spoken or in the topics addressed as it is in the manner in which the participants listen to one another.

The discussion might be characterized as "coordinated action"[10] in which the respective speakers are attempting to impose their perspectives on the other. Their concerns, then, are for the articulation, explication, and defense of their own views. In more adversarial forms of discussion—those more resembling debates—more energy is directed toward attending to the other's perspectives, but this attendance is with the goal of dismantling those opinions, not for understanding their origins, let alone for seeking consensus.

The conversation, in contrast, is less oriented to pointing out differences and more concerned with arriving at shared understandings. Put otherwise, the discussion is an analytical rhetorical structure; the conversation is a place of listening. An analysis of the origins of the two words helps to make this point clearer: To *discuss* originally meant to "shake apart," and its emphasis on separation continues to echo in our current use of the term. To *converse*, much in contrast, had a meaning more toward "to live with" or "to keep company with." This is why we use "conversation" when referring to interactions with friends and "discussion" when speaking of meeting with strangers, professional colleagues, and business contacts. The conversation-discussion distinction also points to a, perhaps unfortunate, trend in teacher-student interactions: as recent developments have alerted us to the importance of active interaction while learning, we have tended to opt for "classroom discussions" rather than conversations. Not surprisingly, there doesn't seem to be much listening happening within such settings, although (in my own experience with classroom discussions, at least) the demands that others listen tend to increase dramatically.

The conversation, thus, offers a rich territory for an exploration of listening. As Taylor explains:

[Conversations] move beyond mere coordination and have a common rhythm. The interlocutor not only listens but participates with head nodding and "unh-hunh" and the like, and at a certain point the "semantic turn" passes over to the other by a common movement. The appropriate moment is felt by both partners together in virtue of the common rhythm.[11]

Taylor contrasts such "dialogical acts" with "monological acts"—acts of a single, ostensibly autonomous and isolated, agent. Taylor's use of "dialogical" is, I believe, similar to Varela, Thompson, and Rosch's use of "co-emergent," suggesting that a conversation is more than an intertwining of two separate voices (or, in Taylor's terms, two "monologues"). Rather, the conversation involves a merging of subjectivities as, together, we are conducted toward new questions and new understandings. Unlike the discussion, which lacks the qualities of rhythm and of "living with the other," the conversation's path is neither predictable nor controllable. Nor would we want to prescribe its route or its outcome because, again in contrast to the discussion, the "purpose" of the conversation is as much the act of conversing (i.e., "living with others") as it is the development of a deeper understanding. There is no winner, no gaining of the upper hand, no final word, no compulsion to stick with the topic. Rather, the conversation allows us to move freely and interactively toward those questions that animate us while enabling us to explore not just the topics that emerge, but why such topics capture our interest in the first place.

Gadamer has written extensively on the nature of the conversational relation. In his formulation, the conversation is a triad involving you, me, and the topic or subject matter. The subject matter exists only in the conversation[12]—neither in you nor in me, but between or about us—and we are "conducted" by it.

For Gadamer, the conversational relationship is an intimate one—an idea that is echoed by Merleau-Ponty who suggests that human interaction involves a merging or an intercorporeality.

[As I listen to another, my body] discovers in that other body a miraculous prolongation of my intentions, a familiar way of dealing with the world. Henceforth, as the parts of my body together comprise a system, so

my body and the other person's are one whole, two sides of one and the same phenomenon, and the anonymous existence of which my body is the ever-renewed trace henceforth inhabits both bodies simultaneously.[13]

We are thus joined in conversation, a theme that is common in the writings of both Merleau-Ponty and Gadamer. Elsewhere, for example, Merleau-Ponty describes the communicative act as "one system with two terms (my behavior and the other's behavior) which function as a whole."[14] Husserl, similarly, described such coordinated action as a phenomenon of "coupling" where, according to Merleau-Ponty, the notion of "coupling" is "anything but a metaphor."[15] He goes on to explain that it is our capacity to perceive—to sense and to make sense of—the other that enables this phenomenon: "In perceiving the other, my body and his are coupled, resulting in a sort of action which pairs them (*action à deux*)."[16] The conversation, and hence listening, thus involves a sort of ego-loss where the culturally constructed barriers between self and other are dissolved.

Maturana and Varela,[17] working from a basis in the biological sciences, have arrived at a similar formulation. In their terms, the interactive unity of the conversation involves a "structural coupling" that brings about a system of higher order. The conversation is thus not a "third thing" that is made up of two people; nor is it something happening between them. Such interpretations—like the suggestions that the human body is just a compilation of organs which, in turn, are mere assemblages of cells—miss the essential element that bodies and organs (and conversations) have integrities proper to themselves that are analogous to the integrities of their subsystems.[18]

Complementing Gadamer and Merleau-Ponty, then, Maturana and Varela would agree that, in conversation, we set aside our illusions of subjectivity, allowing a collective consciousness to emerge. In this relational unity, we become capable of greater insight and deeper understanding,[19] capable even of cutting beneath the conscious intent of the speaker.

A goal of the conversation is to deepen understanding and, in that deepening, to create knowledge. It "has a hermeneutic thrust: it is oriented to sense-making and interpreting that notion that drives or stimulates the conversation."[20] The key to such sense-making, and that which enables the interpretation, is listening, itself hermeneutic. It is our capacity to listen—that is, our ability to attend to and to interpret what is said—that makes conversation possible. Levin suggests:

When listening really echoes and resonates, when it allows the communication to reverberate between the communicants, and to constitute, there, a space free of pressure and constraint, it actively contributes, quite apart from the speaking, to the intersubjective constellation of new meaning, *meaning actually born within this intercorporeality; and it promises, because of this, the achievement of mutual understanding—if not also consensus.*[21]

The conversation, enabled by our capacities to listen, is a "meeting of (embodied) minds."

Listening Is Not a Technique

Robert Pirsig describes the title character of his book, *Lila: An Inquiry into Morals*, in the following way:

What he'd told her . . . was valuable if she'd been listening. But she wasn't. She wasn't a listener. She had a fixed set of static patterns of value and if you argued with her, she'd get mad at you.[22]

The statement, "She wasn't a listener," is immediately comprehensible. In so describing Lila, Pirsig is suggesting not that she was incapable of hearing, but that she was not normally open to others and to their ideas, limited by her "fixed static patterns." Listening thus is not primarily an act; it is an orientation. Everyone is capable of listening, but few, it seems, are in the world in a listening way. Listening, then, is a way of being in the world, an "*ontologically oriented* capacity"[23] that is directed toward bringing ourselves and others into being.

We are all acquainted with people who are not listeners. When we talk with them, they might ask the correct sorts of questions and perhaps even display the appropriate mannerisms, but our contributions either seem to be ignored or misinterpreted. We get an uneasy feeling because, even though we find ourselves within the interaction, it does not seem that we are part of it. We feel rushed, unheard, not listened to, excluded—not present. We quickly become unwilling to "share" even the most mundane thoughts.

Nevertheless, in keeping with the modernist tendency, efforts have been made to reduce listening to a technique. Text after text on the topic of improving listening skills is now available, almost all of them suggesting that success (usually in business) is tightly linked to mastering this ability.[24] These manuals, it seems, are founded on the premise that the acquisition of particular skills will change the person and the sorts of relationships that person is able to maintain, in contrast to the perspective that how one listens—and hence, the nature of one's relationships—emerge from the way one is already standing in the world.

One notable contribution was made by Carl Rogers[25] in the development of his "Active Listening" program—a system by which particular skills, intended to enable the listening of psychologists and counselors, were identified and described. Unfortunately, in many cases, Rogers' program was misinterpreted as focusing on the development of these skills rather than on the development of one's listening. Among the victims of this technical reduction was a guidance counselor and colleague named Jean. Shortly after being appointed to the position of school counselor (by an administration that was impressed with the sorts of relationships she had with her students), Jean attended a series of seminars and inservices where she was to develop a better understanding of her role. Based on what she had learned in these sessions, she tried "active listening" by paraphrasing, repeating, requesting clarification, and affirming student articulations. The general response was one of confusion, frustration, and anger—and Jean quickly recognized the impairing effect of focusing on the skills rather than on the listening. As is typical of modernist projects, this effort resulted in a separation and a distancing rather than a facilitation of communicative interaction.

And so listening cannot be reduced to a set of prescriptions or guidelines. It is something that we enter into, something that we are, emerging from our occupation with others and with their meanings.

Listening as *Embodied Action*

Listening is a way of being which surpasses our efforts to formalize or articulate. It is not so much a conscious effort as it is a way of participating with others. Unfortunately, with our cultural desire toward clear and unambiguous language, listening has been understood as strictly auditory, passive, and subjective.

Each of these notions is challenged in the suggestion that listening is embodied. The separation of listening from other sensory modalities, for example, is not so easily made when one considers the overlap between touch and listening. As Schafer explains, "hearing and touch meet where the lower frequencies of audible sound pass over to tactile vibrations (at about 20 hertz). Hearing is a way of touching at a distance."[26] Further evidence of the whole-bodily status of hearing can be found in examinations of the psychological and physiological consequences brought on by the modern phenomenon of noise pollution. Pervasive noise does more than restrict hearing. On the individual level, it impairs concentration and memory; it affects mood and performance; it contributes to fatigue, high blood pressure and other stress-related disorders. On the collective level, noise undermines interaction and sociability, thus disrupting the "collective body"—that is, our capacities for joint or shared action. (Unfortunately, but not surprisingly, noise pollution seems to be almost a non-issue beside the more visible—but no more serious—problems of air, land, and water pollution.)

As for the belief that listening is passive, Straus[27] reminds us that this pervasive notion is founded on a troubling distinction that tends to be drawn between perception and action. The inappropriateness of that idea is evidenced by our bodily actions in listening: we raise, tilt, and turn our heads, we move closer, we hold still other parts of our bodies. Listening—likes smelling, tasting, touching, and looking—is a reaching activity, a motor activity, an en-activity.

Further to this point, Charles Taylor[28] writes of two sorts of action: formulated and unformulated. The former he describes as those thoughts, behaviors, and bits of knowledge that we have written into the text of our experience—those we are aware of, speak of, and tend to link in narrative or causal chains. Such formulated actions, Taylor argues, represent only a small portion of our total action, even though they dominate our conscious awarenesses. The bulk of our moment-to-moment living is a matter of unformulated action—a negotiated movement through an interactive world during which our knowledge of that world and our way of being in that world are continuously enacted. The evidence of such knowledge and understandings is our survival, not our ability to identify or explain (narrate) our actions in formal terms.

Understood in the context of our daily lives, then, listening is embodied, enacted and not necessarily formulated. An important implication of this idea is that listening cannot be considered as merely an auditory capacity that can be understood in behavioral science terms. We listen not just with our ears and minds, but also with our bodies. It is an activity of all the senses, attuned not only to the text of the conversation, but to the subtexts, the contexts, the pretexts, and the textures. It is not strictly—nor even primarily—an academic or intellectual activity; it is a fully human endeavor that also evokes physical and emotional responses. As Merleau-Ponty suggests, "I echo the vibration of the sound with my whole sensory being."[29] We listen with our ears, with our eyes, with our touch, with our stomachs, with our bodies, bringing the collected weight of our experience to bear on our emerging understandings.[30]

Listening Is Not the Same as Hearing

Part of my research has involved making audio-recordings of classrooms. Each time I sit to transcribe bits of the teacher-student interactions from one of these recorded lessons, I am struck by the muddle of sounds the machine has captured. There are rustling papers, falling pens, and textbook covers slapping against desktops. There are whispers, sighs, and laughter. But when I was there, I was unaware of this hum of the classroom; I quite simply did not hear these sounds.

I am able to induce the same phenomenon at this moment as I pause from my writing to listen, becoming once again aware of the sounds in which I am immersed. It seems that only when my attention is drawn or directed to particular sounds—like the rumbling of the traffic outside my window—that I am able to hear them.

Moreover, returning to the recordings, as I listen in on the classroom through the mechanical ear, I must struggle to hear particular voices that are woven unevenly and that are tangled with one another. Cut off bodily, I am unable to hear interactions that were easily heard when I stood in the classroom. Cut off bodily, I cannot enter the ebb and flow—to become part of the tone and the tempo—of the lesson. I can do little more than rehear a now-blurred rendering of that lesson. I can do no interrogation, and so I can do little listening.

Hearing and listening, then, are different phenomena. Consider, for example, the difference in intended meaning between the two statements: "I can't *hear*" and "I can't *listen.*" In uttering the former, my concern is that the sound isn't loud enough. It is something I say when I want to hear but, for whatever reason, cannot. The concern is strictly sensory.

In uttering the latter, however, I am suggesting that *I am able* to hear the sound without difficulty. When I say, "I can't listen," I'm not saying that I *can't* hear but that I *won't* hear. To make this point clearer, the statement "I can't hear" is often followed with "Turn *up* the volume." But the statement "I can't listen" tends to be accompanied by requests more along the line of "Turn *down* the volume." Listening is thus a capacity which is founded upon hearing but which goes beyond hearing. It is orienting (we listen *to* something) and oriented (we listen *for* something). Hearing, in contrast, lacks such intentionality.

A comparison to the visual—to seeing and looking—may be helpful here. *Seeing* is the sensory capacity; *looking* is the intentional action through which particular "objects" are pulled into focus (brought forward). Hearing and seeing, the sensory capacities, present us only with an undifferentiated background. It is our capacity to draw something out of that background of experience, to focus on it, and to bring it into our selves—that is, to listen and to look—that enables our perceptions.

The first distinction between hearing and listening is thus made. Hearing is the sensory capacity that underlies our ability to listen. In the classroom, what I heard was determined by what I was listening for: the teacher's questions, the students' answers, the range of pitch and tone in their voices. In one sense I heard everything, because I was aware of no gaps in my perception; the experience was seamless. But in truth, I heard hardly anything.

This also points to a second important distinction between hearing and listening, one that is suggested by the phrases, "I hear you" and "I'm listening." At a recent parents' meeting, a school principal responded to each of the parents' concerns with "I hear you." But it was clear to every parent that she was not listening. In repeating,

"I hear you," she was suggesting that she understood all that was being said, that the speakers' meanings were apparent to her, that there was no need for further listening. Put differently, the parents were not participating in a conversation; rather, they were *having input*—a truth that was altogether apparent to them.

Hearing presumes understanding and, when we cannot comprehend someone, "we can't hear a word he's saying." In contrast, the statement "I'm listening" implies a recognition of the preeminent role of interpretation in our interactions. It is when we perceive gaps in our understandings that we are compelled to listen. Indeed, when someone challenges or fails to grasp the point we are attempting to make, we do not respond with, "There is a problem with your hearing," but by saying, "You're not listening." Recalling Gadamer's notion of the prejudices that shape our perceptions, hearing is inattentive to them while listening entails an active interrogation of the biases that frame our interpretations.

The distinction between hearing and listening is an important one because much of our interaction tends to be undertaken in "hearing mode" rather than "listening mode"—that is, on a knowledge of the other's subjectivity, but not on an awareness of the intersubjective bases of emerging conceptualizations; on knowing, but not on understanding. While perhaps not inappropriate for much of our daily existence, the consequences of operating strictly in the "hearing mode" within the classroom, as will be developed later, can be devastating.

Listening *for*—Our Listening Is Oriented

Listening implies an attunement to the "voices" of others in all their richness. But it would be a gross overstatement to suggest that, by listening, we can somehow transcend the constraints on our perceptions. While I believe it a route to greater openness and richer relationships, we must acknowledge that our listening always and inevitably occurs against the backdrop of personal histories that are set in and shaped by cultural, historical, social, and environmental factors. It is here that the notion of "voice" as a unified projection of the speaker begins to break down, because one's voice can never be singular. Rather, it seems, it is more appropriate to think of our selves as choruses of voices or—to use Gadamer's term—as *conversations.*

In other words, persons are never merely individuals; "they are always also representatives of institutional power, bringing with them a multiplicity of vested interests—and many virtually inaudible agendas."[31] Each of us carries not only the history of our personal experiences, but the accumulated experience of the culture in which we are embedded. (It is thus that, merely by acting, we are participating in the evolution not just of our selves but of our society.) These experiences simultaneously enable and impair our listening—at the same time facilitating interpretation and limiting the possibilities for that interpretation.

But the central point is that listening is not a matter of accurately representing auditory input. Quite the contrary, what we listen for and what we hear are primarily a matter of what we expect and/or anticipate.

Philosophers and scientists alike have elaborated upon this point. One example, as already mentioned, is Gadamer's explication of the "prejudices" that both limit and enable our listening and observing. In his conception, these prejudices are not negative, but necessary; perception is not possible without some sort of anticipation or prejudgment to impress on what is sensed.[32] In a related vein, Varela Thompson, and Rosch[33] discuss the implications of a provocative study of human perception. Briefly, subjects were presented with various stimuli while their brain functions and their retinal activity were monitored. To the researchers' surprise, there was little correspondence between the qualities of the stimulus and the activity in the brain. However, there was a very strong correlation between retinal activity and brain function, indicating that "the flow of information" was not primarily from the object to the mind (from the outside to the inside) but from the brain to the eye. In effect, this result demonstrates that one's perception is more the product of what is "projected" than what is actually "sensed"—that the observers' perceptions are determined by their structures. Put simply, we are not born with the ability to perceive the world in the way that an adult does. Seeing, hearing, smelling, tasting, and feeling are learned.

This inference is supported by a growing collection of case histories of persons whose sight has been restored after long-term blindness. In an account of one such incident, neurobiographer Oliver

Sacks[34] describes how Virgil, through a cataract operation, regained the vision he lost several decades earlier. What is surprising about this case is that the immediate consequence of overcoming his blindness was despair and depression rather than happiness, for, although Virgil was no longer blind, he could not yet see. When the bandages were removed from his eyes, he was bombarded with a frightening mélange of undifferentiated images, which—lacking "prejudice" or interactive experience with this aspect of the world—he could not reduce or translate into meaningful sights. He was thus trapped in the visual equivalent of "noise."[35]

Of course, these studies focused on vision, but there is no reason to suggest that hearing and the other senses are differently constituted. In an auditory analog of Virgil's story, for example, a friend who recently began to wear a mechanical aid to compensate for a rather severe hearing loss found herself unable to "screen out" unwanted noise when in a restaurant. Compelled to hear everything, she could hear nothing, and soon chose to turn off the hearing aid. (She has since learned how to listen with it.) I experience a related—but in many ways opposite—phenomenon when I visit noisy restaurants. At particular moments I hear fragments of background music which, for the most part, go unnoticed beneath the layers of other sounds. Occasionally one of those fragments "registers" and I am able to identify the tune. From that instant, I can hear the whole song, with remarkable clarity, despite the noise that prevents others from hearing it. Put differently, once aware of what I should be hearing, I can hear it. When unaware, the song goes unheard.

A third illustrative example emerges from this study of listening. As I listen *for* listening, I hear the term everywhere—voiced in every politician's promises, embedded in every text. Like my name mentioned across a noise-filled room, the word "listening" demands that it be heard.

In brief, then, we are compulsive sense-makers and, discounting some sort of handicap, have become adept at pulling bits from a sea of sensorial possibilities. Hearing is really more a matter of *not* hearing—a truism that is evident in those frustrating interactions where you have attempted to make a point but, regardless of what you say, the other person hears the wrong thing. "He hears only what he wants to hear."

The point I am trying to get at, then, is that "perception" and our "perceptual capacities" are far more than means of "taking in the world." Quite apart from the capacity to "pull in sound," hearing is more a process of imposing order on noise—of bringing forth a sound—and there is physiological evidence to support this contention. There are approximately 10 percent more neural connections running from the brain to the ear than from the ear to the brain, indicating that sensory organs do not merely "take in" incoming information; they go fishing for it. To listen, then, is to subject our hearing perceptions to scrutiny, endeavoring to disrupt the "taken for granted" which precedes, constrains, and (in effect) determines those perceptions. "Listening" does not suggest an ability to transcend such constraints, but a willingness to "unfix" our selves or to position our selves differently.

The phrase "listening for" points at the inevitability of approaching interactions with a particular set of expectations or biases. That we cannot help but take a particular stance in our listening is usually revealed very quickly when my background differs markedly from that of my partner in conversation. In the extreme case, when languages differ, listening is reduced to attempts to interpret simple signals because there are few shared signs. But conflicting interpretive frames present even more imposing barriers to listening as they bring about a reluctance to adopt the other's stance. Similarly, if the subject matter is not something that commands my interest, my listening becomes labored, more easily distracted, and sometimes resentful.

But what is listened *for* is not strictly determined by personal prejudices. What we are able to hear (understand) is also dependent upon the context, which provides us with clues to interpret the speaker's words and actions. It is thus that the same statement made in a different setting can take on a new meaning—or perhaps lose meaning entirely. This particular phenomenon is well illustrated by referring to the effect of replaying audiotaped interactions. Like rereading a book or re-viewing a landscape, such re-listening brings with it something new, in part because the context has changed, in part because the actual listener is different. And so, inappropriate interpretations are not always a consequence of one's inability to listen; they may emerge from a failure to attend to contextual clues.

Listening *to*—Our Listening Is Orienting

As suggested earlier, listening is intentional. It is directed toward a particular "object"—that is, toward bringing it forth out of an undifferentiated background of experience. In listening, I am drawing an object into myself, the subject, and so we are brought forth together; we are intertwined in our being and becoming; we co-emerge. Thus, an orientation to listening brings with it an awareness that there can be no rigid subject-object split. Additionally, this point illustrates that listening benefits the listener as well as the listened to.

But what is the nature of this "object" of listening in the mathematics classroom? At first, there is a temptation to suggest it must be either the speaker or the subject matter. Arguably, our proclivity to answer in these terms betrays persistent Cartesian perspectives on subjectivity and knowledge—perspectives that are challenged by Gadamer's, Merleau-Ponty's, and Maturana and Varela's accounts of the communicative relationship.

These are issues that I will deal with in later chapters as I explore the natures of mathematical knowledge and the teacher-students relationship. For the moment, I will point to an answer to the question What is the object of our listening? by suggesting that this object is analogous to a "game." As in other forms of interaction, details such as the participants, the setting, the rules of play all serve to circumscribe the boundaries of the game, but they are not the game. Rather, the game exists only in the playing. Similarly, the "object" of listening exists in the interplay of the participants, the setting, and the subject matter.

Three Modes of Listening

In the final section of each of the subsequent chapters, I will be developing the discussions around a report of an extended collaborative investigation into mathematics teaching that I conducted in conjunction with a middle school mathematics teacher. Intended as a forum for both explication (of the varied ideas presented in the chapters) and implication (i.e., exploring some of the practical ramifications of the ideas), these sections are constructed around three teaching episodes that are drawn from different stages of our collaboration.

Each of those teaching episodes, all of which will be introduced in the next chapter, will be characterized in terms of a different mode of listening. In an effort to frame these discussions, and in an attempt to gather together some of the important points of this chapter, the following "modes" of listening are offered. Before differentiating between these sorts of attending, however, it must be noted that the intention is not to suggest that they are somehow mutually distinct. This framework is intended to serve as a useful conceptual tool, as qualities of each mode of listening are inevitably enacted in the others.

Evaluative Listening In terms of our day-to-day interactions, "listening" and "hearing" tend to be virtually synonymous—that is, we are not often aware of the biases that frame our auditory perceptions. Our listening is not always—and perhaps not often—put to use, and thus tends to be rather limited and limiting. Nevertheless, this manner of listening is sufficient to meet our daily needs. As Levin describes it, it is "a hearing that is personal, adequately skillful in meeting the normal demands of interpersonal living, and ruled over by the ego, which habitually structures all the auditory situations in which it finds itself in terms of subject and object."[36] Within the mathematics classroom, this manner of listening is manifested in the detached, evaluative stance of the teacher who deviates little from intended plans, in whose classroom student contributions are judged as either right or wrong (and thus have little impact on lesson trajectories), and for whom listening is primarily the responsibility of the learner. This mode I will be referring to as "evaluative listening" in subsequent sections.

Interpretive Listening Recent discussions of how we learn, most notably those framed by radical constructivism, have prompted calls for listening differently. Teachers have been encouraged to attempt to get at what learners are thinking, and so a need has arisen to present opportunities for more elaborate demonstrations and articulations by students. All of this is based on the realization that the teacher and learner alike are actively constructing conceptualizations: the learner constructs the mathematics; the teacher constructs the learner. As such, the teacher is compelled to move away from an "evaluative listening" and toward an "interpretive listening" in order to open up spaces for re-presentation and revision of ideas—to *access* subjective sense rather than to merely *assess* what has been learned. "Interpretive listening" is founded on an awareness that an active interpretation—a sort of reaching out rather than a taking in—is involved, whereby the listening is deliberate and aware of the fallibility of the sense being made. As Levin describes it, in this mode of listening, "we are essentially involved in developing our listening as a practice of compassion, increasing our capacity, as listeners, to be aware of, and responsive to, the interrelatedness and commonality of all sonorous beings.[37]

Hermeneutic Listening Both "evaluative" and "interpretive listening" are premised on conceptions of human identity and agency as essentially subjective, autonomous, isolated, and insulated. Further, in the context of mathematics teaching, these modes of attending are founded on an irreconcilable split between the role of the teacher and the role of the student. Theirs are different tasks. These conventionally enacted boundaries are problematized in "hermeneutic listening," a third mode. This manner of listening is more negotiatory, engaging, and messy, involving the hearer and the heard in a shared project. "Hermeneutic listening" is an imaginative participation in the formation and the transformation of experience through an ongoing interrogation of the taken-for-granted and the prejudices that frame perceptions and actions. The focus is on the dynamic interdependence of agent and setting, thought and action, knowledge and knower, self and other, individual and collective—rather than on autonomous constitution or construction. It is this manner of listening that I offer both as a metaphoric lens to reinterpret practice and as a practical basis for the reformulating of teaching action.

In sum, then, evaluative listening is an uncritical *taking in* of information that is *out there*, interpretive listening involves an awareness that one is *projecting onto* one's understandings particular biases that are *in here*, and hermeneutic listening is a *participation in* the unfolding of possibilities *through collective action.*

Chapter 2

An Ear to the Ground

The Subject Matter

Mathematics is not a book confined within a cover and bound between brazen clasps, whose contents need only patience to ransack; it is not a mine, whose treasures may take long to reduce into possession, but which fill only a limited number of veins and lodes; it is not a soil whose fertility can be exhausted by the yield of successive harvests; it is not a continent or an ocean whose area can be mapped out and its contour defined; it is as limitless as that space which it finds too narrow for its aspirations; its possibilities are as infinite as the worlds which are forever crowding in and multiplying upon the astronomer's gaze; it is as incapable of being restricted within assigned boundaries or being reduced to definition of permanent validity, as the consciousness of life.

—*James Sylvester*[1]

No other locus, no other topos, *within the senses at man's disposal is so directly linked with mathematics as the ear.*

—*Joachim-Ernst Berendt*[2]

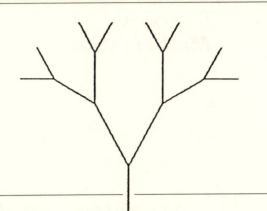

Section A
Mathematics

[N]ature never blazons her secrets with a loud voice but always whispers them. And the mathematician must listen attentively . . .
—*Morris Kline*[3]

The world is out there, but descriptions of the world are not.
—*Richard Rorty*[4]

The "nature of mathematical knowledge" has been a topic of debate within the field of mathematics education from its inception, but it is only recently that the issue has taken center stage alongside discussions of learning processes and teaching approaches. This rise to prominence has been a welcome development in a field where research projects have often begun with definitions of mathematics that are given in terms of the contents of curriculum manuals.

My own interest in this topic—and part of the reason for its prominence in this text—emerges largely from reactions to my posing the question, What is mathematics?, to students and colleagues. More often than not, my efforts to discuss the nature of the subject matter have been regarded as irrelevant time-wasters. I must confess to a certain despair when faced with this sort of response, especially when it is manifested among pre-service and practicing teachers. In simplest terms, I hold little hope for any meaningful change in the teaching of mathematics until we are willing and able to interrogate earnestly the subject matter we are claiming to teach. A failure to do so, I fear, will compel us to reenact the same fragmenting and reductive practices that have recently come under such harsh critique.

In this section, I deal specifically with the question of mathematics. Consistent with the investigative framework outlined in the previous chapter, these discussions will be based on and will provide an elaboration of various principles of enactivism—as well as extending sonorous and auditory metaphors. In particular, this chapter will deal with the nature of collective action, the dynamics of our *body* of mathematical knowledge, and the contribution of ecological thought to discussions of epistemology. The two main themes of this first section are that modern mathematics has largely lost touch with its ground and that a return to auditory (rather than visual) framings of its subject matter might help us to recover that ground. In the other sections of this chapter, the discussion is broadened to include issues of curriculum-making and preparation for teaching.

The chapter's first task, that of investigating mathematics through the lens of ecology, is not an easy one. Mathematics itself—or our privileging of it—has been cited as a primary contributor to our "ecological crisis,"[5] and this is an accusation that I am inclined to support. Nevertheless, I believe it is possible to describe an "ecological mathematics" that is aware of the relational world from which it emerges and that is sympathetic to the natural world onto which it is imposed. I approach the topic through a brief history of the discipline in which some of its major transitions are identified. The goals here are twofold: to trace the evolution of the modernist conception of mathematics—that of a static, formal, hierarchical, and truthful body of knowledge—and then, by attending to our own traditions and to recent developments within mathematics itself, to explore alternatives to this modern conception.

I must preface this section by noting that no discussion of the nature of mathematics would be complete without delving into the moral and ethical status of the discipline and its subject matter. While these issues are briefly touched on here, they are more specifically addressed in Chapter 3 as I begin to explore the "why's" of mathematics education.

"Ecological"

I begin by drawing a distinction between the terms "environmental" and "ecological." Although not synonymous, the two words tend to be used interchangeably in reference to the plethora of problems faced by our modern society. Many commentators[6] contend that this confusion has contributed to the obfuscation of the causes underlying these problems. The crises, they argue, are not *environmental,* but *ecological.*

The term "environmental" is used to direct attention toward our *environs*—our surroundings—and hence away from ourselves. This tendency gives rise to an immediate problem. As Wendell Berry explains, "once we see our place, our part of the world, as *surrounding* us, we have already made a profound division between it and ourselves."[7] Describing a crisis as environmental, then, leads to attempts to develop (usually scientific) solutions—in effect, to fall back onto the same mode of thinking that precipitated the original difficulty. Implicit in the notion of "environmentalism" is a reification of the Cartesian separation of individual and world. These are two distinct categories, connected only by chains of causality which are generally perceived as uni-directional.

Identifying a problem as *ecological,* in contrast, places it in our *oikos,* our household—that is, in the web of relationships in which we find ourselves and against which our identities are established. The focus thus shifts from outward gazes to a reexamination of the assumptions and the actions that gave rise to the crisis. *Ecology* is about interrelationships and interconnections. It involves an attunement to codependencies, mutual affects, and codeterminations—in essence, to the fundamental intertwining of all things. When we speak of *ecology,* then, we speak of everything that shapes our being—their effects on us and ours on them. Folding back to earlier discussions of enactivism, hermeneutics, and listening, such notions are founded on an awareness of this sort of deep ecological interweaving.

The difference between *environmentalism* and *ecology,* then, is analogous to the difference between sight and hearing, as developed in the previous chapter. It is thus not very surprising to note that ecological theorists—whether focusing on natural, social, or cognitive realms—are founding their discussion on metaphors of sounds and harmonies, thus casting the place of the cognizing agent in terms of a participatory listening to and in those sounds. On what might be considered a more "radical" extreme, some thinkers go so far as to suggest that "all is sound"[8] building on frequent reference to the notion of "waves" in describing phenomena ranging from elementary particles to brain activity to social movements to the "echo" of the Big Bang. Whether or not one accepts the idea, there can be no denying that the fleeting, situated, and implicating qualities of sound (and listening) do seem to be better attuned to postmodern sensibilities than the separating and fixing of vision-based metaphors.[9]

Ecological Mathematics

If the current philosophical and theoretical debates are any indication, the question, What is mathematics?, is an unanswerable one—and fortunately so. Were we able to decide once-and-for-all what mathematics is, we would doubtlessly give in to our modern tendencies of exorcising ambiguity and mechanizing complexity, in effect reducing a fluid form to a static formula.

A review of the history of mathematics reveals a dynamic and ever-evolving field of inquiry which could never be technologized. To illustrate this point, I describe several "eras" of mathematical history, attempting to show how the era helped to define mathematics and how, in turn, mathematics helped to define the era. Implicit in this analysis is the notion that mathematics is time- and context-dependent. Philip J. Davis and Reuben Hersh, two professional mathematicians, comment on the issue:

> *A detemporalized mathematics cannot tell us what mathematics is, why mathematics is true, why it is beautiful, how it comes to be, or why anybody should care a fig about it. But if one places mathematics squarely within human time and experience, it becomes a warm and rich source of possible meanings and action. Its ultimate mystery is never dispelled, yet it is exhibited as one of the prime creations of the human intellect.*[10]

I must precede this quick tour through mathematics history by acknowledging my inability to escape the modernist (mathematical?) tendency to abstract, reduce, and impose structure on an amorphous mass of largely unformulated, and far from validated, experience and observation. It is thus that I have identified five mentalities[11] in the emergence of mathematics, and will use the terms "Oral," "Pre-Formal," "Formal," "Hyper-Formal," and "Post-Formal" to refer to them.[12] The centrality of the term "formal" in these titles is intended to point toward the relative importance of formality, formalization, and the formulaic in the various conceptualizations.

Of course, mathematics is not and has never been an isolated discipline. The perspectives that are implicit in the field have always spilled into and have always been affected by the perspectives and the developments in other areas of inquiry. For this reason, those readers familiar with the field of literary criticism may wish to replace the word "formalist" with "structuralist" and, in so doing, note the relationships between the emergence of current conceptions of mathematics and the evolution of literary interpretation theory. Similarly, some of the relationships between mathematics and postmodern thought will be made more apparent by substituting "modern" for "formal."

Mentality 1: Oral Knowledge The oft-heard suggestion that the philosophy of René Descartes gave rise to modernist perspectives is, perhaps, somewhat reductionist and facile. Although he certainly announced a changing of mind-sets, and more than likely contributed to the rise of a new era, Descartes was as much a product of modern thought as he was an instigator.

Some, in fact, have traced the roots of modernism back several millennia. Walter Ong,[13] for example, suggests that the construction of the radical subject (of the sort implied by Descartes' *cogito*), did not begin with the work of Descartes but with the advent of literacy. Starting with the contention that the invention of writing (and, in particular, of the alphabet) prompted a separation of earlier ways of thinking from modern modes, Ong undertakes to demonstrate how oral societies differ from literate ones. This task is made difficult by the fact that he and his audience are thoroughly inscribed by literate traditions; so constituted, we can at best struggle to imagine how members of an oral culture might think.

Using as his starting point those relics from earlier cultures that have been preserved (albeit primarily in written form), as well as studies of contemporary societies that are predominantly nonliterate, Ong argues that knowledge in oral traditions exists only in action.[14] It is thus local, current, practical, and fluid—as necessitated by the fact that ideas exist only in an oral milieu. Put differently, ideas find form in the transient immediacy of sound, a medium that exists only when going out of existence.[15] As such, knowledge resists the objectifying and solidification pressures of written (visual) forms. The oral culture is thus one of activities rather than artifacts.

By consequence, oral cultures are uninterested in definitions; meanings are implicit by usage and through enactment. Where there are gaps in understandings between persons, these are immediately negotiated. In contrast to the literate's location of meaning in language, the meanings of oral traditions are located in contexts and actions. Spoken words come into being in situations (whereas written words tend to be isolated from the setting in which they were recorded). It is thus that persons from oral societies resist—or may simply be unable to—provide definitions for familiar words; for them, words are not items but patterns of acting.

Because of the temporal and contextual embeddedness of all knowledge in oral societies, Ong contends, reasoning does not consist in the abstract logical-deductive modes that we literates associate with rationality. Ong uses the work of Luria,[16] a student of Vygotsky, to illustrate this point. Luria studied some of the nonliterate citizens of remote parts of the Soviet Union, noting that these people, for example, identified circles or squares in terms of concrete objects (e.g., plates and mirrors) rather than assigning them abstract names. Further, objects were classified by practical situation rather than in formal categories (e.g., they had difficulty selecting the object that "did not belong" from among a hammer, a saw, a hatchet, and a log, regarding them all as having to do with workmen and wood. Although "tool" was in their vocabularies, it was an object of immediate practical use for them and could thus not serve as a conceptual category). And, perhaps most significantly, each nonliterate was virtually unable to speak of himself or herself, modulating self-evaluations into group evaluations. Ong sums up:

> *[An] oral culture simply does not deal in such items as geometrical figures, abstract categorization, formally logical reasoning processes, definitions, or even comprehensive descriptions, or articulated self-analysis, all of which derive not simply from thought itself but from text-formed thought.*[17]

Edmund Carpenter, in a study of Inuit conceptions and perceptions of "reality," provides support for Ong's conclusions. In particular,

Carpenter offers us a glimpse into Inuit senses of "space," arguing that these tend to be framed orally rather than visually. Noting that he is aware of "no example of an Eskimo describing space primarily in visual terms"[18] and that they have no system of linear measurement, he suggests that their spatial apprehension is vague, local, and dynamic—much in contrast to our own senses of well-marked, thoroughly measured, and long-fixed territories. Theirs is a space structured by sound.

The Inuit people in Carpenter's study had no concept of equal portioning (i.e., knowledge of fractions or processes that we would describe in terms of fractions); a universe structured auditorially need not be divided into "equal shares." That is to say that the concept of *ratio*—the term from which "rational" and "reason" are derived—is not part of their oral culture. Furthermore, the counting systems of Inuit peoples typically extended only to five or ten (and, in some cases, only to two or three) before the quantity of "many" was invoked.

At first hearing, statements such as these might be taken to imply that oral societies have no mathematics. In one sense, this is likely true. Mathematics certainly does not exist as an independent discipline in these settings, nor is there a clearly articulated *modus operandi* that can be called "rational" (i.e., deductive). However, as revealed by the poems, the songs, and the stories that are left to us from oral cultures, there was certainly some knowledge of number, statistic, pattern, and meter. (These latter elements, in fact, infuse the oral narratives, serving as mnemonic devices and providing structure for poets and performers.) The essential difference, however, is that numbers and statistics were never divorced from human activity, just as the oral stories were never presented in absence of active listeners. Numbers, in other words, were always adjectives and never nouns. Similarly, the varied processes employed for calendar reckoning, commerce, agriculture and other activities seem to have consisted in disconnected and simple rules, neither linked together nor pursued for anything other than immediate practical use. (These, too, appear to have been written into verse form so that they could be easily memorized and passed on.)

The "mathematics," then, like the "literature," was a language of action, encompassing, engaging, and implicating both speaker and hearer. More appropriately, perhaps, there was no mathematics (like there was no literature); there was rather the spectral presence of a mode of thinking that might be called "mathematical" and out of which formal mathematical thought eventually arose. As Joseph argues:

If we define mathematics as any activity that arises out of, or directly generates, concepts relating to numbers or spatial configurations together with some form of logic, we can then legitimately include in our study proto-mathematics, which existed when no written records were available.[19]

This "proto-mathematics" might be thought of as a mode of thought that, among other qualities, involved the noting and deliberate extending of patterns—activities that were always contextually and temporally bounded (and, hence, always in danger of being lost for want of rehearsal). Knowledge, in every sense, was situated eco-logically—that is, in the knotted logic of one's *ecos* (dwelling place).

Mentality 2: Pre-Formalist Mathematics Formal mathematics, then, does not exist in oral cultures, although some form of what we would call "mathematical thought" does. The manner in which the objects of mathematics came into being has thus been a topic of intense and diverse speculation for centuries, with recorded contributions to the discussions dating back beyond the ancient Greeks and Egyptians. Commenting on its possible origins, Alfred North Whitehead[20] has conjectured that formal mathematical thought began with the conceptual leap of thinking of seven fishes or seven days to thinking of seven. In this realization of samenesses, the first objects of mathematics—pure numbers—were created.[21] Interestingly, as time passed and as this abstracted notion of number began to permeate human interaction, pure number came to resist embedding in any human context, gaining an existential status on par with that of colors and sofas.

Exactly how such abstract notions came to escape their situatedness—how the adjectives (and, later, verbs) became nouns—is an interesting question. Ong suggests that the ability to draw such abstractions is linked to the invention of the written word, a technology that, he argues, brought about a transformation of human consciousness. According to Ong, writing pushes the *known* into the visual field, detaching it from its author and its audience by assigning it permanence and reducing its mutability. Because of this detachment, the author's intention can no longer be interrogated. Moreover, through writing, thought becomes a solo (although still social) activity. By writing, the author separates not just descriptor from described, but knower from known and self from other. New senses of subjectivity and autonomy thus arise.

The written text also enables the reader to work on individual bits—to extract, or abstract, knowledge from contexts and to fragment it into autonomous facts and independent disciplines. In fact, in a very real way, words (like numbers) come into existence through the technology of symbolization. They become things with objective status, and thus objects that can be operated upon. Writing also demands that these fragments be presented linearly, and the resulting chains of reasoning mark a profound break with the all-at-once thinking modes of the oral traditions. In a further break with orality, definitions become important as one moves to the visual milieu of writing; lacking the space to interrogate the author, usage must be clear, unambiguous, and uniform.

As a result of these changes in human modes of thought, Ong provocatively suggests, logical-deductive reasoning—which relies on abstraction, linear thought, causal links, fragmentation of ideas, and word-objects (for logic operates on the *logos*—the word)—was a consequence of literacy. He suggests, in fact, that formal logic was invented by the Greeks (and other civilizations) soon after they perfected their alphabet:[22]

We know that formal logic is the invention of Greek culture after it interiorized the technology of alphabetic writing, and so make a permanent part of its noetic resources the kind of thinking that alphabetic writing made possible.[23]

In his own account of mathematics history, Carl Boyer[24] provides support for Ong's contention as he notes that the emergence of formal mathematics has tended to lag some centuries behind the development of literary forms. He also comments that "few subjects depend as heavily on a continuous bookish tradition . . . as does mathematics."[25] He does not, unfortunately, develop the possibility of a relationship between these phenomena.

It is important to emphasize that the association being made here is not between formal mathematical reasoning and language—the latter of which Ong would contend emerged long before logic—but between modern mathematics and literacy. In terms of the shape of our knowledge, this connection represents a shift in traditions from the auditory to the visual. Presented to the eye in the written text, in effect, ideas[26] were abstracted from the lived sonorous realm. They came to have an existence of their own, one that was in many ways superior to the immediately experienced, for the reified forms of these ideas could be applied across experiences. (This is not to say, however, that mathematics sprang, fully formed, from an emergent literacy. On the contrary, and particularly outside of the Greek world, mathematics appears to have begun as a series of simple but disconnected rules—not entirely unlike conventional school mathematics—which were concerned with questions of daily life. These rules were likely determined empirically—that is, through trial and error—and approximate rules for calendar reckoning, agriculture, and other exploits seem to have been satisfactory for most cultures' needs. As well, in terms of the mode of thought underlying the development of mathematics, Kline[27] reminds us that analogy, and not strictly deduction, was often the dominant mode of thinking, particularly within Hindu and Arab cultures.)

The transcendent nature of mathematical objects (that is, the way in which abstract mathematical ideas can be applied to situations with no surface similarities) likely contributed to a pervasive conception of mathematics as mystical and magical. Indeed, as Donaldson[28] points out, at some point in our history, mathematicians were thought to be dabbling in "black magic," perhaps as a result of the tremendous predictive capacities of the discipline. (Descartes himself, it appears, actually suppressed many of his mathematical insights, fearing that he might be accused of some form of sorcery.)

Mathematics was thus woven into the spiritual lives of our ancestors. At least since the time of Pythagoras,[29] who proposed that nature is fundamentally mathematical, numbers were seen as the true essence of things; concepts were understood to have emerged from the mind of God; the elegance and "power" of mathematical knowledge hinted at an ultimate "perfection." Mathematical ideas were understood to be the strands from which the universe was woven. One's hold on these threads permitted access to the hidden and true meaning of existence itself. Very often, then, mathematical inquiry was the domain of the priest classes.

Mathematical ideas were thus entangled with all aspects of existence and all areas of knowledge. They were not something imposed on, but qualities inherent in, all things. Correspondingly, as George Steiner[30] suggests, all mathematical concepts could be represented in conventional linguistic terms—that is, a concept was always interpretable against one's everyday experience. According to Steiner, and as will be developed later, this perspective on mathematics persisted until the time of Galileo, Descartes, and Newton.

In the hands of the ancient Greeks, the tight links with daily experience and familiar language contributed to a conception of mathematical truths as "forms" or "unchanging aspects" that governed the world. Their great contribution was to make mathematics rigorous and definite (understood in terms of logical consistency), as epitomized by Euclid's geometry. The mathematics of Ancient Greece thus represented a departure from the pragmatic "tool collection" mathematics of its contemporary cultures.[31] Far from being a collection of theorems or established truths—that is, a distinct discipline or body of knowledge—mathematics came to be powerfully regarded as a particular mode of inquiry that was, for the most part, as tightly linked to the arts of divination as to other areas of inquiry. As Heidegger explains, mathematics (or, more accurately, the *mathematical*) was "the fundamental condition for the proper possibility of knowing" which involved an awareness of "the fundamental presuppositions of all knowledge and the position we take on such knowledge."[32] In different terms, the *mathematical* was regarded as a particular and disciplined approach to thinking, which began with the statement of fundamental propositions (the *axioms*, arrived at by consensus) and, through the applications of particular rules (the *logic*), the deduction of further truths. (It is thus that Thales, to whom the first deductive proof is generally attributed, is hailed as the first true mathematician.) The validity of the results, assuming no rules were violated, was assured by the rigor of the derivation process—not by some external measure.

This is not to say that mathematical thought disregarded experience. On the contrary, the purpose of such analysis was to enrich those experiences, locating them in the web of creation by referencing all postulates to their bases in axioms. Nor should we make the mistake of associating all of pre-formalist mathematics with the logico-deductive structures of the *geometria.* While the Greeks were exceptional in their concern with formal knowledge, their predecessors, contemporaries, and immediate successors tended to focus on the practical aspects of mathematical inquiry, mixing derivation and approximation with little apparent concern for what we would consider an inconsistent application of principles. Nevertheless, the contribution of this more pragmatic orientation toward mathematics—which was perhaps most evident in Arab and Hindu cultures—was to become as important to the evolution of mathematics as the contribution of the Greeks. Developing such areas as arithmetic, number theory, and algebra—not to mention preserving much of the mathematics of Ancient Greece, Babylonia, and other cultures—non-European societies helped to set the stage for the emergence of a modern mathematics.

In sum, contrasting the pre-formal conception of mathematics with the sense of "mathematical" that exists in oral traditions, one notes a dramatic departure. Still shared are the senses of order and pattern; however, with the influence of symbolization, the mathematical has acquired an almost magical capacity to pull objects of reason to material form. These "objects," it must be borne in mind, were always considered as part of the universe—always attuned to the ground *from* which and *on* which they were drawn.

Mentality 3: Formalist Mathematics As mentioned, an important transition in mathematics was initiated in the time of Descartes and Newton. As Steiner[33] explains, mathematical methods were turned upon themselves, producing a realm of knowledge that could no longer be meaningfully reduced to or captured by conventional language. As might be illustrated with the example of Newton's *Calculus,* mathematics broke from the everyday and ceased to be understandable or representable in terms of immediate experience. This "break"—which amounted to a removal of intuitive restraints—had a number of important consequences, among them a tremendous surge in research and a corresponding increase in mathematical knowledge.

As such, mathematics ceased to be regarded merely as a mode of reasoning and became a distinct discipline, separated from other areas of inquiry. That is to say, the *mathematical* began to be overshadowed by the *mathematics*—i.e., the mode of thinking was in some ways hidden by the corpus of knowledge that it spawned. The central concern in this formalist movement was the manner in which the forms comprising this corpus were linked together via formal proof. Descartes played a central role in this project by bringing together the diverse strands of thought (represented by geometry, arithmetic, and algebra) into the single unified field of analytic geometry. With the masterstroke of imposing a grid to slice up the plane, Descartes was able to pull together number and shape—in the process assigning a new, much broadened character to mathematics.

At the same time, and largely through the work of Galileo, Descartes, and Newton, science was mathematized as the rigorous guidelines for mathematical inquiry were applied to the study of diverse physical phenomena. These events mark the (formal) beginning of the modern era, and it is thus not surprising that the person most often credited (or blamed) for the rise of modernity, Descartes himself, was a mathematician. Reacting to the current state of knowledge, which he considered to be a mixture of fact and fancy:

[Descartes] had been the first to embark upon a programme to establish a firm foundation for human knowledge of the world and had singled out mathematics as the only reliable route to unimpeachable knowledge.[34]

In other words, Descartes called for nothing less than "the primacy of world mathematization"[35] whereby all truth—and not just that of mathematics—would be determined through a formal system, complete with a predefined and carefully articulated alphabet, grammar, set of axioms, and rules of inference. This transitional period is thus marked by three critical shifts in thinking: mathematical ideas came to be seen as something apart from human experience; the mathematical and the scientific were given identities distinct from the religious, the magical, and the spiritual; and mathematics acquired the status of *the* model of reasoning for a modern era. The overarching goal of this movement—or, perhaps more appropriately, its net effect—was prophesied in 1637 by Descartes in his *Discourse on Method*:

> *[My discoveries] have satisfied me that it is possible to reach knowledge that will be of much* utility *in this life; and that instead of the speculative philosophy now taught in the schools we can find a practical one, by which, knowing the nature and behavior of fire, water, air, stars, the heavens, and all the bodies which surround us, as well as we now understand the different skills of our workers, we can* employ these entities *for all the purposes for which they are suited, and so* make ourselves masters and possessors of nature.[36]

All sense of our ecological embeddedness was cast aside in this formulation. Similarly, the experienced, phenomenal world was rendered suspect, fallible, and unreliable as logical consistency, not correspondence with experience, became the criterion of truth. It is thus that mathematics displaced religion, history, and narrative as legitimate routes to knowledge and became "the unifying glue of a rationalized world."[37] Descartes' emphases on the detached, technical, and utilitarian qualities of mathematics contributed to an emerging conception of the universe as a deterministic machine—and our relationship to that machine, as revealed in Descartes' own words, came to be expressed in the language of control and dominance via mastery of the underlying mathematics.

Importantly, though, mathematics did not quite lose its grounding in this formulation. Although valued for the structure of its argument (as opposed to its conclusions), in the turn to modern philosophic traditions, mathematical reasoning remained the one human capacity that was believed able to keep us in conversation with the now separate nonhuman universe.

As noted, the privileged place and status of mathematics benefited those areas of inquiry that could employ or emulate the discipline, but it was devastating to other modes of human thought. As is evidenced by the preeminent place of mathematics within modern universities and government agencies, Descartes' dream of world mathematization has largely come to pass. Mathematics, primarily through our science and our technology, has come to permeate our existence.[38] The result has been that, adapting Gadamer's words on history, "In fact [mathematics] does not belong to us, we belong to it."[39]

It is this formalist view of the discipline and the consequent pervasiveness of mathematics which have drawn such intense criticism from various theoretical perspectives. Postmodernist thinkers[40] have identified mathematics as one of the "grand narratives" which have compelled us, the victims of modernity, to suppress our own personal narratives. The consequence has been a feeling of profound personal displacement broadly inflicted upon the citizenry of Western nations. Non-Western societies have also suffered at the hands of Western mathematics, which (in Western sensibilities) has tended to be regarded as culturally neutral. This perception has been discounted by postcolonial theorists who have characterized mathematics as a "weapon of cultural imperialism"[41] and by those interested in ethnomathematics, who have criticized Western mathematics as being destructive of other cultures' mathematical forms.[42] These criticisms are closely aligned to those of ecological philosophers,[43] who suggest that the equating of mathematics and rationality has caused us to ask only "Can we do it?" rather than the more ecologically sound "Should we do it?" The result has been the nearsighted, and often disastrous, application of our mathematized scientific knowledge. This form of "conventional rationality" has not only eclipsed other forms of reason, it has allowed greed to replace the tradition of wisdom. Various feminist scholars[44] argue that, far from being the "neutral" discipline it is held to be, mathematics is biased culturally, socially, and by gender. Our modern tendency to make a fetish of mathematical knowledge has thus contributed greatly to social inequities. Even mathematicians have joined in the attack on formalist mathematics. Davis and Hersh,[45] for instance, discuss the consequences of the fulfillment of Descartes' dream in their survey of the contexts in which and the phenomena onto which mathematics has been applied—including the inappropriate application of its principles to various social situations and the insidious use of its insights in the enabling of our military culture. David Levin powerfully sums up these critiques as he points to "the terrible violence, the subtle repression of difference and otherness, hidden within the 'benevolent universality' of Reason."[46]

Mentality 4: Hyper-Formalist Mathematics Despite the privileged position of mathematics within modern society, its foundations have long been questioned. The seemingly endless dispute on the issue of the criteria for a valid proof, for example, suggests that mathematics' reputation for certainty may be no more than an illusion.

In particular, the emergence of non-Euclidian geometries nearly two centuries ago signaled an important transition in mathematics as it became clear that one could question and manipulate the very foundations of geometry. This startling result was generalized to all mathematics systems in the middle of the nineteenth century with Hamilton's creation of quaternions—an algebra with practical utility that lacked some of the commonsense properties of existing arithmetics. As a result of these sorts of developments, leading mathematicians David Hilbert, Albert North Whitehead, and Bertrand Russell set out to reconstruct mathematics as a strictly formal system at the beginning of this century. In effect, one of their goals was to articulate the inner consistency (and hence the independent nature) of mathematics by divorcing it from the experiential world[47]—a project that, as noted earlier, had its origins in the work of Newton and his contemporaries. Their goal was to recast all of mathematics in symbolic form—in the process transforming mathematics from a means of inquiring in the universe to a closed, tautological system—driven by the belief that by ignoring (necessarily limited and limiting) physical interpretations, one's deductive abilities would be powerfully increased.

While their purpose was hardly to wring the meaningfulness out of mathematics, the effort to formulate a fully consistent system served to distance the discipline even further from its already obscure associations with the realms of the phenomenal, the superstitious, and the mystical—not to mention the very ground we walk on. This conception was bolstered by an emerging division within the field itself, as "applied" began to be distinguished from "theoretical" mathematics. To this point, mathematics had been "the servant of science and technology,"[48] with efforts centering on such applications as land surveying and astronomical calculations. In the last century, however, the inferior status of mathematics was pushed aside as mathematicians "invented their own problems and played gratuitous games whose rules they made up themselves."[49] Hubert Reeves suggests that this led to an astonishing discovery:

> *The questions posed by science and technology represented only a tiny fraction of the problems that could be formulated. Most theories devised by mathematicians . . .* had no application in reality. *In no way did they describe the world around us. Their axioms did not correspond to nature as we know it. They existed only for the pleasure they gave to the mathematicians who invented them. Their sole justification was their own internal coherence.*[50]

One can see the emerging separation between "discovered" and "invented" mathematics here. Once not an issue—for mathematics was believed to permeate the universe—the tension began to deepen the chasm between experience and mathematical interpretation. The effect—on popular (public) opinion, at least—was to promote a conception of the discipline that had very little to do with the "real" world. In this formulation, as it was torn from its ground, mathematics became the quintessential "grand narrative," transcending not only experience, but human existence.

During this time, the mathematization of scholarly study crept beyond the physical sciences and into such realms as economics, politics, language, and law. This movement was, as Davis and Hersh put it, "based on the questionable assumption that problems in these areas can be solved by quantification and computation."[51] The extent to which a discipline relied upon mathematics came to be taken as a measure of its rigor and, hence, its relevance. Moving away from the conception of an "established body of knowledge," mathematics came to be defined as something that mathematicians do. Nevertheless, perhaps as a result of its growing influence, beliefs in its neutrality, its pristine structure, and its objective truthfulness were further entrenched.

Mentality 5: Post-Formalist Mathematics In the 1920s, mathematician Kurt Gödel demonstrated that Hilbert's hope of devising a decision algorithm for all of mathematics and the Whitehead-Russell project of deducing all of mathematics from the axioms of logic were unrealizable by proving that any sufficiently complex mathematical system is necessarily incomplete. The hyper-modern project, in effect, came crashing to the ground as the issue of the nature of mathematical knowledge was torn open. For the first time in the modernist/formalist era, absolutist beliefs in mathematical knowledge began to be eclipsed by more fallibilist accounts which acknowledged the social dynamic of knowledge generation.

Discussions in the area have come a great distance since Gödel's earth-shaking pronouncement, with important contributions coming from the likes of Karl Popper,[52] Thomas Kuhn,[53] and Imre Lakatos.[54] More recently, a few mathematicians have dared to suggest that mathematics might more appropriately be considered as one of the *humanities*.[55] Inherent in such a conception is the suggestion that mathematics, as a human construction, is fallible, ill-structured, and implicitly biased. More importantly, mathematics so-conceived tells us more about ourselves than about the universe, which was once believed to be written in mathematical characters. In other words, concerns for the qualities of the *mathematical*, versus the objects of *mathematics*, have reemerged.[56]

Other recent developments in mathematics have served to further debunk realist and formalist perspectives (which, in spite of these events, continue to have a pervasive presence in the discipline). Notably the tremendous advances in computer technology, coupled with the increased availability of such technology, have had profound effects on both the approaches one might take to mathematical investigation and the ways one might go about proving particular ideas.[57] Two events stand out in this regard. First, in 1976, a group of mathematicians proved the century-old four-color conjecture[58] by combining graph theory and sophisticated computing. Second, the dynamic and increasingly popular new field of nonlinear dynamics (Chaos Theory), sparked by an unexpected result from a computer-simulated weather system, opened the possibility of using computers as an investigative tool in a more "experimental" and tentative approach to mathematical research.[59] These sorts of events have helped to displace the formal proof as the primary concern of mathematical inquiry. Lynn Arthur Steen sums up recent developments in mathematics as follows:

Not since the time of Newton has mathematics changed as much as it has in recent years. Motivated in large part by the introduction of computers, the nature and practice of mathematics have been fundamentally transformed by new concepts, tools, applications, and methods. Like the telescope of Galileo's era that enabled the Newtonian revolution, today's computer challenges traditional views and forces re-examination of deeply held values. As it did three centuries ago in the transition from Euclidian proofs to Newtonian analysis, mathematics is undergoing a fundamental reorientation of procedural paradigms.[60]

These developments, while contributing to a renewed public interest in mathematics, have hardly been welcomed with open arms within the discipline. Many feel that they do not represent mathematics at all; others question the trustworthiness of programming or the accuracy of digital computers. There are continued calls for the rigorous paper-and-pencil proof—even though, with specialization and complexity both on the rise, the task of validating such proofs without technological aid is becoming a significant challenge.

While the debate rages on as to whether such branches of inquiry as chaos theory and fuzzy logic are indeed mathematics, these areas of study have served to demonstrate that mathematical knowledge is not preexistent; nor does it exist in any one of us. Rather, it emerges from our actions in the world and from our interactions with one another. On this former point, as the images generated by fractal geometers have recently demonstrated, there is an uncanny tendency for even the most esoteric of mathematics constructions to have some practical utility in the comprehensible, experienced world. Kline argues that this result should not be surprising:

The unexpected . . . uses of mathematical theories arise because the theories are physically grounded to start with and are by no means due to the prophetic insight of all-wise mathematicians who wrestle solely with their souls. The continuing successful use of these creations is by no means fortuitous.[61]

In these postformalist times, then, mathematics is once again aware of its ground, however tentatively.

As Kline hints in the above quote, it is also more attuned to its intersubjective basis. An indication of the social nature of mathematical inquiry is provided by John Barrow:

[An] intriguing aspect of mathematics that seems to distinguish it from the arts . . . is the extent to which mathematicians . . . collaborate in their work. . . . [In] mathematics the collaborative process goes much deeper to entwine *the* authors *in a process . . . by which they are able to produce a result that could not have been half-reached by one of them.*[62]

This statement is worthy of further analysis, more because of what is suggested than because of what is explicitly stated. The implication is that the modernist and formalist orientation to the discovery of truth has given way to a sense of creativity. The mathematician is an *author*—not a theorist, scientist, or explorer—who is *entwined* with his or her coauthors. The myth of the isolated mathematician (and of isolated mathematics) is thus also put to question. We have moved to an awareness that mathematical meaning, like scientific meaning, "derives from both social interaction and interaction with the physical world."[63]

In a sense, then, the postformalist era involves a reclaiming—an *informed* reclaiming, that is—of past perspectives on knowledge. It offers the chance to recover some of the preformalist wonder associated with mathematics—or more particularly, the *mathematical*—as it resituates us in a social-and-natural world of actions, interactions, and interpretations. Mathematics is once again understood to emerge as we seek to understand the transcendent complexity of our universe. As such, it provides us with a sense of the "pattern which connects"[64] us to our world.

In conceiving of mathematics in this way, it becomes apparent that the popular understanding of a "mathematical concept" is in error. In the movement toward a formalist mathematics, our actions within the world (such as counting, comparing, and pattern noticing) have become solidified into objects (like number, size, and order) whose existences have somehow become conceptually independent of—and even prior to—the actions, experiences, or insights that brought them forward. It also seems that mathematics, rather than representing a distinct mode of reasoning, is entangled with other forms of rational thought, including narrative and metaphorical. Once again, mathematical understanding is closely aligned with one's experiences and—in opposition to the formalist tendency toward the dissociation of concepts from their originary experiences—personal meanings are considered to be fundamental to understanding.

Discovery or Creation? Or . . . ?

Even though recent events have pushed the issue of the nature of mathematical knowledge to the foreground, it seems that Gödel's Theorem, chaos theory, computer-assisted proofs, fuzzy logic, and other developments have served to complicate rather than to simplify the debate. As Ernest[65] demonstrates in his overview of various philosophical orientations to the field, characterizations of mathematical knowledge are almost as diverse as the activities of mathematicians. The varied descriptions can be grouped into two broad categories, however, since discussions of the nature of mathematics tend to be developed around attempts to locate mathematics either "in here" (as subjective and constructed) or "out there" (as objective and discovered, placed on either a Platonic or a social plane). That is, for the most part, the question, What is mathematics? tends to be answered either in terms of knowing subjects or in terms of known objects.

Certainly, the current discussions in mathematics education favor the perspective that mathematics is essentially a mental activity. But many theorists and researchers continue to find the idea that mathematics is something we develop (and subsequently impose on an unsuspecting universe) to be as untenable as the opposing Realist perspective that mathematical truths, quite literally, are hiding in the bushes awaiting discovery. How, for example, can we account for the tremendous descriptive capacities of mathematical ideas if they are only mental activities?[66]

That we feel we must believe one way or the other, I think, is evidence of our inability to escape the modern mind-set that we are essentially independent and isolated entities. Not only are we distinct from one another, we are set apart from the universe. To maintain that mathematics is extracted from the world, that is, discovered, is to subtract the creative genius of the mathematical community and to deny our role in shaping the world in which we exist. To argue the contrary point, that mathematics is created, is to ignore the world which provides the occasions for and the constraints upon our own thought. In its extreme form, this argument leads to the conclusion that human thought is somehow unnatural—not of nature. Our ecological situation cautions us against maintaining this naive belief.

I am arguing, then, that neither subjective nor objective accounts of mathematical knowledge—alone or in tandem—are powerful enough to help us understand the nature of mathematics. Characterizing the subject matter in terms of individual constructions is clearly inadequate; such a description would reduce the fluid and harmonious movement of the collective to mechanically coordinated actions of fully autonomous agents. Similarly, characterizing mathematics as a field of objectified, pregiven truths toward which mathematicians are progressing is also unsatisfactory—as demonstrated by the fact that systems of mathematics have been developed that flatly contradict one another. (There are, in fact, *many* mathematics, not one.)

Given that the interpretive power of the subjective-objective dichotomy is inadequate to address the question of knowledge, we are compelled to look elsewhere for other theoretical possibilities—such as that offered by enactivism. The key to the enactivist alternative is found in its challenges to two premises of the subjective-objective debate—namely, the belief that mental operations and physical actions (i.e., mind and body) are in some way independent and separable, and that individual knowing agents are isolated from one another and from the known world.

Interestingly, in modern analytic terms, knowledge tends to be understood as a sort of bridge that links subject to object, knower to world, individual to collective, and mental to physical. Knowledge is popularly regarded as a "third thing" that links two opposites—a notion that underlies such statements as Kline's "mathematics . . . is a bold and formidable bridge between ourselves and the external world"[67]—and it is this conception that presents us with the problem of determining whether that third thing should be anchored in the subject/knower/individual/mental or in the object/world/collective/physical.

Much has recently been written challenging the mind-set that places the cognizing agent (i.e., the mind) and the world into two distinct categories. For example, as noted in Chapter 1, Merleau-Ponty argues that this formulation is lacking because it has forgotten the body. In his terms, the body is simultaneously a biological structure and a lived-phenomenological structure—it is, all at once, of the world and of one's self. Our bodies separate us from one another at the same time that they place us in relationship with one another. Our bodies are shaped by the world that they participate in shaping; they render mind-and-world, subject-and-object, individual-and-collective, mental-and-physical inseparable. These phenomena are coemergent: fluidly defined against one another.

An assumption being made here is that, contrary to popular belief (particularly as maintained by those working from more subjective versions of constructivism), the phenomena of *joint* action and *shared* understanding are quite possible. To state the point differently, Descartes' assertion that each of us is isolated from one another and insulated from the world—assertions which serve as the foundation for modern analytic philosophy—are in error. Recent studies in the field of complexity theory[68] also support the notion that we are capable of joint action—that is, of acting collectively in ways that give rise to structures that transcend each of us. A comparison that is often made to illustrate complex (joint) action involves that of the subsystems that comprise our bodies. Just as cells come together to form organs and those organs, in turn, come together to form bodies, higher order unities can emerge in joint action. Important in these instances of coupling is that the properties and behaviors of higher order unities tend to be highly complex—in general, far more complex than might be predicted from a knowledge of the unity's subsystems. Moreover, the higher order unities are capable of patterns of acting that could likely never be attained separately by any of the individual subsystems.

An analogy can thus be drawn between one's body and a collective's body of knowledge. Just as mind and world are made inseparable by our physical-phenomenological body, so knowers and known world are brought together in a body of knowledge. (This latter body is a fluid structure consisting entirely in the complex choreography of knowers.) Similarly, just as my changing body is the locus of my personal identity—simultaneously setting me apart from while situating me in the world—so our dynamic knowledge is the locus of our collective identity, providing an integrity that distinguishes us from a background while placing us in communion with that background. Our body of knowledge—that is, our established and mutable patterns of acting—can thus be thought of as our collective self: dynamic as, co-emergent with, inhabiting, and en-habited by the world.

As part of this body, we constantly participate in its shaping, just as it serves to shape our own perceptions and identities. In a sense, then, mathematical knowledge is like the subject matter of a conversation. It exists only in conversing, and its nature, its structure, and its results can never be anticipated, let alone fixed.

Our mathematical knowledge, like our language, our literature, and our art, is neither "out there" nor "in here," but exists and consists in our acting. As such, the character of our knowledge changes with every action, as do the characters of the agent and of the world. And so the patterns of acting that we refer to as our collective knowledge, and through which we formulate our part of this unfolding conversation, can be understood in terms of neo-Darwinian evolutionary processes. The evolution of mathematics, like the emergence of a species, is subject to the same sorts of twists, turns, and dead-ends. The path that mathematics follows—what mathematics comes to be—is a path that is laid down in walking, not one toward a pregiven end.

The question of the nature of mathematical knowledge can thus never be determined once and for all. Further to this point, if our knowledge and our action are coimplicated, then we are also compelled to acknowledge that the character of our mathematics changes as a result of engaging in mathematical activity. Instead of thinking of our body of mathematical knowledge as essentially unchanging (and of mathematics learning as conforming to that fixed body), this enactivist interpretation suggests that individual conceptions and collective knowledge take shape simultaneously. The questions of whether mathematics is "in here" or "out there" and whether mathematics is a process or a product, are thus replaced by the assertion that such notions are inseparable. To draw an analogy between this shift in thinking and recent developments in mathematics, one might say that a new geometry of knowledge has been proposed in which a previously uninterrogated axiom (which might be called the "Axiom of Authenticity"), by which the individual is cast as the locus of cognition, is rejected in favor of an "Axiom of Collective Action" whereby consciousness, cognition, and knowledge are thought to arise in shared social action. This enactivist twist, in effect, helps us to reconcile the Rationalist/Empiricist tension. For the enactivist, collective knowledge is necessarily something "larger" than the solitary cognizing agent. Thus it is, in a sense, "out there," beyond the individual, as the empiricist would contend. Similarly, by identifying the individual as a specifiable but inextricable part of the complex collective, the enactivist is able to appreciate the role of individual thought and action—the "in here-ness" of knowing—in the emergence of the shared body of knowledge.

So, what is mathematics?

The critical task seems to be not so much determining the nature of mathematics, for in posing the question in those terms, there is an implication that we can somehow consider the body of knowledge as determinable, fixable, and separable from ourselves—as though we could somehow step outside of our mathematics. An enactivist turn on the question of knowledge would be to ask how we are knitted together in this particular body. How does the discipline contribute to our perceptions and define our actions? How does the subject matter help to shape the responsive world that we perceive, within which we act, of which we are part?

Far from merely representing the universe (thus setting us apart from it), then, our mathematics presents[69] the rhythms of the planet and the patterns that are repeated in all forms and at all levels of life. It does not reduce the universe, but places us in conversation with it, hinting at the complex orders and the tangled relationships that inevitably exceed our attempts to understand and surpass our efforts to control. Conversely, our mathematics also presents us (i.e., "makes us present") in these harmonies, enacting not the modernist separation, alienation, and exile from the natural world, but an attunement to the pulse of the planet.

The "unreasonable effectiveness of mathematics" in describing and predicting the physical world should hardly be surprising. In the work of the Egyptians, the Babylonians, and others, mathematics was built directly on the surface of the earth, and, in spite of modern efforts to yank it away from its grounded beginnings, it remains inextricably woven into our physical experience. Mathematics is truly about us and our world.

A New Question

The more important question, then, is not, What is mathematics?, but, What are *we* that we might know mathematics?[70] And herein lies an important difference between enactivist and modernist perspectives: in the move to embrace the complexities of existence, the focus shifts toward understanding being and away from questions of knowledge and validity. Put differently, priority is given to ontological concerns rather than epistemological, thus reversing Descartes' *cogito*. The implications are profound, extending culture-wide to encompass virtually every niche of human endeavor—for, in our modern age, little has been untouched by formalist perspectives on knowledge and the divisive and destructive patterns of acting that are supported by such perspectives. This issue is explored further in the next chapter where the issue of formal education is addressed.

Before leaving this section, however, I wish to state in clearer terms that, by invoking ecological theories, I am not attempting to establish a new ground for mathematical knowledge. Rather, I am trying to embrace the "groundlessness" that has emerged in all areas of academic inquiry, aligning myself with Varela, Thompson, and Rosch, who contend that we must work toward a "planetary world." In their words:

> *[T]he solution for the sense of nihilistic alienation in our culture is not to try to find a new ground; it is to find a disciplined and genuine means to pursue groundlessness. Because of the preeminent place science occupies in our culture, science must be involved in this pursuit.*[71]

The concern for "groundlessness" in this admonition, at first hearing, may seem to contradict one of the themes running through this section: that we must recall the (physical) ground on and out of which we draw our mathematics. The contradiction is resolved, however, when we recognize that two senses of ground are involved, one meaning certain (as in "solid ground") and one meaning connected (as in "grounded"). "Ground," in this latter sense, is a constantly changing form, both in terms of its impermanent formations and the ever-evolving manner that we construct and perceive it (as determined, in part, by the conceptual lens provided by our mathematics). It is, in fact, a groundless ground, with the same sort of transience, immediacy, and locality of sound.

We would do well, then to recall that sound sense of knowledge enacted in oral cultures—that is, the intertwining collection of patterns of acting. Within this conception—where the concern is for maintaining adequate fit rather than progressing toward optimal fit—there is a possibility for educational renewal, for we can begin to rid ourselves of the desires to determine the most important things to know and the best ways to teach them. (These are the topics of the next two sections.) Such a sense of knowledge might also enable us to cure what Max Horkheimer calls the "disease of reason": "The disease of reason is that reason was born from man's urge to dominate nature; and 'recovery' depends on insight into the nature of the original disease, not a cure of the latest symptoms."[72]

The last word in this exploration of mathematics I give to two mathematicians, Philip J. Davis and Reuben Hersh:

We should never forget that a stroll in the woods or a deep conversation with a new or old friend are beyond mathematics. And then, when we go back to our jobs as administrators, teachers, or whatever, let us still remember that numbers are only the shadow, that life is the reality.[73]

Section B

Mathematics Curriculum

> *The material composition of the waterfall changes all the time; only the form is permanent and what gives any shape at all to the water is the motion. The waterfall exhibits a* form in motion, *or a* dynamic form.
>
> —*Susanne Langer*[1]

> *In order for curriculum to provide the moral, epistemological, and social situations that allow persons to come to form, it must provide the ground for their action rather than their acquiescence. It must be submitted to their reform, be accessible to their response. . . . Curriculum is a moving form.*
>
> —*Madeleine Grumet*[2]

I recall visiting the bedroom of my niece a few months before she began grade one. There she introduced me to her horses—a large and varied assemblage of playthings, porcelain, and pictures.

It was immediately clear to me that this sprawl of objects had prompted her to count, to group, to order, to compare. As I followed her movements through the room, I became aware of the subtle and exquisite patterns in her arrangements. Her interest lay—to my hearing—not in the images or in the physical presence of the horses, but in the play that they invited.

Today my niece is in grade three. Today she hates "math." And she's afraid of it. It's not surprising. She can't do it. From the instant her teacher tells her and her classmates to begin the *Mad Minute*[3] to the sound of the timer's bell, she is confronted with the menacing reality of her incompetence.

Which is not to say she can't do the addings and subtractings.

Given enough time (and a table under which to hide her still active hands) she can produce answers without error.

But to her, that's not math. In her math class, fingers and the symbols on the page are only coincidentally related in the word "digits." Her manipulations (that is, etymologically, the actions of her hands) and the arithmetic manipulations are worlds apart. The math, to her, is in the insanity of the *Mad Minute.* It is a work of the mind that demands the suppression of the body.

Thankfully, she still plays with her horses. And she'll still talk about them with anyone willing to listen.

The topic of this section is curriculum. It is about the business of sifting through what is known and selecting those aspects of our knowledge that are deemed important for the ongoing viability of our society. Curriculum thinkers thus locate themselves between the culture's established knowledge and the individual's emergent knowings, with "one foot in the camp of curriculum visionaries. . . . [t]he other foot in the real world where teachers and principals deal with day-to-day problems."[4]

The central purpose of this section is to move the discussion from the topic of collective knowledge to the question of what to teach. Once unproblematic (i.e., when mathematics was valued for its usefulness, one simply selected those bits of knowledge with the greatest utility), this issue has taken on a renewed relevance. With emerging insights on the evolving nature, the implicit prejudices, and the cultural status of mathematics (not to mention the changing needs of society), the question has been taken up with renewed vigor by curriculum theorists—and so, another purpose of this section is to introduce readers to that field and some of its current concerns.

In particular, a goal of this section is to offer a challenge to modern outcome-based perspectives that dominate discussions of mathematics curriculum, while taking care to point toward what may be the starting place for an alternative. It is, in effect, a call to discard the orientation to mathematical knowledge underlying and promoted by the *Mad Minute* and to seek our curriculum amid the chaos of a child's collection of horses. It is a call to recognize the moving form of curriculum.

Conceptions of Curriculum

It often comes as something of a surprise to those educationalists working within a single subject area, such as mathematics, to hear that there is an entire field devoted to curriculum studies. Nevertheless, with beginnings traceable to the early nineteenth century, curriculum has both an extensive history and a rather broad literature.[5] It has, in fact, been called the only field of study that is proper to education—as all its other subdisciplines (e.g., educational psychology, educational administration, educational philosophy) might be described as versions of other scholarly endeavors that have been adopted and adapted.

The most notable quality of curriculum studies is, perhaps, the range of interpretations to which the term "curriculum" has been subject—most of which share little beyond an acknowledgment that curriculum has something to do with what happens in schools. I begin this discussion by tracing out perhaps the most prominent orientation, one that finds its roots in the work of Franklin Bobbitt.[6]

Bobbitt began from understandings of society and schooling as essentially static entities, insisting that curriculum development should begin with scientific determinations of that knowledge and those qualities that are necessary for adult life. These elements could then be dissected into teachable bits by curriculum makers. It is thus that, for him, schooling amounted to a preparation for life; it was not part of life itself.

In terms of current beliefs and practices surrounding curriculum, the sorts of ideas announced by Bobbitt figure prominently. This point is well-illustrated in the survey of conventional perspectives on curriculum that has been prepared by William Schubert.[7] Among the more prominent of current orientations, Schubert identifies and elaborates upon the following: curriculum as content, as subject matter, as a program of planned activities, as intended learning outcomes, as cultural reproduction, and as discrete tasks and concepts. Common to each of these orientations are a desire to predetermine what is valuable to know and a belief in the possibility of controlling learning outcomes once the topics of study are selected.

In other words, each of these perspectives is predicated on the assumption that it is possible for the contents of a curriculum to have a transcendent validity—one which, for all intents and purposes, is independent of the era, the culture, the classroom, the teacher, and the learners. Such an assumption arises from the modern notions that the world is pregiven and objectively knowable and that established knowledge of both the physical and the social world is essentially value free—conceptions that support curriculum developers' goals to identify knowledge objectives that reflect that world and to organize those objectives in ways that are suited to the linear and tiered structure of the schooling system.

Conspicuously absent in this formulation is a reference to the learner, and so, not surprisingly, there are those who argue for a more "student-centered" curriculum. Rejecting the stifling effects of imposed formal structures and ostensibly value free "facts," these student-centered approaches concentrate on personal expression, authority, autonomy, and self-image.

As might be expected, then, an objectivist-subjectivist tension figures prominently in much of current discussion in the field of curriculum. Supporters of a knowledge-centered perspective worry that the child-centered approach is relativistic and potentially solipsistic. Proponents of a more child-centered curriculum criticize their adversaries' project as being dehumanizing and oppressive. This "world versus child" conflict was first announced in Dewey's *The Child and the Curriculum*[8] and it has since become a foundational issue in curriculum studies.

Exactly which side of the debate seems to be "winning" is easily established. One need only step inside a typical mathematics classroom and make note of the teacher's position at the head of the room, the program of studies' place in the center of his or her desk, and the standardized textbooks located in front of each learner. Student authority and self-image are not priorities in today's math class.

What must be borne in mind, however, is that both objectivist and subjectivist perspectives on curriculum are founded on the belief, à la Bobbitt, that those qualities most critical for successful living can be identified and taught. In terms of the nature of mathematics in this formulation, there is a predictable emphasis on the utilitarian and mechanical qualities of the subject matter. That is, for the most part, mathematics is valued for the very qualities that serve to crystallize the discipline into a completed and static hierarchical structure of absolute concepts and rigid procedures—a resource to be mined and exploited, as it were. In this conception, understanding is reduced to rightness and wrongness and doing math is made equivalent to applying memorized rules.

Some Issues

The difficulty with the development of mathematics curricula, I would like to argue, springs from two sources: a narrow definition of curriculum and a naive understanding of the nature of mathematical knowledge. Having already touched on the latter issue, I will focus here on alternatives to the predominant instrumental and prescriptive orientation to curriculum (predominant, that is, among those agencies responsible for the creation of curriculum documents).

Reflecting the mode of thinking that underlies Bobbitt's writing, "curriculum" is generally understood to refer to those mandated programs of study that are to be offered in our schools. As already noted, for the most part, such curricula take on the physical form of an ordered list of objectives to be met over a period of study and, in the case of mathematics at least, to be assessed through a battery of regularly scheduled standardized examinations. In this incarnation, a curriculum document inevitably and necessarily is comprised of bits of already established facts that are to be passed from one generation to the next.

An immediate difficulty arises, however, when one considers the nature of the well from which the "facts" are drawn, for what seems to be forgotten in the construction of such impositional curricula is that, in Jerome Bruner's terms, "a culture is constantly in process of being re-created as it is interpreted and renegotiated by its members."[9] Unfortunately, like the static appearing glacier, the transitional rate of a culture's collective knowledge has traditionally been so much slower than that of an individual within that culture that this knowledge tends to be "taken for granted"; it is the given that precedes the preparation of curriculum documents. Losing sight of its movement and the mass that lies behind it, we have tended to excavate bits from the front end of this glacier and to offer them as reasonable representations of the remainder.

As such, modern curriculum has forgotten its past. Moreover, in our efforts to distinguish one discipline from another and one concept from another, our curricula have come to embody the modern ideals of fragmentation and isolation. As Pinar, Reynolds, Slattery, and Taubman put it:

> *It seems to us that most textbooks present a field of study as if it were an army of disembodied ideas, marching across the blank space of time, inevitably annexing unincorporated space, establishing cities of systematized thought.*[10]

In consequence, again with reference to school mathematics, the subject matter has come to be regarded as having little to do with the "real world" and as bearing an even more tenuous relationship to the lived experience of learners.

A number of critical commentaries on this orientation to mathematics curricula have been offered from a range of perspectives. Valerie Walkerdine articulates a feminist critique of the preeminent place assigned to mathematics within the modern curriculum—a practice which she regards at the foundation of the "bourgeois and patriarchal rule of science, it is indeed inscribed with domination."[11] Social ecologist Murray Bookchin[12] comments on the devastating cultural consequences of our privileging of an ostensibly neutral "conventional reason" modeled after mathematical thought. David Orr,[13] an environmentalist, discusses the contribution of our near-sighted application of mathematized scientific knowledge to the destruction of our ecosystem. A host of critical theorists have echoed and elaborated upon these critiques, all arriving at a similar conclusion: that in our teaching of mathematics, we are maintaining a series of gender, racial, class, cultural, and ecological barriers, some of which are a consequence of teaching methods, but much of which can be directly traced to the discipline of mathematics itself.

These thinkers are presenting quite a different message from those few theorists and researchers within mathematics education who offer a social critique of mathematics teaching.[14] For them, the focus seems to be almost exclusively on instructional approaches and institutional biases. There are thus two levels of critique that must be considered: analyzing the biases implicit in the subject matter and investigating the more hidden prejudices that are enacted as the subject matter is re-presented to students.

Re-Membering Dewey

John Dewey, who was a contemporary of Franklin Bobbitt, articulated a conception of curriculum that was much different from the prevailing modernist perspectives. Briefly, he argued that curriculum had to do with the dynamic and complex relationships among children, teachers, and culture. He thus sought to erase the rigid boundaries that had been drawn between the learner and the curriculum, contending that the two were not distinct but intertwined. For him, the same fluid and co-emergent relationship existed between knowledge—a source of curriculum—and society.

Unfortunately, through the contributions of Bobbitt and others (among whom Ralph Tyler figures prominently), Dewey's work was pushed to the side, and it is only recently that this trend has been seriously challenged. In the mid-seventies, William Pinar[15] introduced the term "reconceptualist" to the field of curriculum inquiry in an edited volume of essays from theorists who had begun to question the field's underlying instrumental (and, arguably, mathematical) rationality. Arriving from backgrounds in literary, existentialist, critical, feminist, and phenomenological thinking, these scholars called for a greater awareness of the ecologies of our existence, the agency of the learner, the interconnections and interdependencies of knowledge areas, and the value of diversity, thus opening the door to a new form of curriculum study. They did so not merely by offering an effective critique of conventional practices, but by reminding us that education is never merely concerned with questions of knowledge.

Put differently, curriculum reconceptualists called into question the modern priority of epistemology over ontology[16]—an emphasis that perhaps arises from the Cartesian assumption that the mind has an existence that is independent of experience. If one accepts the notion that there is a stable Self which precedes learning and which is able to maintain its integrity through learning, then the practices of preselecting what is valuable to know and predetermining how it is best learned are entirely unproblematic. But if one rejects this notion—as do the reconceptualists (along with thinkers such as Merleau-Ponty, Bruner, Varela, and others)—the alternative is that we are, in fact, the product of our experiences and, because we are social beings, our minds and our identities emerge and evolve relationally. The issues of learning, teaching, and curriculum, then, are fundamentally ontological, regardless of one's opinions on the moral status of the subject matter at hand.

Further to the issue of knowing, curriculum reconceptualists also challenge the very possibility of predetermining what is to be learned. A complex and poorly understood phenomenon, human learning has proven itself to be tremendously adept (but wildly unpredictable) at adapting to the contingencies of existence: one never knows exactly what one will learn—just as, on a broader level, one can never predict the directions in which mathematics and other facets of collective knowledge might evolve. Curriculum makers, it seems, have disregarded these commonplace understandings, electing to work from the maxim that what is to be learned can be controlled through careful articulation. The reconceptualist movement, in contrast, might be understood as a return to an acknowledgment of the ambiguities and uncertainties of life. Curriculum is thus not conceived of in terms of distinct (but coherent) knowledge bits, but as having to do with the existential qualities of life in schools.

Not surprisingly, then, part of the reconceptualist project has involved an effort to "free" the notion of curriculum from its modern divisive, prescriptive, and instrumentalist frame. To this end, Pinar and Madeleine Grumet[17] have reminded us of the verb *currere* from which "curriculum" (along with a host of other terms, including "course," "current," and "au courant") is derived. *Currere* refers to "the running of the course" rather than the "course to be run, or the artifacts employed in the running of the course,"[18] and Pinar and Grumet use the term to refocus our attention away from the impersonal goals of conventional curriculum projects and onto the meaning-making process of moving though the melée of present events. In rendering experience meaningful, one recovers and recreates one's history and simultaneously creates new possibilities for one's future. Such sense-making is understood to be both enabled and constrained by language and, as such, fundamentally social and relational. In brief, "curriculum"—far from popular conceptions—is conceived as the interpretation of lived experience, and is thus valued for its transformative rather than its transmissive potential. Implicit in the notion of *currere* are an acknowledgment of the relational basis of our knowing (and being) and a recognition of the happenstantial, constantly negotiated nature of our existence.

It is important to emphasize that Pinar and Grumet are not recommending that standardized curricula be abandoned and new documents reflecting the fluid natures of cultural knowledge and personal identity be developed. On the contrary, such action would miss the point by supporting, rather than challenging, the belief that learning outcomes can be managed. Rather, they are inviting us to think differently—not just about the topics of study, but within the context of study.

Mathematical *Currere*

How, then, do we move from instrumental formulations and interpretations of mathematics curriculum? A possible tack might be found in the suggestion that the more fluid form of *currere* points away from the prescriptive (retentive) efforts of conventional perspectives on curriculum and toward a more proscriptive (attentive) orientation. Following Varela,[19] the difference between prescription and proscription is essentially the difference between "what is not allowed is forbidden" and "what is not forbidden is allowed"—a shift which might enable us to overcome our modern desire to fix what is learned by mandating outcomes.

Common to both *prescriptive* and *proscriptive* is the root "script"—to write or to draw. *Pre*script*ion* is a writing that occurs in advance, a charting of a particular path; *pro*script*ion* is a scribing not of route but of boundaries. Proscription does not seek to converge onto what is perceived as ideal, but to open one's perceptions to the divergent, the possible. Temporally, in the movement from prescription to proscription, the concern shifts from a privileging of the future to a greater attentiveness to the present and to the immediacy of interpretation and action. One's focus is thus set not on the path (because the course has not been predetermined) but on negotiating a path: on *currere*, running; on the instant of interpretation; on doing. The contents of a mandated program of studies might thus be interpreted as outlining areas for exploration, rather than as specifying where each step will land. ("Curriculum" thus comes to be something that can only be discussed in retrospect, as the path that was taken, in all its experiential richness.)

Such an interpretation is in greater harmony with the enactivist premise that our identities are established in the dialectical play of biology and human culture. Translating this notion into the realm of mathematics learning gives rise to the suggestions that, first and foremost, learners must come to understand that mathematics is *about* them—where the word "about," in an ambiguous play, invites at least a four-fold interpretation. "Mathematics is about oneself" simultaneously suggests senses of being surrounded ("round about"), of being the object of focus ("about this idea"), and of being active ("about one's business"). "About" also points to the fundamental interpretability of things. "Tell me about . . . " is an invitation to explain and to rethink. For the current purposes, then, the term is a reminder of the ecological, enactive, and hermeneutic foundations of this project.

How might one foster a sense of *about*-ness in a mathematics classroom? I think that Heidegger[20] provides us with a possibility as he draws a distinction between *mathematics* and the *mathematical*. As I understand him, *mathematics* is that more-or-less static, widely accepted assemblage of concepts and activities that have emerged through centuries of inquiry. Different sorts of mathematics can and do arise, as illustrated in the preceding section, depending on the era, the culture, and the needs or events that present themselves. (I might add that one need not go far to observe the emergence of mathematics that diverges significantly from established systems. Indeed, it may not be unreasonable to suggest that, in spite of our efforts to prescribe understandings, the mathematics of any given classroom setting will likely diverge in some way from the expected norms. As teacher and learners interact, as they establish their own body of knowledge (i.e., patterns of acting that give rise to a particular collective identity or character), their mathematics will drift from "standard knowledge," even while being framed by that knowledge. It is thus that an investigation into combining fractions might be deflected into a study of partition theory, or a lesson in ratios might shift into a discussion of various forms of reasoning. While the understandings may lack the rigor to qualify as formal mathematics, such contextually specific knowledge is certainly appropriately labeled "mathematical.")

The *mathematical*, in contrast, is that orientation to inquiry which has allowed our *mathematics* to emerge. It involves a noticing of sameness, pattern, and regularity amid one's explorations. It involves comparing, ordering, creating, and naming. It is, true to its etymology and to Pythagoras' definition, about learning. And it is thus that, as some historians contend, *mathematics* (as an independent discipline) may be only a recent phenomenon, whereas there are traces of the *mathematical* in the earliest of human records.[21]

In our own (formal and literate) traditions, we have tended to focus only on the endpoint of mathematical inquiry (i.e., where the *mathematical* becomes *mathematics*)—that is, on the logical situating of a "truth" amid an already established set of propositions. These propositions can be, and often are, modified, as might be the rules of logic that govern the mathematical play. But the issue is neither the content of a specific system of mathematics nor the mysterious qualities that enable mathematical intuitions. It is, rather, the particular structure of a mathematical argument—and it is this structure that, in Western history at least, has remained more or less constant. As such "situating" or "proving" has become the hallmark of acceptable mathematics, the underlying mode of deductive reasoning has been made equivalent to mathematical thought.

As such, with regard to our modern heritage, particular aspects of the mathematical have been privileged over the past few centuries, including abstraction, formalization, rigor, and generalization—and perhaps the quality that most distinguishes modern mathematics from the mathematical activity of our ancestors is its current level of formality (i.e., the assigning of form through some manner of representation). The resulting mathematics has risen in status alongside the "power" it has offered in the Empiricist project in controlling our world through a knowledge of it. But, as has been noted, this mathematics is not without its shortcomings. We hardly need to know it better or to apply it more effectively. Consider, for example, mathematician Richard Courant's admonition:

Abstraction and generalization are not more vital for mathematics than individuality of phenomena and, before all, not more than inductive intuition. Only the interplay between these forces and their synthesis can keep mathematics alive and prevent its drying out like a dead skeleton.[22]

Rather, we must begin to understand that, contra Descartes' belief, mathematical thought simply does not work everywhere. Perhaps, then, we need to seek or to reclaim a different orientation to the mathematical—one that makes it local, immediate, personal, part of the way we participate in the universe.

On this point, curriculum makers (reflecting the modern tendency) have concentrated almost exclusively on the utilitarian and analytic qualities of the mathematical: abstraction, generalization, classification, rigor, deduction, formalization, "power." While important, these qualities have eclipsed others, such as elegance, patterning, rhythm, intuition, and contextualization—elements which clothed the mathematics of oral traditions. Further, the conversational or dialogical nature of mathematical inquiry—that is, the aspect of learning that involves an active and intersubjective questioning of the world—has given way to a perception of mathematics learning as solitary and monological. It is here, it seems, that we might most effectively direct our efforts in moving from an orientation toward curriculum as a plan to an understanding of curriculum as *currere.* Stated otherwise, the particular concepts (i.e., the *mathematics*) that we select to study, while important, are not as central a concern as the manner in which we choose to portray the *mathematical.*

By drawing this distinction between mathematics and the mathematical, then, a space is opened to develop a critical understanding of some of the defining qualities of our culture and, hence, of our selves. It further serves to emphasize the temporal and contextual nature of mathematics. Finally, it compels us to connect ourselves to the mathematics, for it is we who think this way, and it is this that affects the way we think. Mathematics curriculum, then, can serve as a location for hermeneutic interpretation—a sense of curriculum which makes explicit that there is a dynamic, complex and ecological relationship among individual identity, collective identity, individual understanding and cultural-collective expressions of knowledge. The core of mathematics pedagogy, in this light, is neither product nor process, neither knowledge nor knower, but the fuzzying of such distinctions. Within this focus on the interpretive process, the varied relations involved in the doing of mathematics become present for interrogation.

"Doing Mathematics"

Implicit in this formulation is the suggestion that "doing mathematics" is something other than memorizing prespecified facts and mastering preselected procedures. Of course, this redefinition of mathematical activity hardly represents a new insight—as the NCTM Standards documents[23] have plainly stated and as, for example, the broad movement toward process-oriented problem-solving in the 1980s has demonstrated.

That movement has continued into the 1990s, rejuvenated somewhat by a trend toward the activity of "problem-posing"—an idea that derives from the activity of professional mathematicians. In brief, learners are not merely asked to solve multi-step, multiple-operation, nonroutine problems, they are offered situations and activities in which they are encouraged and expected to define mathematical problems for themselves. This trend reflects an emerging conception of what it means to "do mathematics." As mathematician Jerry P. King describes it:

[To do] mathematics means to produce new mathematics. Realistically, it means to produce mathematics that is new and that is simultaneously significant. . . . [In] a technical sense, you are doing research in mathematics whenever you are producing mathematics that is new to you. . . . *If you have invented the problem yourself and then solved it yourself, your work is close to what mathematicians actually do.*[24]

On the surface, this pronouncement seems fully compatible with the conventional emphasis on problem-posing among mathematics educators. It takes on a deeper significance, however, as one considers that this sort of activity brings the classroom learner into the space of mathematical research. That is, there is an *explicit* recognition that school children (and their teachers) are part of the mathematics community, part of our dynamic body of mathematics. (The important point here is that this inclusion is made explicit. As noted in the first section of this chapter, each of us is necessarily implicated in the shape of mathematical knowledge by virtue of the fact that we are literate and numerate.) To do mathematics, then, is to engage in a transformative process: transformative of the learner, the community, the culture, and, ultimately (since we cannot extricate what we know from how we act), the world.

By coupling this notion with an emphasis on the *mathematical*, as presented earlier, senses of the sorts of qualities, activities, and features that one might look for in a mathematical task (for the purpose of preparing to teach) begin to emerge. Regarding important qualities, we might be guided by Richard Courant:

> *The* interplay *between generality and individuality, deduction and construction, logic and imagination—this is the profound essence of* live *mathematics. Any one of these aspects of mathematics can be at the center of a given achievement, In a far reaching development all of them will be involved. . . . In brief, the flight into abstract generality must start from and return again to the concrete and specific.*[25]

That is, the qualities of individuality, construction (creation), imagination (intuition), and concretization should complement the conventional emphases on generality, deduction, logic, and abstraction. And if Morris Kline is anywhere near the mark in his suggestions that "free creation must precede formalization and logical foundation"[26] and that "mathematics rests not on logic but on sound intuition,"[27] we might do well not merely to introduce these former elements, nor merely to note their interplay with the latter. They may well be the most important points of emphasis.

In addition to such lists of qualities, particular sorts of activities might also be identified as mathematical. Alan Bishop,[28] in describing commonalties among mathematical systems across cultures, suggests the following: counting, locating, measuring, designing, playing, and explaining. While he does not take it to the level of individual activities, I would propose that an important feature of a mathematical task would be that it include most or all of these elements—all-at-once.

In addition to being all-at-once, other features of a mathematical task are that it be variable-entry[29] (i.e., constructed so that learners, regardless of their backgrounds in mathematics, are able to locate themselves and negotiate the difficulty of the tasks they set for themselves), rich (i.e., presenting the possibility for diverse, unexpected, and extensive mathematical interpretation), and open-ended (i.e., raising more questions than answers). As well, I believe that a mathematical task should involve more than a single mode of reasoning (i.e., rather than focusing exclusively on logico-deductive thought, one should be able, for example, to draw analogies between mathematical constructs and other categories of experienced phenomena and to locate mathematical activity in the context of stories), include opportunities for both independent and collective action, and present an opportunity for embracing the emotional/affective dimensions of mathematical inquiry (and, in particular, the possibility of profound personal engagement—and perhaps even obsession—of the sort that one rarely witnesses in the context of a fragmented and decontextualized mathematics). Finally, and perhaps most importantly, a mathematical task should have the capacity to serve as a focal point for joint, collective action. That is, it should allow for both solitary and shared exploration: as a sort of common text around and through which learners can come together. In sum, a mathematical task should impose "liberating constraints"[30] which are intended to strike a balance between "complete freedom" (which would seem to negate the need for schools in the first place) and no freedom at all.

While much of the remaining text is focused on an exploration of these ideas, a preliminary example of the sort of task to which I am referring might help to make clearer—or at least to announce—some of its important points. In a recent senior undergraduate course, on the topic of methods for elementary mathematics teaching, I required students to engage in some "original mathematical inquiry" (in the sense described by King earlier in this section) within a fractal geometry setting. I presented a cursory introduction of the field by pointing out some important terms, providing some examples of fractal images or figures that could be generated with pencil and/or scissors and paper, and identifying some possible directions for inquiry.[31] Class members were then given one week to conduct their investigations and to submit a brief summary of their "findings" along with an account of how, to their minds, their activity was mathematical.

I was quite surprised by the results. As I had expected, most students were initially quite apprehensive about the task, not in the least because of the rather open and somewhat ambiguous way in which it was presented (relative to their previous experiences with mathematics). However, almost everyone reported that, upon sitting down to "play" with fractal images, they became intrigued by the patterns and the sequences that presented themselves. Several students, in fact, commented that they could not recall ever having been so engaged by a task that had been explicitly labeled "mathematical." From my teacherly perspective, the most important (and unexpected) result was that these persons' investigations, in general, prompted serious re-cognitions of the nature of the discipline and how it serves to frame our thinking. In being asked to interpret various phenomena through a different mathematical lens, they became more consciously aware of the previously unnoticed (mathematical) interpretive frames that shaped their prior perceptions. As such, the exercise in fractal geometry not only contributed to immediate perceptions (as, for example, ferns, broccoli, trees, and sea shells came to be seen differently), it prompted a re-formulation of past perceptions and projected actions (as what it meant to "do mathematics" and to "be mathematical" were fundamentally redefined). The mathematical inquiry became a location—a common text—for hermeneutic interpretation.

"Subject Matter"

So far in this chapter, I have been using the term "subject matter" rather indiscriminately. Given its prominence in the pages of the curriculum guides and standardized textbooks that line teachers' bookshelves—where uses of the term are significantly different than mine—it would appear to be a phrase that bears closer scrutiny.

The phrase was also used in the first chapter in a discussion of the conversational relation. According to Gadamer, it was noted, the subject matter of the conversation is something to which the participants subject themselves without reserve; it conducts them, engages them, unites them. (In terms of complexity theory, the active subject matter of the conversation might thus be thought of as a transcendent unity.) That is the sense of the term that has guided my use.

The subject matter to which learners are subjected in many conventional classrooms is quite another issue. In another example of our language forgetting itself, the subject of mathematics—whether one believes it to be discovered, created,[32] or otherwise—is assigned an objective status, and the goal of teaching is to toss out to learners the subject's objects. The hope is that they catch onto or grasp them. Perhaps not surprisingly, relatively few seem to do so. And, even less surprising, few are conducted, engaged, and united by the subject matter of mathematics.

The calls for *currere* to complement curriculum, proscription to complement prescription, the mathematical to complement mathematics, and doing to complement knowing thus amount to a call to regard the "content" as potential "subject matter" (in the Gadamerian sense). It is a call to consider mathematics more as an approach to knowing than as an established body of knowledge. As Max van Manen reminds us:

> *To know a subject does not only mean to know it well and to know it seriously in the fundamental questions it poses. To know a subject also means to hold this knowledge in a way which shows that it is loved and respected for what it is and the way it lets itself be known. We learn* about *the subjects contained in a school curriculum. It is also true that the subjects* let *us learn something about them. It is in this letting us know that subject matter becomes a true subject: a subject which makes relationships possible. Our responsiveness, our "listening" to the subject, constitutes the very essence of the relationship between student and subject matter.*[33]

The teacher is called to listen, and the focus of that listening is an emergent knowledge—the individual's conceptualizations and the collective realizations—by which the mathematics is not (and indeed cannot be) considered apart from the mathematizers. The mathematics, like the curriculum, is in the realm of the sonorous rather than the visual, thus merging with and emerging from experience. The notion of curriculum, then, involves more than the study of particular ideas; it becomes an integral part of the constantly emerging text of our existence as enacted in the relationships of the classroom. Issues of knowledge and understanding are thus woven into and cannot be considered apart from the notion of identity.

Of course, such "subject matter" can exist only in the conversation. For the teacher, then, the critical issue preceding his or her entrance into the classroom is how he or she might transform a curriculum objective into a potential "topic of conversation." The task is not an easy one, for militating against the possibility of falling into a conversation, the mathematics classroom is founded on a particular disdain for that sort of happenstantial interaction. The mere practice of assembling at a specific time and in a specific place thirty persons with diverse interests and concerns might be considered a daunting barrier to any sort of sincere and profound engagement.

As such, simple attempts to rethink the subject matter, although necessary, are patently inadequate. A range of other issues must also be addressed—not the least of which are the natures of the relationships between the teacher and the learners and among learners. These topics are discussed in the next chapter.

For the moment, however, I would like to more specifically address the issue of "planning a lesson." I do so through a specific example drawn from my research. That presentation is preceded with an acknowledgment of its necessary "flatness" and a reminder of my conviction that the content is only one aspect of the classroom's rich texture of relationships. As such, a "learning objective" can become subject matter only through the sensitivity of a listening teacher—one who is attuned to the larger context and who is able to bring learners to the ontological significance of the mathematical.

Section C
Mathematics Curriculum Anticipating

[We] need to see . . . that curious consequences flow from planning when this planned instructional program becomes too fixed, too inflexible, too prescriptive for life with children. For one thing, inflexible planning may freeze the body of knowledge that is otherwise dynamic, vibrant, and alive.

—*Max van Manen*[1]

[W]e tend to encounter people and things, and enter into situations, with closed minds and deaf ears . . . *[with] our course of action fixed, and our experience prejudged, predetermined.*

—*David Levin*[2]

One aspect of my research into understanding teaching as a listening endeavor has been to work alongside a few mathematics teachers within their elementary, middle, and secondary school classrooms. Together, we have explored many issues relevant to the teaching of mathematics, and, in this section (as well as in parallel sections of subsequent chapters), I present some of the topics of our discussions and some of the happenings within their classrooms.

Consistent with the theme of this chapter, I focus on two issues here: first, the manner in which a teacher enacts his or her conception of the subject matter (and how that enactment contributes to the movement of the classroom collective) and, second, the role of planning in teaching. The latter concern emerges from the discussion of the former: If indeed one's conception of mathematics is critical to one's manner of teaching, how does one go about preparing to work with learners?

At the end of the first chapter, I introduced three modes of listening, using the labels "evaluative," "interpretive," and "hermeneutic" to distinguish them. Here I connect these modes of listening to three teaching vignettes—brief episodes drawn from mathematics lessons and through which I attempt to demonstrate how one teacher's evolving style of teaching (that is, of listening) might be linked to his or her enacted conceptions of the subject matter.

Wendy

Wendy is a middle school mathematics teacher with whom I took up the question, How might we teach mathematics? Spanning more than two years, Wendy's and my collaborative effort included a variety of shared tasks: observing and interpreting one another's teaching, reading and discussing relevant texts, planning and reviewing mathematics lessons.

For the purposes of this report, I had originally intended this account of Wendy to be a faithful portrait of one of the persons with whom I explored the theoretical and practical issues addressed in other parts of this text. But, as I have written and rewritten various accounts of our experiences, I have come to the realization that the Wendy presented here, in spite of my best efforts toward an accurate rendering, is more a *collage* of personages than a single, coherent, and accurately represented personality.

The character I portray here, in fact, might better be thought of as a reformulation of my own complex history as a learner and teacher of mathematics as it is read through my interactions with one particular teacher. In this rereading, I have come to regard Wendy as an elaborate fiction, even though the details that are provided are, to the extent possible, factual. Having said this, however, it must thus be noted at the outset that, in electing to present some of my perceptions through these vignettes, my concern is not exclusively—nor even primarily—with the accurate portrayal of events. Rather, the descriptions of these classroom incidents are offered more as prompts than as proofs, founded on a recognition that an objective representation of complex happenings is impossible.

Following Rorty[3] my concern here is with developing a location to use vocabulary more as an instrument of change than as a means of (f)actual depiction of events. As Rorty explains, we must develop new vocabularies (either by introducing new terms or by using old ones in novel ways) if we hope to effect changes in action and perception. My project in these closing sections of the remaining chapters is thus to explore the possibilities for listening, both as a means of interpreting classroom phenomena and as a useful starting place for transforming mathematics teaching practice.

Notes on Validity, Reliability, and Generalizability

With the juxtaposition of the announcement that this section of the text is founded on an actual in-school research project and my comment that the central character of this report, namely Wendy, is a fictionalized collage, it behooves me to comment briefly on the issue of the accurate representation of objects and events as it pertains to a hermeneutic inquiry.

As briefly noted in Chapter 1, a tenet of hermeneutics is that the desire for factual reports and objective analyses is something of a self-deception, founded upon a failure to notice that what is perceived is more a function of the perceptual frame than the object of study. Focusing on *this* rather than *that*, then, already involves us in the process of interpretation—as I attempted to highlight in the preceding chapter's phenomenology of listening. And so, while I strive to be true to the details of my collaboration with Wendy, I approach this "report" keenly aware that what I saw and heard in her classroom says more about me than anything else. In other words, "who is speaking" matters here—and it is thus that I have struggled to include my own signature in this text, both directly (through these sorts of statements) and indirectly (through such devices as narrative details, selection and sequencing of topics, and use of the first person).

Conventional concerns for validity, reliability, rigor, and generalizability—notions that are founded on a belief that reality is "out there" awaiting our efforts to capture it in our language—are replaced with an acknowledgment of the contingency of interpretation. The concerns of this account, then, lie more with issues of viability, reasonableness, relevance, and applicability—that is, more with the qualities of an engaging tale which implicates teller and listener alike than with an account that is sanitized of any particular human involvement. As explained by educational theorist Deborah

Britzman, "a practice of narration is not about capturing the real already out there. It is about constructing particular versions of truth, questioning how regimes of truth become neutralized as knowledge, and thus pushing the sensibilities of readers in new directions."[4]

The report is thus valued for its tranformative potential rather than for its unrelenting faithfulness to particular occurrences. At the same time, however, the text has a responsibility for being "true" to the intentions and motives of those portrayed. It is important, for example, that our collaboration occurred over two years, that we talked extensively about the nature of mathematics, and that Wendy had only been teaching a few years when we began.

Three Vignettes

Vignette 1: Evaluative Listening The first lesson under consideration took place a few months into the school year. The topic in this eighth-grade classroom was addition of fractions, and the following account is drawn from one of the first sessions in the month-long unit.

The opening activity for the lesson involved correcting the homework assignment consisting of a series of textbook exercises on the topic of comparing fractions. A complete list of answers was displayed using an overhead projector and each student, quite familiar with the routine, marked his or her own work in relative silence. A few raised their hands to ask questions about difficulties with their answers and Wendy dealt with these individually, moving between the desks of those seeking clarification.

That activity completed, Wendy wrote a series of addition statements on the chalkboard:

$^1/_5 + {}^1/_5 \qquad {}^1/_8 + {}^5/_8 \qquad {}^1/_4 + {}^1/_2 \qquad {}^1/_2 + {}^2/_5$

and instructed students first to copy these "questions" into their notebooks and then to write a response for each. A few moments later she asked for students to volunteer their answers.

Tim gave the first one, $^1/_5 + {}^1/_5 = {}^1/_{10}$.

"Now, let's think about that one," Wendy suggested. "Pretend we have a chocolate bar and that we cut it into fifths." On the chalkboard she drew a rectangle and sliced it into five equal-sized pieces (see Figure 2.1). "If you take one fifth," she said as she shaded in the first of the five

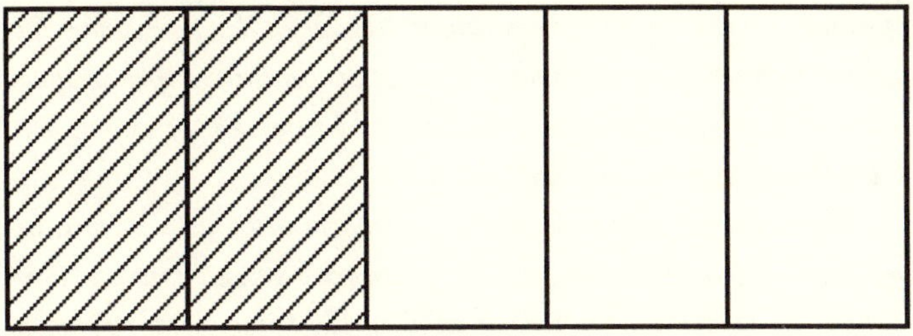

Figure 2.1. The chocolate bar example

sections, "and I take one fifth," shading in the second section, "how much is gone altogether?

"Two fifths," Tim responded correctly.

"So," Wendy continued, pointing to the shaded parts of the diagram, "what's one fifth plus one fifth?"

"Two fifths."

"Two fifths. That's right. How many of you got that?" Most of the students raised their hands. "Good. Adding fractions is just like adding anything else. One horse plus one horse is two horses; one tree plus one tree is two trees; one fifth plus one fifth is two fifths."

"Now," she continued, pointing at $^1/_8 + {}^5/_8$, "What about this one?"

"It's six eighths," Reena offered immediately.

"Good. One rabbit plus five rabbits is six rabbits; one eighth plus five eighths is six eighths. . . . We can write that differently if we want, can't we?"

Several hands were raised and the fact that six eighths could be rewritten as three fourths was quickly established.

"Now, what about one fourth plus one half?" Wendy asked, pointing at the fifth example and waiting for a show of hands. "Laura?"

"It's three fourths," Laura responded.

"That's right. How did you get that?"

"If you take half of something and then take another fourth of it, you'll have three fourths of the whole thing," Laura elaborated.

"That's right, but can you explain it mathematically?" (As became clear in a later interview, Wendy was requesting that Laura justify her solution by framing it in relation to ideas that had already been discussed.) Laura was unable to explain her reasoning in such "mathematical" terms. Nevertheless, this question served as the starting place for Wendy's presentation of the addition algorithm, first described in fairly

informal terms to "prove" Laura's answer and then developed more formally around the final example, $^1/_2 + ^2/_5$. Students were then assigned several seatwork questions along with their homework assignment, both of which were drawn from the textbook.

They worked independently for several minutes until Wendy announced that it was time to mark the seatwork exercises. This was done quickly as she called out the correct answers. The balance of the class was spent on the homework assignment, and during this time the teacher moved around the classroom, repeating bits of previous explanations to students whose hands were raised, checking students' work over their shoulders, and asking an occasional question of particular students.

Many issues can and should be addressed in an analysis of this brief account. Presently, the two central concerns are the manner of listening and the enacted conception of the subject matter. Using the terminology developed in Chapter 1, I would describe Wendy's listening in this lesson as "evaluative": Wendy did not seem to be listening *to* learners, but listening *for* something in particular (e.g., specific answers, a "mathematical explanation"). Moreover, the motivation for her listening appeared to be to evaluate the correctness of contributions, judging them against a preconceived standard. Thus, for example, even though Laura's explanation indicated a clear intuitive understanding of the relationships among the fraction amounts involved—despite its lack of mathematical rigor—it was quickly labeled as nonmathematical by Wendy's follow-up question. Student contributions—and Laura's explanation is a cogent example—were thus largely ignored and had virtually no effect on the prespecified trajectory of the lesson.

In this case, then, it seems that the manner of teaching—that is, this manner of evaluative listening—is also associated with a particular conception of the subject matter. Her use of the phrase "explain it mathematically" might suggest that Wendy regards mathematics primarily as a system of already established, formal truths whereby "doing math" consists in logically locating one truth against another. Further, her desire for streamlined and clear explanations indicates beliefs that mathematics is fully consistent, value-less, and socially-inert, and that teaching mathematics is a process through which, above all else, one strives to avoid ambiguity. The mathematics teacher is imperceptible in this conception of the subject matter: due to a host of enacted separations, she does not seem to be implicated in either the (objective) mathematics or the (subjective) learnings, let alone in their conflation.

As such, and as suggested by a teaching sequence that seemed impervious to student input, it appears almost as though the lesson that Wendy presented could have been taught to any group of students. "Curriculum," here, is pregiven and imposed: a path of preselected, predissected steps to follow. The particular context and the particular backgrounds of learners had little to do with the structure or content of the lesson. Wendy herself announced this in an interview that followed this class: "I'm quite proud of that lesson. I've almost got it to the point where it feels like everything's in place." It is a lesson, consistent with the enacted conception of mathematics, which transcends the particularity of learners. As such, little more than an evaluative listening—a mode of attending that is used primarily to ensure that learners themselves are listening—seems necessary.

Vignette 2: Interpretive Listening The lesson described in this second vignette occurred in the latter half of the school year, a few months after the preceding vignette. The topic of study for this lesson was the addition of integers and it, like the addition of fractions lesson, was situated near the beginning of a four-week unit.

When the class began, Wendy was standing beside the overhead projector. Displayed on the screen behind her were two different piles of transparent colored BINGO chips and a series of uncompleted adding statements:

$(+3) + (+5) =$ $\quad$ $(-4) + (+6) =$

$(-2) + (-4) =$ $\quad$ $(-4) + (+2) + (+3) + (-5) =$

$(+3) + (-1) =$

"Today we're going to talk about adding integers. Can anyone remind us what an integer is?" she began.

"A number with a sign," Ian offered.

"Okay. 'A number with a sign.' You mentioned two things there: a number and a sign. Can you say any more about those things?" Wendy asked, probing for the informal definition that had been established in the previous day's class.

"The number part tells you how far it is away from zero, and the sign tells you which side of zero it's on."

"Great. Okay, today we're going to talk about another way of showing integers: with BINGO chips. I have two colors here: red and blue," she explained, pointing at the pieces on the projector. "One color is going to be the positive and the other will be the negative. Which should be which?"

Several opinions were called out before Jaime offered, "Doesn't 'in the red' mean that you're in the hole?"

"Could you say more?" Wendy requested.

"You're out of money. You owe money when you're 'in the red.'"

"So 'in the red' means negative," Wendy responded. "Right. We talked about that expression a few days ago, didn't we? That's a good reason for calling the reds 'negatives' here, isn't it?"

Wendy then moved to the first of the addition statements, representing +3 and +5 with piles of three and five blue counters, pushing them together (to indicate the addition) and recounting them (to determine their sum). Following the demonstration, she asked for a volunteer to move to the front and "explain" the second sum, (–2) + (–4).

Amanda came to the projector. "This [pointing at the (–2)] is the same as this [pulling out two red counters]. And negative four is four reds [pushing four more reds to the center]. When you put them all together you have negative six."

"Good work, Amanda. Did everyone understand?" No one indicated that they didn't. "Good. Now, before we do this next one, you have to know something new. What do I have if I put a blue chip and a red chip together? . . . Tim?"

"Nothing. They'll balance."

"That's right. They'll cancel one another out. What number would this be?" Wendy asked, pointing to a blue and a red chip placed side-by-side.

"Zero," several voices called out.

"Okay. That's a zero. What would this be then?" Wendy asked, placing two red chips beside two blue ones.

"Still zero," came the reply.

"Right, because they cancel one another out," she said, pushing the opposite pairs to the side of the screen. "Now, let's see who can do this question: positive three plus negative one. . . . Ryan?"

Ryan came to the front and, with some prompting, produced the sum of +2. The remaining questions were explained by students from their desks as Wendy moved the counters according to their instructions.

Students were then divided into their preestablished working groups of three or four and a lengthy list of adding statements on a worksheet, along with packets containing BINGO chips were distributed to each group. They began in earnest, with almost every student making enthusiastic use of the chips for the first few questions. Fairly quickly, however, their use declined and, by the end of class, the chips served more as a distraction than a learning aid.

On the surface, there are many aspects to this lesson that resemble the previous one. Most obviously, the overall structure is similar, having begun with a brief presentation of the day's topic and ending with seatwork. The structure of the brief presentation is also similar, moving from more straightforward (and familiar) instances to those that are less intuitively obvious.

A closer inspection of Wendy's manner of attending, however, suggests that the style of teaching is not quite as similar as it might appear at first glance—in this case being more toward "interpretive" than "evaluative listening." For example, Wendy posed questions for which she did not (and could not) know the answers, and so she was compelled to listen *to* the students (to make sense of the sense they were making) and not merely *for* particular responses. However, perhaps because her questions did not actually foster much divergence, like the previous episode, student articulations seemed to have little impact on the trajectory of the lesson.

The enacted conception of mathematics knowledge, similarly, is little different from the preceding account: math still seems to be about constructing associations between signifiers. If we examine the use of the chips, for example, while they served as a means of illustrating the concept at hand, it seems that that concept is still thought to be something that transcends such physical manipulation: mathematics exists independent of and prior to these sorts of representational experiences. This interpretation is supported by Wendy's comments during an interview, "Now that I see that every student's understanding is a little bit different, it makes teaching harder. . . . It makes it really hard to make sure that they get the right understanding."

There is an important change, however. In spite of the continuing sense that there are "true" and knower-independent mathematical forms, Wendy appears to have moved toward a conception of personal mathematical understanding as inevitably subjective and necessarily implicated in various aspects of the learners' existences. It is thus that she is more attentive to personal interpretations. The underlying sense of "curriculum," as manifested through the structure of the planned lesson, involves a more tentative traversing of the prespecified territory. While the learning objectives are still explicitly stated, Wendy is no longer attempting to specify every footfall of the path of learning.

Vignette 3: Hermeneutic Listening Wendy took a personal leave shortly after the teaching episode just discussed, and so the in-school component of this research was interrupted for several months. However, she and I continued to meet on a regular basis to discuss various issues surrounding her classroom practice. In particular, considerable time was devoted to the question, "What is mathematics?," centering the discussion around various popular texts.[5] While never arriving at any sort of definitive answers, the possibilities that mathematics is subject to change, that it is inscribed with particular social, gender, and political ideals, that some of its conventions are quite arbitrary, and that mathematics—appropriately or inappropriately—has permeated virtually every aspect of our lives served to disrupt much of what Wendy had brought to her teaching.

Midway through the year following the addition of integers lesson, the research in Wendy's classroom resumed. Once again, the topic of study was fractions, and the lesson from which the following vignette is drawn occurred two weeks into that unit. The sequence begins with the correcting of homework "questions" that were to be done using Fraction Kits (pieces of paper cut into halves, thirds, fourths, sixths, eighths, twelfths, and twenty-fourths).[6]

"Number one [writing $^1/_6 + {^3/_{12}} + {^2/_{24}}$]: one sixth plus three twelfths plus two twenty-fourths. How much is that . . . Elaine?"

"One half."

"Can you tell us how you got that?"

"I can draw it."

Wendy held out the chalk and Elaine came to the board to draw a picture of her arrangement of the pieces (see Figure 2.2). "It covers the same area as a half [piece]," she explained. "The sixth [piece] is as tall as a half [piece] and these three pieces [motioning across her diagram] are as wide as a half."

"So they're exactly the same size and shape as a half piece when you lay them out that way. Good. Did anybody get any other answers . . . Truong?"

"Six twelfths."

"Can you show us how you got that?"

"You can use that picture," Truong responded, pointing to Elaine's diagram. "You have three twelfths already; two twenty-fourths together is another twelfth, and the sixth can be cut into two twelfths. That's six twelfths altogether."

"Okay. Good answer. Any other answers? . . . Van?"

"Four eighths."

"Four eighths? How can you get four eighths using these pieces?"

"Easy," Van announced," rising to go to the chalkboard. "One fourth of a sixth plus one twenty-fourth plus a half of a twelfth is an eighth," drawing a dotted line across Elaine's diagram (see Figure 2.3).

"You do that twice, so you can trade that for two eighths. Then, across the bottom, you have one fourth of a sixth and two halves of twelfths, twice, so that's two more eighths," adding more dotted lines and then simplifying the diagram by erasing the unwanted marks.[7]

The lesson continued with an exploration of other possibilities, and students presented similar cases for other answers (which included $^{12}/_{24}$, $^{2}/_{4}$, *and 1.5 thirds). More than half of the 45-minute time block*

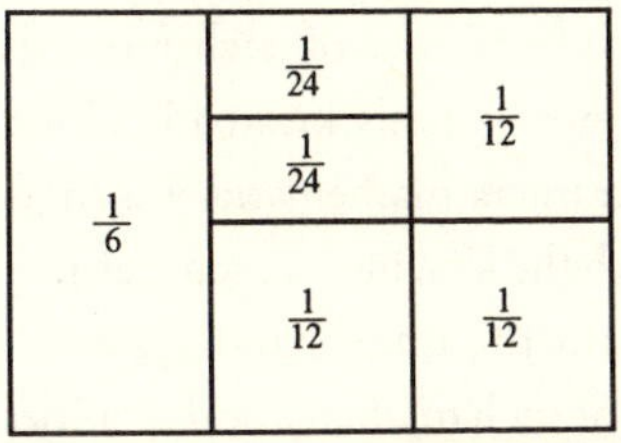

Figure 2.2. Elaine's diagram for $^{1}/_{6} + ^{3}/_{12} + ^{2}/_{24}$.

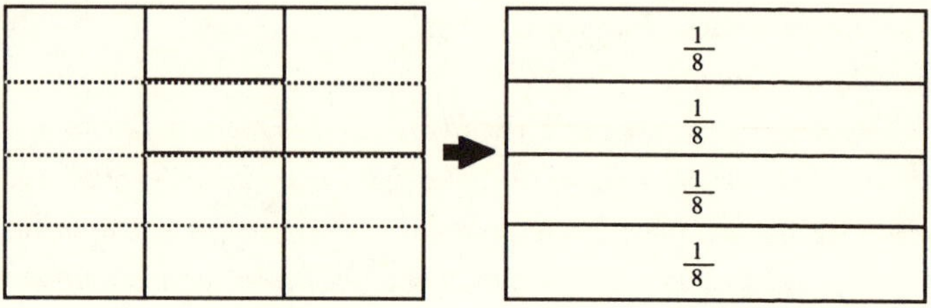

Figure 2.3. Van's diagram.

was taken up in reviewing the homework "questions." The remainder of class time was spent in group work on another, similar, set of addition exercises that were developed by the students themselves. Wendy gave the additional instruction that groups were to find several different answers for each question and to explain why those answers were correct.

There are some clear points of divergence from the previous lessons in this teaching episode—most notably perhaps, the absences of a clearly structured format and a set of prespecified learning outcomes. Following the framework presented in the preceding section, the sorts of activity that were occurring during this lesson might be described as *mathematical*, for the class members seemed to be jointly exploring a mathematical issue rather than attempting to master already formulated bits of knowledge (as is the case for *mathematics*). Put differently, the subject matter in the first two teaching episodes was drawn from established or "front-end" mathematics, and the mathematics concepts were treated as though they had some sort of material and transcendent existence, independent of learners and their experience. Some consequences of this conception become evident when Wendy's use of the BINGO chips in the second teaching episode is contrasted with the use of the Fraction Kits in the third vignette. The chips were largely illustrative and, hence, not considered to be part of the concept under study. The opposite was true for the Fraction Kits (as indicated by students' uses of such terms as "cover," "cut," and "trade" which cannot be tidily located in either mental or physical realms). There the learners' mathematics was thoroughly tied up in their experiences with the kits, just as each learner's understandings were intertwined with the understandings of all others present. Further, the interplay of such mathematical qualities as free creation-and-deduction and individuality-and-generality—

along with a host of mathematical activities, including counting, locating, designing, playing, and explaining—are enacted here.

Knowledge and understanding, in this frame, cannot be thought of in strictly subjective terms; the collective knowledge and individual understandings are dynamically co-emergent phenomena. In response to the question, Where is the mathematics?, one might thus say that it is located in the activity—or, perhaps more descriptively, in the interactivity—of learners. As the events of the lesson are retraced, it becomes apparent that it was not so much the possibility for individual action as it was the opportunity for interaction that contributed to the flow of the mathematics.

Importantly, while there appears to be a joint or collective project in the lesson, not everyone is working on the same problem. Because the Fraction Kits setting is variable-entry (i.e., learners are able to adjust tasks to their own level of difficulty—as indicated by the range of responses given in the brief vignette), learners have been able to negotiate their own problems and modes of responding, thus freeing the teacher from the unrealizable demand of setting appropriate tasks for thirty learners whose abilities, backgrounds, and interests inevitably vary dramatically.

In sum, in contrasting this episode with the two preceding episodes, it is tempting to suggest that the differences are all a matter of greater fluidity. The rigid structure, the preset goals, the formulated explanations, the entrenched roles have all been dissolved to some extent as the unanticipated, the surprising, and the intuitive find places for expression. The mode of teaching thus seems to be more a matter of flexible response to ever-changing circumstances than of unyielding progress toward imposed goals. The importance of listening in enabling the teacher's ability to respond is evident.

It is thus that I would characterize Wendy's mode of listening in this episode as "hermeneutic," as evidenced in the negotiated and participatory manner of her interactions with learners. The "subject matter" of the setting is not a detached, objective mathematics, but a dynamic form in which all present are implicated. Mathematics—that is, the body of knowledge that we call mathematics—is different for this event having occurred. There are senses in this setting, albeit enacted and unformulated, of dynamic interdependence of agent and setting, thought and action, knowledge and knower, self and other, individual and collective. The focus in this classroom is not on particular mathematics concepts, nor on particular learners' conceptions, but on the possibility of mathematical (and hermeneutic) interpretation whereby interpreter, interpreted, and mode of interpretation are all simultaneously presented, all simultaneously affected.

This is not to say that Wendy has somehow abdicated what are normally regarded as the teacher's responsibilities (vis-à-vis curriculum guidelines). In fact, her students' demonstrated understandings indicate quite the opposite. What seems to have been abandoned is the belief that teaching is a matter of causing learners to acquire, master, or construct particular understandings through some pre-established (and often learner-independent) instructional sequence. In this case, learning is a social process and the teacher's role is one of participating, of interpreting, of transforming, of interrogating—in short, of hermeneutic listening.

From Teacher Preparation to Preparing for Teaching

There are at least two problems with presenting, as I have, three snapshot images which are intended to indicate a transition over time. First, I risk deflecting readers' expectations toward an account of what might have precipitated the noted transformations—a digression that is somewhat at odds with the announced intention of exploring the relationship between one's conception of mathematics and one's style of teaching. Second, one might be left with the impression that each of the episodes represents a distinct phase in a teacher's development. However, there were no clear "phases" in Wendy's teaching; all change appeared to be gradual—of the sort that goes unnoticed until one episode is contrasted with another, sufficiently distanced, event. Any effort, then, to chart such transformations must be presented as a side-note and involves considerable conjecture, included because some important issues regarding teacher education and ongoing development seem to have been raised.

With regard to my collaboration with Wendy, it is tempting to focus on particular events in our discussions (or during some other aspect of the research) and argue that *this* suggestion or insight *caused that* action or response. This sort of account would commit the error of "confusing essential participation with unique responsibility."[8] In an attempt to avoid suggesting such cause-effect relationships, I identify the four happenings as important watersheds in the evolution of Wendy's enacted conception of mathematics teaching: (1) the presence of an interpretive community; (2) an engagement with the issue of the nature of mathematics; (3) the practical exercise of working through various theoretical ideas in considering the possibilities for teaching; and (4) an occasion of actually *doing mathematics* (in the sense described in the preceding section). The following brief discussions of these happenings are intended to highlight important moments in our interactions; I leave it to the reader to determine their applicability in other contexts.

A first key element in the evolution of Wendy's teaching seems to have been the presence of an interested colleague who was willing to offer support and assistance and able to disrupt some of what was being taken for granted (with regard to, for example, conceptions of the subject matter, learning processes, and teaching practices). With time pressures and professional obligations, there is normally very little space for such community in a teacher's life. Like mathematics, the social phenomenon of teaching seems to have become a solitary activity within the fragmented and fragmenting modern school.

It is thus very significant that Wendy took a personal leave in the midst of this research. Several months away from the busyness and the demands of the classroom afforded us an opportunity to delve into issues which, quite simply, she would never have had the time or energy (and perhaps not even the interest or inclination) to address otherwise. There is no doubt that the separation from the immediate responsibilities and the constraints—the "realities"—of the classroom allowed us to be somewhat more free-ranging in our thinking. (This separation, however, also served to limit our discussions and conversations as it demanded that knowledge be considered apart from the particular knowers. We thus found ourselves continuously resisting the tendency to speak of the ubiquitous and generic—and therefore nonexistent—"student." Nevertheless, we were firm in our conviction that, even if one could not predetermine the path that would ultimately be taken, the teacher could not abdicate the responsibility to point to particular aspects of the world. Positioned between the learner and society, the teacher has a primary responsibility in shaping the occasions for learning—a responsibility, demanding a response-ability, that moves in both directions. Put differently, the task of exploring teaching ideas—whether in the learners' presence or in their absence—has the effect of broadening the possibilities for teaching responsively. In particular, with reference to the notion of teaching as listening, such planning tasks compel the teacher to consider not just the classroom activities, but a range of student responses. The teacher is thus loosening up or expanding the prejudices that constrain his or her listening. The possibilities for his or her attentiveness and responsiveness are correspondingly enabled.)

The importance of establishing some distance from the immediate demands of teaching was most evident in our discussions and conversations of the nature of mathematical knowledge. Typical of many teachers (including myself until only very recently), Wendy had not previously thought to look beyond the curriculum guides or her own schooling for an understanding of mathematics. Not surprisingly, then, when I first visited her classroom, hers was a "textbook" approach to mathematics teaching. She was thus somewhat taken aback when first presented with the possibilities that mathematical knowledge might be incomplete, dynamic, fallible, and not universally or objectively true. One of Wendy's comments, made early in our reading of John Barrow's *Pi in the Sky*, is telling:

I read this and I worry. If math isn't out there . . . if it isn't "true," then I've been completely wrong in the way I've been teaching it. And I wonder about the ways I was taught too.

While we were discussing this topic we were also exploring its implications for teaching through the development of a unit of study (as discussed below). As that project progressed, Wendy gradually moved away from teaching the mathematical concepts as items for mastery. Instead, she began to approach them as locations for exploration: Why are these classification schemes used? What happens if that assumption is dropped? How has geometry contributed to the shape of our living environment? And vice versa? Why are these topics worthy of study? And, more practically: Recognizing the cultural, governmental, and institutional constraints that had to be negotiated, what sorts of lessons could one prepare that would be informed by recent philosophical developments and yet remain viable in the given setting? And how does one go about planning for such lessons?

Although never coming to any conclusive formulations, Wendy and I did develop some preliminary answers to these and other questions, most of which are reflected in the various discussions of this text. The question of how one goes about planning for teaching turned out to be the most straightforward, with some "guidelines" for such activities falling out of our own mathematical "doing." In attempting to identify potential mathematical settings and activities for students, we found ourselves immersed in the process of inquiry. And, while we developed nothing that hasn't already been put forward in other contexts, we were certainly setting our own problems and contriving our own means of solving them—in effect producing new (to us) mathematics.

The significance of the event should not be left understated. Wendy's remark, "I've never done math like this before," voiced in the midst of our mathematizing, signaled an important transition in her own conception of what it means to do mathematics—a transition that was soon to be reflected in her teaching. Given this event, and others like it to which I have been party, I would hazard to suggest that one of the greatest weaknesses of current mathematics pedagogy is that teachers, in general, have not been adequately engaged in mathematical inquiry in their own educations. Unlike virtually every other area of activity and study—music, athletics, literature, etc.—it is difficult to identify another where a teacher could successfully fulfill his or her responsibilities with such a desolate history of participating in the subject matter. At the risk of stating the case too strongly, I would contend that an important part of the preparation and ongoing development of mathematics teachers is the continued engagement in such inquiry . . . and, given that it can be accomplished in the context of planning lessons and working with learners, such involvement seems well within the realm of the possible.

An interesting side-note, and one that pertains to both the matter of our mathematical activities and the significance of an interpretive community, is that, of the many pages of records and field notes that were assembled over our lengthy collaboration, it was the interactions on the topic of the nature of mathematics (and on the companion project of planning for teaching) that were the most difficult to transcribe. They lacked the I-speak-then-you-speak structure of most of our discussions. Instead, they were filled with interruptions, pauses, incomplete thoughts, exclamations, laughter. In short, they were conversations, and they thus resisted the flattening process of transcription. Unlike many of the other recorded interactions, the tone of these conversations was not what-I-think; what-you-think, but more toward what-we-think. The ideas were thus neither hers nor mine, but ours. (Significantly, this same sort of comment could be made of the third teaching episode, as contrasted with the other two.)

In these conversations we also, I would contend, set a foundation for a "community of professionals" of a sort that is conspicuously (and tragically) absent in most "educational" settings. Lacking such a community, a teacher might understandably not be enthusiastic about departing from "what works"—falling back on planning outcomes rather than anticipating possibilities—for they have no interactive model on which to found their teaching. It is doubtful that the same richness of ideas would have come about were Wendy and I to have independently undertaken the task of planning. Within the forum we created, we simultaneously anticipated learner actions and enacted the very model of teaching and learning that we hoped could later be brought to life in the classroom. In effect, the multi-layered, self-similar, recursive, and negotiatory natures of teaching and learning were revealed in this rather ordinary (as we perceived it at the time) event.

Introductory Geometry

The goal that Wendy and I set for ourselves was thus to identify and develop some teaching ideas for a given unit of study—in this case, introductory geometry. Our hope was that these ideas, when appropriately revised for introduction to a particular group of learners, would support a model of classroom mathematics that foregrounded the *mathematical* while avoiding the modern tendency to sever knowledge from action, interaction, and context. It was thus necessary to consider how one might approach a collection of concepts in a way that would do more than simply sidestep the problems of fragmentation and absolutism; we wanted to create the sorts of conditions that would challenge and disarm the expectations of "math" and "math class" that would likely precede a group of school-weary adolescents into the classroom.

Wendy chose the topic of geometry, prompted in part by her feelings of dissatisfaction with previous teaching efforts in that unit. She was also concerned that her own knowledge of the area did not extend far enough beyond the contents of the approved textbook. These issues will be taken up in the next chapter.

Although it did not figure into her selection, the topic of introductory geometry proved to be an ideal one, in part because the strand of geometry runs clearly and distinctly through the history of mathematics. It was a prominent area of inquiry for most, if not all, ancient civilizations. It also served as the centerpiece for the mathematics of ancient Greece and, as such, heralded the rise of formalist mathematics. Indeed, it was this *geometria* on which Descartes founded his rationalist program. And it was the introduction of non-Euclidian geometries that first hinted that mathematics need not be constrained by intuition, thus prompting the hyper-formalist project. More recently, nonlinear dynamics and chaos theory—central movements affecting the emerging shape of our postformalist conception of mathematics—rely heavily on "fractal geometry," a geometry that "mirrors a universe that is rough, not rounded, scabrous, not smooth,"[9] to break from the modernist ways of thinking.

Geometry has also figured prominently in various incarnations of school mathematics, and the topic has actually been identified as the "problem child of the mathematics curriculum."[10] Much of the debate surrounding topic area arises from our general inability to resolve the issues of, first, what geometry is, and second, why we should study it. It is thus that, as curriculum changes have been proposed and implemented, the face of geometry has altered dramatically and its revised images have reflected the shifts in our thinking about mathematics and education. For example, the changes that occurred in formal curriculum during the early 1960s, popularly known as the "new math," could be accurately illustrated with a brief description of the increased emphasis on formal geometric proof. More recently, some mathematics educators have recommended that learners be introduced to a few ideas from fractal geometry, a change that could have profound implications not just for mathematics teaching, but for the prevailing conception of mathematics.

It probably won't come as much of a surprise, then, that a reinterpretation of geometry figures prominently into the conceptions of mathematics and mathematics education underlying this document. At the risk of sounding overly "romantic," I would note that, in its very title, *geometry* still echoes the name of *Gaia*, calling us back to the earth, to the source of our being, to the genesis of our knowledge. Further, through *metron* (a Greek word from which *meter*, *measurement*, and *mensuration* are derived), there is a re-membering of our body. All of our base measurement units (for length, area, volume/capacity, weight/mass, temperature, and time) are in bodily scale—and some of them (most obviously, the *foot*) are derived explicitly from body parts, capacities, functions, or needs. Most systems of measurement, it seems, began with the body and moved outward to the not-body, the objects of one's world. (Within the metric system, apart from the base of ten, the relationships between our units of measure and the body are distanced by several layers of abstraction. The base units, although still in scale to our bodies, are defined against "external" objects—yet another instance of modern mathematics pushing the experiencing body into the background.) "Measurement," then, particularly for young learners, might be thought of as a collection of activities that takes us back to the body. It is thus tempting to suggest that mathematics did not begin with number, but with measuring . . . or, more precisely, with geo-metry—that is, with comparing one's body to the objects of one's world, an activity that might be argued to precede (or, at least, to implicate) such competencies as numeration, fractionation, rationation, and logical thought.

Geometry, then, is not merely earth-measurement; it might be thought of as a pressing of one's body (*metron*) against the living world (*Gaia*). And so, in its remotest origins, geometry was, perhaps, an exemplar of ecological thought. Rising out of the efforts of our ancestors to, quite literally, measure the earth, one can envision those earliest mathematicians on their hands and knees—ears pressed to the ground, as it were—coaxing secrets from the living Earth.

Curriculum Anticipating

Wendy's and my joint project of "curriculum anticipating" (versus the narrowing process of "curriculum planning") served to familiarize us with some of the possibilities for the teaching of an introductory geometry unit while it presented an opportunity to enact an ecologically minded model of teaching and learning. Our investigations were motivated by sincere interests and oriented by particular questions. We were not seeking *the* truth, *the* answer, or *the* way; the goal was to understand more deeply an issue that we held between us. As such, the talk ranged widely: we brought in what we knew and did not know of history, philosophy, and mathematics; we compared teaching and learning experiences; and, most importantly, we created a forum in which to reinterpret what we already knew. Put more formally, the conditions necessary for a hermeneutic inquiry were established, leading naturally (although still demanding considerable discipline and effort) to back-and-forth movements between our conceptions and the web from which those conceptions arose and between the particularity of our teaching practice and the social context in which that practice occurs. The effect of this aspect of the research, not surprisingly, was that more questions were raised than were answered. This consequence was not a negative one, however, for it instilled a thoughtfulness—that is, it prevented a thoughtlessness that springs from certainty—that deepened the interactions rather than disabled them.

It was for the express purpose of anticipating possibilities for teaching that we entered into this aspect of the research. Underlying our conversations was the assumption that the teacher has a responsibility to carefully think through what might happen and to make particular decisions as to the possible shapes of lessons. It is thus that, contra the conventional emphasis on planning (which is guided by a desire to control all aspects of the learning setting), I have elected to use the term "anticipating" to draw attention to our hope to prompt rather than to prescribe appropriate action. The shift in orientation has two important effects. First, as already elaborated, it enables one's listening as it widens the range of one's hearing. Second, by creating a sense of direction and a feel for the territory to be covered, it helps to promote a sense of when to let things diverge and when to redirect action. In effect, they serve to open a space in which to learn from what the learners are doing and, from there, to select what might be done next. To repeat, such anticipating activities enable the teacher's response-ability while not permitting an abdication of his or her responsibility.

A brief account of the process of our anticipating will help to set the stage for the "plan" that we eventually prepared. The activity occupied several meetings, arising out of and occurring alongside our ongoing explorations of the nature of mathematical knowledge. After deciding to translate some of the concepts we were investigating into classroom ideas, we began by reporting to one another some of our past teaching and learning experiences. To our initial surprise, there was considerable correspondence between our histories, and the many "coincidences" quickly became the targets of our analysis as we began to interrogate the taken-for-granted notions that we had brought to our respective professional practices. Key issues that arose in these pre-anticipating moments included the roles of textbooks and resource manuals (which had been central to both our geometry units) and—as topics of relevance and interest arose—the rather daunting question of why we were bothering to teach the subject matter in the first place.

This latter issue proved to be quite troublesome for us. With our extensive histories of justifying particular topics and tasks in terms of their future value—that is, of deeming particular activities worthy because of uninterrogated beliefs that they will contribute to future mathematics learning, or that they will at some point be of use in "real life," or that they will eventually promote thinking skills—it was difficult for us to think of developing activities that were not principally founded on that sort of deferment.

It was at this stage that the ideas of considering the *mathematical* (rather than concentrating solely on the *mathematics*) and of endeavoring to present a subject matter that was about (and not apart from) learners came up. Our orientation as we began our anticipating activities might thus be expressed by the question, How might geometry help learners to better understand their worlds? Or, phrased in a way that makes more explicit reference to the teacher, What occasions could be presented that might prompt learners to act so that their mathematical perceptions and patterns of acting—their structures—are broadened and enabled?

We set off by gathering ideas through exploring curriculum-support documents, inviting others to participate, and jotting down things that came to mind. We soon had a collection of possibilities to begin "playing around" with. At one point, for example, a pile of rulers, compasses, protractors, string, roadmaps, and paper polygons—among other items—was stacked between us.[11] There we tested out ideas, guessed what sorts of things might happen, and tried to articulate the necessary preconditions for such events. We then selected activities and made a tentative outline (see Table 2.1) of the teaching ideas along with the content those ideas might support. Having chosen the sorts of spaces that we thought might foster the development of rich repertoires of experience and common action among learners, we then sought to draw out of our own "playing" the elements of the mathematical that seemed to be announced by these activities.

Throughout these explorations, we endeavored to leave as much space for movement as possible, electing to give only brief orienting descriptions rather than detailed mappings. The extent of our investigations is thus not at all represented in the conciseness of the "unit plan." Simply put, we worried that greater detail might prompt us to reenact the scripts of our explorative activities—an effort that would, in effect, narrow the prejudices we had struggled to broaden.

Further, we felt the sparse detail would compel us to reanticipate possibilities as the event of teaching approached. This must be a continuing act, preceding, accompanying, and following the introduction of any learning activity. This ongoing attentiveness is essentially a listening to (that is, a participation in and an interrogation of) the mathematics of the setting.

Necessary but Not Sufficient

Curriculum anticipating is thus a necessary—but far from sufficient—condition to enacting a listening orientation to teaching. The teacher is able to consider how particular ideas are connected to other concepts, to bodily experience, to the community of knowers, to the relational world in which it is constituted—in short, to create a basis for an ecologically sound mode of teaching.

But such preparation inevitably falls far short of the ideals set out in the preceding parts of this chapter. The teaching ideas remain

Table 2.1. *An Overview of Some Curriculum Anticipating*

Activity	Possible Content	Rationale/ Underlying Concepts
1. Bag of Shapes Students are given a bag filled with various polygons. They are asked to devise various means of classification.	• various means of classification; • reasons for classification; • development of various skills (angle and linear measurement, property noticing); • (possibly constructing and using a stretch protractor to compare and measure angles).	Mathematics involves • *abstraction* (i.e., extraction, reduction, and simplification—focusing on a particular trait to the exclusion of others); • *classification*; • *naming* (i.e., we classify to make things simpler. The precise classification scheme is often a matter of convenience. Conversely, technical names may encode the conceptual framework in which we organize things).
2. Triangles The triangles are separated out of the *Bag of Shapes* for further examination.	• property noticing: a) properties of all triangles (e.g., sum of angles, etc.), b) classes of triangles (e.g., classifying by sides, by angles, by symmetry, etc.); • skills: - measuring angles and sides; • constructing (other triangles are constructed looking for more properties. May be a nice segue to quadrilaterals—two congruent triangles make a parallelogram).	• *generalization* (i.e., we abstract in order to generalize and predict. Certain properties are common to all Euclidian triangles, other properties can be used to distinguish among triangles); • *standardization* (i.e., the importance of establishing a set of common terms to refer to the units, properties, or categories that are developed).
3. Quadrilaterals As with triangles, the focus shifts to examining quadrilaterals.	• property noticing: a) properties of all quadrilaterals (e.g., sum of angles, etc.), b) classes of quadrilaterals (e.g., classifying by sides, angles, symmetry, diagonals, etc.); • skills: - measuring sides and angles; • construction (other quadrilaterals are constructed looking for more properties. May want to return to idea that a quadrilateral is two triangles, because subsequent polygons with n sides can be constructed using $n-2$ triangles).	• *symbolization* (i.e., our ability to express our ideas in symbols allows us to operate on those representations, enabling us to move to other levels of abstraction); • *power* (i.e., if our abstracting and generalizing were appropriate, we can begin to make fairly powerful predictions about other related topics/ shapes/concepts); • *elegance* (i.e., some ideas are simple, yet powerful. Mathematicians tend to prefer these ideas).
4. Polygons The exploration of triangles and quadrilaterals is broadened to include other polygons.	• property noticing; • constructions with ruler, protractor, and compass.	• *aesthetics* (i.e., mathematics has long been associated with beauty—principles and products alike).

Table 2.1. *An Overview of Some Curriculum Anticipating (continued)*

5. Roadmaps Start with identifying triangles, quadrilaterals and other polygons on the map. Then move more specifically to angles formed by turning corners (turning left versus turning right [supplementary], the sum of the angles when turning around and going the other way [supplementary again], the sum when turning all the way around, the sum when turning twice to change directions, etc.). Then move to parallel lines and transversals (which can be seen to be producing the polygons under study).	• further property noticing; • using grids (first quadrant, where street number gives *x* coordinate and avenue number gives *y* coordinate); • applying knowledge of polygons by identifying them on the map (IDEA: If you start from some point, go somewhere, and come back on a different route, you've traced out a polygon: a CLOSED figure with STRAIGHT sides); • supplementary and complementary angles; • F, C, Z, and X angles[12]—and maybe others—as useful ideas for studying shapes, etc. (i.e., means and not ends); • using angle relationships to predict, calculate, and justify other angles; • "least number of angles" questions (i.e., given a complex figure, what is the minimum number of angle measurements so that all the angles can be determined?); • naming angles—the three ways (interior, point, 3-point)—when and why would each method be used?	Math principles are extracted from our experiences. They are useful not only because we can use them to generalize about experiences we've had, but because we can use them to predict future actions (What angle will we have to turn?) and to structure or arrange our world (as in the way we set out our cities). Many mathematical ideas are simply conventions that people have agreed on. These include the terms used to refer to pairs of angles, the way we name angles, etc.
6. Complicated Questions Devise hard questions. For example: First on the roadmap and then on a separate piece of paper where you draw the lines, develop questions where certain measurements (angles and otherwise) are missing. Then set questions for classmates such as: • What's the least number of points needed to name all the angles? • What are the missing measurements? • If this angle changed, what would happen to that one?	• problem solving; • applying understandings and skills.	Much (most?) of mathematical inquiry involves identifying problems and attempting to solve them. Through this process, new ideas are developed, which are used to work on even harder problems. Another essential element of mathematical inquiry is *justification.* While not asking for formal proofs, it's important to foster a sense of the sequence of reasoning involved here.

largely confined to the mathematics classroom, physically separated both from the "real" world and from other disciplines. Its possibilities for promoting understandings of the pervasive shaping force of mathematics within our culture are thus similarly constrained. Also at risk are the desired ends: developing a critical awareness of the consequences of the application of one's mathematics and promoting a certain wisdom toward such application.

On the other side of the issue, however, I'm not sure we should even attempt to write these things into a proposal for teaching, for the mathematics can only present a context for the possible exploration of the mathematical (and other epistemological and ontological concerns). I believe that we must bear in mind that, as Madeleine Grumet points out, curriculum is a "moving form," and so:

That is why we have trouble capturing it, fixing it in language, lodging it in our matrix. Whether we talk about it as history, as syllabi, as classroom discourse, as intended learning outcomes, or as experience, we are trying to grasp a moving form, to catch it at the moment that it slides from being the figure, the object and goal of action, and collapses into the ground of action.[13]

It is not easy for us to talk about moving forms and dynamic structures; it seems that it is the nature of our language (and perhaps of languaging, in general) to freeze, to fix, to isolate, and to present one-word-after-the-other a thread of some interpretation of the world. The same fixing tendencies are evident in our planning. It is only in the actual teaching—a phenomenon that remains to be investigated—that the subject matter, that the living body of knowledge, actually comes into existence.

Some Anticipating

A summary of some of the ideas that Wendy and I explored is presented in Table 2.1. Given the preceding discussion, I am not going to elaborate on the chart's contents other than to direct the reader's attention to the third column. On the surface, the activities that are described in the first column (and the corresponding formal curriculum objectives that might be addressed during these activities, as presented in the second column) would appear familiar and unremarkable to an experienced mathematics educator, although they may mark a dramatic departure from a textbook-based program. (This observation is an important one: to recast mathematics teaching in an enactivist frame does not demand another round of curriculum revision.)

But it is the emphasis on the mathematical, as outlined in the third column, that signals the difference between this and more traditional program emphases, for the focus in teaching is shifted from "this is what you must know" (i.e., column two) to "this is what it means to think mathematically." As such, mandated objectives become incidental and serve merely to proscribe the lesson setting.

The status of the third column might appear somewhat ambiguous. By including it, I do not mean to suggest that these things should be taught directly, nor even that the teacher should try to steer the activities in a direction that would "make them fit." Rather, these ideas are intended as a persistent reminder that the mathematics content, while interesting, should not be construed as the end point to learning. In simple terms, if all we learn about angles is how to identify them, we miss the whole point.

Additionally, it must be noted that the chart's contents are not intended to represent a linear progression, nor to prescribe everything that is to be done. In fact, it is unlikely that all (or even most) of these activities would be undertaken, and even more unlikely that the presented sequence would be maintained. It may well be, for example, that the introductory activities serve as a basis to address all of the noted issues; alternatively, some entirely unanticipated event may render these ideas unnecessary. There is no predicting what ideas will come up, what interests will emerge, what insights will arise. This "plan" is thus best thought of as a series of possible prompts or nudges to encourage movement through a mathematical space. It is not a scheme to be implemented, but a series of possible entry points for teaching action. It is, then, merely a starting place for a continuous process of anticipating; it is more along the lines of a strategy for an as yet unplayed game than an algorithm for reaching a particular destination. It is a way of stepping into the current of a curriculum.

In this conception, this unit outline merely marks some places where learning might happen.

Chapter 3

Stood on One's Ear

The Educational Endeavor

There is a powerful Australian aboriginal belief that everywhere you walk, you walk where others have walked before you, but also that as you walk, you are leaving your footprints for others to walk in. This resonant image speaks of continuity and community, of chains linking past to future through ourselves. It accompanies a belief in the importance of the naming of the dead, and trusting the power of language both to carry the culture and to allow us to recreate it continually while investing the storied events and forms with new meanings and significance.

—*David Pimm*[1]

That is what education is—the continual "challenge of rethinking Everything." . . The new challenge becomes an exploration of self, a quest for a beginning, and, in my personal case with this class, how to communicate—how to listen to each other, comprehend each other, understand each other.

—*Hannah Merker*[2]

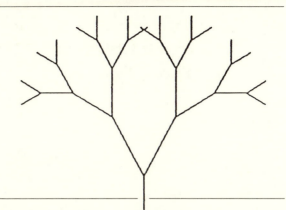

Section A
Culture Making
The Place of Education

Teach your children what we have taught our children—that the earth is our mother. . . . Man does not weave the web of life; he is merely a strand in it. Whatever he does to the web, he does to himself.

—*Chief Seattle*[3]

It is necessary to strain one's ears, bending down toward this muttering of the world, trying to perceive the many images that have never turned into poetry, so many phantasms that have never reached the color of wakefulness.

—*Michel Foucault*[4]

If the space of curriculum is between our collective knowledge and the knowledge of the learner, then education is situated between the society and the child, between the actual and the possible, between certainty and chaos, between past and future.

Education exists and consists in such relational spaces. They are not difficult to identify; as teachers and learners, we continuously negotiate them. But it is quite another matter to point out the boundaries that mark the *place* of education within these spaces.

Such is my present task. In this section I begin to develop an enactivist response to the question, Why educate? I commence with a brief tour through some prominent orientations (political, theoretical, and personal) to formal education and to schooling. Following the pattern already established, this exploration involves a critical investigation of a range of modern conceptions, and is followed by an examination of an alternative that is derived from (and through which I take the opportunity to further develop) pragmatist, ecological, enactivist, and hermeneutic notions.

But first, an elaboration. In the previous chapter, I tended to use the word "pointing" to describe the curriculum-maker's task of orienting the learner's attention toward particular aspects of our culture. In this discussion of education, as I move closer to the vibrancy of an actual classroom, I am compelled to replace the passive detachment of pointing with the active engagement of interpreting, for, in standing between, in selecting *this* and not *that*, the educator does more than merely direct. The teacher inserts himself or herself into the events—the places—of education.

Notes on "Places" and "Boundaries"

As might be gathered from the titles of its sections, this chapter is framed in terms of "place"—a notion that, in Western societies at least, implies the drawing of boundaries. True to the modern tradition, we unproblematically separate one location from another, all in an effort to put and to keep things—persons, objects, and events—tidily where they belong.

What is it that makes a place a place?

The answer to this question is simple if one chooses to define "place" formally. It is a location in space, a fixed point (or collection of points) in a given domain. In the most uncritical terms, as evidenced by the phrase "Person, place or thing?" a place is an object, not dissimilar from Cartesian conceptions of objectified personal identity.

This very modern definition of place reveals the influence of one of Descartes' major contributions to contemporary thought and formal mathematics: the Cartesian coordinate system, by which each point in a space is defined in terms of its location relative to an arbitrarily positioned set of axes. This system of *placing* places cuts up a territory with complete disregard for the surface features, the events, and the relationships that are associated with it. Room numbers, city addresses, roadmaps, and schedules are often presented in Cartesian or quasi-Cartesian forms.

But while these coordinates might help us to locate places quickly and accurately, they reveal nothing about the places themselves. In fact, they make places placeless—devoid of the experiential qualities and features that distinguish them. As David Orr points out:

> *[M]uch of Western history has conspired to make our places invisible and therefore inaccessible to us. In contrast to "dis-placed" people who are physically removed from their homes but who retain the idea of place and home, we have become "de-placed" people, mental refugees, homeless wherever we are.*[5]

It seems, then, that place is more than mere location; in fact, such locating usually occurs only after a place has become a place. Only then are we concerned with exactly where it is. So what is it that brings a place into being?

Again, we tend to have ready answers. A place, for example, may be defined according to its topographic features: some places include "the river valley" and "the education building." Or it may be identified by the sorts of activities that it sponsors (or for which it was intended), or by the sorts of people who gather there.

However, from an enactivist position, each of these means of characterizing a place is inadequate for the purpose of understanding what a place might be. The placeness of a place is never merely a singular matter of physical features or social activities. Rather, such qualities are co-implicated: the topography of a place selects and shapes the actions and relationships that occur there; inversely, in *taking* place, these activities and relationships shape their landscape. We and the places we find ourselves co-emerge; we inhabit and enhabit one another.

One etymology of *place* suggests that the word originally meant "the sole of the foot." A *place*, in other words, was that part of the body that touched the earth. In the moment of contact, the ground conforms to the foot just as the bottom of the foot molds itself to the contours of the surface. Occupant and occupied take shape simultaneously. In other words, we are part of the places we occupy, just as these places are part of us. This point is powerfully illustrated by the way we describe ourselves, for these descriptions invariably make reference to particular places—to nations, to hometowns, to classrooms, to relationships. Moreover, we tend to implicate our own identities in our descriptions of familiar places. (It is thus that we find ourselves feeling violated when a childhood playground is destroyed or a favorite river is polluted.) We do not define places; they do not define us. Rather, in dynamic interplay, we come to form together.

An inquiry into the place of education and of teaching, then, is not merely an exercise in identifying the location assigned by society, for education and teaching are active in shaping their own landscapes. Their places cannot be reduced to statements of purpose, descriptions of role, or delineations of demographics (as many modern efforts would have it). They are, rather, dynamic and autopoietic (that is, self-shaping and self-maintaining) within a cultural setting, just as they are contained and shaped by that setting. As I explore the places of education and teaching, then, I am not attempting to fix them spatially, temporally, or socially. Rather, I am seeking out where they place us as I explore where they are placed and where they take place.

To state this goal in different terms, this study of the place of formal education might also be thought of in terms of an exploration of its boundaries—where, like place, boundaries are thought of as fluid, dialogic, evolving. By calling attention to the edges that separate *this* from *that*, we can come to a deeper appreciation of the inextricable intertwining of both the identity of the object of study and the background out of which that identity is carved. Dennis Sumara[6] frames this idea in terms of the us/not-us relationship, whereby he points to the shifting boundary between (and the simultaneous definition of) the figure of "us" and the ground of "not-us."

To tie this notion to an idea mentioned earlier, it seems that one of the reasons we have difficulty accepting the possibility that boundaries are unfixable—and that, for example, even our selves are not self-contained—has to do with our predisposition toward defining objects and phenomena according to Aristotle's axioms of logic: *A* cannot be both *B* and *not-B* (the Law of Contradiction) and *A* must be either *B* or *not-B* (the Law of the Excluded Middle). However, recent developments in mathematics, such as fuzzy logic and complexity theory, have suggested that it is important to blur and complexify the constructed boundaries between *B* and *not-B*, just as identity theorists have blurred the distinction between *self* and *not-self.* This is not to say that such boundaries should not be drawn. Rather, they cannot be fixed.

I begin this exploration of places and boundaries with the premise that our system of education is an integral part of our culture, shaping not just individuals but the collective psyche. As such, it is a profoundly moral endeavor, and so we dare not consider its place with the indifference and detachment of a (Des)cartographer.

(Mathematics) Education—Some Perspectives

To educate is to engage in an intentional activity—one that is directed toward some already-anticipated end. This end varies according to one's perspectives on knowledge, one's ideology, one's social group, and a host of other factors ranging from the subtle to the imposing.

Given the multi-textured surface of our own society, it is to be expected that there are profound disagreements among persons regarding the role of education (and, correspondingly, on such issues as the structure of the schooling system, the approach to instruction, and the nature of the teacher-student relationship). And, given the pervasiveness of modern (rationalist and empiricist) orientations to dealing with the world, it is not surprising that the predominant perspectives on education tend to be framed in terms of either "the progress of society" or "the good of the child."

Paul Ernest[7] provides a clear illustration of this point. In a brief survey of various educational ideologies he attempts to identify the perspectives on mathematical knowledge, moral values, society, the child, and other facets of the educational endeavor that, to his analysis, are aligned with each of the prominent orientations. Because his examination serves as a cogent example of not just a modernist analysis (i.e., one that, in the end, is founded on Cartesian assumptions), but of the spectrum of modernist views, I will use it as the springboard for my own interpretations.

Directing his account at the British context (but not irrelevant to our own), Ernest begins by tracing the development of the currently dominant *Industrial Trainer* and *Technological Pragmatist* orientations to education, suggesting that formal schooling has for some time now been controlled by the interests of industry and technology. Emerging from the demands brought on by the Industrial Revolution (and, more recently, the technological revolution of this "computer age"), society had need of disciplined, trained workers who would accept their place in the social hierarchy. Mathematical knowledge, in this radically conservative account, is valued for its utility rather than its truthfulness or its transformative potential. For the purposes of educating the populace, then, mathematics (like most other subject areas) is regarded as an unquestioned body of knowledge that is taught because of its usefulness for the technically literate worker. With a guiding metaphor of mathematics as a set of tools, the focus of instruction is on basic facts and rules. Exposition, repetition, and drill are at the core of the preferred teaching method.

Associating mathematical competence with the enabling of technology, this orientation to education underlies the oft-heard calls for "back-to-the-basics," supporting the belief that, in times of restraint, "unnecessary" courses such as music and art should be the first ones cut. The technical orientation has also given impetus to the increasingly popular practice of international comparison testing—a practice whose justification rests on the unquestioned, and certainly unproven, assumption that there exists a direct link between economic potential and instrumental mathematics competency.

Ernest contrasts this perspective with the more liberal attitudes of the *Progressive Educator*[8] who holds a more person-centered view of education. In place of the technologist's authoritarian and practical emphases, progressive educators advocate a more nurturing relationship with the child. Mathematics, as with the other disciplines, is seen as a means of promoting creativity and self-realization. It thus continues to be viewed as neutral knowledge, although its absolute nature is abandoned in favor of a more personal, subjective account of knowing. Privileging the relativistic ideals of independence, personal autonomy, and self-expression, the progressive educator espouses a teaching approach that is based on the facilitation of activity, play, and personal exploration through the provision of "rich" environments.

Finding fault with the ideological, epistemological, and educational implications of both technological and progressivist orientations—primarily on the grounds of their failure to address political and social issues—Ernest proposes his own model of *Public Education,* the central goal of which is the preparation of an informed citizenry capable of full participation in a democratic society. Not unlike the *Academic Rationalism* of Mortimer Adler[9] and E.D. Hirsch,[10] Ernest's *Public Education* is designed to provide essential knowledge and to promote critical intellectual skills (such as thinking, observing, and communicating). Rejecting the extremes of absolutist and relativist perspectives on knowledge, he calls for an awareness of the social basis of knowledge production. Such an awareness, he argues, will serve to foster critical consciousness and democratic citizenship.

A fourth movement in educational thought, and one that might be considered a more radical version of Ernest's Public Education, is *Critical Pedagogy*. Its proponents, who include Paulo Freire[11] and Henry Giroux,[12] come from a range of backgrounds, including Marxism, postmodernism, and various feminisms. It aims more toward the rupture of the oppressive tendencies of political regimes (democratic or otherwise) than toward mere conscientious participation. Formal education is thus more tightly linked to activist politics. Giroux explains that:

> *[M]aking the pedagogical more political means inserting schooling directly into the political sphere by arguing that schooling represents both a struggle to define meaning and a struggle over power relations.*[13]

As Peter McLaren points out, this perspective is closely aligned with the Foucauldian notion that "all regimes of truth [are] contemporary strategies of containment. The point . . . is to purge what is considered truth of its oppressive and undemocratic elements."[14] Not surprisingly, mathematics, identified as the model of reason and situated at the core of the modern curriculum, is a particular target of these critical theorists.

What's Left Unsaid?

On the surface, it appears that each of these perspectives has its own particular agenda; and, while some are in many ways compatible, proponents of any one are quick to find fault with the others. In this section, I would like to argue that, in spite of their differences, these orientations are really much more alike than a cursory glance would reveal. And they are certainly more similar than any of their proponents would admit.

To begin, in acts of monologic authority, proponents of each of the above perspectives start out by assigning education its place. Boundaries, rationales, and purposes are given in concise terms, and little space for negotiation is permitted. With such clear-cut guidelines, then, all of the orientations are, in one way or another, modern.

The clearest example is the industrial or technological perspective. Guided by the ideals of competitiveness, efficiency, productivity, and progress, the educational system of the Industrial Trainer and the Technological Pragmatist is premised on the separations of knowledge from knower and society from individual. Preference is given to the first terms in these dyads, as the latter are valued only insofar as he or she is an adequately functioning component of a machine-like whole. A powerful criticism of this perspective is offered by a number of postmodern and poststructuralist theorists who argue that industrialist ideologies and philosophies are founded on untenable structuralist and positivist assumptions. Cleo Cherryholmes provides an insightful analysis of this orientation, concluding that:

> *[C]ontemporary education is constructed on outmoded and dangerous structural, utilitarian, and instrumental assumptions. They are outmoded because they make rhetorical claims for textbooks, teaching, research, and practice that their logic subverts. They are dangerous because they rhetorically promise foundational, final, and efficient answers about which their logic is silent. They dehumanize by demanding that we adjust to structures imposed upon us while remaining silent about the exercises of power within those structures.*[15]

The central themes of this criticism are thus that the interests of the individual are subordinated to those of the institution and the maintenance (or progress) of existing social structures is given precedence over the enabling of learners to rise above their current status.

The Progressive Educator, in contrast, reverses the technocratic priority by placing the "innocent" and ostensibly autonomous child at the center of the educational endeavor. Far from preparing the learner for the marketplace, the role of the educator is to protect the child from the corrupting influences of the world. As such, the Progressive Educator maintains the same rigid distinction between child and society, although spaces are opened for deeper and richer relationships between teacher and learner and between learner and knowledge. Nevertheless, the progressive education movement appears to have fallen short of its goal to liberate the child. Edwards and Mercer, for example, suggest that even among teachers who describe their practice as progressivist, the instruction is characterized by the teacher "retaining tight control, dominating the agenda and discussion, determining in advance what should happen and what should be discovered," leading to situations in which learners are unable to function "outside the precise context and content of what was 'done' in the classroom."[16] In other words, unaware of the modernist ground on which they are founded, and ignoring the social matrix in which they exist, the dynamics and the outcomes of "progressive" classrooms are very similar to those that are more technical in orientation.

Valerie Walkerdine provides another critique, contending that the progressivist movement has failed not because of its emphasis on the individual but because of its focus on "the child." She argues that the progressivist notion of "'the child' is an object of pedagogic and psychological discourses. It does not exist and yet is proved to be real every day in classrooms and laboratories the world over."[17] Put differently, progressivist discourse has failed to recognize that "the child" is not coterminous with actual children.

The most positive quality of the progressivist orientation—an attentiveness to the relationship between teacher and learner—is maintained in the Public Education model, which also attempts to consider more productively the interplay of the individual and the collective. Nevertheless, with such descriptors as "clay molded by environment," it is clear that the learner is still considered as a distinct (albeit somewhat shapeless) entity—for the emphasis here is on considering the individual in its environment, not on considering the ecologies of the learner. Further to this point, a criticism that could be leveled against both Ernest's Public Education and Adler and Hirsch's Academic Rationalism is that both models begin with the premise that they represent the most enlightened and culturally advanced perspective. Like the technocratic argument, this orientation privileges a masculine and Western view of the world.

It is thus that the criteria for determining which aspects of mathematical knowledge are "essential" do not differ greatly between Public Educator and technocratic orientations. Indeed, as Ernest goes into great detail on his model, he finds a means of justifying the rigid and impersonal examination regime of the British educational system—a program that was initially founded on industrialist needs and which has contributed significantly to the maintenance of the social inequities that the Public Educator supposedly seeks to reform. As such, the modern qualities of competition, stratification, and productivity continue to be foregrounded.

The Critical Pedagogy movement might be criticized on the same grounds, for its entire project is founded on the assumption that human relationships are necessarily political and competitive. These relationships are characterized as perpetual power struggles that inevitably result in control and oppression. The modernist influence is clear here, and it is expressed in active (rather than merely descriptive) oppositions: we versus they, emancipation versus subjugation.

But, although the movement has had a valuable and potent effect in alerting us to many of the social inequities of our society, it bears the seeds of its own destruction. Some aspects of Critical Pedagogy might be described as being radically objectivist, for forgotten are the metaphorical origins of the power structures, the social barriers, and the regimes of truth. Once intended as conceptual tools, these constructions have themselves become obstructions in the discourse field, and their reification has forced proponents to assume adversarial postures; no position other than one of strife and struggle is tenable when one refuses to entertain other models or possibilities for human interaction.[18]

In offering this critique of Critical Pedagogy, I do not mean to suggest that the issue of "authority," a central target of the movement, is not an important one. Quite the contrary, it is perhaps *the* issue, for, as Karl Jaspers[19] argues, education might be thought of as a dialectic between authority and freedom. The point being made here is that authority should not be identified with oppressive power or intrusive violence; these place it on a foundation of fear. Rather, authority might better be aligned with reasonableness. Gadamer says this on this issue:

This acknowledging authority is always connected with the idea that what authority says is not irrational and arbitrary but can, in principle, be discovered to be true. This is the essence of the authority claimed by the teacher, the superior, the expert. The prejudices they implant are legitimized by the person who presents them.[20]

In this formulation, power is not simply something that is possessed by one and arbitrarily imposed on another; power is a function of knowledge as much as social positioning. While not divesting the notion of power from its political implications, power is suggested to be more "the ability not to have to learn"[21]—and by recasting power in such terms, we can begin to formulate alternatives to the power-invested relationships of the classroom. Noting that the teacher, too, is a learner—an idea that I take up in Chapter 5—for example, prompts a leveling of the hierarchical structure of the conventional classroom, as does a recognition that we are all complicit in the body of knowledge that we call mathematics.

For the current purposes, another characterization of power might be, "the privilege of not having to listen." So defined, I find myself in much greater sympathy with the arguments and conclusions of the Critical Pedagogues, for it is clear that mathematics learners, in being compelled to listen, are the powerless ones in the classroom. Small wonder that they often don't listen, then. In failing to attend, they are exercising what limited power they are afforded.

A Middle Way

And so, although the perspectives discussed above appear to be diverse—and even contradictory—they "share a core set of Cartesian/liberal assumptions."[22] As Bowers and Flinders elaborate:

That each, while dealing with important issues and appearing to make a convincing case (depending on which part of the Cartesian/liberal paradigm the reader takes for granted), is totally silent about the connection between cultural beliefs and practices and the ecological crisis suggests the basic limitations of the Cartesian/liberal paradigm. Its blindness to the long-term interdependence of cultural patterns and natural environment is reflected in the blind spots of [their positions].[23]

In particular, modernist assumptions or ideals that are common to the perspectives presented include the primacy of the epistemological, the construct of a static Self, the distinction of self from other, a desire for progress, a goal of optimalization, and a belief that competition is a central defining characteristic of existence. In proposing alternatives to these notions, enactivist and ecological theorists also offer a starting place for rethinking educational philosophy. In this section I attempt to sketch out a basis for these alternatives, setting the stage for an enactivist response to the question, Why educate?

To begin, the issue of the modern tendency to privilege the epistemological over the ontological has already been addressed in the preceding chapters. Briefly, the position taken was that, on issues of knowledge, the question of what we know is not distinct from the question of who we are. Nor can our knowledge be considered as "prior to" or "dependent upon" our identities, for the two are established together. This argument, in effect, is the foundation of the enactivist challenge to the modern construct of a static Self. Not held to be pregiven or fixed, the self, in enactivist terms, is historically and relationally established and is therefore contextually and temporally dependent. Nor can the self be considered apart from others. In simple terms, the qualities I invoke to give shape to my identity and the stories I construct to give this self a historical coherence are linguistically (and therefore socially) constituted.

The desire for "progress" lies at the core of all modern educational philosophies. Implicit in the ideal of progress is a preconceived goal, which one must strive to attain. In itself, this notion is not problematic; it is not the goal that presents the immediate difficulty but the inability of the goal-makers to define their goals in terms other than "progress." As David Denton explains:

[Our] assumption of one overarching purpose, namely, progress has blocked any serious discussion of alternative ends to education. The ends or purposes of education come, without serious reflection, from external units of the society: the state, churches, military, industry, or "the market place."[24]

When the activity of progress-oriented goal-setting is undertaken from a strictly modernist mind-set, the means of attaining those goals are inevitably articulated in prescriptive terms. Therein lies the problem. The goal of the Industrial Trainer is an efficient and complacent workforce; the means is a technical fact-based use-oriented education. The goal of the Academic Rationalist is a smoothly functioning democratic society; the means is the provision of a homogenous and "truthful" (and therefore uncritical) knowledge base. The goal of the Critical Pedagogue is emancipation; the means is a provocation of the oppressed to some form of violence against their oppressors. In each case, both goal and means can be stated in terms of control or management—modern ideals which bring along the baggage of cost effectiveness and resource-use efficiency—founded on the dream of optimization and on the threats of a more capable competitor or more devious adversary.

This thoroughly Western take on the "progress" of society is consistent with, if not predicated upon, a survival-of-the-fittest mentality that is appropriately associated with the notions of competitiveness and optimization. Challenging this orientation, enactivist theorists Varela, Thompson, and Rosch offer the metaphor of *bricolage* in the context of their discussion of evolution. In their words, bricolage refers to "the putting together of parts and items in complicated arrays, not because they fulfill some ideal design but simply because they are possible."[25] Phrased differently, a neo-Darwinian conception of evolution is not founded on optimization (survival of the *fittest*), but on satisficing (survival of the *fit*). The sole criterion for continued existence is viability—that is, an adequate compatibility with the given context. Replacing the ideal of optimization with the criterion of satisficing, in effect, destroys the basis of our culture's desire for progress, because the goal of that progress—some form of best-ness—were it even within our capacity to anticipate, is (at the most optimistic level) a moving target.

The modernist understanding of "progress" is tightly linked to the privileging of vision over the other senses. If we compare, for example, our visual space to our sonorous space, we note that we are placed differently in these sensory realms. We stand at the edge of our visual space, looking into it, whereas we are placed at the center of our sonorous space, surrounded and immersed. Visual awareness is unidirectional and forward, and a vision-dominated consciousness is thus occupied with projecting, foresight, speculation, and seeing ahead—the roots of a desire for progress. Audio awareness is omni-directional and centered, and so the listener is more concerned with locale and immediacy.

Hence the listener is not primarily interested in progress but in movement, for movement—and not progress—is a defining characteristic of life. All living things have some capacity for motion. But it is not a movement toward a prespecified goal (i.e., progress); it is more an intricate dance with other elements of one's ecological sphere in which the players select in one another particular actions or qualities. It is not a machine propelled by competition, but a structure defined by co-emergence.

It is this contrast between modernist and enactivist perspectives which offers the basis for rethinking the place of education in our society, for it offers the hope that education might be something more than a training ground as it is freed from its role of supporting progress. The focus of the educator's efforts are shifted from unattained learning outcomes to current relationships—relationships on levels ranging from the species-biosphere to the learner-classroom. It makes little sense, in this framework, to study the emergence of an individual's understandings without considering the social and political contexts in which those understandings arise. Conversely, the broader context cannot be understood as fixed, oppressive, and all-pervasive, but as subject to the movements of individuals' conceptions.

Education is thus not about attaining the best but about "living well in particular places."[26] It moves from an "almost occult yearning of the future"[27] to an embracing of the here and the now. In Robert Young's terms, the goal is "education for life," an education "for reflective change and adaptation of the self, for co-operative change in relationships with others, and holistic and respectful change of the environment we share."[28] And, as argued in the preceding chapter, it is an education that must include studies of mathematics and of the mathematical.

Mathematics (Education)—Why Teach Math?

Shifting the discussion to focus more specifically on the reasons for studying mathematics affords me opportunities both to elaborate on these ideas and to revisit the conclusions of the preceding chapter. Just as that analysis of the nature of mathematical knowledge pointed to the necessity of reconsidering what is meant by "subject matter" and "curriculum," this examination of education through the lens of enactivist thought demands a reevaluation of the practice of situating mathematics at the core of the schooling experience.

Our answers to the simple question, Why teach math? can be particularly revealing, for we tend to have a range of responses at our fingertips. Embedded as they are in a modernist setting, these responses are often expressed in a tone of certainty that belies their shaky commonsense groundings. I recently posed the question to a colleague, for example, and her matter-of-fact answer was a terse, "You need it." In spite of my efforts to place a more critical edge on our discussion, her perspective on the issue was neatly summed up in those three words.

My efforts to compile a more comprehensive list of reasons have been frustrated by statements that reflect little more depth. (Indeed, this inability to "justify" the teaching of mathematics has been the source of considerable unease throughout my professional career.) In this section I present and briefly discuss some of the more popular rationales. To facilitate the discussion, I have arranged them according to the presumed benefactor—one of: the learner, the educational system, or society.

The most commonly cited argument for studying mathematics is that the subject matter has a particular utility within our culture—an argument that, if made in reference to the actual concepts studied, is simply wrong. Beyond basic arithmetic, it would be difficult to name anything as essential. Of course, the argument that the subject matter has a utilitarian relevance might also be interpreted in terms of the contention that engagement in mathematical activity promotes reasoning skills, a notion that likely emerges from the alignment of mathematics and reason in our culture. James Fey's remark is typical: "Without question, the most important goal of school mathematics is to develop students' ability to reason intelligently."[29] The difficulty with these sorts of statements is not so much the narrowness of their conception of reason, but the correspondence between the goal as stated and the actual consequences of living through one's mathematics education. Mathematics learning may well support thinking abilities—the research has been contradictory on this issue—but there can be little debate of the point that, at least as often as not, conventional mathematics instruction has quite the contrary effect as students resort to memorization and rote application of largely meaningless procedures.

That is, mathematical concepts tend to be reduced to mere tools rather than means of exercising one's thinking. In my home province, for example, the Ministry of Education offers as one of its three goals and objectives for the Junior High Mathematics Program that students will be able to "use mathematics as a tool in the pursuit of personal goals and aspirations."[30] The modernist ideals of individualism, competitiveness, objectivity, utility, progress, and exploitation permeate the statement.

Mathematics instruction is also defended as a measure of rigor in a learner's program. The number of mathematics courses taken by a student is commonly regarded as an indicator of his or her potential and ability, not in the least because mathematics wears the mask of objectivity and impartiality so effectively. Thus, courses in mathematics have assumed a "weeding out" or "gatekeeping" role. That this role might be antithetical to the notion that the purpose of education is to present opportunities—not to deny them—is often not considered. It is perhaps fortunate, then, that we are continuously confronted with the inappropriateness of this rationale and this practice as a parade of successful public figures flaunt their feelings of mathematical incompetence.

The most pervasive reasons for studying mathematics—and certainly the reasons that are most in harmony with the dominant technical-pragmatic perspectives on education—are those that are couched in terms of societal need: A mathematically-literate citizenry is essential in our technologized world. But here we would do well to question not only the role of school mathematics, but the worthiness of the perceived end. Is it best that we attempt to perpetuate our technological culture in light of the toll it has exacted from the planet? Might it not be more appropriate to shift our educational emphasis to other disciplines and modes of reasoning that can more powerfully connect us to the earth, to our past, to one another?

Also on the societal level, there has been considerable attention devoted to the notion that mathematical study will enable children of economically disadvantaged or socially marginalized backgrounds to escape the disadvantaged status of their parents. The National Research Council is one agency among many that has advanced this argument for mathematics education through its pronouncement that "inadequate preparation in mathematics imposes a special economic hardship on minorities."[31] There is little evidence to support this argument, however, and it may even represent an attempt to maintain rather than to alter the status quo. As Nel Noddings has responded:

> *The truth might well be almost the opposite of such statements. Innumeracy and illiteracy are almost certainly the products of divisions long present and maintained by practices largely outside of the control of the school. . . . [Further], there is no morally or practically persuasive reason why lack of mathematical preparation should impose a debilitating economic hardship on minorities or on any of the individuals who contribute significant work to our society.*[32]

Noddings thus further problematizes the gatekeeping status of mathematics, adding fuel to the argument that we might do better to displace the discipline from the center of the modern curriculum.

This discussion would be incomplete without at least a brief glance at a rationale that has become a favorite of government and media alike. Success in the study of mathematics has somehow become closely linked to our nation's economic prosperity. Study after study indicates that Japanese and German students outperform their Canadian and American counterparts. Leaving aside cultural and methodological issues that would render problematic these studies' findings, and ignoring the Cartesian assumptions that underpin this practice of comparative examination, there seems a need to question how it might be that our economic ills can be in any way attributed to the performance of twelve-year-olds on a standardized test that is of little consequence to those writing. Madeleine Grumet[33] contends that this practice represents an attempt by the governing males to deflect the blame for their nearsighted decisions onto those who will suffer the consequences: the children who fail and the women hired to teach them. David Orr suggests that our misplaced concern over our children's lack of competitiveness in science and mathematics has prevented us from attending to whether or not they "will know how to protect the biological resources upon which any economy ultimately depends."[34]

In sum, then, when analyzing the situation through an ecological or enactivist framework, we are unable to provide a satisfactory defense for the mandatory study of mathematics in its present form. Quite the contrary, it is easier to argue for a relaxation of current requirements—and this is certainly the position of certain feminist[35] and ecological[36] theorists.

A Possible Rationale

It seems that we are trapped in an untenable position: between seeking to preserve what we hold to be a valuable part of our intellectual heritage and avoiding the perpetuation of a dehumanizing practice.

But what must be borne in mind is that, as elaborated in Chapter 2, with the realization of Descartes' dream of world mathematization, we have become as much the products of mathematics as it is the product of us. We see the world in mathematical ways as aspects of the discipline infuse our language and frame our experiences. To understand the universe in which we find ourselves and in which our selves are established, the study of mathematics, like studies of language and history and art and music, is critical. The suggestion that we disregard a discipline is tantamount to the recommendation that we ignore who we are and who we might be—and what our society is and what it might be. We study mathematics not to master its processes or to possess its objects, but to understand the world into which we are thrown and which we participate in creating.

Further to this line of reasoning, in pointing to the notions that our personal and collective identities are interactively established, that the fundamental unit of survival is not the organism but the "flexible organism-in-its-environment,"[37] and that we belong to our history and not it to us, enactivist and ecological theories have effectively thrust the educational endeavor into the realm of the ethical.[38] As Wendell Berry argues, "Under the discipline of unity, knowledge and morality come together. . . . To know anything at all becomes a moral predicament."[39] And in highlighting the notion that even the slightest perturbation can have the most profound effect when processes of repetition and recursion come into play, they have also provided us with the moral imperative to intervene in a particular way.

A compatible notion has recently been articulated by complexity theorists Jack Cohen and Ian Stewart,[40] who have attempted to push discussions in this field into the realms of the moral and the ethical through the development of their idea of "complicity." Briefly, complicit systems are ones that are not dependent on initial conditions and, as such, cannot be simulated by mechanical devices like the modern computer. (That is, complicit systems are living systems, and so the sorts of computer simulations that are being developed and researched by most complexity theorists are not necessarily useful in helping to understand the complicit systems. A key limitation is that such models are dependent on initial conditions and so the space of the possible is defined at the start.) In cases of complicity, of which evolution and cognition are key examples, subsystems interact in ways that change each and that erase their dependence on initial conditions—that is, they interact in ways that open up new possibilities and, hence, enlarge the space of the possible. By this definition, formal education and teaching are examples of complicity.

Cohen and Stewart's choice of terms is more than mere word play. "Complicity," with its popular sense of being implicated in or serving as an accomplice to, announces a need to be attentive to one's own participation in events. In effect, for example, we are complicit in the way our personal and collective identities unfold, and it is this fact that compels us to participate in discussions of moral and ethical import alongside our interpretations of the varied phenomena associated with teaching.

In our discussions of education, then, we can neither privilege societal interests nor focus on the whims of the learner, but must seek to understand their interdependencies and our own complicity in them. Formal education can neither cling to what is given nor relentlessly pursue the limitless imagination, but must explore the transformative possibilities of thought and action; it can neither strive for certainty nor dwell in chaos, but must embrace the complexities of existence; it can neither grasp for the future nor hold only to the past, but must be sensitive to what was and what might be as represented in the context at hand. Education is thus neither this nor that, but dwells in the movement between the two. Just as the capacity for motion is an essential quality of all living things, education is a necessary trait of our living culture. As Bruner puts it:

[A] culture is constantly in process of being recreated as it is interpreted and renegotiated by its members. In this view, a culture is as much a

forum *for negotiating and re-negotiating meaning and for explicating action as it is a set of rules or specifications for action. . . . Education is (or should be) one of the principal forums for performing this function—though it is often timid in doing so.*[41]

And so, whether we wish to assume moral responsibility or not, we who are involved in education are also actively engaged in the transformation of our culture—even while we attempt its transmission. This is not to say, however, that through education we should seek to "overcome" the past. Because we are "historical beings," we must rather situate ourselves—seeking, in Heidegger's terms, a "conversing with that which has been handed down," so that there is no "break with history, no repudiation of history, but . . . an appropriation [*Aneignung*] and transformation [*Verwandlung*] of what has been handed down to us."[42] An attitude of listening for that which speaks to us in our traditions—recalling that listening is not a passive attendance but an active participation—is thus demanded.

In sum, a theory of enaction prompts us to work conscientiously toward cultural reform (while acknowledging that we cannot help but participate in the cultural transformation). In effect, we must acknowledge the co-implicative structure and the dynamic nature of the place of education. To fail in this task is to be complicit in promoting what Varela, Thompson, and Rosch describe as "the sense of nihilistic alienation in our culture"[43] and what Charles Taylor has labeled "the malaise of modernity."[44]

Section B
Artistry
The Place of the Teacher

The right stuff is not the same from great teacher to great teacher, so the art of teaching is frustratingly elusive—we know it when we experience it, but as soon as we talk about it, we also know it is constantly slipping away.

—Timothy Crusius[1]

[T]hat family of art forms referred to as improvisatory, such as jazz and epic recitation, actually depend upon endless practice and the recombining of previously learned components so that each performance is both new and practiced.

—Mary Catherine Bateson[2]

At the moment of this writing, someone somewhere in this province is planning for or participating in a protest of the government's proposal to reduce spending on education by 20 percent. Most people are not at all happy about the projected cuts.

Much of the discontent arises from the apparent contradictions that surround the undertaking. At the same time that legislators are lamenting the economic consequences of our grade eight students' lack of academic competitiveness, they are cutting the funding that supports the educational system. It is thus that these politicians are attempting to change their song on schooling: the issue today is inefficiency, eclipsing yesterday's concern for ineffectiveness.

The premier, who assured voters that "He listens. He cares," in the recent election, has promised a series of public forums on the issue. Not content with the format of these forums, teachers and their association have been sponsoring more open debates. Apparently they have also engaged in more devious activities, for it seems that some have discussed the issues (and their own views) with their students. And some may have actually encouraged learners to voice their own concerns publicly.

The government is not happy. The premier and his supporters have broadcast their contempt for both the "irresponsible teachers" and the "disobedient students": "Teachers have no *place* meddling in the affairs of government;" "Their *place* is to teach."

In the middle of this debate about money, then, the issue of *the place of the teacher* has moved into the spotlight, for it is clear that the government authorities are not willing to allow (nor even to recognize) the place of teachers in shaping society. And it seems that the teachers are not going to ignore their place in culture-making.

What is the place of the teacher? That is the topic of this section, and I approach it through an exploration of a metaphor: "teacher as artist." In terms of the preceding section, this discussion is about how we might make explicit our own complicity in the subject matter through our defining of a mathematics curriculum. It may be regarded as an imperative to recognize that we, in fact, are the curriculum.

Teacher as Artist

"The art of teaching" is a common enough phrase. Most often, it is used to draw our attention to the capacity to negotiate the interplay of the assigned program of studies and the lives of learners, and so we usually hear it in arguments that deal with the impossibility of constructing fully scientific bases to teaching and to education. Placed in direct opposition to the scientific mentality in this conception, the artistic is thought to be flexible rather than rigid, sensitive rather than violent, synthesizing rather than analytic, and inclusive rather than reductionist. Art is skill or knowledge acquired through experience, and it is offered as a counterpoint to the sort of knowledge that comes about through experimentation and rigorous verification.

However, the conceptions of both art and science that underlie the popular notion of "teaching as art" are shallow ones, emerging from a this-or-that mentality that has, since the beginning of the modern era, sought to distinguish between scientific insight and artistic awareness and to separate mechanization from creativity. We thus have need to re-explore the question, What is a work of art?

Gadamer discusses the issue at length. One of his conclusions is that the work of art has a two-fold function. First, it *represents* something that is not immediately present—that is, it recalls to our senses, it makes present, it stands in for something that is not here. But that is its minor function, for the work of art also *presents.* In Gadamer's words, "a picture is an event of presentation . . . an increase of being."[3] Put differently, the artwork not only points to something that is not at hand, it offers to us something new—something that was not available to our previous seeing or hearing, something that demands that we look again and that we listen anew. The artwork is both an imitation and an interpretation, with the function of making the familiar strange and the strange familiar.

A contrast might thus be drawn between the work of art and those visual and auditory products that are intended only to represent—such as photographic snapshots and recorded interviews. Unlike a work of art, the photograph aims to make itself invisible. It is not the snapshot, but the image it bears that we notice. The artwork, however, never disappears. Its purpose is not just to represent something else, but to remind us of how we "see," thus challenging the taken-for-granted (the prejudices) that frame our perceptions.

Gadamer thus assigns the work of art an ontological status, in accord with Susanne Langer's contention that

> *a work of art expresses a conception of life, emotion, inward reality. But it is neither a confessional nor a frozen tantrum; it is a developed metaphor, a nondiscursive symbol that articulates what is verbally ineffable—the logic of consciousness itself.*[4]

The work of art, then, is not intended to transmit a message, but to open a space for personal transformation. It encourages the onlooker or the listener to think otherwise, to consider the possibilities that exist at the edge of our awarenesses and that have not yet found form in our common language.

The artist, then, is situated between the actual and the possible, between what is and what might be. The artist must be attuned to—listening to—both this and that, for he or she has consciously thrown himself or herself into the zone of tension between the two. The point, as Madeleine Grumet elaborates, "is that to be an artist is perpetually to negotiate the boundary that separates aesthetic from mundane experience."[5] It is here that the connection to teaching might be made, for both the teacher and the artist are in a place "to challenge the taken-for-granted values and culture that one shares with others."[6] Grumet is thus suggesting that understanding curriculum as an aesthetic text offers us a way of replacing its technical function with a revelatory function.

Aronowitz and Giroux[7] use the phrase "transformative intellectual" to describe their sense of the teacher's role. They, like Grumet, Varela, and others, point to the inevitability of effecting transformation of one's self, one's students, and one's culture through one's teaching. In spite of our persistent timidity in acknowledging the impact of teaching, the teacher, in pointing and representing, is also and always interpreting and presenting. More importantly, perhaps, and much contrary to the seemingly invisible or nonpresent role of the teacher in transmission-based conceptions of education, the teacher is necessarily present and implicated in the subject matter of the classroom. Always and inevitably, he or she simultaneously re-presents and presents ideas while presenting his or herself.

A deeper understanding of art, then, can provide us with a profound sense of the place of the teacher. Sadly, it is a sense that has been all but lost with the commodification of art and knowledge in today's consumer culture.

The Art of Mathematics

For the most part, statements about mathematics that include reference to art are rarely heard outside of discussions of Escher prints or, more recently, computer-generated fractal images. Such items are among the few points of intersection of these two disciplines . . . areas of scholarly activity that are normally considered not just distinct, but in seeming opposition. Indeed, the suggestion that mathematics might have some aesthetic value often appears in flat contradiction to the instrumental emphases that framed our school mathematics experiences. The question thus arises, Can mathematics be an art form?

The beginnings of a response to that question might be offered through a few etymological notes on the words "art" and "arithmetic." Both are derived from two proto-Indo-European roots, *ar-* and *Rt.* The former, as Berendt[8] explains, signifies both coming together or unifying (as in *harmony* and *aural*) and series or order (as in *arrange* and *rhythm*). The latter, *Rt,* is the root of a host of terms (including, and of relevance to the current discussion, *right, rhetoric, ritual,* and *root*). Extrapolating from the meanings of its linguistic descendants, Pirsig offers the following definition of *Rt*: "first, created, beautiful, repetitive order of moral and aesthetic correctness."[9] In bringing the two roots together, a more fluid, collective, and auditory sense might be added to Pirsig's formulation.

It thus seems that art and mathematics (not to mention the auditory) are not quite so far apart as one might imagine, given the clear boundaries enclosing the two categories of activity within popular conception. Within the mathematics literature, in fact, statements linking the two abound. Mathematician Lynn Arthur Steen, for example, suggests:

[T]he motivation and standards of creative mathematics are more like those of art than of science. Aesthetic judgments transcend both logic and applicability in the ranking of mathematical theorems: beauty and elegance have more to do with the value of a mathematical idea than does either strict truth or possible utility.[10]

Another mathematician, Jerry P. King, echoes the sentiment: "To *do* mathematics is to do research, which means to create mathematics as a poet creates poems."[11]

King speaks at length about the relationship between art and mathematics, his central thesis being that it is the aesthetic dimension of their work that most motivates professional mathematicians. He thus argues for both a rethinking of why we teach mathematics (i.e., emphases on utility and disciplined labor no longer seem to be appropriate) and, correspondingly, to reconstruct how we teach mathematics (i.e., the conventional disciplinary boundaries between art and math, and other subject areas, may need to be dissolved). In effect, King seems to be joining with many others in calling for a remembering of our bodies of knowledge, moving away from the current fragmented curriculum landscape that arose at the same time as (and largely as a result of) the modern school.

There thus seems to be the possibility of an art-full mathematics. But, prompted by Gadamer, it is important to note that it is not merely the potential for beauty or an aesthetic engagement, but the capacity to reconfigure experience that makes art what it is. Can mathematical inquiry succeed here?

I would contend that the potential for mathematical inquiry to prompt reformulations of perception and action (and, hence, identity) is quite astounding, although difficult to appreciate in a culture that is saturated with mathematized interpretations of phenomena. (A quick browse of the morning newspaper will confirm this statement. Few articles are free of quantified interpretation, and virtually all follow a logical formula that is directly derived from the model of argumentation advocated by Descartes.) Given the pervasiveness of mathematized interpretation, as blindingly obvious as it is, it seems not only possible but necessary for mathematical study to move beyond the conventional emphasis on representation (i.e., of standing in for or pointing to some phenomenon) to also encompass presentation (i.e., enabling us to experience that phenomenon differently and, in the process, noting our complicity in our perception of that experience). Mathematician Philip Davis makes the point this way:

The subconscious modalities of mathematics and of its applications must be made clear, must be taught, watched, argued. Since we are all consumers of mathematics, and since we are both beneficiaries as well as victims, all mathematizations ought to be opened to public forums where ideas are debated. These debates ought to begin in the secondary school.[12]

We must understand what it means to live in a mathematized world—on both collective (social, political) and individual (perceptual, physical) levels. But I would differ with Davis on two issues. First, the sense that we are complicit in our mathematics—that we are not merely consumers and victims, but accomplices—does not seem to be adequately foregrounded in his admonition. As such, he might be interpreted as implying that (art-full) mathematical inquiry does not engender a certain interrogation of circumstances; such interrogation seems be something of an add-on rather than in integral part of mathematics schooling in this formulation.[13] Second, on his last point, I do not believe these debates should begin in the high school, by which time patterns of routinized action, expectation, and examination pressures often militate against this sort of critical engagement (in my experience, at least). Rather, these debates ought to begin with the earliest formal teaching of mathematics.

Wherefore Art?

Whether young learners are capable of appreciating the subtleties of these sorts of discussions is, of course, an issue to be considered. I personally believe that they are, and that the key to successful interrogation of the manner in which we and our world have been mathematized lies in incorporating such discussion into mathematical inquiry as an integral part—not as a supplement to mathematics.

Before taking this discussion into the elementary classroom, it might help to insert a few illustrations of the point being made, ones drawn from among my own mathematical experiences. I might begin, for example, by pointing to such mathematical formulations as the Fibonacci Sequence, through which it is possible to link our experiences of phenomena as diverse as spirals and sunflowers to music, hinting at a mysterious "pattern which connects" (to borrow Gregory Bateson's phrase) not only the seen to the heard, but the singular to the cyclical and the part to the whole. Another example might be drawn from my first introduction to the topic of fractal geometry. Just over a decade ago, I was first introduced to fractals through a computer simulation of a developing fractal tree (not unlike the one that is growing on the title pages of this book). After that initial and altogether brief exposure, I found that I could no longer regard trees, ferns, flowers, snail shells—or anything organic, for that matter—in the same way. I could not help but to be attentive to the self-similarity of their forms, amazed both at these simplicities and at the fact that we, collectively, had taken so long to come upon this obvious quality. This bit of mathematics, for me, was aesthetic and art-full—and, like the Fibonacci Sequence, has come to offer yet another link between the seen and the heard, the piece and the whole. Not only was a familiar object (i.e., a tree) *represented* to me, a whole host of phenomena (collected under a new category of pattern in the world) was *presented.* This transformation served to alter not only those immediate perceptions, but also past and projected perceptions, in the process prompting considerable reflection on the phenomenon of perception. Such is the transformative potential of mathematical inquiry.

A moment very similar to this one, but on an entirely different mathematical principle, occurred in a recent third-grade classroom during a lesson on rational numbers. Asked to identify fractions equivalent to $^2/_6$, one student began with the list, $^1/_3$, $^3/_9$, $^4/_{12}$. Before she could announce another, a classmate, Jiema, interrupted, protesting that $^3/_9$ did not belong. After a brief discussion, Jiema did agree that $^3/_9$ of a piece of paper did indeed cover the same area as $^2/_6$, but still maintained that it was "not as equal as the other fractions" on the list.

The teacher in this classroom did, to my mind, a wonderful thing on this occasion. Rather than rejecting Jiema's conclusion as false—for it is common sense that equality cannot occur on a relative scale (in mathematics, at least)—he fostered a conversation on the matter, and actually ended up agreeing that a fraction like $^{63}/_{189}$ "is not very equal at all to $^2/_6$," whereas $^4/_{12}$ and $^8/_{24}$ "are very equal."

At first I was somewhat concerned that he did not correct Jiema's obvious misconception, but further thought on this moment of listening has brought me to the belief that it is necessary to examine the logical assumptions underlying both the traditional conception of equality and the conception that Jiema announced. Regarding the former, for the most part, Western systems of logic are founded on a belief in the possibilities of clean definitions, crisp edges, and unambiguous categories. Our numeration systems as well are developed around the assumption that those things that are to be counted, sorted, added, or compared can be unproblematically defined and grouped. The same 1–0, all-or-nothing mentality is evident in much of our formal interaction, and likely has been at least since Aristotle formulated his axioms of logic.[14] Those phenomena that belie clear-cut classification or quantification tend to be dismissed as mis-defined or not-yet understood. The art-full question to ask here seems to be, Is this the way we really think?

It is clearly not the way Jiema was thinking in the reported classroom situation. And, according to fuzzy logicians, it is not the way we think most of the time. Cups that we consider full are usually less than full; a robin is a better example of a bird than a penguin; some blues are more blue than others. And, it seems, some equivalent fractions are more equal than others. The contention of fuzzy logicians is that the crispness suggested by whole numbers and our 1–0 logic is an illusion—founded on an assumption that, through uninterrogated habit, has been elevated to the level of a fact too obvious to question.

Fuzzy logic—along with non-Euclidean geometries, complexity theory, and other areas of mathematical study—has helped us to uncover some of what we have assumed to be universally, and not just mathematically, true. Most phenomena cannot be clearly defined or rigidly bounded; parallel lines might meet or they might diverge; the whole really can be greater than the sum of the parts. It is interesting to note that, both in the mathematics community and in society at large, these ideas have not always been readily embraced. Very often, in fact, extensive effort has been made to explain them away as special cases, matters of definition, or not really mathematical. It seems that we are not completely comfortable with the challenges they offer to what we believe to be true.[15]

Why are we so reluctant to welcome these sorts of ideas? Might it be that the traditions that they challenge are so much a part of the way we think that we are unable to acknowledge their relevance? Or might it be that these sorts of ideas present challenges not only to what we know and believe, but also to who we are?

These questions can be addressed only if one has a strong sense of how mathematics helps to shape the way we perceive and act—or, in Gadamer's terms, how our perceptions are simultaneously enabled by and constrained by our mathematical prejudices. With our traditional emphasis on utility, we have focused on the enabling possibilities, blind and deaf to that which gets pushed into the background. We are thus compelled to undertake what I would call a "mathematical anthropology" that might begin with what Hans Freudenthal describes as the "phenomenology of a mathematical concept." He uses this phrase to refer to the process of situating a concept in "relation to the phenomena for which it was created, and to which it has been extended in the learning process of mankind."[16] Freudenthal's purpose in articulating this notion (and in providing rather extensive illustration) is to offer the mathematics educator a "didactical phenomenology"—"a way to show the teacher *the places* the learner might step into the learning processes of mankind."[17]

In terms of the legitimate potential of mathematical inquiry to accomplish this sort of introspective anthropology, I would say that there is good reason to be hopeful. Relative to other areas of inquiry, mathematics is a fairly self-aware body of knowledge—in that an important part of any mathematical inquiry involves explicitly laying out what is assumed. And, as enacted in non-Euclidian geometries and non-traditional logics, these assumptions are available for renegotiation. Mathematics thus, perhaps more than any other field, offers us a route to interrogating the way we think.

That the reported occasion with Jiema took place in a unit on fractions is important, for it demonstrates that even with the most *basic* of topics, opportunities for mathematical anthropology do present themselves to the listening teacher. What is needed to investigate how our mathematics shapes us is not so much a revised syllabus as a change in mind-set. It is thus that, I would contend, the current list of topics in a typical grade-school curriculum already offers a rich ground for exploring what tends to be taken for granted—not just in mathematics, but in virtually every area of inquiry typical to our society. The laws governing our systems of logic and numbering, as noted earlier, have been identified as a possible site. We might also, for example, explore the relationship between rational numbers, ratios, and "rationality"—noting that this last term is derived from the same logical processes that underlie our work with fractions. Similarly, the foundational truths of geometry, having long ago been demonstrated to be anything but universally applicable, offer a site for investigating how we think. These are a few of the possible locations for interrogating our mathematics—or, more accurately, for studying ourselves and the prejudices that shape our world.

Which is not to say that we should not be considering for study some of the more recent topics in mathematics such as chaos dynamics, complexity theory, and fuzzy logic. With each of these challenging, on some level, conceptions and assumptions of traditional mathematics—not to mention offering vivid examples of the dynamic face of mathematics—there seems to be good reason to be optimistic about the possibility of mathematical study that makes a difference. In particular, through such topics, the fact that mathematics provides only models or metaphors for phenomena of the lived world (as opposed to laws or underlying structures of that world) is an important understanding that might be fostered through an introduction to these sorts of developments.

A Way of Putting Things

I recall a teacher, her name was Miss Orcutt, who made the statement in class, "It is a very puzzling thing not that water turns to ice at 32 degrees Fahrenheit, but that it should change from a liquid to a solid." She then went on to give us an intuitive account of the Brownian movement and of molecules, expressing a sense of wonder that matched, indeed bettered, the sense of wonder I felt at that age (around ten) about everything I turned my mind to. . . . In effect, she was inviting me to extend my *world of wonder to encompass hers.*

—Jerome Bruner[18]

Bruner uses this anecdote to illustrate the disparate educational consequences of two modes of speaking: that which is characterized by certainty, and that which is more tentative.

Citing a study in which the sorts of statements teachers made to one another (regarding their subject area knowledge) were compared to the way they spoke to students in their own classrooms, Bruner comments that:

[T]he world that the teachers were presenting to their students was a far more settled, far less hypothetical, far less negotiatory world than the one they were offering their colleagues.[19]

Positioned in front of their students, teachers gave little or no sense of the tentative nature of knowledge—a sense that was willingly communicated to colleagues—and, in so doing, tended to close down invitations to further thought. One might say that these teachers stopped listening to themselves when they entered the classroom. In Bruner's personal history, Miss Orcutt stands out as an exception: "She was a human event, not a transmission device," standing apart from other teachers whose "stances were so off-puttingly and barrenly informative."[20] These teachers endeavored only to represent. Making no deliberate effort to treat the subject matter as something that also presents, that opens, that challenges, that engages, the teachers offered "flat declarations of fixed factuality"—something hardly worth listening to. Bruner sums up:

To the extent that the materials of education are chosen for their amenableness to imaginative transformation and are presented in a light to invite negotiation and speculation, to that extent education becomes part of . . . "culture making." The pupil, in effect, becomes a party to the negotiatory process by which facts are created and interpreted. He becomes at once an agent of knowledge making as well as a recipient of knowledge transmission.[21]

The preceding discussion of the possibilities of mathematical study to art-fully reorganize experience is thus only part of the story. Mathematics is about people, and what matters is the presence of teachers who are interpreters of (and hence participants in) the subject matter. The art of teaching, then, is to be attentive to the interpretations offered, concerned not merely with assimilation or mastery, but with fresh perception. On this issue I believe it is important that we locate and consider the examples of those teachers—in their enacted artistic specificity, rather than their formulated general competencies—who brought the subject matter to life in our own experiences. We need to point toward examples such as that of Miss Orcutt whose willingness to share her fascination with something as mundane as water freezing—that is, her unwillingness to allow her interest to be doused by familiarity—open the possibilities for important (transformative) moments in children's educations. In my own experience, I recall Mr. Heuver, Mrs. O'Brien and Dr. Cristall who, for all their eccentricities, were genuinely animated by the mathematics they taught. It always presented something new for them; it was never offered as something to be mastered, but for what it hinted at, where it led, what it presented. For them, teaching was not a matter of *telling*, but about *listening* for possibilities.

These persons were "transformative intellectuals." I return to this phrase because there remains one issue to address more directly: that these teachers were indeed *intellectuals*. They knew and enjoyed their subject matter, and these qualities provided them with the ability to move beyond the prescribed limits of a curriculum manual. In a sense, these teachers were able to enact the mathematics they taught—the sort of person described by van Manen: "A math teacher is not (or should not be) just somebody who happens to teach math. A real math teacher is a person who *embodies* math, who *lives* math, who in a strong sense *is* math."[22]

A person who is only "one page ahead" of the learners is not likely to do much more than fixate on the image and ignore the substance, in effect, to rob learners of the very reason the subject is worthy of study in the first place. This issue is not a simple one, for as Alba Thompson[23] explains, one's approach to mathematics teaching arises from a host of influences, including one's history with teachers, teaching, learners, and learning. The extent of one's mathematical knowledge, while important, can be eclipsed by one's perspectives on knowledge or made irrelevant in the face of institutional constraints. A broad knowledge base hardly ensures a pedagogy that is not prescriptive or mechanistic in nature. Perhaps, then, the issue of teachers' mathematical knowledge, should not be addressed (as it often is) in terms of the number of mathematics courses that should be taken. Given the importance of one's perceptions of the subject matter, a count of arts and humanities classes might well be every bit as valid.

The Place of the Teacher

What is the place of the teacher?

If we are to conceive of the teacher's role as that of a transformative intellectual, then he or she is that artist who is attuned to and who moves back and forth between the collective and the singular, past and future, actual and possible. He or she is the one who interprets and who, in that interpretation, opens a space for transformation. The teacher's task is thus not merely to re-present and in that objective representation, to make himself or herself invisible. Rather, the teacher is in every way implicated—complicit—in the subject matter.

But, like any metaphor, "teacher as artist" obscures as much as it illuminates. The artist, for example, is an artist by virtue of the sort of work he or she produces—and "work" in this context has a very particular meaning. An artwork is a performance, the result of a likely prolonged, but largely invisible, labor. It arrives to its public already formed and it thus masks both its history and the intricacies of the relational web from which it arose. Thus, although the metaphor may well challenge and provoke us to think otherwise about some matters (for example, in addition to bringing the teacher into the teaching, it helps us toward an understanding of "work" that distances it from the repetitiveness of factory-like labor), its usefulness for informing teaching is limited.

For the "work" of the teacher is unlike the "work" of the artist; a teacher's work cannot be "finished" or "performed" in the same way. We do not gaze at the endpoint of teaching (although there is a pervasive tendency to fixate on the consequences of teaching performance: student achievement), but rather at the sustained effort, the mundane day-to-day-ness of life in the classroom. The artist's work is an endpoint—albeit one that is continually transformed through performance; the teacher's work is a labor that never sees its completion.

And the artist's work acquires a certain autonomy. Indeed, we tend to construct clear and distinct boundaries around such work by framing or binding or staging. The teacher's work does not have such boundaries. Lacking these bounds, it becomes difficult to talk about where teaching takes place, even if we are able to agree upon the place of the teacher. I thus move to a discussion of the more immediate and specific places that teaching happens, within the fluid, constantly renegotiated spaces of our interrelationships.

Section C
Pedagogy
Where Teaching Takes Place

> *[Talk] of teaching must consist in symbols, metaphors, which signify in a plurality of ways not only what we are doing in the moment but the possibilities of the moment, the negations and affirmations in the moment which open us up to projections beyond the moment.*
>
> —*David Denton*[1]

> *Our responsiveness, our "listening" to the subject, constitutes the very essence of the relationship between student and subject matter.*
>
> —*Max van Manen*[2]

In this section, I seek to explore the nature of the relationship between teacher and learner—or rather, a possibility for how that relationship might be conceived. The need for this exploration emerges from Gadamer's explication of the conversation (as elaborated in Chapter 1). For him, the conversational relation is a triad involving three elements: you, me, and the subject matter. Having looked at the issue of our relationship to the subject matter already, I turn to an investigation of the you-me part of the conversation.

My contention at the outset of this discussion is that there is little reason to raise the issue of listening in the context of teaching if we are not willing to critically analyze and explore alternatives to the sorts of relationships that typically exist between teachers and learners in the modern mathematics classroom. In my own experience, I have found myself enacting that relationship in terms of manager/managed, employer/employee, businessman/client, enforcer/deviant, master/apprentice, expert/novice, facilitator/sense-maker, and (most recently) listener/conversationalist . . . among many others.

Following this chapter's theme of "place," I develop this section around a discussion of the "bounds" of the places where teaching happens. My selection of this polysemous term as the focal point of the discussion is deliberate. In contrast to the convergent tone of the previous section, here I would like to more fully acknowledge the ambiguities, the contingencies, and the complexities of the sorts of relationships that are enacted in the classroom.

The first part of this section involves a further explication of the three modes of listening introduced in Chapter 1 and of the three classroom vignettes presented in Chapter 2. The current discussion is also founded on those teaching episodes, and so the reader may wish to take a moment to recall some of the details of the accounts. The emphasis in this elaboration of the three modes (and moments) of listening is on the relational texture of the teacher's manner of interacting with learners.

Three Listenings

Mode 1: Evaluative Listening ("Adding Fractions" Lesson) The patterns of interaction in the first teaching episode might be characterized as separating and distancing. The roles are clearly defined, as are the power and authority structures. The teacher determines what will happen next, what is appropriate, what can be said—in brief, where the boundaries are drawn—with a sort of 1–0, black-and-white style of demarcation.

The relationships between teacher and learner might be best described as business-like and managerial—a style that is consistent with the fragmented, instrumental, and technicized subject matter of the setting. This analysis was borne out during a brief teacher-students interaction that was noted early in the unit, near the time of the reported lesson. In response to a student's query, "Why do I have to do this?" (made in reference to a series of repetitive practice exercises from the textbook), Wendy remarked, "When you have a job, you'll be expected to do what your boss tells you to do."[3]

This employer/employee metaphor for the relationship between teacher and student was evident in the very manner that Wendy positioned herself in the classroom. She stood at the front, outside of the area occupied by students, monitoring, supervising, watching, scrutinizing their actions—an instructive stance that hardly called for any sort of engaged attendance.

This authoritarian positioning, interestingly enough, was only evident during class time. When the bell rang to mark the beginning of the lunch break, for example, a transformation seemed to occur. Wendy set aside her "teaching identity," becoming more personable, attentive, and interactive as she moved among the students. (I recall having undergone similar transformations upon stepping outside of my own classroom during my teaching career.) I mention this point to underscore the fact that the stance that Wendy assumed relative to her students during the lesson did not arise from any lack of concern for them, nor as a result of an inability to interact with that particular social group. Rather, it seems that Wendy was enacting the role of teacher as defined by her history within formal educative contexts. Her detached, impersonal, and authoritative mode of attendance—her evaluative listening—is thoroughly consistent with her relational and spatial positionings in the setting.

Mode 2: Interpretive Listening ("Adding Integers" Lesson) In the second teaching episode, many of the rigid separations enacted in the first seem to have been relaxed to some extent. For example, while distinct power and authority structures are still in place, the pronounced differences between teacher and student have been evened out somewhat. Such leveling appears to have been accomplished largely through an emerging emphasis on student voice, which Wendy has embraced both as an essential component of personal sense-making (i.e., consistent with a constructivist epistemology, vocalizing one's understandings is regarded as an important part of subjective sense-making) and as a means of personal empowerment (i.e., consistent with varied commentaries critiquing the imposed silence of learners, such vocalizations are seen as honoring student theories and, hence, promoting more critical thinking).

But a careful listening in this classroom suggests that the relationships continue to be defined in fragmenting and fragmented terms. Those present are still regarded as isolated, fully autonomous agents whose voices must compete against one another. The teacher continues to stand apart from learners, still situated at the edge of the space, still overseeing the activities of the classroom. Her primary concern continues to be control or management, albeit that this concern has come to incorporate a more tentative, negotiated understanding of communication.

And so, while Wendy's manner of listening has prompted a redefining of roles in the classroom—learners are more active and vocal and the teacher is more facilitative and attentive—the interpersonal relationships cannot be said to have changed dramatically. Once again, evidence for this contention came when the bell rang to end each class. As in the previous episode, Wendy's in-class manner changed remarkably as her efforts to control the direction of events gave way to a relaxed movement with the students as they proceeded to their next classes.

Mode 3: Hermeneutic Listening ("All-at-Once Fractions" Lesson)

In reviewing the third teaching episode, I find myself wondering who was learning the most. For me, the most significant departures in this lesson from previous ones are the conflation of the roles of teacher and learner and, correspondingly, the blurring of boundaries between them. This is not to say, however, that power relationships have been obliterated. Rather, they are differently configured, with power being cast more in terms of the capacity to redirect collective action through a thoughtful contribution than by administrative fiat. The voices in this room are not competing; they are conversing, existing in a particular fluid harmony.

There is thus a smoothness to the unfolding of classroom events, arising from a shared sense of pacing. Similarly, the previous concern for management has given way to a sense of control as a shared quality, a partnership through which teacher and learner alike have become immersed in the flow of the subject matter. The positioning of the teacher is thus more of a listener—immersed in acoustic space—than that of supervisor, scrutinizer, or overseer who is perched at the edge of visual space.

The relationships in this setting, then, are different from the preceding episodes, and this difference is perhaps most clearly announced in the way that the lesson overflowed its boundaries. The manner of interaction between teacher and learners did not suddenly end when the bell rang to dismiss the class. Although the topic of conversation changed for most (but not all), the interactions continued for the most part with the same tone and tempo. And, unlike the other episodes, Wendy did not assume another persona—there were no rigid breaks in enacted identity—with the completion of the lesson.

The critical point here is that a hermeneutic listening implies more than a different mode of attending. It is a different mode of relating, of being in relationship, that implicates listener and listened to. In what follows I undertake a deeper exploration of the many bounds that we use to frame those relationships in which hermeneutic listening occurs.

The Bounds of Teaching

bound *n.* **1**: a limiting line ⟨out of *bounds*⟩: BOUNDARY

The *bounds* are the limits that separate this place from that place; the marking of bounds is the first step in transforming a space into a place. It assigns a shape or a form. In setting the bounds of teaching, we might begin by pointing to the physical bounds of the schoolyard or the classroom, the temporal bounds of the school year or the class period, or the interpersonal bounds of the school population or the class members.

But, prompted by the sorts of transitions that Wendy went through at the ends of the first two teaching episodes, we must be cautious here. David Denton speaks against our tendency to scribe these sorts of borders, arguing that such delimitation "of teaching constitutes an imposition on that situation, an imposition with normative force: the situation must be made to conform to this definition."[4] One of Denton's purposes in writing is to suggest that there is something indescribable, something that cannot be bounded, that makes teaching what it is. For him, teaching is not a set of actions, nor a role, but a "mode of being." As such, while we may choose to speak of bounds, we cannot impose them. At best they can serve as traces of where teaching has been.

Dwayne Huebner echoes this disdain for our tendency to impose bounds on teaching, a proclivity that seems more closely aligned with vision than with hearing: "The closed classroom door can be very deceptive and illusory; it merely hides the inherent communal nature of teaching. The vocation of teaching is living a life in the real world."[5] Later he adds that "teaching is a way of living, not merely a way of making a living."[6] It is thus, for example, that a teacher's favorite stories about teaching are often situated outside of the defined and imposed bounds of the school or the classroom: in grocery stores, at home, during the summer, after school, with friends, among strangers.

Nevertheless, there is still something to be gained in exploring this issue, but we must first loosen the bounds on "bound." Mathematics, I believe, offers a means of doing this, for "bound" is a notion that has been borrowed and elaborated upon by mathematicians. As with any term that has been co-opted for the purposes of mathematics, it returns to us with a new richness.[7] In his wide-ranging exploration of issues surrounding artificial intelligence, prominent mathematician Roger Penrose distinguishes between a recursive set with a simple boundary ("so that one can imagine it being a direct matter to tell whether or not some given point belongs to the set"[8]) and a recursively enumerable but non-recursive set which has a complicated boundary—"where the set on one side of the boundary is supposed to look simpler than that on the other."[9] As Penrose elaborates, for such a non-recursive set, "there is no general algorithmic way of deciding whether or not an element (or 'point') belongs to the set."[10]

It is this sort of bound that enframes teaching and teachers. For those who fall outside the bound, the line of demarcation is a simple one. But for those standing inside—for teachers—it is complex, and the question of whether this act or that issue belongs to teaching is not always easily resolved. Indeed, whether or not the bulk of those activities that we hope fall into the category of "teaching" are actually educative can only be determined by someone normally perceived to be outside the bounds—by the learner.

Yet, there is a bound; some actions clearly belong to teaching, while others clearly do not. That they cannot always be specified—that no algorithm or definition can help us to decide where teaching begins and ends—does not mean that it lacks bounds.

Otto Bollnow develops a similar idea using the metaphor of atmosphere in discussing the sorts of places where teaching might happen. For him, the "pedagogical atmosphere" refers to "all those fundamental emotional conditions and sentient qualities that exist between the educator and the child and which form the basis for every pedagogical relationship."[11] (Regarding his use of the term "atmosphere," then, Bollnow's concern is with the preconditions of adult-child relationships that are necessary for the rearing of our children, and not with the "emotional and sentimental undertone" which is often associated when "atmosphere" is used to refer to relationships.)

Bollnow is not just interested in the virtues of the teacher, but with the virtues of the child, and his exploration is thus conducted from the perspectives of both educator and learner. For the teacher, Bollnow identifies and elaborates on the qualities and attitudes of confidence, (reciprocal) trust, love,[12] expectation, patience, hope, serenity, humor, and goodness. Rather than doing an injustice to his work by attempting a summary, I will let this list stand as it is, for Bollnow has identified those virtues which, I feel, are the markers that give shape and form to the place where teaching occurs. They are the proper bounds of teaching, following Heidegger's reconceptualization: "A boundary is not that at which something stops but, as the Greeks recognized, the boundary is that from which something *begins its essential unfolding*."[13] The qualities (boundaries) of the pedagogue as identified by Bollnow thus provide us not just with a sense of the form of teachers' relationships with children, but with an idea of the place from which they unfold.

A basis is thus established for approaching teaching with an orientation to listening. (Indeed, if we were to identify the qualities of a good listener, I suspect that we would generate a list similar to Bollnow's, above.) If we look to Wendy's listening—as opposed to the lunch bells and the classroom walls—for insight into the bounds of her teaching, a very different sense of where that teaching begins and ends emerges. Mathematics pedagogy comes to be understood as being about relating and relationships: between teacher and learner, between learner and knowledge, among learners.

bound *adj.* 2: intending to go ⟨homeward *bound*⟩: ORIENTED

Much of the difficulty we experience in trying to talk about the borders of teaching arises not from the fact that they are ill-defined, nor because the bounds of teaching might better be thought of as necessary qualities rather than limiting lines, but because the bounds of teaching are in constant motion. The place of the teacher is continuously being negotiated as those elements that frame teaching move (that is, as society evolves, as the learner learns, etc.) and the place where teaching happens can never therefore be held still.

Saying that teaching is oriented and that it is impossible to pin down the place where teaching happens is not the same as suggesting that teaching has a specific goal (i.e., in the progress-insistent modernist sense of the term). Teaching is intentional; it *takes* place. A more appropriate sense of where teaching is bound is captured by Max van Manen in his elaboration of the notion of pedagogy:

Pedagogy refers only to those types of actions and interactions intentionally (though not always deliberately or consciously) engaged in by an adult and a child, directed toward the child's positive being and becoming.[14]

The guiding principle of the pedagogue, then, extends beyond the reductive epistemological frame of the modern school. In this way, recalling an earlier citation from Levin, a pedagogical orientation has much in common with a listening orientation:

In listening to others, accepting them in their irreducible difference, we help them to listen to themselves, to heed the speech of their own body of experience, and to become, each one, the human being he or she most deeply wants to be.[15]

Of course, characterizing the educational intention in this way gives rise to several questions. Is the criterion that teaching contribute to the "child's positive being" an adequate basis to select one's teaching actions? How might we separate our own personal intentions from the pedagogic endeavor? How might we resolve the conflicts between our own pedagogic hopefulness and the child's intentions? The answers to such questions, I believe, are to be found by first understanding that pedagogic intentionality is in no way prescriptive. It cannot determine or serve as a measure for a particular action. Rather, the notion of pedagogy points more toward a way of standing in the world, and it is founded not on a desire for perfection, but on the knowledge that indecision, ambiguity, and tension are inevitable parts of living.

As such, in terms of Wendy's classroom, we must take care to attend both to deliberate and to accidental actions. The intentions of the mathematics teacher are not to be found only in the explicit instructional objectives or in the formulated lesson outlines. Rather, they are enacted in the complex weaving of chance and planned encounters. We must, therefore, attend to the relationships within the classroom setting to understand the bounds, the directedness, of the teaching. And, once again, Wendy's manner of listening, of situating herself in relationship to learners, becomes a focal point. In the first two lessons, for example, Wendy left little to chance; where the lesson was bound was predetermined by imposed guidelines and imported texts. In the third lesson, as happenstance begins to figure into the current of the action, a different sense of how Wendy is oriented to the learners and to the subject matter emerges. Her listening in that episode is directed toward educing, toward educating.

bound *adj.* **3:** under moral obligation ⟨honor *bound*⟩: COMMITTED

There are deliberate moral dimensions to Bollnow's and van Manen's explications of pedagogy; part of their project in writing is to redirect our attention to the human and relational elements of educating and away from the impersonal and distancing tendencies of modern schooling.

The point has already been made that our identities are affected by historical contingencies and are tied up with social relationships. If we pause to think about the classroom context, it is not difficult to produce a list of the sorts of personal relationships that are either indirectly affected by or directly mediated by the teacher. Most obviously, there is the teacher-child association (the locus of van Manen's "pedagogy"). But the teacher also helps to shape the learner's relationship to knowledge, to others, and to the collective. Conventional schooling, which seems to be founded on an aversion to the topics of morality and ethics, chooses to acknowledge its role in affecting only one of these relationships, the epistemological—and, even there, the system seems non-cognizant of the ontological status of one's knowledge.

Enactivist theorists make a profound contribution to this discussion, a contribution that is perhaps best articulated through their notion of "being and becoming"—on *identity* or *self*hood. Briefly, enactivist theorists join in their rejection traditional (Western) conceptions of the Self (understood in modern terms as a unified, coherent, singular, and insulated agent). Some, including Varela, Thompson, and Rosch, and Charles Taylor, suggest that it is our grasping after the objectified subject that underlies much—and perhaps most—of human suffering. In its place, they offer a constantly evolving self—one that brings with it not only a history of personal experience, but the accumulated cultural and biological histories of the species. "Self," so-conceived, is "a social linguistic construct, a nexus of meaning rather than an unchanging entity."[16]

These thinkers do not wish to dissolve or discard popular notions of self and identity. Their point is not so much that the modern conception of the Self is useless (or even destructive), but that it is misconceived. In their view, rather than existing as a pregiven transcendent object, the self is *enacted* and *embodied*. It exists and finds its form in bodily action and interaction. And so, enactivist theorists seek to reawaken our awareness of the active, negotiated, storied, and relational natures—that is, to give a dialogical rather than a monological account—of our selves. As Foucault explains:

> *[The] subject should not be entirely abandoned. It should be reconsidered, not to restore the theme of an originating subject, but to seize its functions, its intervention in discourse, and its systems of dependencies.*[17]

To illustrate this point, we might return to Gadamer's investigation of the role of a work of art. For him, art is art in the fact that it can become an experience that changes the experiencer. Gadamer uses the concept of "play" to describe this experience, stating that "play fulfills its purpose only if the player loses himself in the play."[18] There is a forgetting of the Self in play (and, correspondingly, in experiencing a work of art), and a subsequent returning to subjective awareness—but, upon return, the Self has been transformed. (The topic of play will be more thoroughly explored in the next chapter.)

If we are to regard the educator as a transformative intellectual, one who endeavors to open these places for play, then the ethical implications are clear: the teacher "shares in, but does not cross the boundaries of the other person's being."[19] Pedagogy—that acknowledgment of the moral status of the teacher-child relationship, or of any relationship, for that matter—is an area of scholarly inquiry that must be brought into our research in mathematics classrooms. Unfortunately, it is a notion that is notable in its absence from much of the research in mathematics education, where methodology is often substituted for care and technology tends to replace personal contact.

Such absence of pedagogical relationship certainly seemed to be the case in the first two teaching episodes. Wendy appeared to be bound to teaching objectives, bound to plans, bound to a fixed conception of the subject matter. These became barriers, obstacle illusions, militating against (and perhaps substituting for) her relationships with learners—and the evidence of this contention was revealed when the bell to end class pushed them aside. At that point, Wendy related in a different, pedagogical manner—in the manner, in fact, that she enacted throughout the third episode.

bound *adj.* 4: fastened by or as if by a band ⟨tightly *bound*⟩:RELATED

"The practical consideration for a teacher is that he or she must believe there is a pedagogic way of being with children that sets a teacher-child relationship apart from any other kind of adult-child connection."[20] It is a relationship *sui generis.*[21]

Bollnow, Spiecker, and van Manen have elaborated on the *pedagogical relationship*, and so extensive explication will not be attempted here. For the current purposes, a few additional statements will suffice to provide a flavor of this relationship:

In pedagogical situations the adult and the child do not just happen to be in the same spot; rather, they are together in a special way. They are together in an interactive unity that constitutes a relation, a pedagogical relation.[22]

The theme that I have used to structure this chapter is *place*, or, more specifically, how particular places come to be. An understanding of relationships is central to this discussion. Like humans, the identities of places are established relationally—that is, by the sorts of relationships that they invite, define, or facilitate, and which, in dynamic reciprocal action, continuously re-form their landscapes. A place is a locus, an ecology.

The pedagogical relationship is a place—one that is bounded by particular virtues and one that has as its reason for existence the education of the child. It is where teaching takes place, for within this relationship there is the possibility for setting aside one's agenda, one's desire to predetermine outcomes, one's drive to control. Within this relationship, one is able to attend to possibilities, and not merely to the actualities that are imposed by conventional curriculum-making and instructional practices.

The point here is that, as we seek to determine where teaching takes place, as we explore the *bounds* (in all its polysemous splendor) of teaching, we return to relationships—to the everydayness of life. The place where teaching happens is not found between bells or classroom walls, it is in the immediacy and the intimacy of the interactive unity of one person with another.

Teaching is a fabric of relationships. It is an identity. These ideas are implicit in the notion of *pedagogy*, and it is thus that an understanding of the special relationship between teachers and learners provides us an opportunity to heal the modernist separation of life and work; it challenges the belief that we can live differently and apart from the way we make our living. It allows us to act on Wendell Berry's warning: "If we do not live where we work, and when we work, we are wasting our lives, and our work too."[23] It is thus that, when I say that I am a teacher, I am not saying how I make my living, but how I live. I am announcing where my work—and therefore my life—take place.

Back to Listening

A colleague[24] recently conducted a series of interviews with several high school English students. The intended focus was a unit of study that had just been completed. However, even though he never intended it to be a central issue, the discussion inevitably turned to the teacher. Asked what it was that separated her from their other instructors, most students responded immediately that it had to do with the way she listened.

What is interesting here is not that this teacher might have been paying more attention to what these students had to say, but that these students independently—yet almost unanimously—selected the idea of *hermeneutic listening* to describe their relationship with her. The fact is that only a small part of her time was taken up in attending to their spoken words, so the listening that these students were pointing to was much more than the complement of speaking. I suspect that, had they the word to use, they would have described their relationship with this teacher as pedagogical. These students knew her concern was genuine, that she lived as a teacher, that there was a particular intimacy between her and them. In this case then, pedagogy and listening were synonymous.

It has been interesting over the course of this study, while working with Wendy and others, to note how such relationships tend to be described in the language of the auditory rather than the visual: we talk of tone, rhythm, harmony, resonance, attunement—*listening.* These terms speak not just to the interactive unity of the teacher and child, but to their harmonious situation within the world. In contrast, it is when pedagogical concern is wanting that we turn to the visual and speak of perspectives, views, supervision, surveillance—*watching.*

This contrast is an important one. A teaching founded on seeing is a teaching that stands apart from students; it positions itself at the edge of the classroom so that it can oversee all that happens. In this conception, the "good" teacher is the one with "eyes in the back of her head." A teaching founded on listening places itself in the midst of events as a full participant. Like the "good" supervisor, the listening teacher is aware of what is happening outside of his or her visual field . . . but not because he or she maintains a silent vigil. Rather, he or she is attuned to the rhythms of the classroom.

The last word in this quest to determine where teaching takes place, then, is about listening. Perhaps our frustration in locating this place—and the inability of conventional educational theory to define or manufacture it—is that we have been *looking* for it. There is much to be said for turning formal education on its ear and *listening* for it instead. As Levin explains:

Good listening draws out, educes, the child's readiness for autonomy; and succeeds because it is a means that is consistent with, in harmony with, its intended end. In the education of children, such consonance is absolutely essential. One can hear *its presence and absence.*[25]

Chapter 4

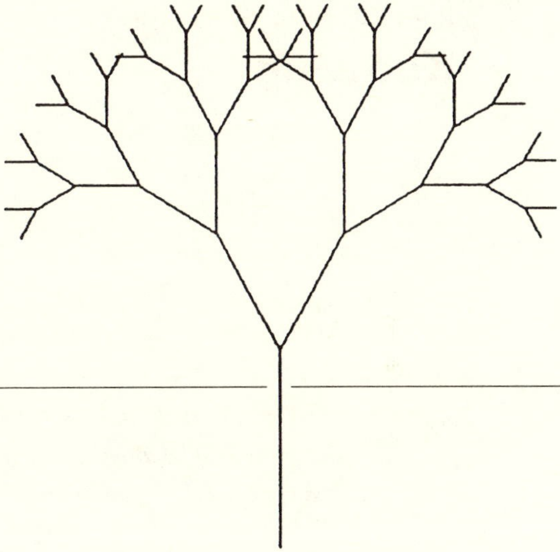

All Ears

Cognition

Mental activities . . . each draws its metaphors from a different bodily sense. . . . Thus, from the very outset, in formal philosophy, thinking has been thought of in terms of seeing. . . . *The predominance of sight is so deeply embedded in Greek speech, and therefore in our conceptual language, that we seldom find any consideration bestowed on it, as though it belonged to things too obvious to be noticed. . . . [But] if one considers how easy it is for sight, unlike the other senses, to shut out the outside world, and if one examines the notion of the blind bard, whose stories are being listened to, one may wonder why hearing did not develop into the guiding metaphor for thinking.*

—Hannah Arendt[1]

At its core, the process of thinking depends on our ability to tell a good lie and stick with it. Metaphors R Us. To think is to force one thing to "stand for" something that it is not, to substitute simple, tame, knowable, artificial concepts for some piece of the complex, wild, ultimately unknowable natural world. Much of the hard work of thinking has already been done for us by those anonymous ancestors who originated and shaped the earth's human languages. Language is surely one of our most useful tools of thought, giving conceptual prominence to certain things and processes, while relegating the unnamed and unnamable to conceptual oblivion.

—Nick Herbert[2]

Section A
Knowing

What is my *answer to the question of the nature of knowing? I surrender to the belief that my knowing is a small part of a wider integrated knowing that knits the entire biosphere or creation.*

—Gregory Bateson[3]

We are to a degree continuous across the intervening air with what moves with us in one commonality of vibration, because the sounding air has been galvanized by the source of sound into acting as a vibrant connective tissue.

—David Burrows[4]

How do people learn? What does it mean to *know* something? What sorts of experiences lead to changes in behavior, attitude, and conceptualization? These questions—or, more precisely, our answers to these questions—frame our actions as researchers, teachers, and learners.

Among mathematics education researchers, by far the most prominent discussions are focused on issues of knowledge—which are collected under the term "epistemology"—along with the implications for teaching of varying perspectives. The purpose of this chapter is to examine some of the historical and current models of cognition, moving toward an enactivist alternative that might be helpful in both challenging and complementing current "commonsense" accounts.

As was noted with the phenomena investigated in the preceding chapters, metaphor continues to play a powerful defining role in our perceptions of what it means to think, to know, and to act intelligently. The focal points of this first discussion, then, are the figures of speech we use to frame cognition.

Historical Movements

Historically, the perspectives on learning and knowing that have risen to prominence among educators have been diverse and (seemingly) disparate. Three schools of thought that have had significant impacts in the field of educational psychology are the currently disparaged but still visible *behaviorism*, the now pervasive *cognitivism*, and the persistent *humanism*. Briefly, *behaviorism* concerns itself primarily with the observables of cognition; notions such as thought and emotion are defined in terms of visible actions or responses. For *cognitivism*, the predominant (although not exclusive) orienting metaphor is "brain as computer" and, as such, this discourse system tends to be preoccupied with knowledge structures, information processing, and decision-making activities. *Humanism* refers to both a psychological and a philosophical orientation, and is centrally concerned with those characteristics that are thought to make us most human.

A quick review of the texts and professional journals in the field reveals that the *cognitivist* framework is by far the most prominent and broadly accepted by the public at large, educators, and educational theorists alike. However, this circumstance can hardly be taken to mean that there is widespread agreement among cognitivist theorists on the consequences of employing a computer metaphor for the thinking part of us. In particular, two very different perspectives, both of which can be traced to the emergence of Descartes' Rationalism and the consequent Empiricist movement, have found the "mind as machine" notion to be a powerful tool in helping to explicate their positions. These two branches of cognitivist thought I will refer to as Realism and Representationism.

Realist theories are those materialist epistemologies that favor facticity and by which knowledge is regarded as actual or objective bits of information. Whether discovered or created, these bits are treated as though they have a substantive existence: ideas are to be *grasped* and *held*; facts are *cold* and *hard*. Communication is a matter of passing these knowledge bits from one person to another, and the critical aspect of human interaction is thus the selection of the words that are to contain and carry the knowledge. "Thinking," correspondingly, is a matter of processing newly-inputted information by moving it about along neural networks and re-organizing it into new and increasingly complex patterns.

In educational circles, this commonsense orientation to cognition is popularly known by the monikers of "the acquisition model" and, more deprecatingly, "the banking metaphor." It is closely associated with a model of communication that has been described and critiqued by Michael Reddy[5]—the "conduit metaphor." In the conduit framework, communication is understood to occur as a speaker (sender) packages his thoughts into word-containers and sends them through some sort of conduit (e.g., the medium of spoken language) to a receiver who extracts the intended meaning. As will be developed in the next chapter, these are the orientations to knowledge, cognition, and communication that underlie the (predominant) transmission model of teaching.

Bruner notes that, in Western cultures at least, we seem inclined toward Realism: "At our most unguarded, we are all Naive Realists who believe not only that *we* know what is 'out there,' but also that it is out there for *others* as well"[6]—a mode of being that might well be necessary for us to function. (Having to continuously take into consideration the varying perceptions and interpretations of all present would likely be debilitating.) Nevertheless, critiques of the orientation have been extensive and condemning, focusing on its inappropriate formulations of both information and interaction. However, the underlying notion of "mind as computer" tends, for the most part, to slip past the criticisms. In fact, most opponents use the same metaphor, seemingly unaware of its recent and figurative origins.

Such is the case with many Representationist theorists, who focus not on facticity, but on the ideal of consciousness. Continuing with the project of Descartes, Representationism implies the construction of an internal (mental) model of the outer (physical) world, and so is founded on the premise that it is impossible to know the world in any direct way. Building on the Cartesian belief that knowing and thinking involve the development of increasingly accurate representations of the world, Representationists use metaphors of theory-making and knowledge construction. Such constructing was originally understood as a sort of map-making by the "mind's eye"—a conception that has been replaced with the advent of computer metaphors. Presently, the internal representations tend to be discussed in terms of digital encodings in neurological networks rather than sensorial reconstitutions of outer realities, but they are representations nonetheless. Not surprisingly, the resulting emphasis on internal structures, strategies, and schemas is heavily influenced by our understanding of electronic computers, as evidenced by references to processing, input and output, retrieval, and programming in their accounts of cognition. Cognitivism (i.e., "mind as computer") might be regarded as an updated model of cognition that utilizes a comparison to prevailing technologies (i.e., just as previous accounts of brain functioning drew on technologies of the time, such as hydraulics, telegraphs, and switchboards).

The common ground of Realist and Representationist models of cognition extends beyond their reliance on computer metaphors. Both, for example, are predicated on the notion that learning, while perhaps not smooth, is nevertheless linear and cumulative. And both are founded on the belief that the realm of the mental is utterly distinct from the realm of the physical. Knowing is a matter of the former; Truth is a matter of the latter. As discussed in Chapter 2, in so separating knowing agent from known world, a *third thing* called "knowledge" is posited as a means of bridging the gap created. Knowledge is thus assigned a somewhat ambiguous status—it is neither a full account of the objective world (and so, it is not "out there"), nor a possession of a single cognizing agent (and so, it is not "in here").

This then is the form assumed by a dualistic mode of thinking about thinking: on the objectivist side, cognition is a matter of employing the senses to extract knowledge bits from the universe. In this way, one comes to know the world as it is. On the subjectivist side, the learner does not come to know *the* world, but creates *a* world. Cognition is thus understood to be a process of autonomous "theory-making" by which the individual develops increasingly accurate (but inevitably unique) representations of the universe. In both cases, a foundational premise is that one's thought or knowledge is valid only insofar as it reflects or corresponds to the pregiven universe.

As noted in Chapters 1 and 2, these sorts of dualistic models can be aligned with the logic underlying the "Natural Selection" account of evolution. This *survival of the fittest* logic—by which it is argued that only the organisms that are best adapted to a pregiven, actively selecting environment will succeed—is analogous to the Realist/

Representationist tenet that superior ideas will supersede inferior ones as cognizing agents seek to understand the world. The better representations, like the fitter species, will always prevail. And, just as species (and collective knowledge) seem to steadily evolve toward an optimal fit with their environment, we think of our cognizing selves as progressing along a linear path toward a more accurate understanding of the universe—both individually and collectively.

As suggested earlier, this is the orientation toward knowing, knowledge, and Truth that undergirds most of our actions within schools. Evidence for this claim can be found in curriculum documents which carefully delineate what is to be internalized, in the shelves of textbooks designed to guide learners through an unambiguous journey of learning, and in a barrage of diagnostic and achievement tests that promise objective assessments. The "real world" (of, for instance, mathematics) is always defined in opposition to—and given primacy over—the learner's world, which is inevitably cast as incomplete and deficient.

"Knowing agent versus known world" is not the only dichotomy associated with this model of cognition. All of the previously noted dyads are enacted in this formulation in some way: self is made distinct from other, fact from fiction, right from wrong, teacher from student . . . all with the same 1–0 binary logic upon which computers are constructed. Moreover, in making such tidy distinctions, and by equating the brain with the computer, knowledge is reduced to data or information that not only has a material existence which is independent of knowing agents but, significantly, comes to be regarded as personally and socially inert. It is the knower, not the separated and autonomous knowledge, that is subject to corruption.

A Step toward a Middle Way: Constructivism

There has been a rising tide of criticism in recent years directed against the tendency to frame phenomena in such cut-and-dry terms. Coupled with a growing awareness that we don't seem to be converging onto some coherent, universal theory of existence, the cognitivist model and the Representationist paradigm have been largely rejected by educational theorists. In the wake of this rejection, constructivism has emerged as a possible successor to Representationist accounts of cognition.

Ernst von Glasersfeld[7] tells us that the cognitivist's link between knowledge and reality is one of the distinguishing characteristics of both traditional views of epistemology and conventional orientations toward cognitive psychology. Founding his own work on the theories of Vico and Piaget, von Glasersfeld critiques this taken-for-granted relationship which he describes as "always seen as a more or less picturelike (iconic) correspondence or match."[8] Such matches are the foundation of conventional notions of *truth* (i.e., representations that accurately reflect the way things really are). It is at this point—that is, the quest for such truths—that the epistemological orientation of constructivism[9] departs from traditional perspectives.

Briefly, constructivist *knowing* (a term that is used in contrast to "knowledge," in part to emphasize the dynamic nature of one's conceptualizations) is recast as "a search for fitting ways of behaving and thinking" rather than the conventional "search for an iconic representation of ontological reality"[10] (i.e., facts[11] or truths). It makes little sense, it is argued, to speak of *representations* of a reality that, as even Descartes acknowledged, is unknowable and inherently inaccessible. Rather, following Vico, constructivists consider knowledge to be a human construction that is to be evaluated according to its fit with the world of human experience. "Representation" is thus redefined by constructivists as "not the mental representation discussed in cognitive science . . . but, rather, the process of transforming the contents of consciousness into a public forum so that they can be stabilized, inspected, edited, and shared by others."[12] It is thus that the criterion of *truth* (in the modern sense of matching with an objective reality) is abandoned in favor of a requirement of *viability*.

The meanings of *fit* and *viability* here are the same as those used by those evolutionary theorists working from a "Natural Drift" perspective (as presented in Chapters 1 and 2), and it is at this point that we note Piaget's influence. In biological terms, the criterion for an organism's survival is its fitness—that is, the environment inexorably eradicates whatever does not fit the constraints it imposes. The logic here is not *prescriptive* (whereby some external and monological agency predetermines the qualities necessary for survival), but *proscriptive* (whereby an entity remains viable so long as it is ecologically sound). At best, then, the environment is responsible for extinction, not for existence.

Put differently, in neo-Darwinian theories of evolution, there is no causal link between an organism's survival and the world, since the theories are not based on the idea of cause-and-effect but on the principle of constraints. As this notion is applied to discussions of cognition, we arrive at a very pragmatic orientation to knowing: the sole criterion for the existence of a conceptualization is that it be feasible within a given setting. It must "work," in that it must provide a basis for appropriate (in the sense of non-self-annihilating) action. (This quality also serves as the pragmatist measure of truth.)

The emphasis on action is critical here, because, unlike the epistemological orientations it aims to supplant, constructivism does not draw a rigid distinction between mental and physical "objects." As Piaget puts it:

> *[T]he empiricist tradition . . . regards knowledge as a kind of copy of reality and intelligence as deriving from perception alone. . . . As if there were nothing more in mental life than sensation and reason—forgetting action!*[13]

Body and mind cannot be considered as distinct. In the constructivist conception, all knowing is founded on bodily action or sensation; conversely, the evidence of one's body of knowledge is found in one's behavior. It is thus that we arrive at the two main principles of constructivism, as identified by von Glasersfeld:

> *(a) knowledge is not passively received but actively built up by the cognizing subject;*
> *(b) the function of cognition is adaptive and serves the organization of the experiential world, not the discovery of ontological reality.*[14]

For the constructivist, then, cognition is not about representing a real world, but about organizing (and constantly reorganizing) one's own subjective world of experience. In this frame, cognition (unlike the associated process of evolution) is seen to occur in fits and starts, involving the simultaneous revision, reorganization, and reinterpretation of past, present, and projected actions and understandings. It is thus that both constructivism and evolution replace the defining imagery of Representationist accounts of cognition—that of causal relations and linear equations—with the intricate and fluid imagery of nonlinear dynamics.

Again, it must be emphasized that these principles mark a radical departure from traditional notions of knowledge, truth, objectivity, and reality. As von Glasersfeld puts it, "instead of an inaccessible realm beyond perception and cognition, it now becomes the experiential world we actually live in."[15] It is thus that, as conventional understandings of knowledge and truth are set aside, constructivism must posit itself as merely a hypothesis, not an absolute truth—a situation that, from a modern perspective, seems paradoxical.

With the constraining demands of a match with the real world erased, constructivism is often misinterpreted as suggesting that the cognizing agent's conceptualizations emerge freely and in completely arbitrary ways—and, thus, that the theory tends toward solipsism. In fact, constructivists argue quite the contrary: that, according to the requirement of fit-ness, the individual's interpretations of and abstractions from experience are shaped by the learning context and, in particular, by the social milieu. The needs and opportunities for collaboration and communication thus demand that the person's "knowing" fall within the bounds of the social setting's construction of normalcy. The role of the environment, albeit proscriptive rather than prescriptive, thus remains central to the construction of one's understandings.

In spite of its movement away from many of the modernist assumptions that frame commonsense orientations to cognition, constructivism appears to share some of the shortcomings of the more traditional theories it has aimed to supplant. In particular, in attempting to position itself as "merely" an epistemology (in contrast to a philosophy, which also addresses matters of ontology), constructivism has situated itself in that modernist niche that attempts to disregard issues of moral and ethical import. Existence and established knowledge, in this frame, are unproblematic givens.

This criticism is not a minor one for, as has been illustrated by the pervasive acceptance of constructivism within the field of mathematics education (which also attempts to locate itself in the same neutral corner), it has allowed researchers to reorient themselves theoretically without compelling them to more critically examine the nature of their task. The modernist ideal of "How can we do this better?" has thus continued to eclipse the perhaps more urgent "Why are we doing this?" (It is interesting to note, in retrospect, how these two questions framed my own schooling experience. The former guided my actions as a teacher; the latter has figured prominently in my learning.)

A second point of critique is constructivism's inability to account for cultural knowledge. Simply put, constructivism has failed to place things into the larger social-historical context. In denying the possibility that knowledge exists "out there," and in failing to address the issue of human interactive capacities, constructivists are compelled to locate all knowledge within individual knowers. The critique of the theory's tendency toward solipsism, although perhaps extreme, is thus in many ways justified. Constructivism is a theory of how the individual comes to know—and "individuals," for the most part, are understood in modern isolating and insulating terms.[16] As such, a space has been opened for other, contrasting accounts of cognition.

Another Step toward a Middle Way: Social Constructionism

The recent movement in mathematics education away from objectivist and toward subjectivist theories of learning (e.g., from "banking"-related to "constructing"-based metaphors) has been, in effect, a movement from the privileging of an external authority (i.e., pre-given or pre-established fact) to the privileging of an internal one (i.e., the learner's emerging conceptions).

The difficulty here is not the location of the authority but that, in both cases, the authorities are monological. In the more traditional conceptions of education, the monologic authority is the assumed-to-be knowable *real* world. The teacher, the program of studies, and the textbook, as depositories of knowledge of this world, are thus granted primary authority in the classroom. In more child-centered perspectives, the monologic authority is found in the learner's own subjective conceptions—and in this way, a learner's actions can never be considered "wrong" (because they can always be justified in the world that the individual has constructed). However, as Taylor[17] demonstrates, there can be no such single authority. Rather, issues such as "what we know" and "who we are" are dialogical; they are negotiated through our interactions with one another within the context of our culture. That culture, in turn, is negotiated within the wider contexts of history, civilization, and environment.

And so, while constructivism has risen to the position of the dominant discourse among theorists and researchers in the field of mathematics education, it is hardly unchallenged in this status. In particular, an account of cognition that finds its roots in the theories of Vygotsky rather than those of Piaget has risen to prominence: *social constructionism.*

The differences between the two epistemological frameworks is most clearly announced in the modifier, "social." For the social constructionist, cultural situation and social mediation are the critical elements in knowledge construction. As Vygotsky put it, "every function in the child's cultural development appears twice: first, on the social level, and later, on the individual level; first between people (interpsychological), and then *inside* the child (intrapsychological)."[18] A defining assumption of social constructionism is thus that "human beings are not self-contained, self-sufficient subjects contingently and externally related to one another, but beings who are formed, from the very beginning, in and through their social interactions."[19] Social constructionism is thus a call for dialogical understandings of knowing and learning, a recognition of the ways in which knowers and knowledge are situated historically, culturally, and politically. The main point of critique, then, of a constructivist epistemology is its rather narrow focus on the cognizing agent—that is, on the privileging of subjective rather than collective knowledge.

This point of departure is not so surprising when Piaget and Vygotsky are considered in their historical contexts. Piaget, a biologist, focused on individual organisms and founded his theories of cognition on evolutionary and other life-science metaphors; Vygotsky, living in a newly founded communist state, developed his ideas around metaphors of co-laboring, collective phenomena, and Marxist analysis.[20] (Not unexpectedly, social constructionism has been picked up by those in mathematics education who are working from more critical perspectives, such as Valerie Walkerdine and Jean Lave.[21] These and other theorists and researchers tend to be critical of constructivism for its lack of emphasis on the importance of language and social factors in learning—although, to be fair, constructivists have acknowledged the roles of such elements in learning, albeit considered only from the subject's perspective.)

It thus appears that the essential difference between constructivism and social constructionism, arising from their contrasting root metaphors, has to do with the priority of events in learning. Constructivists suggest that the subjective construction of knowledge occurs before social mediation, whereas, social constructionists suggest that social mediation occurs before the subject's construction of knowledge. Of course, neither framework regards the events in such simplistic chronological terms; rather, both recognize that individual and collective evolution are inextricably intertwining processes. Paul Cobb sums it up as follows:

> *[W]hereas a sociocultural theorist [i.e., a social constructionist] might see a student appropriating the teacher's contributions, a constructivist would see a student adapting to the actions of others in the course of ongoing negotiations. In making this differing interpretation, sociocultural theorists would tend to invoke sociohistorical metaphors such as* appropriation, *whereas constructivists would typically employ interactionist metaphors such as* accommodation *and* mutual adaptation. *Further, whereas sociocultural theorists typically stress the homogeneity of members of established communities and eschew analyses of qualitative differences in individual thinking, constructivists tend to stress homogeneity and to eschew analyses that single out pregiven social and cultural practices. From one perspective, the focus is on the social and cultural basis of personal experience. From the other perspective, it is on the constitution of social and cultural processes by actively interpreting individuals.*[22]

A closer look, then, suggests that it is not so much that these perspectives are incompatible as that they are focused on seemingly disparate phenomena. Constructivism has its lens fixed on the individual's learning; social constructionism is concerned with the context in which it occurs—and, in terms of cognition, the influence of these phenomena seem to flow in opposite directions. Can they be reconciled?

A Middle Way: Enactivism

Social constructionism is more attentive to issues of collective knowledge—aware that individual understandings of the world are shaped and motivated by political and other social factors and willing to grant the possibility that individual cognition is not located "inside" a mind but distributed across the objects and locations of one's world. But the phenomenon of knowledge remains a problem for the social constructionist. As with the Representationist, knowledge seems to be cast as some sort of *third thing*—in this case, something more fluid and negotiated, but still serving to bridge the gap between individual and collective. And so, while social constructionism makes the important contribution of positing a dialogical relationship between individual and collective knowledge, the framework appears to be premised on conceptions of cognizing agents as subject to the shaping pressures of social forces, but nevertheless isolated and independent from one another. Cognition remains a solitary, subjective phenomenon, and culturally sanctioned knowledge continues to be framed in terms that exclude particular agents (although, importantly, such knowledge is no longer cast in neutral and strictly objective terms).

In other words, both constructivism's monologic authority of the individual and social constructionism's dialogic authority are founded on a modernist separation of self from other. Cognizing agents are regarded as separated—not only from the world, but from one another. While interaction among agents is deemed possible, it is reduced to coordinated mechanical action whereby we can never transcend our subjectivities. The best we can hope for is that the persons with whom we interact will have compatible understandings to our own; ultimately, conceptions can never be shared. In this way, these epistemologies retain an idea that was announced by Descartes—the primacy of the subject—and, in retaining this ideal, they have fixed and maintained not just separations of self from not-self, but of (mental) thought from (physical) action.

The difficulty here amounts to an inability to rid ourselves of the notion that knowledge has some sort of physical, material existence—something solid, grasp-able, manipulable. So long as we are wedded to that idea, we are compelled to assign it a location. As discussed more extensively in Chapter 2, knowledge comes to be cast in terms of existing "in here" or "out there." In Realist and Representationist accounts of cognition, true knowledge is thought to lie outside of the cognizing agent who must somehow take it in. For constructivists, knowledge is internal and a critical part of cognition is externalizing (i.e., vocalizing) it. For the social constructionist, knowledge is a hot potato that is neither inside nor outside, but tossed between agent and social context. But what happens if we take seriously the notion that, as Gregory Bateson[23] puts it, there is no such *thing* as information? Or, placed on the level of the individual cognizing agent, what if we complement the pervasive knowledge-as-object metaphor with something more toward knowledge-as-action? Or, to frame it in still different terms, what if we were to replace the s*elf*-evident axiom that cognition is located *within* cognitive agents?

This is the starting place of an enactivist account of cognition: to challenge the commonsense divisions that tend to be drawn between one individual and another and between our selves and the world. Just as the development of alternatives to the parallel postulate by mathematicians gave rise to completely different understandings of the nature of mathematics, a rendering problematic of these axioms of theories of cognition opens the door to radically different models of thought and action. As elaborated in Chapter 2 in the discussion of mathematics, enactivists (along with complexity theorists) conflate knowledge and action—both on collective and individual levels—and, in so doing, point to the co-emergence of individual knowing and collective knowledge and to the self-similarity of their underlying processes.

As such, one might describe enactivist theory as being concerned more broadly with the collaborative construction of a subjective world. The concern is focused on the ecological interface of mind and society rather than on a solitary mind seeking to make sense of an ontological given. In response to the previously announced shortcoming of constructivism, then, enactivist theorists offer a perspective on cognition that involves both becoming part of an ongoing existing world *and* the shaping of a new one. Acknowledging the role of the individual in affecting this world's form, as discussed earlier, effectively pushes enactivist thought into the realm of the moral. And by addressing the issue of how the world has come to be as it is, enactivist thought places itself in the space of ontology.

It is also this premise of co-emergence or deep interdependence that enables enactivist theorists to sidestep the solipsistic quagmires that seem to tug at constructivists, in spite of their best and most persistent efforts. In positing the autonomous knower—or, more precisely, the goal of the autonomous knower—constructivists create for themselves the problem of accounting for the interactive capacities of ostensibly independent beings. How is it that we can communicate so freely and effectively if we are isolated from one another? Enactivists, in contrast, take mutual affect and historical effect as fundamental tenets.[24] (It is thus that these theorists tend to align themselves more closely with Buddhist and Taoist thought than with the Judeo-Christian and Aristotelian traditions.)

The point can be illustrated by reference to a particular implication of constructivism. As stated by von Glasersfeld, the individual's "experiential world is constituted by the knower's own ways and means of perceiving and conceiving, and in this elementary sense *it is always and irrevocably subjective.*"[25] In this formulation, the possibilities for "joint action" or "intersubjectivity," as elaborated upon by Merleau-Ponty, Gadamer, Maturana and Varela, and others, are effectively discounted. The bounds of the individual, as constructed by constructivists, are impassable. For enactivists, such bounds—while "real" in the sense that they have become for us an experiential reality—are illusory. (With regard to schooling, as will be noted in the next chapter, the consequence of the constructivist notions of subjectivity and intersubjectivity place severe constraints on discussions of what teaching might be.)

This most fundamental distinction between enactivist and constructivist theorists can be illustrated with reference to the notion of "self." Piaget insightfully departed from conventional wisdom by suggesting that one's identity was constantly undergoing transformation and so the process of change was something that was continuously happening to the self. Enactivist theorists take this one step further: the transformational process is not something that *happens to* the self, it *is* the self. Gallagher phrases this idea in terms of narration: "The 'self' . . . is not a totalized self-identical essence, but a 'self-narrative,' a self-process which never stops being a process in play."[26] "Play" (which is the topic of the third section of this chapter) is used here polysemously and is intended to call to mind a movement which, in Gadamer's words, "has no goal that brings it to an end; rather it renews itself in constant repetition."[27] Within play, there is the possibility for a setting aside of subjective awareness and for coupled action, as illustrated with the examples of the performance of a piece of music, the conversation, the staged production, and the game—each of which we commonly describe in terms of play. An important further note is that, in each case, the phenomenon exists only in the playing. So it is with the (enacted) self, a self-in-process, which might be understood as merely another level of (inter-)play.

The self, then, is defined as a network of relationships, and so, as histories, contexts, and participants vary, identities (or, in Maturana and Varela's terms, structures) change. (This idea is closely aligned with the postmodernist contention that we do not "don different masks"—that is, behave differently—as we move from one setting to another. Rather, different selves are enacted: we change.) Our identities do, however, retain an integrity as we move from one setting to the next, held together by particular habits, language (patterns of acting), stories (narratives), and other knowings.

Just as the self is complexified in this formulation, so is cognition. Played out in the complex choreography of existence, knowing cannot be separated from action, nor can it be extricated from interaction. Cognition/knowledge—the parallel, co-implicated, co-emergent process—is what knits us together, and it is where both individual and collective identities (selves) come to form.

In sum, then, cognition does not occur in minds and brains, but in the possibility for (shared) action. Enactivism thus embraces the insights of constructivism, but does not privilege the individual as the truth-determining authority. Similarly, enactivists are able to appreciate the social constructionist's concern for the transcendent (i.e., beyond the individual) nature of knowledge, but do not frame collective knowledge in opposition to subjective knowing. Truth and collective knowledge, for the enactivist, exist and consist in the possibility for joint or shared action—and that, necessarily, is larger than the solitary cognizing agent. Enactivism thus offers a way of bringing these discourses into conversation; for example, constructivism's subject and social constructionism's collective are regarded as self-similar forms. Contrary to the Western tradition of consciousness, whereby the subject is seen as apart and distinct from the world, enactivism understands the individual to be part of—that is, embedded in and a subsystem to—a series of increasingly complex systems with integrities of their own, including classroom groupings, schools, communities, cultures, humanity, and the biosphere. The notion of "embodied knowledge" extends to bodies much larger than our own.

From the Formulated to the Unformulated

Returning to the issue of knowledge and knowing, Charles Taylor[28] provides us with a useful distinction between two orientations to human action: the *formulated* and the *unformulated.* Traditional epistemologies have focused exclusively on the former—on established, validated truths, or on the quest for such truths. This emphasis springs, at least in part, from the rigid division between cognizing agent and world, which requires some sort of intermediary step (in this case, formulated representations) to bridge the gap.

With enactivism, the emphasis shifts to the unformulated whereby, in Maturana and Varela's terms, every act is an act of cognition: "to live is to know (living is effective action in existence as a living being)."[29] This notion is founded on the belief that we are not apart from, but "coupled" to our situation or context. As such, we are constantly and inevitably enacting our knowledge; we are continuously knowing, as determined by our structures and our situations. However, much of this knowing is not, and may never have been, formulated in explicit terms. Much of what we do and know, in other words, is unformulated: we just do it; we just know it. It is thus that, as mentioned earlier, the measure of one's knowledge shifts to effective action in a specific context—and these actions may or may not be (but likely are not) subject to conscious awareness. Knowing is doing, and all doing arises from a rich and ongoing history of structural coupling with a complex and active environment.

It is important to emphasize here that "formulated-unformulated" is not presented as a *this-or-that* sort of dichotomy. These are, rather, complements of one another and thus cannot be separated. Nor would we want to do so: our formulations continually emerge from our unformulated actions, even while they fade into such action in a process that might appropriately be compared to the gradual literalization of a metaphor.

As we move to a more specific discussion of the schooling context, the implications become profound, for we can no longer focus our educational efforts on the formulated pregivens of programs of study or institutional structures. Rather, our attention inevitably must move toward emergent understandings and toward offering occasions for *play*.

It is interesting to note, as I end this section on the varied perspectives on knowledge, that the alternative offered by enactivist theorists bears many of the same characteristics and draws many of the same conclusions as behaviorist and humanist schools of psychology—orientations that have been completely overshadowed by cognitivism.

Section B
Understanding and Meaning

Thinking begins only when we have come to know that reason, glorified for centuries, is the most stiff-necked adversary of thought.

—Martin Heidegger[1]

Logic is goal-orientated and passes judgment. Analogy ponders and establishes relationships. The logician sees. The ana-*logician listens.*

—Joachim-Ernst Berendt[2]

Course:	Math 10, Section 2C - Mr. Wallace
Time/Place:	Block 3, Friday, May 19; Room 214
Lesson Topic:	Factoring Polynomials
Activity:	Seatwork (textbook exercises)

Mr. Wallace [passing by a student's desk and deliberately moving into her visual field]: What are you doing, Loren?

Loren [casually]: Thinking.

Mr. Wallace [in a reprimanding tone]: What are you supposed to be doing?

Loren: Working. [She leans forward, lowering her gaze onto the textbook and reaching for her pencil.]

I must confess that when I witnessed this brief exchange, I found myself quite appalled. How could it be that Loren's response of "Thinking" was unacceptable in this context . . . and that "Working" was appropriate?

With a little thought, however, I realized that it was unlikely that Loren's "thinking" had much to do with focused concentration.

Rather, it was more toward "daydreaming," and that meaning was well understood by student and teacher alike.

The meanings and understandings here, then, did not exist in the words spoken, but in the participants' joint action. And so, the error of my initial interpretation was to assign definitive senses to their verbal utterances—that is, I failed to recognize that the meaning was not in any particular object or action, but in the constellation of events that made up the classroom setting. As an external observer, I saw what I thought to be a rupture in communication. There was none, however. The exchange was smooth and unambiguous for both Loren and Mr. Wallace.

That is to say, the understandings and meanings in this episode were shared—an assertion that pushes these phenomena outside of individual minds and into the space of collective action.

This, then, is my starting point as I seek to move the preceding discussion of knowing and knowledge toward the immediate concerns of the mathematics teacher—namely, how we might conceive of "understanding" and "meaning" in ways that will help us to avoid the conventional tendency of locating them in the heads of ostensibly autonomous agents. My particular intention here is to investigate the possibilities for a physically engaged, embodied sense of cognition—as it pertains to mathematics teaching—thus setting the stage for the final section of this chapter.

"Subjective Mental States"

The volume of literature that has been generated on the topics of understanding and meaning within the field of mathematics education is quite remarkable, and it is certainly well beyond both my current project and my personal capacity to summarize or to thematize what has been written. Nevertheless, in part because of the extent of this literature, it is necessary to discuss the topics, however briefly.

But the main reason I focus on understanding and meaning in this section is because of the currently-pervasive admonitions from mathematics education researchers, mathematics teachers' organizations, departments of education, and other stake-holder groups to "teach for understanding" and to "ensure the meaningfulness of the concepts"—all articulated as though the meanings of such statements are self-evident, as though teachers' understandings will be unproblematic. Given the extent of the literature, and the diversity of opinion expressed in that literature, such assumptions might be seen as somewhat worrisome. And, considering that I would have likely characterized most of my actions as a mathematics teacher as having been directed toward promoting meaningfulness and understanding (and, in retrospect, they were not), it seems reasonable to suggest that there is a need to be explicit about these issues.

One of the purposes of this section is thus to touch on popular senses of understanding and meaning through an exploration of both the common ground and the points of divergence implied by the notions. The task is somewhat complicated, however, by the current uses of these words among mathematics educators. Overwhelmingly, understanding and meaning are regarded as private and autonomous phenomena. Indeed, with the conventional emphasis on individual sense-making, it is not unusual to see the adjectives "personal" and "subjective" used as modifiers of the terms. And, for the most part, even when not explicitly modified, a sense of subjectivity is implied. The most popular reasons given for the conventional emphases on group work and class discussion, for example, are quite revealing. Such activities are regarded as means of fostering or promoting (subjective) understanding and meaning.

Such senses are challenged by an enactivist interpretive frame. For the enactivist, the space of collective action is not merely a device in promoting individual sense-making; it is a *location* for (shared) meaning and understanding.

Further, as touched on in the preceding section, enactivism also challenges a two-pronged assumption of the current discourse: that understandings and meanings are mental states. For the enactivist, these phenomena are neither "mental" (again, the distinction between thought and action is problematized) nor "states." On this latter point, our commonsense *static* orientations to understanding and meaning undergird such activities as the *stating* of curriculum *objec*tives and formal testing (of learners' mental *states*, as determined by their capacities to re-*state* formal learning *objec*tives). These orientations also contribute to the perspectives on education in which listening skill is regarded as a necessary capacity of the learner and not of the teacher—for if understanding and meaning are to be measured through re-presentation of one's sense of preformulated terms, all that is needed to assess such phenomena is an appropriately constructed template.

The difficulty here is, of course, not the act of stating or fixing—which, I suspect, is a necessary activity if we are going to make sense of the otherwise quivering sea of possibilities in which we are immersed. Rather, the problems seem to be our reluctance to un-fix what has been stated, our failure to ask about was has been left unstated or pushed into the background, and our inattentiveness to the personal and social consequences of stating our selves.

Understanding *versus* Meaning

Within mathematics education, understanding and meaning tend to be used somewhat interchangeably. Given the similarity of interpretation of such queries as, "What is your understanding of this?" and "What meaning do you attach to this?" it is clear that there is considerable gray area between them. My intention here, then, is not to draw any sort of clear distinction, but to attempt to outline some of the subtle—but significant—differences between the two notions.

Such differences are more evident, I believe, in their non-mathematics education uses. An *understanding person*, for example, is one who is sympathetic, tuned in, caring; a *friendly understanding* is a mutual (and often unannounced) agreement or promise; the phrase "*on the understanding that . . .* " suggests a sense of contingency, of inevitable uncertainty. In each of these instances, "understanding" invokes senses of social interaction, negotiation, fluidity, engagement, conversation.

A similar examination of the uses of "meaning" points to a somewhat different sense. A *meaning look* is one that is intended to broadcast some deliberate message; a *word's meaning* is a clarification, a statement in other terms, with the ultimate authority assigned to an external source such as a dictionary; a *deeper meaning* involves moving toward a more truthful sense of an event. In each of these cases, there are senses of intention, of directedness, of pointing, of referring *to something* in particular (whereas "understanding," as suggested in the above expressions, does not necessarily require or imply such a referent). There also seem to be concerns for clarity and formulation; desires for unambiguous definition and careful articulation.

To frame the two words in terms of ideas already presented, then, understanding seems more closely aligned with the interpersonal realm of ever-evolving conversation (which I have associated more closely with auditory sensory modalities), and meaning seems more closely linked to the objectifying realm of definition-seeking discussions (which I have associated with vision). Indeed, as I engage in this writing project, I am attentive to this distinction. Lacking the opportunity to negotiate understandings with readers, I am obligated to attend carefully to the meaning of the text.

Both meanings and understandings, then, are interpersonal phenomena and of principal relevance in the context of social interactions. Understandings, however, seem to be more immediate, more fluid, more negotiable. Meanings, while still dynamic and still subject to bargaining processes, are more authoritative, as the term connotes stronger senses of unilateral fixing, of definitiveness, of stating. It is thus that, in terms of a mathematical idea (outside of a teaching context), we are more concerned with meanings (on a broader, socially sanctioned level) than with understandings (other than our own).

But the gray area between the two terms is also important. The distinctions I have drawn between understanding and meaning are insignificant beside their common ground, which is the space of interpretation. Our concerns for understanding and meaning are shared by those who study interpretation. They are, in fact, the focal point of hermeneutic inquiry.

Understanding Understanding

Von Glasersfeld has offered us a means of moving beyond conventional state-ic conceptions of understanding by providing a constructivist definition of the term: understanding is a continuing process of organizing one's knowledge structures.[3] So understood, understanding is dynamic and necessarily caught up in a web of meanings (which, to the teacher's perspective, may or may not be appropriate).

This redefinition of understanding, however, offers only a first step in rethinking the notion, for at least two elements of more traditional interpretations remain unchallenged. First, the subjective constraints on understanding continue to prevail; second, a focus on the formulated aspects of one's knowing is retained.[4] Both of these shortfalls are overcome by enactivist theorists in the suggestion that cognition might more productively be understood in terms of adequate functioning in an ongoing interactive world. First, as personal identities are reinterpreted to be emergent, relational processes rather than self-creations, understanding is placed in the realm of interaction rather than subjective interpretation. The possibility is thus opened for shared, rather than merely subjective, understandings. Second, those understandings that are enacted in our moment-to-moment, setting-to-setting movement are acknowledged.

Constructivists, in critiquing the conventional state-ic orientation toward understanding, have argued that understandings are founded on a history of experience that is subject to continual reinterpretation. Since each person's background is different, each subject's understanding of a given phenomenon, word, or mathematical concept is necessarily unique. For the constructivist, then, when we speak of personal knowledge, we must speak in terms of compatible rather than shared understandings.

But from an enactivist perspective—whereby "understanding" is discussed in terms of effective action rather than conceptual structure, and whereby words and concepts are interpreted as patterns of acting—shared understandings are quite possible.[5] Our social natures—that is, our capacity to function harmoniously—is evidence of such phenomena in action. Understandings are thus not merely dynamic, they are relationally, contextually, and temporally specific. As one moves away from a particular situation, one's understandings, as revealed in one's actions, may change dramatically. And so, while understandings might be shared during moments of interactive unity, they inevitably diverge as the participants come back to their selves.

The critical departure from constructivism here is not the semantic move from compatibility to sharing, but the more foundational shift from formulated (the state-able) to unformulated (the enacted). By way of practical example, a learner's understanding of the commutativity of addition might just as well be revealed in a setting where he or she is manipulating a set of wooden blocks as in a situation where he or she is encouraged to represent interpretations by vocalizing thinking. The essential point here is that both the physical manipulation and the vocalization are critical elements to cognition. As Vygotsky phrased it,

Children solve practical tasks with the help of their speech, as well as with their eyes and hands. This unity of perception, speech and action, which ultimately produces internalization of the visual field, constitutes the central subject matter for any analysis of uniquely human forms of behavior.[6]

Or, to paraphrase Maturana and Varela, every act is an act of cognition.

Such enacted understandings are bodily, and, if Mark Johnson's[7] thesis that our linguistic capacities are founded on metaphorical extensions of bodily experience can be trusted, these understandings serve as a sort of repository for the knowledge that underpins more formulated conceptions. (The difficulty here, however, is that, with the current emphasis on formulated knowledge in mathematics education, many concepts tend to be covered without regard for the experiences that might support them.) They are a part of our acting in the world—an acting that "understands" the difference between a single or a pair of raised fingers before it can count, an acting that "understands" that a sequence of two perpendicular cuts produces four pieces before it realizes the process is multiplicative. These are understandings that are aspects of the body's doing, and are thus conditioned by that which is encountered in moving through the world. The bulk of our understandings fall into this category, with only a small portion ever coming to formulation. In this sense, we simply have no (formal) understanding of the extent of our (enacted) understanding. The role that the body plays in this formulation is not unlike the role played by Freud's "unconscious,"[8] unaware of itself as it moves through the world.

Our teaching of mathematics is founded, at least in part, on the premise that formulated understandings are in some way better than those which remain unformulated. This is not a difficult point to argue; one need only call attention to the tremendous organizing and predictive "powers" of certain concepts. However, it is a premise that becomes troublesome when the statable is privileged over—

or considered in ignorance of—the enacted. Rather than focusing strictly on the promotion of abstracted (and therefore formulated) understandings, it might be more appropriate if mathematics educators were to also look at the interplay of formulated and unformulated understandings. How do they affect—that is, support, negate, or shape—one another?

Important inroads into this question have been made by a number of theorists and researchers in mathematics education. Worthy of note are those constructivists[9] who contend that the learner's actions, and not socially-sanctioned preestablished truths, are the most important source of one's mathematical understandings. Regarding the interplay of these informal actions and formal conceptualizations, Thomas Kieren and Susan Pirie[10] have developed a model of mathematical understanding that serves to bring out the complex back-and-forth movement between immediate and interpreted experience. Their model, which they illustrate with a series of concurrent circles (see Figure 4.1), is intended to portray the *non-linear* movement from one's current knowledge (in their terms, "Primitive Knowings") through to more formalized understandings. The various levels of mathematizing behavior represented in the different circles are arranged in order of increasing abstraction. They are not intended to represent a series of incremental steps one must take on the path to formal understanding, but the range of possible ways of acting mathematically. As such, one might skip several layers in a flash of insight, or one might be compelled to "fold back" to account for an unexpected result.

The Kieren-Pirie model of mathematical understanding is not intended to serve as a basis of predicting mathematical behavior. Quite the contrary, it is predicated on the belief that such behavior is complex and unpredictable. It is thus a model to enable the observer or listener's description of what has happened—what the learner has done and the invocative or provocative (i.e., causing the learner to "fold back" or to skip ahead) consequences of a teaching intervention. Its important contribution, for the current purposes, is the formulation of different modes of acting, replacing the rather unhelpful and rigidly dichotomous concrete-abstract distinction. Understanding, as Kieren and Pirie's model and their supporting research indicates, is a dynamic and active process of negotiating

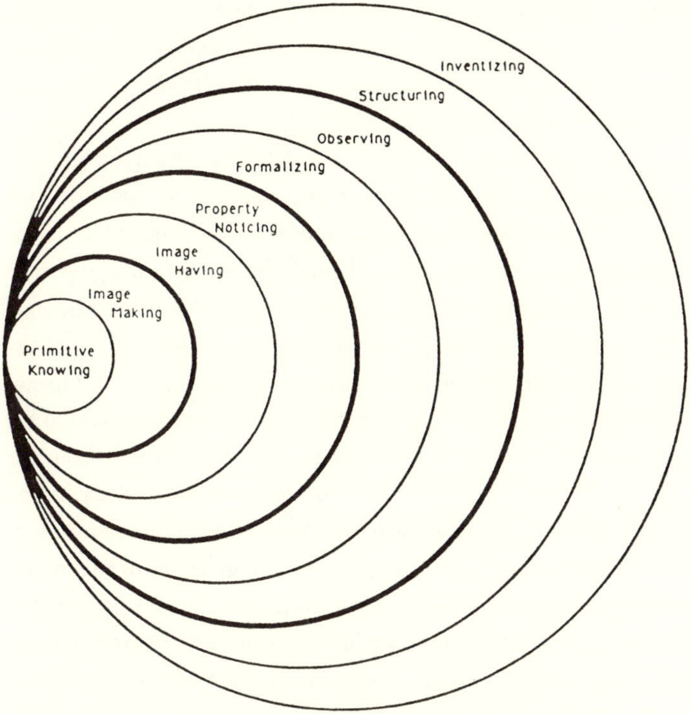

Figure 4.1. The Kieren-Pirie Model of Mathematical Understanding[11]

and re-negotiating one's world whereby the abstract can never be severed from the concrete.

In addition, a significant strength of this model is that it can be used to interpret the mathematical actions of either individuals or groups of learners. In particular, as it has been applied to collective sense-making, the model highlights the manners in which collective understandings do emerge—senses that cannot be located in any of the participants but which, rather, are present in their interactions.

Each level of the Kieren-Pirie model is associated with particular styles of logical reasoning—beginning on the most primitive levels with what might appear to an observer to be a sort of random "mucking about" or playing and extending through more deliberately creative actions—and so a researcher using the model must be aware of the sorts of activities and expressions that might be considered proper to each level. (These "logics" are hinted at by the descriptors included in the diagram.) For the listening teacher, this is an important aspect of the model, for the movement from one level to another might be (and often is) occasioned by questions or other teaching actions. The teacher must thus be able to listen for the characteristic logics.

Further, as regards the distinction that I have been drawing between formulated and unformulated knowings, Kieren and Pirie have developed the idea of "don't need boundaries" (indicated by the darker circles in the diagram) to highlight particular events in the growth of one's dynamic understandings. As one crosses a "don't need boundary," one is able to operate at a more sophisticated level without having to rely on previous modes of thinking and acting. For example, a learner whose understanding of fraction addition has been tied to his or her actions in manipulating materials might begin to talk about the additive process in terms of those materials but without having to actually manipulate them. Later still, he or she might begin to formally operate on mathematical symbols without having to refer to the original manipulative activities. In each instance, the learner has moved to a level of understanding in which previous actions or processes, while still available should he or she need to fold back, are not explicit parts of the current understandings. In terms of formulated and unformulated knowings, we observe in such examples the manner in which each unfolds from and is en-folded in the other. What was once formulated (e.g., manipulating fraction pieces) comes to be taken-for-granted (unformulated), but still remains available for interrogation.

Formulating one's understandings is regarded as a process analogous to *storying*, whereby the learner incorporates new experiences into the text of previous understandings. In this process, both past knowings and interpretations of current experiences are revised—one rewriting the other, as it were. This revisionary and recursive *storying* process stands in stark contrast to the cumulative and linear *storing* process of transmission-acquisition models of learning (especially those founded on "mind as computer" metaphors), thus highlighting not just the *reproductive* nature of understanding but its *productive* aspects as well. Understanding is generative—both of the selves that participate in the understanding and of the world that is opened (or "brought forth") by that understanding.

The Kieren-Pirie model might thus be interpreted as a framework for listening, for it places the teacher/researcher in a necessarily attentive relationship to the learner. The model demands not just that one be more mindful of student articulations and actions, but, because such activities are argued to be of benefit both to teacher and to learner, one must present occasions for learners to express themselves verbally and in action. It is thus that this model acknowledges the dialogical structure of our mathematical knowings. The teacher is seen as part of the action and is hence implicated in all the emerging understandings.

Meanings of Meaning

To repeat an earlier point, a distinction between a meaning and an understanding is not easily drawn—and our difficulty with constructing one is perhaps attributable to the ranges of understandings of "meaning" and meanings of "understanding" that are present in our day-to-day language. In many cases, the words are used interchangeably; in others, they are separated through rigid definition. I am considering meaning apart from understanding here, not principally because I believe it important to separate them, but because the word "meaning" has taken on a particular status within the field of mathematics education. There the meanings of "meaning," for the most part, demonstrate the same tendencies to privilege the formulated and to neglect the bodily as the most popular understandings of "understanding."

Conventionally, "meaning" tends to be understood in terms of connective associations. On the more objectivist side, the meaning of a concept has to do with its relationships to other concepts, its possible applications, its derivation, etc. In short, a meaning is something that can be identified and subsequently taught. More subjectively, "meaning" is understood in terms of personal associations to other ideas, and it is a quality to be either supported or contradicted, depending on its appropriateness. In both cases, "meaning" is understood in formalized and formulated terms: it is something that can be, and usually is, stated. As such, meanings reside in the domain of language, and language, in turn, is generally cast as a mental (in contrast to a physical) capacity.[12]

To the enactivist, however, the bulk of our meanings are neither formulated nor strictly linguistic. They are, rather, lived through or enacted. For the purposes of illustration, we can turn to Hilary

Putnam,[13] who describes two opposing conceptions of the meanings of words. In formal terms, to know a word's meaning is to be able to provide a definition without using the word itself. However, as Putnam points out, most of the time we are unable to readily offer such definitions, and yet we clearly *know the meaning* of the words we are using—simply by virtue of the fact that we are using them. (Conversely, one's ability to provide a formulated definition is no assurance that the word can be used meaningfully.) Their meanings are thus enacted, and it is to this unseen (or unacknowledged) part of the iceberg that enactivist theorists invite us to focus our attentions in our discussions of education. The measure of learning is not what can be stated or re-stated, but what is performed. Put differently, thought and action are not precursors to or consequences of meaning; they *are* meaning.

In a similar vein, Richard Rorty refers to such enacted meanings (i.e., our languaging behaviors) as "patterns of acting," a phrase that underscores the notion that our language is not a "third thing" that exists between you and me. Rather, our language (i.e., our speaking, our conversing, etc.) is an element of our moment-to-moment acting and interacting. Applying Putnam's and Rorty's notions to a discussion of the meaning of mathematical terms, symbols, and concepts is not difficult. We need not delve too deeply into our own ways of interacting with the world to find that we are continuously enacting particular meanings or understandings of mathematical ideas—we compare, we note patterns, we prove, we group, we abstract, we deduce—all in ways that are particular to a culture in which mathematical reasoning is privileged.

Returning to the issue of linguistic competence, it is generally believed that we learn our language through a process that begins with noting inadequacies in vocabulary (e.g., noticing an object for which a name is not yet known, or recognizing that a term or phrase is inadequately understood). We then proceed through a conscious interrogation of possible meanings, and a deliberate period of "experimentation" in social context, after which the term or phrase becomes part of our natural lexicon. While not disputing the possibility of this sequence, enactivism suggests that other processes might also be involved. Many of us, for example, have had the experience of spontaneously using words that we never knew we knew—

a phenomenon that is especially prevalent among adult learners of a second language. That we are able to utilize terms in this way—without prior inquiry into their formal meanings—points to another mode of learning, one that is sometimes metaphorically described in terms of "osmosis" or of "picking things up along the way." For the enactivist, this side of learning is vital. There is so much to know about living in a complex world that the epistemological assertion that every cognizing agent must go through a process of formalizing everything that he or she knows—in effect, the contention that it is possible to separate mental from physical functioning—becomes untenable.

Our enacted meanings are thus embodied meanings. Arising from the background of unformulated experience, sometimes passing through some manner of formulation, these meanings return to silently shape the actions of the body. They become part of our being—part of the way we stand in the world. They become our "commonsense," our taken-for-granted, the "way things are," sometimes so blindingly obvious that they resist re-formulation and re-presentation. There is thus a dialectic between formulated and unformulated meanings. Learning is a process of affecting one's meanings—formulated and unformulated, for the two cannot be considered apart. It is a restructuring of being. The key element is that what is learned must be in some way meaningful.

Herein lies the problem with conventional approaches to mathematical instruction that begin by presenting a concept and proceed by attempting to render it meaningful. We are, in effect, saying, "Here is something that is not about you; here is how you make it into something that is about you." Sometimes this approach works. Most of the time—as evidenced by popular (Realist) belief as to the nature of mathematical knowledge—it holds knower apart from known. With regard to mathematics education, this separation is a tragic one, for the bases of almost all of the meanings and understandings that we seek to promote in grade school can be found in everyday—albeit unformulated—experience.

Perfinking

One quality of "meaning" that I haven't touched on so far is its affective dimension (which is not associated so strongly with "understanding"). People, events, objects, and memories can become meaningful for reasons that we very often are unable to comprehend.

This facet of meaning has been virtually unaddressed in mathematics education, where thought and emotion are separated in yet another modernist dichotomy—a split that is supported by the pervasive opinion that the discipline is objectively neutral. Any personal or emotional associations to the subject matter are, in consequence, thought inappropriate and irrelevant—although perhaps inevitable. Indeed, the word "rational"—used as it is to describe both mathematical modes of reasoning and sane, sensible, unaffected behavior—points to a sharp distinction between reasoned thought and irrational feeling. In the modern frame, thought is considered to be of the mind, and feeling of the more primitive, animalistic body; and so the thought-emotion split might be considered another relic of our Cartesian heritage.

As Walkerdine[14] persuasively argues, the disdain for the emotional—and the belief that the rational might provide us with a means of overcoming our irrational proclivities—has exacted a toll from learners of mathematics. In the classroom, where a sometimes "complex" and "painful" suppression of experiential knowings is required to attain a mechanical proficiency, learners are stripped of a dimension of their being.[15] Often the ignored feelings and suppressed emotions are manifested in a hatred of the subject matter or an indifference toward the teacher. Other times it creeps in more subtly in the throw-away remarks that students so often make: "My family's bank account is in the negative integers," "With my mother gone, only four fifths of my family remains." We underestimate, for the most part, the emotive powers of our numbers, forgetting the way they permeate our existence.

In many ways, the severance of thought from feeling is an odd one, especially for those of us who, like young children, have retained the capacity to be excited about what we do and do not know. As Margaret Donaldson puts it, "passionate curiosity empowers the intellect. . . . [The] achievement of new understanding is normally accompanied by delight."[16] There is a devotion that animates the existence of those who seek after new truths—a passion that is very often absent in both the teachers and the students of conventional school mathematics. The evidence of this statement is found in the school definitions of "discipline," a word that has lost its original sense of devoted following to become associated with two modernist impulses: control (imposition, regulation, punishment) and separation (as in "subject area disciplines").

The connection of emotion and reason is not without scientific support. Antonio Damasio,[17] in his exploration of the manner in which modern medical science has severed the mental from the physical, outlined the role of feelings in the construction of rationality. Locating the "drive" for each of these intertwining phenomena in both the biological and the phenomenological/social, Damasio offers compelling scientific evidence to support Walkerdine's, Donaldson's, and others' arguments.

In response to our tendency to separate these phenomena, David Krech[18] has coined the term "perfink," drawing attention to the way we perceive, feel, and think all-at-once. Bruner, elaborating on Krech, adds that action is an important element of our perfinking. All of these elements are present as we learn—as we interactively make sense of our world. That only rational thought has been the domain of mathematics teaching, then, has been its most dehumanizing trait—one that has been supported by a unidirectional teaching style (teacher-to-learner) that has seen no value in attending. The perfinking teacher, however, cannot help but listen.

The Space of Learning

The Western notion of the Self—that thing that thinks, understands, means, feels, and acts—is inadequate for the purposes of understanding learning and teaching, primarily because it obscures the transformative process that is the self.

I return to this issue to add a note of elaboration, for even with a more fluid definition of identity, we still tend toward thinking of our selves as agents that "have" or that "shape" understandings, meanings, and feelings. While I am uncomfortable in suggesting that this notion is without value, I do think it lacks a necessary symmetry. Our understandings, meanings, beliefs, feelings, and actions, in other words, are not so much things that we give shape to, but events that give shape to our selves. As Rorty puts it, "Just as the brain is not something that 'has' . . . synapses, but is simply the agglomeration of them, so the self is not something which 'has' the beliefs and desires, but is simply the network of such beliefs and desires."[19]

This point is an important one because, in many ways, learning involves an attempt to resolve the tensions that arise between tacit and explicit knowledge, between emotional and reasoned actions, between intuitive and calculated responses. At times these move in harmony; at times they exist in contradiction. In colloquial terms, the issue here is the level of agreement between "what we say and what we do." Unfortunately, this phrase tends to be expressed derisively—as a statement of bad faith. We are critical of someone who says one thing and does another.

These inconsistencies of our behavior might more profitably be regarded as small tears in the fabric of our existences—ones that offer a hand grip or a toe hold for movement. Lacking them, there is little need to learn. And so, putting it into more formal terms, there is always *play* between the formulated (stated) and the unformulated (enacted)—where the latter provides evidence for or contradicts the former; where the former validates or reframes the latter. It is in this *play*—the movement, the divergence, the synchrony—that we find a space for learning.

An illustration. In the middle of a unit on decimal numbers, Melinda, a seventh-grade student, asked her teacher for assistance with the textbook exercise: "Calculate $3 \times {}^{1}/_{4}$. Express your answer as a decimal." The teacher's first attempt at assisting was to ask, "If you had three quarters, how much money would you have?" Without hesitation, but with a decidedly quizzical look, Melinda responded, "Seventy-five cents."

Melinda saw no connection between the original question and the one posed by the teacher—between the formal mathematical concept and her enacted mathematical competency. As she and the teacher explored the play between the two, however, Melinda's understanding of both was broadened.

In the last section of this chapter, I delve more deeply into the place of this sort of play in the learning of mathematics. My orienting theme is that we, as educators, need both to open spaces for and to locate existing instances of tensions between stated and enacted meanings, understandings, and knowings.

Section C
Play

Play—a sacred activity which, in our see-and-work world, has been made profane.

—*David Denton*[1]

[Child, arriving home from school, to parent]:
"They don't give us time to learn anything; we have to listen to the teacher all day."

—*Jim Unger*[2]

The importance of play for learning about the world has been a prominent theme among educational theorists and psychologists alike, with notable contributions having been made by such figures as John Dewey and Jean Piaget. Normally regarded as a sort of random exploration of the features of a space or experience, play tends to be regarded as foundational to sense-making.

Within mathematics education, the importance of play has not been overlooked, although it might be argued to have been undervalued. Contrasted with the goals of teaching and learning that, for the most part, are stated in terms of formal competencies, we often lose sight of the playful beginnings of our knowledge—not to mention the inevitable play in the most certain of our truths. In this section, I explore the nature of play, seeking to understand its place in the emergence of mathematical understanding and, hence, in the listening teacher's classroom.

As with the corresponding sections of preceding chapters, I include a further discussion of the three modes of listening introduced in Chapter 1, this time framing them as three styles of participation. The focal points of this elaboration are the roles of play and creativity within both the varied modes of attending and the associated flow of classroom events.

That elaboration is preceded by a discussion of the notions of play and creativity within educational contexts—both in terms of the actual and the possible.

Education and Play

If I might be permitted for a moment to think of the word "play" as a box filled with meanings and possibilities, then it is the sort of container that lures the person intent on play. It invites itself. It announces itself. It enables itself.

As I examine its many dictionary definitions, it seems that I am faced with a choice. I might treat it as a word with numerous and divergent applications—used in the contexts of sport, frolic, drama, jest, love, and risk, to name a few—or I might play with it as an essential quality of life that is hinted at in each, but never fully revealed in any of its definitions. In the spirit of play, I have elected to do the latter, but begin the discussion by acknowledging the futility of attempting to capture and tame this play-full thing/no-thing. It cannot be found or created; it cannot be planned or manipulated. It exists in the immediate. Play is only play in the playing. And so, I play.

In English, the link between education and play is not readily apparent. Not surprisingly, then, in the conventional school, play tends to be discounted as childish, haphazard, ineffective, and inefficient—and is often defined in explicit opposition to the goals of formal education. Among the subject areas, mathematics classes are perhaps the least playful. There, even the words governing what is to be learned have been stripped of their play: they are rigid and restrictive, defined in ways that belie their sensual origins and that discount their associated experiences.

In Greek, however, the distinction between play (*paidiá*) and education (*paideía*) is not so obscured. Both terms arise from an original reference to the activity of the child (*pais*), an echo of which can be heard in the word "pedagogy" (*paidagogos*). Plato incorporated this play-element in his *paideía* as he recommended that the guards' children learn their lessons through *paidiá*. But, even for Plato, the connection between play and education was quickly lost as he moved to the "higher form" of his dialectic. There, learning became a matter of earnestness, of not-play.

Piaget regarded play as the most powerful of the child's learning activities. In play, the child takes what surrounds him or her and, in effect, re-structures that which was given into a range of imaginative possibilities. His or her physical action and "make believe" enable an internalization of certain parts of the world, leading to a broader range of possible actions. Play, in Piaget's conception, is thus a creative endeavor, which is understood in the child's orientation to the activity rather than in the activity itself.

However, with Piaget's conception of play, the educative import is lost as one progresses to more complex modes of thinking and reasoning. In contrast, John Dewey articulated a perspective on play that can be applied across developmental stages and maturational levels:

> *The first stage of contact with any new material, at whatever age of maturity, must inevitably be of the trial and error sort. An individual must actually try,* in play, *to do something with material . . . and then note the interaction of his energy and that of the material employed. This is what happens when a child at first begins to build with blocks, and it is equally what happens when a scientific man in his laboratory begins to experiment with unfamiliar objects.*[3]

In this conception, play is not merely a physical manipulating of objects, nor simply an unformulated, completely random movement—but, by the same token, it is a far cry from the rigid structures for inquiry suggested by modern formulations of the "scientific method" and the logical proof. Play, here, might be thought of as an undirected mucking about—a quality of action that has been acknowledged in such models of mathematical understanding as the one developed by Pirie and Kieren (introduced in the preceding section).

Unfortunately, the perspective on play in the secondary mathematics classroom is neither that of Piaget nor that of Dewey, having been made synonymous with "off-task behavior" and "goofing around." Its creative and re-creative aspects have been forgotten as it has become associated strictly with recreation; play is now thought of as something that interferes with the serious business of schooling—something to be purged, held down, put off. But the playfulness of learners is not so easily suppressed.

An illustration. Early one school year I asked on a mathematics quiz, "What is the difference between 18 and 8?"—a poorly worded question intended to help me determine who among a class of eighth-grade students knew the mathematical definition of "difference." Perhaps one third of the students gave the "correct" answer of "ten." The rest suggested that the difference had to do with the fact that 8 was smaller, less, lower, or that it had one fewer digit; or that 18 had more factors, that it had "a number in the tens place," or that you could drink and vote when you reached that age. One learner provocatively suggested, unfortunately without explanation, that there really was no difference. All these responses I marked wrong. There was no play in my grading. There was no play in my understanding. Unable to suppress the play-fullness in the learners' ideas, I was compelled to ignore it and to punish them. My inability to listen led me to close the gate on a mathematical playground, rich in its potential.

In the preceding paragraphs, I have deliberately used "play" in many different senses in an attempt to draw attention to our playful understanding of the term. I now move to the realm of more formal explication, drawing primarily on the work of Hans-Georg Gadamer to come to a deeper understanding of play and, in the process, to point at the centrality of its place in the mathematics classroom. Play, like listening, is a phenomenon that has tended to be shallowly understood and, in consequence, almost universally scorned by mathematics teachers. Motivating this discussion is my belief that a deeper understanding of the role of play in learning will not only provide cause to embrace it as an aspect of one's pedagogical practice, but it will also highlight the place of listening in the lives of mathematics teachers and point to the need for evolutionary and ecological—that is, enactivist—senses of knowing and knowledge.

I must note at the outset that my use of the term "play" continues to be somewhat ambiguous, although not entirely deliberately. My inability to assign it a rigid definition—to "pin down" what I am talking about—springs from my firm conviction that there is much more to be learned by playing with the possibilities than by mechanically reducing them to a single definition. That is to say, I am purposefully challenging the modern dichotomy that holds apart the irrational, (re)creative, bodily, sensual, and fictive realm of play from the rational, logical, mental, austere, and fact-ive realm of reason.

The Essence of Play

Exploring the meanings of *play* in such phrases as "the play of light," "the play of the waves" and "the play of forces," Gadamer suggests that the essence of play is "movement as such" which "has no goal that brings it to an end; rather, it renews itself in constant repetition."[4] It is thus that he uses the concept of play as he attempts to decenter the notion of subjectivity, for this movement is impersonal and not subject to subjective control. Rather, within play, subjectivity loses itself; at some point, the game takes over. In retrospect we say, "I forgot the time," "I don't know how I did that." There remains, however, a subject of play, but that subject is *the play itself.* The game takes primacy over the players, just as the subject of play takes primacy over the subjective consciousness of individual players. In Gadamer's words, "all playing is a being played. The attraction of a game . . . consists precisely in the fact that the game masters the players."[5]

It is important to note that, for Gadamer, play is not the opposite of seriousness. Quite the contrary, "seriousness in playing is necessary to make play wholly play."[6] This notion recalls a premodern usage of the term by which, according to David Denton, "to play meant to pledge, to stake one's life, to guarantee, and it also included something of its opposite; that is, the dangers and perils of such mutual commitment."[7] The relevance of this point becomes clearer as Gadamer moves to a discussion of the role of play in one's experience of a work of art. As mentioned in the preceding chapter, a work of art has the capacity, while representing something familiar, to present something new and thus to challenge the taken-for-granted-ness of daily existence. Gadamer explains that artwork has this capacity because it is a form of play. It exists in the play of what is known to be true and what might otherwise be thought. It invites play. It draws the player out of him or her self and, in the interplay, opens a space for transformation. Subjectivity loses itself and re-emerges having learned something—having been changed—and so the playful loss of subjectivity is instructive rather than destructive.

It is thus that play educates. It presents the as yet unexperienced, the unpredictable, the uncontrollable. As Gallagher puts it:

The unfamiliar that we experience in play is first of all interpreted in terms of the world. In play we become so fascinated with the world that we move beyond ourselves, we transcend the limits of the self. . . . The self-transcendence that is essential to play involves a projection toward one's own possibilities. . . . Play bestows reality on the unreal; it gives weight to that which is possible or fanciful.[8]

It is here that the moral significance of play is revealed, for if we accept the earlier conclusion that the self is a process of change, then play is a catalyst for this transformation. Indeed, as we speak of education, it may even make sense to suggest that the movement of play is an essential element of all educational experience. And, in the more specific realm of mathematics education, the artfulness of play and the playfulness of art, as developed in Chapter 3, provide us with a sound basis for including the subject matter in our school curricula.

"Just Playing Around."

Friday was always "Problem Day" when I was a full-time teacher of mathematics. Students would be divided into groups and assigned three or four "nonstandard" (for that was my definition of "problematic") questions from the text.

Most of the time the students dutifully, but somewhat dispassionately, worked at the assigned task. From time to time, however, a question would capture the interest of one student or another, and, on some occasions, that interest grew to a contagious enthusiasm. I could usually tell when we were on the verge of one of these events. The sign was a change in some student's response to my standard intrusive inquiry, "What are you doing?" The normal answers were along the lines of, "We're on number seven," "Thinking," or "Getting back to work." But occasionally someone would say, "Oh nothing, we're just playing around with this question."

Early in my career I interpreted this response as an indication that the students were "stuck." They were trying some things, but could make no progress. More often than not, I immediately ignored what they were doing and undertook to explain the problem into mundane-ness, enabling them (I thought) to get back to the serious business of mathematics. Later I found that by asking them to explain what they were "just playing around" with, interesting things were happening. More recently, I have had occasion to eavesdrop on students engaged in mathematical tasks. It often happens that I am unable to make sense of what they are doing; I can describe it only as "play." And, not surprisingly (any more), they describe it in the same way when asked: "Just playing around."

The key element in these cases is not the making of progress, but the allowing of space for movement. My inability to notice the importance of my students' playing was the "aroundness" of the event; it seemed incompatible with the linearity of the curriculum I sought to follow. "Playing around" suggests a turning and re-turning, a back-and-forth, a repetition and recursivity that are perhaps more in harmony with the ways we learn and live than the lock-step, straightforward structures of many textbooks. "Around," like "play," is a polysemous, playful word that we use to allow ourselves space for movement.

The "just" part of "just playing around" is also important. It indicates two things to me as a teacher. First, playing is something we tend toward. When work is done (or forgotten), when duties are fulfilled, then we can *just* play. It goes along with just thinking, just resting, just kidding. Second, and perhaps more importantly, it hints at a somewhat disparaging attitude toward playing. Such attitudes are to be expected for the conventional mathematics classroom, as mentioned, is not a place for play. Mathematics learning is conceived to be about the *mind*: about stating understandings, about fixing meanings. Play, in this conception, points to the "opposites" of these modern ideals: to loosening and fluidity; to the *body* and to acting. But are these true opposites?

Gadamer's explication of the centrality of seriousness in play would suggest that they are not. The formulated and the stated are critical elements of the unformulated and the enacted. They are the markers that reveal the hidden movement. The problem, then, is not so much that we have focused on the serious, the formulated, and the fixed, as that we have set them up in contradistinction to play. The modernist quest for progress is largely to blame here, for in our desire to move toward prespecified goals, we have become disdainful of "just" moving . . . *just playing*. In focusing on the rules of mathematics, on the limits of the individual players, on the bounds of the playing field, on the time clock, we have lost touch with the play.

Play Time

Perhaps the most devastating phenomenon associated with this loss is the attitude toward time that goes along with mathematics classes. There, time is a commodity. Some researchers,[9] in fact, have gone so far as to prescribe a regimented structure for mathematics lessons that they contend makes the most efficient use of time and produces the most effective results. The de-humanizing metaphors underlying this sort of project are clear. Yet, for the most part, they go uncritiqued. Mathematics learning, after all, is important business.

The criterion of efficiency and the demands of planning compel the teacher to hold a particular perspective on time: a resource that is limited and precious. In Alan Lightman's words, this time is mechanical, predetermined, and unyielding; it is "as rigid and metallic as a massive pendulum of iron that swings back and forth, back and forth."[10] Homework should thus be checked in the first seven minutes, the lecture (with examples) completed in the next ten, and the remaining time fragmented among the other essential lesson elements. If an interesting question arises, one checks one's *watch* to determine if there is time to pursue it. If a student wastes time at play, it is recorded and "made up" at lunch or after school. This mechanical time orders life; it does not obey it.

The time of play is different. It is a "body time" that "makes up its mind as it goes along."[11] It is a time that moves in fits and starts to the rhythms of moods, desires, heartbeats. It is the time that races between the bells that mark the breaks and that slows between the bells that bound classes. It is time that can be frozen by an icy glare, or that can fall away when absorbed in conversation. It is a time that obeys the body.

That is, it *listens* to the body.[12] In our world, and especially in our schools, it is a forgotten time, for in the classroom the body is made to submit to the order of mechanical time. "Put that food away. It's not time for lunch yet;" "No, you can't go to the washroom. Why do you think we give you a break between classes?" And, most commonly, "Get back to work. The time for play is after school."

Mechanical time is the time of *telling*. It is the time of rote, recitation, regurgitation—of *dis*-play. Body time is the time of *listening*. It is a time of pause, passion, persons—of play. It is a time that takes the time that is needed. It is a time that does not move in lock step, that does not parse knowledge into 45-minute gulps, that does not hastily scribe an "X" beside the different answer. It is a time that spills from class into break, from school into home, from one day into the next, from one topic into another.

"Where the two times go their separate ways, contentment. Where the two times meet, desperation."[13] They meet in the modern mathematics classroom—and, in my experience, they meet with a particular violence. In fact, my most frequent response to suggestions for innovation in my teaching was, "Yes, it probably will be more engaging, but how much time will it require?"—which might be translated as, "This sort of activity will likely unfold in body time, but teaching is constrained by mechanical time."

There is no simple resolution to this issue. But, in terms of mathematics learning, as Dewey[14] noted, people are far more likely to learn when they are thoroughly occupied and engaged in what they are doing. This is where recasting teaching as listening enters, for listening involves a forgetting of modern linear time. The listener is not subjected by the object of time. It cannot be an issue. Mathematics teaching, in this conception, is about taking one's (body) time.

Conversations: Word Play

A conversation can be put to a quick death with a simple glance at a watch. This tiny act yanks us back into mechanical time where we must be getting places, where we must be getting things done. Another way to quash conversation is to arrive at some sort of terminal (state-ed) "understanding" that neither requires nor allows for further movement. These sorts of constraints are the rule of the conventional classroom. As far as teaching goes, it is they that make it unnecessary and impossible to really listen, not just because listening happens in body time, but because listening and conversation are sorts of play.

Words *play with us* as they move, twist, and disappear. They *play us* as they tug, push, and taunt. This play is perhaps most clearly evident in a conversation in which, through words, we are conducted through the play of meanings. It is thus that Gadamer notes that play and the conversation have the same hermeneutical structure. If the play (the give-and-take in meaning) of a word could somehow be overcome, there would no longer be any need to listen: either there would be no room for misunderstanding, or there would be no possibility of verbal communication. Listening, then, and *not* speaking, is the human capacity that enables interaction. It is that capacity that makes it possible to make sense of and to maintain sanity amid a sea of linguistic messiness, ambiguity, and play. In David Denton's words, "listening is full participation with that being heard, which surrounds like the water and sun, in depth, multisensually, with no sensation of time."[15]

It is also the play of words that frustrated Descartes' Rationalist project. His goal was to construct a positive and certain philosophy, free of presuppositions and guided by the clarity and rigor of mathematics.[16] He was compelled to use words, however, which, in spite of his efforts to legislate their meanings, could not be detached from the traditions that defined them. Nor could their ambiguity be squeezed away. Put differently, the words had too much play to serve as the building blocks of an unshakable philosophy. It is for precisely this reason that postmodern critics have focused their analyses on language. Their project is founded on the notion that our language, while enabling us to render sensible the meaningless and the chaotic, can always be turned destructively upon itself. Nothing is certain.

(Re)Creativity

Playing must be thought of as a sort of *bricolage*—an engaging in particular activities because one is able to do so, not because they are directed toward achieving any knowable ends. The function of playing is to open a space of possibilities, to "expand the sphere of behavioral possibilities,"[17] to "enlarge the space of the possible."[18]

Creativity arises out of the background of those possibilities, selecting out through repetition and formulation those actions that are new and useful. Creativity is thus a discernment, a choosing . . .

and a phenomenon that has not been well-understood in the modern setting. Like thought, understanding, and meaning, creativity tends to be regarded as a subjective, mental, and progress-oriented capacity.

As regards the belief that it is an individual phenomenon, such a conception denies both the social milieu of creativity and its historical background. As hinted by the word "inspiration" (literally, "breathing in") creativity involves an openness to, a taking in of, a receptivity to possibilities as they occur within—and not in spite of—situation. Further, creativity exists as the edge of past achievement, growing within and out of past achievement, simultaneously overcoming the constraints imposed by and utilizing what is currently known. Creativity thus hardly occurs in isolation. It is a profoundly social phenomenon.

In terms of the contention that creativity is principally a mental capacity, one need only attend to the physicality of children's play, the locus of their incredible creativity. Our use of the word "recreation" as a synonym for play echoes this challenge.

And, with reference to the pervasive belief that creativity is about "making progress," we need only examine the word "innovation." It suggests a newness (nova), a rethinking, whereby the familiar is made strange and the strange is made familiar. In this sense, creativity and art are synonyms, and mathematics would appear to be among the most creative of human endeavors. But it is as much its undirected playfulness as its intentional analyses that renders mathematics a creative undertaking.

Play School

And so *play* is much more than childish or imaginative activity. It is an essential human quality that is evident in everything we do. The argument that play must figure more prominently into the learning and teaching of mathematics is therefore *not* a call for greater activity in a program already packed with too much busyness. Nor should it be interpreted to suggest either that interactive participation is preferable to individual work or that attempts at structure and routinization are ill-advised. On the contrary, implicit in a deepened understanding of *play* is the notion that it can be realized (and is sometimes *best* realized) in stillness, in solitude, or in repetition.

Put simply, play is not so much an activity as it is an acceptance of uncertainty and a willingness to move. Play is thus the antithesis of the modern ideals of certainty, predictability, and linear progress. But it is not an abandonment of our quest for structure, order, pattern, and comprehensibility. Quite the opposite, these are the ends of play.

But these ends are revealed only in the playing, for play is not simply random activity. Rather, by opening the door to the as yet unexperienced, to the possible, play reveals what is not yet known as it simultaneously offers space to support learning. (And, importantly, this is a space of enaction rather than inaction.)

The manner in which this contiguity of play and learning has manifested itself in the modern classroom is somewhat disconcerting at times. As William Pinar, in a critique of current conceptions of curriculum, poignantly puts it:

In schools, particularly in secondary ones, and those for higher learning, one observes countless persons playing at being a student, a professor, an intellectual, a radical, a bohemian, a freak, and so on, playing at being some thing other than themselves. They are not themselves; in Laingian terms, they are out of their minds; they are mad.[19]

There is play; there is learning. But what are the games and the gains? Pinar is arguing, in effect, that the structure of the conventional school compels learners and teachers alike to assume predefined roles, to move along prespecified paths—to play a de-humanizing game—rather than to participate as the persons they are (becoming). It is thus that, in teacher education, we speak of such processes as "developing a teaching identity," inadvertently bringing to being fragmented teaching selves, social selves, learning selves—"playing at being something other than [our]selves." But there are alternatives to playing these roles—alternatives that embrace rather than suppress the play-fullness of learning.

In the classroom, then, the recognition of the vitality of the connection between play and learning points to a participatory sort of teaching—a teaching in which the teacher does not stand outside to direct the play, but becomes a vital part of the action. Immersed in the play, the teacher too is a learner. As van Manen explains:

Etymologically, to learn means to follow the traces, tracks or footprints of one who has gone before. In this sense, the teacher . . . who is able to "let learn" therefore must be an even better learner than the child who is being "let learn."[20]

And so the teacher is a learner with particular responsibilities. He or she is assigned the tasks of presenting possibilities and, through attending to students' responses to these possibilities, opening spaces for play. Such play-fullness is only feasible when one allows for departure from the anticipated (play), fluidity in the structured (play), and uncertainty in the known (play).

Here is the place of listening—of being part of the rhythm and movement of the classroom, of living (rather than merely fulfilling) one's teaching role—a topic to which I now turn in a further explication of the three modes of listening as introduced in earlier chapters.

Three Listenings

Act 1: Evaluative Listening ("Adding Fractions" Lesson) Perhaps the most apt descriptor of the actors' attitudes toward their activities in the first classroom scene is "tolerance." Far from being engaged by what they are being asked to do, those present enact a certain emotionless detachment from the mathematics and from one another as they move, conformingly and in lock-step, through the rigid lesson structure, the common (but not communal) exercises, the mechanically timed class.

This is a place of fixed and imposed definitions: there is no play in the mathematics, no play in the expected learning outcomes, no play in the assigned tasks, no play in the enacted roles. And there is no play between teacher and learner or among learners, for play has been made synonymous with off-task behavior, the opposite of their express purpose for being in this room at this time. As such, there is a certain mechanical character to their interactions—a coordinated teacher-speaks-then-student-speaks-then-teacher-speaks . . . and hence there is little sense of collective action.

In short, there is no real listening happening in this classroom. Neither is the teacher listening to students—apart from evaluating the correctness of their contributions—nor are the students listening to the teacher—save for the trivial activity of obeying her instructions. The students are not much listening to one another either, constrained as they are from participating in one another's thinking by rigid desks that hold them in a forward-looking posture and prescribed tasks that leave little room for creative interpretation.

Act 2: Interpretive Listening ("Adding Integers" Lesson) A sense of play has been introduced in this episode, if only a minor one, through the introduction of a manipulative tool illustrating the concept at hand. But that tool seems to be regarded as only a toy—a location for the more mature activity of mathematical analysis—as the play is quickly set aside for the more serious business of formal algorithms and practice exercises. The play precedes the mathematics, rather than being part of it. That mathematics is straightforward, tidy, clear, unambiguous, thus enabling Wendy to pre-specify the endpoints of the learning in similarly concise and unambiguous terms—terms that are devoid of play.

The status of play in the interactions is similar—and is perhaps most evident in Wendy's manner of listening. While there is increased opportunity for interaction among class members, the goal of the listening seems to be to cut through and to minimize the play—the "noise"—of subjective sense-making, to get to the bedrock of students' conceptions. The discussion thus continues to be metronomic, lacking the fluidity of a collective movement, of a conversation.

Act 3: Hermeneutic Listening ("All-at-Once Fractions" Lesson) This is a play-full mathematics—a subject matter that exists in the interaction and interplay of those present. Theirs is a joint project, one in which the learning objectives are identified collectively. In retracing the events of the lesson, it becomes apparent that it is not so much the particular choice of activity—although the choice is certainly important—as it is the opportunity for interaction that contributes to the flow, the rhythm of the mathematics. The manner in which Elaine's initial diagram serves to frame subsequent contributions and the way those contributions play roles in shaping follow-up activities suggests a complex choreography and not merely a complicated coordination of action. One idea cannot be separated from another; emerging conceptions exist in the realm of shared action. And so, to understand what is happening in this setting, one must step back and consider not individual players, but their collectivity.

Work and play are not dissociated into drudgery and pastime in this lesson, but come together in a concerted engagement with the questions that drive the interaction. Similarly, unlike the BINGO chips in the integers lesson, the Fraction Kits are intended as more than toys, more than illustration, more than precursors to mathematical inquiry. Rather, the learners' physical experiences with the pieces of paper are part of their mathematics, as revealed in their uses of such terms as "trading," "exchanging," "moving," "covering." There is no rigid dichotomizing of mental and physical: they are united in the interplay of action and knowing, of unformulated and formulated, of collective and individual.

In brief, the class members are immersed in the play of the subject matter—situated in the same way that we are immersed in our sonorous field—and so what is occurring is not strictly determined by where the teacher intends to arrive, but more by consensus through what unfolds in the creative play. Amid the possibilities that present themselves, the teaching here becomes a matter of discerning and selecting what seems important and what might be useful. Like learners, Wendy is immersed, complicit, caught up in the unfolding play—a play with its own particular tempo. When Van offers his thoughts, the time is thus taken to hear more, to look further. And so Wendy is not a teller, not a facilitator, but a player, a participant. Hers is a teaching that is attentive, creative, improvisational, hermeneutic—a playing by ear.

Chapter 5

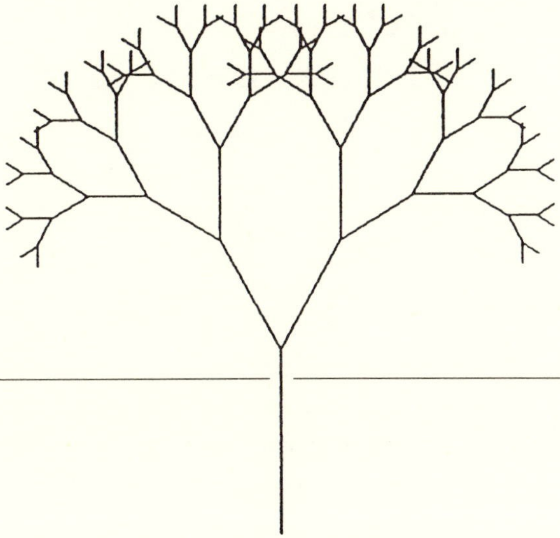

Playing It by Ear

Teaching

Many violinists and violinmakers insist that violins grow into their beautiful throaty sounds, and that a violin played exquisitely for a long time eventually contains the exquisite sounds within itself. Somehow the wood keeps track of the robust lyrical flights. In down-to-earth terms: Certain vibrations made over and over for years, along with all the normal processes of aging, could make microscopic changes in the wood; we perceive those cellular changes as enriched tone. In poetic terms: The wood remembers. Thus, part of a master violinist's duties is to educate a violin for future generations.

—Diane Ackerman[1]

Imagine in your mind's eye and ear a mobile, with thin pieces of glass dangling like leaves off branches, and so on. Any gust of wind will cause the mobile to tinkle, the whole structure changing its speed, torsion of branches, etc. Clearly, how the mobile sounds is not determined or instructed by the wind or the gentle push we may give it. The way it sounds has more to do with the kinds of structural configurations it has when it receives a perturbation or imbalance. Every mobile will have a typical melody and tone proper to its constitution. In other words, . . . in order to understand the sound patterns we hear, we turn to the nature of the chimes and not to the wind that hits them.

—Francisco Varela[2]

Section A
The Nature of Teaching

> *My own view is that it is not much use pointing to the "internal contradictions" of a social practice, or "deconstructing" it, unless one can come up with an alternative practice.*
>
> —*Richard Rorty*[3]

> *[T]he true teacher, no matter what his or her specific field, always instructs us in humanity.*
>
> —*Robert Grudin*[4]

My intention in this final chapter is to pull together the key strands and ideas from the preceding discussions in an effort to respond to the question I set for myself at the start of this writing: What might mathematics teaching be?

As mentioned in the first chapter, when I originally undertook to conduct the study reported here, I did not have this question in mind. It *presented* itself while I was in the process of investigating quite a different issue. Originally, I had sought merely to research the characteristic interactive patterns of the conventional mathematics classroom, a project that was much more comfortable methodologically (since established and validated methods had already been constructed for me to use).

It was thus difficult, when presented with what I knew to be a more important question, to take up a mode of inquiry that seemed far more nebulous, more tentative. Raised and educated in the tradition of reductive certainty, it was not easy for me to appreciate—let alone to convince others of—the importance of a question that is framed around the tentativeness of "might." We want to know what something *is*, not to waste our time exploring alternatives and possibilities that lie outside our current interpretive frames.

This study began with the premise that, in spite of its seemingly sedimented and static qualities, we do not (and cannot) know the precise nature of mathematics teaching. And even if we could provide an unambiguous account that is true for some moment in history, it would profit us little. Both mathematics and teaching are moving forms: mathematics history reveals it to be anything but the epitome of fixed knowledge; the place of teaching and the role of teachers have never been issues of widespread agreement. To suggest that we can know once and for all what they are is to succumb to the pervasive and thoroughly modern tendency to define . . . and in that definition to reduce . . . and in that reduction to mechanize . . . and in that mechanization to lose what is fundamentally human about the endeavor.

Just as it seems we have done in countless mathematics classrooms, where the seating arrangements and the patterns of interaction reflect the same impersonal and rigid structures that are embodied in a fragmented and objectified conception of the subject matter. A major part of my study has involved trying to understand how it is that this highly structured, rigidly controlled, quiz-on-Friday, think-as-I-think conception of mathematics teaching has become so pervasive in the modern setting. What assumptions are being made? Which "theories" or "orientations" are being enacted by students, teachers, and teacher educators? Simply put, I am not interested in knowing how well we're doing whatever it is we're doing; nor am I eager to do it better. I am trying to understand what we might be up to in the first place. And, ultimately, to inquire into an alternative enactment. That is the issue to which I presently turn.

Theory-Practice

Nowhere is the "theory-practice" tension more visible than in the field of mathematics education. If I have been correct in my evaluation of the forms that modernist dyadic perspectives have assumed, then this announcement should hardly come as news. "Theory versus practice" is just one more Cartesian dualism to add to the list already assembled. If I might be permitted to draw a fairly vulgar line between the two "camps" within mathematics education, at the moment we have the theorists and researchers on one side, gathered under the banner of "constructivism," and the teachers (practitioners) under siege on the other, living out a realist perspective within the increasingly unsafe bounds of the classroom walls. That impassable line between them is marked by the corpses of the many ill-fated efforts to define the term "constructivist teaching."

My purpose in this section is to examine this impasse more closely, taking seriously the admonition of Pinar and Grumet:

> *Theory must not hang alienated from practice in some timeless realm of unchanging, arrogant truth. Rather, let us play theory and practice against each other so as to disclose their limitations, and in so doing, enlarge the capacity and intensify the focus of each.*[5]

I thus begin by asking, Why is it that theorists and teachers seem unable to communicate on this issue? And then, How might we go about overcoming or circumventing this most devastating tension?

As I have elaborated in the preceding chapters, the two faces of modernism have created a sort of crisis of identity for mathematics educators, torn as they are between Realist/Empiricist and Rationalist/Constructivist perspectives. The former (whereby knowledge is an object, teaching is the transmission of such knowledge, and learning is a process of acquisition) underlies the entrenched orientations toward and methods for teaching. Backed by current institutional constraints, program demands, public expectations, and the momentum of tradition, the realist perspective militates against any sort of radical reformation. The latter (whereby knowledge is fallible, education is enabling, and learning is a process of constructing) serves as the theoretical foundation of an extensive body of research where only a few—if any—current reports fail to acknowledge an allegiance to constructivist and/or social constructionist orientations.

The realist view of instruction, founded as it is on a "conduit" model of communication, might be succinctly described as a process of *telling*—a notion that I use for both its literal and figurative senses. First, "telling" serves as the practical foundation of much of conventional mathematics teaching. So conceived, the teacher's task involves first selecting the bits of knowledge to be passed on and then re-presenting them with a mechanical efficiency. Metaphorically, and more closely aligned with its etymological roots, "telling" is associated with counting and recording, as well as with communicating and fabricating stories. As Humez, Humez, and Maguire explain, *tell, tale, talk, tally,* and *toll:*

*come from an Indo-European root (*del-*) meaning "number, count" and by extension "recount, relate." Modern German* Zahl *"number,"* zählen *"to count, number, reckon," and* erzählen *"to tell, relate, narrate" are the cognates that remind us that the bank teller counts your money while the fortune teller tells you a plausible tale.*[6]

All of these facets of *telling,* I have suggested, are elements of conventional mathematics teaching—from the notion of bank telling (i.e., tallying of knowledge, assigning a value to a student's acquisition of such knowledge) to the notion of tale-telling (i.e., presenting mathematics as indubitable fact).

The emphases of mathematics teaching in the modern school setting are thus on clarity of expression, depth of explanation, structure of practice, and dissection of knowledge (into appropriately-sized transmittable bits). Madeline Hunter, a prominent proponent of this perspective, frames teaching practice into three categories of decisions (which, ostensibly, are applicable and prior to all teaching action):

(1) What content to teach,
(2) What the student will do to learn and to demonstrate learning has occurred, and
(3) What the teacher will do to facilitate the acquisition *of that learning.*[7]

Not surprisingly, there is an extensive literature critiquing this telling orientation (along with the series of associated realist, mechanical, objectifying metaphors that give it shape). Nevertheless, perhaps in part because our language seems to bias our thought and to mold our patterns of acting, most of current teaching practice appears intent to fit itself into this category.

The constructivist challenge, as might be expected, is founded on the conviction that one's dynamic and unique knowledge is the product of accumulated experience. By redefining learning as a process of experiencing and making sense of that experience, teaching becomes less a matter of ensuring that preselected truths are acquired (i.e., telling) and more a matter of facilitating the process of knowledge construction through the creation of appropriate learning environments. In effect, teaching becomes a matter of *orchestrating* the learners' experiences rather than of transmitting knowledge, and the teacher is more centrally concerned with attending to emerging understandings than with providing unambiguous explications. The teacher seeks to provide opportunities for learners to make sense in their own way and to derive their own theories, in the process attending, responding, and adapting to student action.

One might thus characterize "constructivist teaching" as a process of making sense of the sense students are making (as opposed to trying to foster student sense-making—which, if one accepts a constructivist epistemology, is inevitably happening), founded as it is on the epistemological premise that learning has to do with the active and independent construction of meaning. In other words, the primary concern of the constructivist teacher is not "How might this best be told?" but "How can I tell if the learner has learned?"

This shift in orientation is a dramatic one, and it is not merely a movement from an outer authority (e.g., objective knowledge or an expert teacher) to an inner one (i.e., the learner's subjective conceptualizations). It is a move toward listening—albeit a listening that is cast in terms of a distanced attendance to the other's monologue (i.e., what I have been calling "interpretive listening") rather than an intimate dialogic participation in the sense that is being made (i.e., "hermeneutic listening").

This conception of "constructivist teaching" is not without its problems, however. In particular, with constructivism's self-imposed focus on the individual's creation of subjective meanings (which, admittedly, occur in interactive settings), a host of other issues surrounding the social act of teaching tend to be pushed into the margins (or even disregarded). Topics such as human agency, our tremendous interactive capacities, and the moral dimension of teaching, for example, do not generally receive the same level of critical attention as the processes of sense-making—these are unproblematic givens. On one level, this "oversight" is quite appropriate: constructivism does not claim to be able to provide insight into such topics. On another level, however, this is a serious shortcoming. In failing to address these issues, proponents of constructivism are failing to interrogate the taken-for-granted that they bring to discussions of teaching.

A further problem with the notion of "constructivist teaching" arises from the fact that constructivism, as a theory of learning and knowing (i.e., an epistemology), can at best make us more aware of what we, as teachers, *cannot do*. Indeed, since a key tenet of constructivism is that there can be no such thing as an instructive act (i.e., in the causal sense of the phrase), the teacher can only be considered in terms of a source of perturbations, the purposes of which are to systematically prod learners toward certain prespecified understandings. Put differently, in conventional terms, *teaching* has to do with *causing* someone to learn something. (This definition is fairly standard and seems to work across most educational philosophies.) Yet *constructivism* begins with the premise that no one can *cause* anyone to learn anything in particular. "Constructivist teaching," then, is something of a paradox, if not a complete oxymoron.

It might be expected, then, as these notions have filtered their way from the theorist through the researcher to the teacher, they have collided with enough violence to create an unbridgeable theory-practice chasm. The teacher, who is charged with ensuring that learners develop particular mechanical competencies, is simultaneously stripped of any efficient means of doing so. Rather than enabling us to overcome some of the problems surrounding the teaching of mathematics, then, the constructivist "revolution" has in many ways served to exacerbate them.

A Response

Just as the movement from objectivist to subjectivist accounts of learning and understanding amounted to little more than a transference of monologic authority, the shift from the conventional *teaching as telling* to the constructivist *teaching as orchestrating* amounts to little more than a renewed attempt to prescribe or control the learning that is to occur. That is, in spite of the insights offered by constructivist theorists, recent developments have only served to bolster the modernist desire to dictate outcomes—although the sanctioned means of achieving the desired ends are markedly different.

The problem, I would argue, arises from constructivists' reluctance to step outside the "neutral" bounds of epistemology into the messier and more demanding realms of morality, ethics, identity, and being—ontology. As such, constructivism has not just "gone along with," but has actually provided support for the continued definition of educational practice in terms of modernist ideals. The learner remains autonomous, coherent, and insulated; the curriculum continues to be prescribed, external, and controlled; the subject matter is still perceived as inert, unbiased, and valuable; understanding remains state-able, terminal, and personal. The preceding chapters represent my attempt to pull at, untangle, and reweave each of these strands.

Continuing in that vein, I turn again to enactivist theory to seek an alternative understanding of teaching. My starting place is to invoke once again Varela's distinction between *prescription* (what is not allowed is forbidden) and *proscription* (what is not forbidden is allowed)—a shift which I believe might make it possible to overcome the inability of conventional learning theories to inform teaching. Briefly, enactivist teaching offers a way of distancing ourselves from the constrained consequences of modernist efforts to prescribe learning outcomes and to move toward a more proscriptive orientation whereby diverse possibilities are embraced as the teacher becomes an important interactive and co-emergent part of the learning context.

Current efforts to describe "constructivist teaching" have been crippled by the built-in requirement that they focus on the prescriptive "what is not allowed." Among those things forbidden (or deemed impossible) are predetermined outcomes, transmissive acts (telling), shared understandings, and coupled action. If, however, we shift our focus to "what is not forbidden," and abandon attempts to control learning, then we are no longer compelled to base our teaching actions on as yet unrealized end points—a practice that forces us to privilege what we eventually want to achieve at the expense of what is currently happening.[8] Along with constructivism's constrictive delimitations of its phenomena of study (namely subjective sense-making), this constraint serves to render "constructivist teaching" both difficult to enact and out of step with emerging societal needs.

It is on this sort of issue that the critical difference between constructivism and enactivism might be noted. Enactivism, while sharing many of the conclusions of constructivism on the topic of cognition, casts a wider net in terms of its focus of inquiry. Not merely concerned with individual cognition, enactivism looks more broadly to collective (and other) phenomena. As such, the term "enactivist teaching" is not subject to the same sort of constraining tensions, for it readily acknowledges the complicit nature, the moral dimensions, and the ethical responsibilities of teaching—in the process calling for a particular mindfulness when it comes to teaching.

An Alternative

Enactivist teaching, then, focuses on the *now*—on emergent understandings, on immediate possibilities for action, and on the broader implications of such action. Knowledge, rather than being understood in objective or subjective terms—whereby persons and their understandings are regarded as essentially isolated and autonomous—is recast as those patterns of acting that allow our structures to be coupled, thus entangling us in one another's existence and implicating us in one another's knowing. Teaching, in effect, comes to involve the presentation of occasions for *play* ("play" is understood as referring to the possibility for movement or negotiation rather than the largely aimless and childish activity that is described in psychology texts). The conventional relational, temporal, and spatial *bounds* of teaching are divested of their objective form and invested in terms of pedagogical sensitivities and ecological mindfulness. Efforts to locate mathematics in objects or subjects are replaced by an understanding that mathematics is neither inside nor outside, but *about* us.

In this conception, teaching can be neither about *telling* nor about *orchestrating*. Neither, however, are the acts of telling or orchestrating precluded in the enactivist frame. I, the teacher, can still tell; I, the teacher, can still orchestrate. However, it is the learner, and not I, who determines whether I have told or orchestrated. The teacher must thus be attentive to the consequences of his or her interventions, attuned to the moment-to-moment activity of the classroom, and inquiring into the possibilities of the spaces that present themselves. He or she must be listening.

In no way is this meant to suggest that the teacher must forego all hopes of promoting understandings on particular concepts (that is, those mandated by formal curriculum documents). Quite the contrary, by offering the possibility for joint action (rather than merely coordinated movement), a teaching founded on listening makes tenable the teacher's position between collective knowledge and individual understandings. Rather than attempting to serve as a conduit from the former to the latter, or to shape the latter into the former, the listening teacher, attentive to the play and interplay of both, moves back and forth between them.

Such intertextual movement is implicit in listening. Even in the most naive formulation, listening is necessarily dialogical, involving at the very least the intermingling of another's words with the text of my own experience. As such, on the figurative level, listening offers us a powerful alternative to metaphors[9] of teaching which focus on the monological (such as "transmission," "telling," "voice," or "empowerment"). Similarly, as argued in Chapter 1, a listening orientation denies the possibility of rigid subject-object distinctions, reminding us that the issue of who we are is not separate from where we are, what we are doing, who we are with, and what we know.

More profoundly, because listening occurs (for the most part) in language, in listening we are called to a rich and many-leveled history of human participation in the world. Each sentence, each phrase, each word is meaningful not because it can be defined against other words in some grand tautology, nor because it can be mapped onto an external reality, but because it is situated in the complex web of meaning-making action. It bears the trace of the past, a clue to the present, an anticipation of the future. The modern (and mathematical) tendency to "fix" words and to demand precise usage, in contrast, ignores the past, concretizes the present, and seeks to domesticate the future.

In this regard, the *listening* attitude (which questions the prejudices that shape our perceptions) might be contrasted with the act of *hearing* (which moves along unaware of the play of language). Going about our lives in a *hearing* mode compels us to exist in a modernist frame. A *listening* attitude offers the possibility of another way of being. Both *hearing* and *listening* attitudes are realized in language, but the first is held down by what *is* while the second is (to some limited extent; we can never step outside our language) freed to explore what *might be*. Hearing compels us to move in the fixed patterns of the world; listening invites us into the world's play. In the context of the conventional mathematics classroom, this distinction is an important one because there, it seems, most interaction is founded on hearing rather than on listening—that is, on an awareness of the other's presence, but not on an earnest desire to bring them forward; on definitions, but not on meanings.

Teaching Mathematics Backwards

The point I wish to argue now, and the one that will serve to bridge this section to the next, is that the sequencing of instructional events in conventional textbook-based mathematics classes—if we, as educators, are indeed concerned with promoting understandings, ensuring relevant program content, and being attentive to learners in other than a strictly intellectual capacity—is backward. Reducing it to its simplest terms, this sequence might be described as commencing with a formal concept and moving (via practice, application, proof, or some other "meaningful" activity) toward formulated understanding. It is thus that the typical class period begins with a brief lesson and the balance is given to seatwork.

Experience with this sort of structure is familiar to most in our culture. Some time ago, I was replaying an audio-recording of a mathematics lesson for the purpose of locating and transcribing those teacher-student interactions that I thought might be informative. A colleague from English education entered my office and, after listening for only a moment, demanded that it be turned off. When I complied, he immediately assumed the role of the teacher and proceeded to "reenact" the unheard remainder of the lesson. He did so with an uncanny accuracy, imitating not just the structure and the rhythm of the lesson, but also capturing the voice, the manner, and the bodily aspect of the teacher.

The point here is that, based on his own experience with school mathematics (which was now long behind him), he was able to represent the tone and structure of a "typical" lesson—a format that bears a certain resemblance to the popular image of the subject matter: predictable, hierarchical, precise, fragmented, self-contained; lacking rough edges, rhythm, fluidity, engagement, interaction. This is the mathematics of the textbook, and it is enacted not just in the lesson's structure, but in the teacher's movements, the seating arrangements, and the resultant "understandings." Such fragmented curricula are the inevitable consequences of constructing courses out of textbooks, for, as Ong[10] has noted, writing and print isolate as they obviate immediate human interaction. It is in reference to their experiences in classrooms that are structured around textbooks that we hear teachers in staffrooms and students in hallways complaining that the other never listens.

A listening emphasis in teaching thus begins by shifting from the visual demands of the text to the auditory possibilities of dialogue and cooperative action. It disposes of the formal-concept-to-formulated-understanding sequence of conventional mathematics instruction and provides a space for mathematical play in which appropriate actions (whatever form they may take) are made the focal point. The issue here is not to provoke or to make possible learning actions; they are always and inevitably happening. Rather, the point is to open a space where such actions might be noticed.

The notion of "teaching mathematics backwards" goes much deeper than a reversal of the instructional sequence, however. Daiyo Sawada[11] frames this idea in terms of a resequencing of the questions that define our teaching actions. He suggests that, with regard to the 5 W's (+ H) of decision making for mathematics teaching, we tend to consider matters in order of WHAT is to be taught; WHEN it will be taught; HOW it will be taught; WHY it will be taught; WHO is being taught; and, finally, WHERE the teaching will occur. He proposes a *converse* structure (i.e., one that turns things over and, in the process, implies a more conversational approach), beginning with a consideration of the context (the WHERE and the WHO of the setting at hand), founded on the enactivist premise that what is known is inseparable from who knows it and the situation in which it is known.

From an enactive perspective, one might say that this reversed approach begins with enacted understandings—the *doing* rather than the *stating*—and then *moves*. Exactly where it moves depends on such complex factors as the structures of those present, the context, and what has been anticipated. It may move toward more formulated understandings, if such formulation is relevant to the play space or if it becomes part of a further exploration. It may simply move to other sorts of activities. This, of course, is not to say that we should just allow whatever might happen to happen, thus abandoning our responsibilities as teachers. Rather, it is to say that we cannot make others think the way we think or know what we know, but we can create those openings where we can interactively and jointly move toward deeper understandings of a shared situation. The listening teacher's task in this sort of context is hardly that of a detached observer.

An illustrative example of this point was undertaken in a combined second- and third-grade class on the topic of multiplication. Copies of 10×10 grids were distributed and students were asked to color patterns of six squares in as many different ways as they could. Rectangles of dimensions 1×6, 2×3, 3×2, and 6×1 were quickly generated—and, in the conventional mathematics classroom, the production of these combinations would likely have prompted the teacher to choose another number to work with (since all the whole number factors of six had been identified). This teacher, however did not foreclose on the play, and soon some students had noticed, among other things, that twelve half-squares ($12 \times {}^1/_2$) and that twenty-four quarter-squares ($24 \times {}^1/_4$)—ideas that are normally reserved for students twice their age—also covered an area equivalent to six whole squares. Limited by their dexterity, they went no further, but a few were able to suggest other possibilities in the emerging series of combinations.

The teacher, in allowing the space for play, had opened up a mathematically rich space. She was, at this point, able to move in any of a number of directions. She might have introduced the formal concept of multiplication; she might have let students continue the same activity with other numbers; she might have changed topics completely (to fractions or geometry, both of which figure prominently in the program of studies). The key point here is that, rather than attempting to teach *toward* a narrow, specific, and prestated understanding, this sort of activity made it possible for her to teach *from* embodied understandings. Understanding was thus not a goal to achieve, but a quality to enact. Listening—that attitude of openness to the possibilities that continuously present themselves—is essential to teaching in this conception.

Section B
Assessment

The genuine teacher differs from the pupil only in that he can learn better and that he more genuinely wants to learn. In all teaching, the teacher learns the most.

—Martin Heidegger[1]

[I]f we listen carefully, and take children seriously, we can learn from children themselves what it is important for us to know about their learning.

—Mary Jane Drummond[2]

Sarah's head is down, face hidden in her crossed arms. She doesn't move. One minute. Two.

Mr. Davis notices, and he moves toward her desk as soon as he finishes reexplaining a bit of his earlier lesson to another student.

"Troubles, Sarah?"

"I can't do this," comes the muffled reply.

"Let's see what you're working on."

Sarah lifts her head. She's on question five: "Give the reciprocal of each fraction."

"Okay, the reciprocal is the flip, right?" Mr. Davis utters his question in the tone of a statement.

"Uh-huh."

"So you just flip these. That's easy."

"I don't get *this* one." Sarah points at part C of the question: "12." "It's not a fraction."

"But it's easy to turn it into one." Mr. Davis points at the dividing line between the numerator and the denominator of another fraction. "Here, what does this mean?"

"That it's a fraction." A statement uttered in the tone of a question.

"Yes, but what does this line tell you to do?"

Silence.

"To divide, right?" Another one of those telling questions.

"Uh-huh."

"So a fraction is a dividing statement. Here, three over four means three divided by four. . . . So what could we put under the twelve to make a true dividing statement?"

"Twelve?" Almost too quiet to be heard.

"Is twelve divided by twelve still twelve?"

The answer is once again obvious from the tone of the question. Sarah shakes her head and hangs it a little lower. "I don't get this," she whispers.

"Here." Mr. Davis takes Sarah's pencil and writes "12/☐ " in the spot that's been prepared in her notebook. "What can you put in this box? What will give you twelve?

"Zero?" A spark of hopefulness in her voice.

"You know that you can't divide anything by zero." A bit of frustration seeps into his words. "What can you divide by that gives you the same number you started with?"

"I don't know."

"One." His impatience is now clearly audible. "Twelve divided by one is twelve. So you can put a one in that box." He picks up the pencil for her.

Sarah takes it and writes in the numeral.

"So, what's the reciprocal of twelve?" Mr. Davis asks, just to be sure.

"Sarah's tone is flat. Distant. She has cut her self out of the situation: "Twelve over one."

During my first few years of teaching, I was in the habit of placing myself under surveillance by mounting a video camera in the back of my mathematics classroom and letting it run for the duration of a lesson. My intention was to get an objective look at myself—a practice that I could now thoroughly critique, but which, at the time, seemed like the right thing to do. The above episode with Sarah is a re-presentation of an event that was captured during one of those lessons.

Virtually every issue that I have taken up in this book can be addressed through this interaction: from the mode of listening, to the enacted conception of mathematics, to the unformulated consequences of education, to the tacit conception of understanding. For me, though, this is an episode that is principally about assessment. That is, it is about the complex process of determining what learners know, our attitudes toward the errors they make, the sorts of questions we ask, the manner in which we pose them, the types of answers we expect.

Given the current climate of testing and retesting, no discussion of mathematics teaching would be complete without attending to the topic of assessment. As a means of holding the learner accountable for what is taught and the teacher accountable for what is learned, assessment practices have become the "tail that wags the dog" of formal education. Not surprisingly, then, the issue of assessment is a central and sensitive one for educators. Certainly in my interactions with practicing teachers, the worth of virtually every topic we discuss and every suggestion that is put forward is determined according to our capacity to respond to some version of the question, "Yes, but what about the exam?"

In this section I undertake to examine this concern for examinations, along with the associated model of evaluation through which assessment is regarded as something that, at worst, comes after teaching is done or, at best, is interspersed with instructive acts in a "one instructs, one assesses, one instructs some more" pattern. In summative terms, this section is a problematizing of a conception of teaching that permits such a separation and that, even worse, often surrenders its responsibility for assessing to other agencies.

A purpose and theme, then, is to note the manner in which instruction and assessment are folded inextricably into one another within a mathematics teaching that is founded on our capacity to listen. And a premise of the discussion is that our efforts to assess must be based on sound understandings of our reasons for doing so.

An Object Objection

The following is not a "typical" discussion of mathematics assessment. Conventionally, when the topic arises, the tendencies are to list strategies (e.g., portfolios, journals, self and peer assessments, group projects, monographs, tests, etc.) and to delineate the sorts of artifacts that are inevitably generated in support of such practices (e.g., dossiers, log books, reports, worksheets, exam papers, etc.). Apart from a brief discussion of the formal test, I am deliberately avoiding a focus on methods and their material consequences.

My reasons are threefold. First, while such artifacts provide important records and should therefore be kept (if only in acknowledgment of our cultural need to demonstrate "progress"), I would argue that they should never be the focal point of assessments. An emphasis on the products of learning displaces the teacher from sitting among students to hovering over objects. And, at their most dangerous, certain sorts of artifacts actually serve as substitutes for learners, obviating the need for teacher-student interactions. At a recent parent-teacher meeting, for example, I overheard a colleague say to a parent as he led her to her daughter's portfolio, "Kim is over here." I found the turn of phrase somewhat unsettling, perhaps because it called to mind that, for some teachers, assignments and tests are their only real contact with the persons populating their classes.

My second reason for not taking up an exploration of particular assessment strategies arises from my public school teaching experience. One of the tasks for which I was briefly responsible was the administration and interpretation of standardized diagnostic and achievement tests to middle school students across my school district. Wanting to provide as broad a range of profiles as possible, whenever time permitted I took the opportunity to chat with the teachers of the students I had been asked to assess. Consistently, these teachers were able to anticipate the results and recommendations that would eventually emerge. What I found disturbing about the process was not that they were able to do so—such capacities I did not think altogether surprising, given their familiarity with the "system" and their intimate knowledge of their students—but their willingness to defer to the authority of the formal test. It seemed that they regarded their own informal assessments as mere "suspicions," whereas the test provided objective evidence. Time and again I witnessed tentative opinion solidify into fixed evaluation: "Sarah is only working at a grade 3.6 level"; "Lou is still in a pre-formal stage." And, correspondingly, such authoritative pronouncements seemed to preclude the teachers' prior attentiveness as they became excuses for student achievement rather than prompts for teaching action.

What these teachers (and I) were tending to forget was that the products of these evaluations, like the artifacts of any form of assessment, are inevitably in the past tense—fixed indications of what was known at some point in history. (It might also be added that standardized examinations are also bounded by narrow conceptions of intelligent activity, not to mention limited by the artificiality of the whole formal testing process.) They might thus be used as important background but, given the fluidity and volatility of learner understanding (particularly at younger ages), they should not be mistaken as sound bases for determining what the learner knows here and now. As such, the artifacts of our assessments should provide occasions for our listening, not obstructions. This is an issue that I believe bears careful thought, if only because these objects tend to follow us through our educations in the form of reports and grades.

Finally, there is no shortage of books and articles on the "how to" of conducting assessments. I feel no particular compulsion to add to that pile. What matters to me is not so much the particular strategies that one might employ, but the attitude with which one approaches assessments. And so, I have elected to focus on such issues as what it is that we might be doing when we claim to be assessing and, correspondingly, why it is that we're doing it.

Assessment, Evaluation, "Envaluation"

I begin that exploration of the "why's" by drawing a distinction between "assessment" and "evaluation." While, for the most part, the terms tend to be treated synonymously, I believe there to be some value in temporarily pulling them apart.

Assessment, which is drawn from the Latin *assidere* (to sit beside), is a word that I prefer to use in reference to those teaching actions that are directed toward developing a fuller understanding of both a learner's subjectivity and learners' collectivity for the purpose of adapting one's teaching approaches. Assessment, in this sense, is participatory, implicated in learner understandings, inseparable from instructing—that is, it is an integral part of every teaching act, an idea that is closely aligned with the notion of teaching as listening.

Evaluation, built around the root of "value," is more about assigning a worth to something. The business of evaluation tends to assume that there is an external, objective standard against which such phenomena as calculation speed and understanding can be validly and reliably measured. In its quest for unbiased certainty, evaluation has taken on a certain mechanical character, framed by checklists (that are used to observe what someone else has identified as relevant), explicit criteria (that define not just what we look for, but what we see), and, most obviously, some manner of quantification. Evaluation is thus primarily concerned with tallying, consistent both with the practices and the etymological heritage of an approach to teaching as telling.

A hint of what evaluation "is really about" might be gleaned from a review of the terms associated with evaluative practices, such as "marking," "scoring," and "grading." While their metaphoric origins have been largely forgotten in the modernist quest for objectivity, we would do well to recall that just as one "leaves a mark," "scores a piece of paper," and "grades a road," one's marking, scoring, and grading of a learner involve a certain violence as one leaves "impressions" on that person's body. Evaluation involves a marking for life.

Tom Kieren[3] has proposed the term "envaluation" in an effort to reassert the important social consequences of our unmindful (and often mindless) evaluation practices. Similar to "enculturation," envaluation refers to the processes by which persons are indoctrinated into particular value systems, thus becoming complicit in the patterns of acting that define social organizations. In the case of formal schooling, through a complex and sophisticated envaluation program, a culture of classroom mathematics has been constructed that some have referred to in terms of a tacit (enacted) "social contract"—whereby acceptable action for teacher and learner alike is negotiated and defined. Through the process of envaluation, as enacted through our evaluation procedures, we announce not just what is important to know in terms of mathematical competency, but what qualities are valued in a modern student: among which are included punctuality, conformity, and tidiness. The power of these unformulated procedures is made evident in the manner in which spontaneous and curious learners quickly become students who obey the rules.

A reassessment of our current modes of evaluation/envaluation is thus vital if there is to be any meaningful change in mathematics teaching. In what follows I identify some possible foci which, I believe, are critical in any effort to reformulate and reform assessment (and teaching) practices. A recurring theme in these discussions is that all modes of assessing and evaluation involve comparisons. We must thus seek modes that do not feign objectivity and, correspondingly, that do not presume, assert, or create a "norm" or an ideal standard. If we are going to measure learners against one another, we might as well be up front about who is being compared to whom, and who is doing the comparing.

Why Assess?

With the suggestion that modern evaluation practices are problematic, challenges to the two most commonly cited reasons for conducting evaluations—namely for making learners (and teachers) accountable and for differentiating among learners (and teachers)—are also raised.

In effect, this is an issue I have already addressed in dealing with the question, Why teach mathematics? If high school and first-year university courses are to serve as gatekeepers (to determine who can and who cannot pursue further studies), then the associated evaluation processes are easily legitimated. In arguing against this rationale for mathematics instruction, I have, in effect, also critiqued its accompanying manners of formal assessment.

This position hardly reflects any sort of consensus among mathematics educators, however. More popularly—as indicated in an increasing emphasis on the use of ongoing, formative assessments to complement endpoint, summative evaluations—there has been a shift in emphasis that might be described in terms of moving from an evaluative to an interpretive mode of listening. While marking an important transition in the defining conception of learning (as neither linear nor cumulative), such emphases do not prompt us to move far afield from traditional conceptions of the subject matter and from the conventional reasons for teaching mathematics.

One error that seems to have been made in such rationales (for both mathematics education and formal evaluations) has been, as Mary Jane Drummond[4] points out, an assumption that the purposes and the outcomes of our assessment efforts are reasonably closely aligned. Drummond demonstrates quite the contrary in her analysis of the personal and social consequences of current practices. (Far from facilitating learning, for example, most formal evaluations actually appear to have constraining and narrowing effects on knowledge development.) Such discrepancy between what we think we're doing and what is actually happening prompts me toward the assertion that our assessment practices should be as concerned with assessing the assessor as they are with assessing the assessee—that is, they should be founded on a hermeneutic listening. A critical feature of a hermeneutic listening is that it is attentive not just to the object of perception, but to the listener's complicity in that perception—that is, to the prejudices that determine the sorts of elements that are perceived and the manners in which they are interpreted.

Put differently, we must also interrogate ourselves as assessors, for the questions we ask, the competencies we note, the suggestions we offer are all founded on particular beliefs about mathematics, education, learning, and teaching. Assessments are also about the educational and societal contexts in which they are administered, reflecting the prevailing values on such matters as what should be known and who should be compelled (or permitted) to know it. As such, a key reason for conducting assessments is to understand ourselves—a rationale that is almost identical to the one I gave in arguing for studying mathematics—and, in that understanding, to seek out and to strive to enact alternative patterns of acting.

Such a rationale can be put to immediate practical use, even in the most objectivist setting. It compels us to inquire into, as Drummond admonishes us, both our reasons for assessing and the (frequently incommensurate) results of assessments.

The Error Error

On the issue of the consequences of our formal assessments, it is important to note that, among learners, evaluation in mathematics classrooms is overwhelmingly regarded as a negative process.

There seem to be at least two central reasons for this pervasive perception. First those who are marked and graded tend to believe that evaluation is something that is done *to* them *by* someone else. It is an imposition of authority, a naming, an objectification of one's fluid self. Second, save for those persons who do exceedingly well on such evaluations (and, hence, learn virtually nothing from them), formal evaluations do not focus on the positive side of what we know and what we are now capable of learning, but on the negative side of what we can't do or what we got wrong. In this conception, errors are indicators of incompetence and, as such, things to be avoided.

The well-intentioned attempts by some educators to delve into systematic patterns of student error seem to have contributed to this negative state of affairs. Although founded on the sound notion that learner mistakes generally follow reliable, non-random (albeit flawed) patterns, attempts at "error analysis" are also based on a fragmentation of mathematical understanding into singular competencies. Aligned with the modern medical paradigm of "diagnosis and remediation," in this frame errors are seen as symptoms of underlying illnesses—ones that, in a sort of conceptual chemotherapy, can be located, isolated from other understandings, and removed. Complex knowing is thus reduced to partitioned competencies, enabling elaborate fictions of "normal understandings" and a "normal child"—constructions that do not exist but against which conceptions and learners are nonetheless measured.

The origins of this pervasively negative conception of errors is not difficult to trace. With a mathematics curriculum that seems intent on equipping today's students with all the competencies that they would require to run a turn-of-the-century grocery store, it only makes sense that the mechanical proficiency of isolatable skills should be emphasized. As societal needs shift from developing human resources to promoting resourceful humans, and as mathematics education turns toward the activity of mathematicians for its inspiration, errors take on quite a different status. Among mathematicians, for example, errors are things to be sought out, inquired into, understood—not for the purpose of scoring, nor for remediation, but to build on and to revise. Errors hint at false assumptions, over-generalizations, mistaken analogies, thus raising new questions and opening new possibilities. Far from being something to avoid at all costs, errors serve as important focal points of mathematical inquiry. They offer moments of interruption, of bringing the unformulated (the enacted) to conscious awareness. Errors present for formulation things that we didn't know we knew—or for reformulation aspects of what we might have forgotten we knew.

From an enactivist perspective, then, errors are not negative; they are the bounds out of which learning possibilities unfold. In this conception, errors are not located inside particular individuals, but exist somewhere in the constellation of classroom events. They are instances that call for negotiation as they prompt awarenesses of inconsistencies between subjective conceptions and general consensus—thus, potentially, presenting both for revision.

It is worth noting that there are differences between constructivist and enactivist orientations toward errors. Concerned with subjective sense-making, constructivists often assert that there are no such things as mistakes. Thus, what is normally regarded as an error is merely a departure from socially-sanctioned truths. An error is only an error in the eye of the observer. While enactivists are sympathetic to this interpretation, with their overarching concerns for ecology and intersubjectivity, they not only assert that errors occur, but that we are morally obligated to excavate and interrogate such breeches. The purpose in concentrating on errors, however, is not to remediate them, but to learn from them—that is, to reform collective action every bit as much as to reform subjective action.

An immediate, and perhaps somewhat startling, implication of this assertion is that concerns over such matters as "cheating" or "copying"—concerns that arise from a belief that learning is an individual, self-contained phenomenon—fall by the wayside. No longer preoccupied with avoiding errors, not to mention with arriving at a single right-or-wrong response, cheating is not a concern because there is not much to be gained by copying someone else's answer. Rather, the emphasis is on developing a common text—a basis for joint action—within a mathematical inquiry.

In terms of the enacted social contract of the mathematics classroom, a movement toward an embracing of errors thus amounts to a movement away from that manner of teaching that is concerned primarily with seeing—with surveillance, supervision, scrutinizing, and ensuring that learners' eyes are on their own work. It is a movement toward a teaching that is more concerned with listening . . . and a transition that I suspect would be welcomed by most teachers. There is simply too much happening in a classroom at any moment for one pair of eyes to monitor (and control) it all—especially given the transient and elusive nature of students' learning.

The Question Question

In a way, a discussion of questioning is identical to a discussion of assessment. By asking ourselves about what we think to ask for/about/after, and in examining the manners in which we taxonomize and pose our questions, we are getting to the very foundations of what we believe teaching and assessment to be.

On this issue, Gadamer has identified three modes of questioning: teacherly,[5] rhetorical, and hermeneutic. In his analysis he is critical of the first two categories—i.e., teacherly questioning and rhetorical questioning—because they lack the openness required of a "true question." The teacherly question is one that lacks a questioner (i.e., the person asking already knows the answer, and so the purpose of asking the teacherly question is not to interrogate or investigate an issue; rather, its purpose is toward maintaining students' attention or converting their performances into summative grades). The rhetorical question lacks both questioner and answerer. The hermeneutic question, in contrast, is one for which the questioner does not know the answer and is sincere in his or her desire to learn it. Such questions, in Gadamer's thinking, are the only true questions.

The hermeneutic question presupposes a particular manner of attending. The questioner is oriented toward gaining a fuller understanding and is thus vigilant to the fallibility of interpretation of any response given. In this frame, the associated mode of listening, itself hermeneutic, cannot be held silent; it becomes a kind of speaking, of probing and checking emerging understandings. As Gadamer explains, one *questions*, "one does not try to argue the other person down but . . . one really considers the weight of the other's opinion."[6] Hermeneutic questioning is thus not a solitary act, but a reciprocal engagement.

Hence, whether a question is teacherly, rhetorical, or hermeneutic is dependent not upon the manner in which it is phrased, but on the attitude of the questioner. Consider, for example, the question, "Where might we use positive and negative numbers?" Posed in a conventional mathematics classroom, the teacher would likely allow for a very limited range of acceptable responses, and this point was well-illustrated in an introductory lesson on the topic:

> Teacher: Where might we use positive and negative numbers? [*He draws a T-chart on the chalkboard, placing a "+" in the upper left and a "–" in the upper right.*] First, we call this "positive" [*pointing at the "+" and writing "positive" beneath it.*] If you move this way [*walking and pointing forward*], this is positive. What am I doing?
> Students: [*calling out*] Forward; Walking forward; Moving.
> Teacher: Walking forward [*adding "forward" under "positive"*]. Okay, if I climb a hill, what am I doing?
> Students: Up; Climbing; Upwards; Climbing up; Ascending; Rising.
> Teacher: Upwards [*adding "upward" to the list*]. Can you think of any other words that mean "positive"? Like temperatures rising [*adding "rising"*]. Any others?

Here the questioning is really a thinly disguised *telling*, where the participants are playing a game of "guess-what-I'm-thinking." The teacher is not listening to the responses; he is clearly selecting those words that he wants to hear from among a chorus of answers. In this case, all contributions are assessed as either right or wrong—which is to say, a response is either what the teacher wants to hear (correct, and therefore acknowledged) or what the teacher feels is irrelevant (mistaken, and hence ignored). These are the sorts of questions critiqued by Douglas Barnes:

> *Much teaching leaves the pupils dependent not on publicly established systems of knowledge (if such exist) but on quite trivial preconceptions set up arbitrarily either on the spur of the moment, or when the teacher planned the lesson during the previous evening.* This reduces the part played by the pupils to a kind of guesswork in which they try to home in upon the teacher's signals about what kind of answer is acceptable.[7]

The rapid-fire elicitation of rote-responses is the dominant form of questioning in many mathematics classrooms. Such questions are asked with little interest and framed by "the teacher's own, implicit association of thought and reference."[8] Moreover, they tend to be presented with an attitude of deliberate violence: questions and problems are to be tackled, dissected, taken on, overcome. They can thus effectively close down the very possibility of mathematical thought. (Small wonder that critical theorists regard teacher-student relationships as more political than pedagogical.)

The same question, "Where might we use positive and negative numbers?" might easily have become a hermeneutic question—an open one—the essential quality of which is that the answer not be settled. The questioner participates in the questionability of what is questioned; there is some indeterminacy. It is thus that a hermeneutic question is not about reporting on truth, but about creating it. It is this sort of question that might "break open" a lesson—but only if the person who has posed it is genuinely participating in the question by listening to the actions it provokes.

Such questioning is an art. It moves beyond the teacherly question that calls only for a re-presentation of something that has already been established. The hermeneutic or open question offers the possibility of coming upon something new; it presents possibilities. As such, the emergence of the question is not really under the control of the questioner. Rather, it conducts the person who, once attuned to what is being asked, cannot help but puzzle over it or wonder about it.

In effect, then, the essential difference between the teacherly question and the hermeneutic question is that the former has become a substitute for listening while the latter exists only in listening. That students' responses to teacherly questions are generally not listened to is evidenced by the fact that they generally have little or no effect on the course of a lesson. The same explanations are still given (and re-given); the same exercises are still assigned. They are questions whose relevance is determined in advance by their connection to a prestated objective, by their place in some technologized taxonomy, or by the blind (and deaf) faith that they will motivate learners. The premise underlying this mode of inquiry (or, rather, *inquisition*) is that knowledge, understanding, and identity are states that can be accessed and assessed through the terminal question.

The hermeneutic or open question, however, is founded on the belief that "the path of all knowledge leads through the question."[9] The question does not *follow* learning, it precedes it. It points to the not yet known and to the wondrous. It is thus that the hermeneutic question, like the listening and the understanding that flow alongside it, is more an attitude than an object. It is the sort of question that is quickly transformed by those asked, taking the form of new questions. Conventional worries about how to make the subject relevant and how to motivate learners fade to irrelevance in the presence of a question intended to engage rather than to evaluate.

Thus, in terms of assessment—that is, in terms of sitting beside learners—we might do well to be guided by the ideal of the hermeneutic question, always attentive to both what we are asking and why we are asking it. If guided by genuine interest in prompting thought and opening possibilities, a question is worth asking. If intended as an end to learning, or as a disguised form of telling, we should perhaps be prompted to reconsider our asking.

Testing Testing

Gadamer also makes use of the term "testing" in his description of the sort of probing that is necessary when the listener is seeking a deeper understanding. It is a testing, then, not so much of what the speaker knows, but of one's own hearing. However, like questioning, testing has assumed a very different character in the modern mathematics classroom.

The term "test" has a long and rich history, and it shares its roots with *text* and *texture*. The current (schooling) sense of a (usually written) examination is a modern artifact that belies its origins. For in the regime of testing that surrounds mathematics learning, there is very little concern for the texture of one's understandings, let alone for the texts from which they arise.

Testing, like questioning, has become a substitute for listening. Worse yet, the pervasive presence of standardized mathematics examinations—at levels from inter-classroom to international—has created a performance requirement that stands between teacher and learner: one that, from the vantage point of the teacher administering the tests, not only obviates the need to listen, but militates against it. The instrumental proficiency necessary for success on such tests, at first glance, seems incommensurate with an orientation to teaching that is in deliberate opposition to the mechanical rationality underlying the whole business.

Speaking against the dehumanizing and "evil" practice of external examination (and the accompanying textbook-based approaches to instruction), Alfred North Whitehead has argued that "no educational system is possible unless every question directly asked of a pupil at any examination is either framed or modified by the actual teacher of that pupil in that subject."[10] As noted in Chapter 2, Whitehead was one of the more prominent figures in the hyperformalist project of redefining mathematics as a strictly formal system. That he was so adamant about the contextuality of understandings should thus prompt us to pay close attention. Given such statements, it seems odd that the modern neglect for context that is implicit in current regimes of testing has been taken as a mark of professional competence rather than a serious and devastating error.

It is not my primary purpose here, however, to critique the conventional emphasis on testing. Rather, my intentions are to comment on its unidimensional character and to explore alternatives. Conventional testing can do very little, situated as it is at the end of an assembly line. At best, it provides some information about who could do what on a certain day in a certain place. For the teacher, it might help to pinpoint those skills that require further refinement; for the learner, it might reveal gaps in formulated understandings. But in neither case does it promote communicative action, for that is simply not its purpose. The test is usually administered *after* (instead of during) the study of a given topic; the test is usually stripped of a context of action; the test is usually designed to reveal little about understanding in the first place.

Michel Foucault provides a scathing critique of the test as a mechanism of education. In his words, it "compares, differentiates, hierarchizes, homogenizes, excludes. In short it *normalizes*."[11] In his analysis of the formal test or examination, Foucault describes how this device subjects its subjects (where both verb and noun forms of "subjects" are used polysemously). As Gallagher elaborates:

[Through such procedures as the examination, education] acts as a machine into which we put nonsubjects (children who live on the principle

of play) and by which we produce subjects, *in every sense of that word. These procedures . . . (a) . . . objectify their subjects by making them* visible *in the light of certain measuring criteria; (b) they document their subjects bestowing upon them a personal history which captures and fixes them; and (c) they define each individual as a "case."*[12]

In short, the formal test, as an ostensibly educative tool, serves to distance one person from another, to break play from knowledge, and to assign in nonnegotiable terms an identity to the learner.

Moreover, as noted and as powerfully illustrated by Stephen Jay Gould,[13] modern tests have not merely served as instruments of subjugation, they have also played roles in the creation of the very phenomena they were designed to measure. A Pandora's Box has thus been opened—for in providing "objective" assessments of I.Q., of personality, of aptitude, such tests have enabled objectifications (and, in consequence, subjectifications) of persons through measurements of previously nonexistent traits. Among the disciplines represented in the modern school, mathematics has been the most complicit in this testing movement. Valued for its certainty (rendering the construction of questions and the interpretation of responses relatively straightforward), its privileged status (as *the* model of thinking and reason), and its ostensibly impersonal character (allowing "unbiased" quantification and "objective" analyses), mathematics has both been the preferred site and provided the principal means of interpretation within this testing culture.

And so, if we are to seek an alternative to teaching, we must also seek an alternative to the testing regime that defines it—challenging first such assumptions as the comparability of student performance. As Elliot Eisner explains:

Educational evaluation and measurement have been predicated on the need to compare students with each other or with a known criterion. . . . [Such] a premise is not a necessary condition for any kind of evaluation. As our premises change so that we are open to forms that are distinctive, we will be in a much better position to develop evaluation practices that recognize the cultivation of productive idiosyncrasy as an important educational outcome and thus to honor it in assessment.[14]

It is my contention that a listening orientation to teaching offers a means of moving toward what Eisner is calling for. It begins by returning assessment to its etymological roots of "sitting beside."

A listening emphasis in teaching points to a need to explore alternative frameworks for testing. A starting place might be a redefinition of the word "testing" to include a *scrutinizing of the teacher's interpretations* of students' work—a testing of one's hearing, as it were. The purpose of testing here would be to facilitate classroom interaction, not strictly to assess summatively and retrospectively its effectiveness (nor, as Foucault has argued, to exert one's normalizing authority). One tests to check on *one's own* emerging conceptualizations. Testing, then, is aimed as much at the teacher's prejudices as at the learner's understandings. It occurs in the activity of learning, not after it.

It is important to note that this orientation to testing, arising as it does from an emphasis on listening, is not necessarily incompatible with the current desire to raise "achievement standards." Carpenter and Fennema, for example, reporting on the relative effectiveness of particular mathematics teachers, concluded that "listening to their students was the critical factor"[15] in promoting increased competencies. Such evidence serves to support the contention that an attentiveness to interpersonal relationships—and not to better management, clearer explanations, increased accountability, or more elaborate technologies—leads to better understandings.

The Contingencies of the Classroom

Our orientations toward errors, questioning, and testing, then, are fundamental to the enabling of learning. They are critical to the classroom because of the uncertainties of the teaching process. In effect, a teaching guided by listening (which relies on questioning and testing) is a teaching that embraces the contingencies of existence—the likely but not certain, the dependent but not predictable. It is, in Gallagher's words, a recognition "that we cannot avoid ambiguity and therefore must not deny its operation but find a way to live with it without inflating its effect."[16]

Teaching, in this way, might be thought of as an attempt to "condition ambiguity"—to expose the contingencies of current understandings. Such "conditioning" can be violent and unsettling, or it can be undertaken with sensitivity and tact. It can be imposed, or it can be drawn from immediate experience. It can try to control, or it can embrace the complexity and variation that is present in any social context.

Put differently, in teaching we can either ignore or embrace the watershed moments—those unpredictable and unplannable events that are always happening in our classrooms—that conduct our learning. We can continue in our attempts to structure potentially rich settings and to point fervently to that richness, or we can offer such settings and pursue those elements that capture the attention of learners. We can focus our actions on conducting our lessons, or we can allow our listening to conduct our actions.

Following Weinsheimer,[17] I use the word "hap" to refer to these watershed moments. "Hap" is an archaic word meaning "event"—and referring particularly to those events that come to be associated with good fortune. It is the root of many familiar words, including *happen, happy, perhaps, mishap*, and *happenstance.* Using the notion to critique conventional mathematics education, one might say the efforts to formulate a program of studies and to prescribe appropriate instructional methods are tightly linked to the desire for a *hap*-less curriculum wherein the teacher is able to prescribe all learning and to foresee every possible contingency. Such desire has led to an impersonalized (or, perhaps a more appropriate term would be "depersonalizing") model of mathematics education. Prestated objectives have eclipsed the issue of personal interest, and "fool-proof" explanations have eliminated the need for personal insight. In such mechanized curricula, the hap is something to be ignored or, better yet, avoided entirely.

It is argued here, however, that the hap is the center-point of enactivist teaching. Such teaching is an attendance to the unexpected consequence, to the sudden insight, to the inexplicable interest that is conditioned or occasioned by the teacher's actions. The hap may be anticipated (and, because of this possibility, the teacher has a responsibility to consider what might happen in a given setting), but will more likely be a matter of happenstance.

Section C
Mathematics Teaching as Listening

To be progressively more free is to be sensitive to the conditions and genuine possibilities of some present situation and to be able to act in an open manner. . . . [Freedom] means transformation of our entire way of being, our mode of embodiment, within the lived world itself.

—*Francisco Varela, Evan Thompson, and Eleanor Rosch*[1]

From the teacher's end it boils down to whether or not she is a good conversationalist; whether or not she has the gift or the wisdom to listen to another; the ability to draw out and preserve that other's line of thought.

—*Sylvia Ashton-Warner*[2]

An ecological-embeddedness in the subject matter of mathematics, a complicity in formal education as a cultural institution, being implicated in the emergence of both knowers and their knowing. . . . What then might mathematics teaching be?

I return to my original question in this final discussion, seeking to bring the strands announced in the preceding chapters and sections into a more explicit, but far from whole or settled account of teaching. I develop this section around two projects: first, a final elaboration of the three modes of listening that were introduced in Chapter 1; and, second, a recapping of the main points of this text through a retelling of the third classroom episode (as presented in Chapter 2, and through which I have been developing the notion of *hermeneutic listening*).

I thus do not aim to identify the "educational implications" of my study here. My central purpose, rather, is to try to speak differently about teaching. As such, it is not the closing statement of an argument, but (for me at least) a starting place for a different way of acting. My intention, then, is not merely to summarize, nor just to reassert my principal thesis of the importance of reclaiming our capacities and understandings of listening as we seek alternative enactments and framings for mathematics teaching. I also want to end this discussion in a classroom—the place, ultimately, that all of our theorizing must arrive.

As an ending then, it is not what I would call spectacular. But, true to the sonorous theme, I believe it to be sound.

Three Enactments of Listening/Teaching/Being

Enactment 1: Evaluative Listening ("Adding Fractions" Lesson) By most conventional standards, Wendy's actions during the lesson on adding fractions would be judged as highly competent. In terms of instructional skills, for example, she taught a "textbook" lesson: the levels of her questions ranged from recall to analysis; they were distributed around the classroom; she used appropriate wait time; the structure of the lesson was not inconsistent with the frameworks developed and put forward by various mathematics education researchers. And, while it might be tempting to criticize some of her actions as reflecting a "transmission" approach to teaching, that interpretation seems to be challenged by, for instance, the sequence of examples used to frame her lesson. That movement from like to dissimilar denominators suggests something more than a mere attempt to transmit knowledge. Similarly, her comparison of fractions to familiar additive situations would be consistent with an orientation toward learning that stresses making connections.

However, if we concentrate less on the observable actions of the setting and move into the realms of the invisible and the inaudible—asking, for example, how Wendy seemed to be listening rather than what she actually said—different characterizations of her manner of teaching become possible. In particular, the suggestion that she was enacting a transmission model becomes further problematized. If Wendy actually "believed" that teaching is a simple matter of sending out information, then such actions as asking questions (and listening, in whatever manner, to the responses given) would seem somewhat out of place; implicit in the act of questioning is a certain lack of faith in the transmission process.

Wendy was listening, but it was from a position of singular, unchallenged authority. Representing a subject matter conceived to be valuable for all present, static, and neutral, fulfilling the mandate of an educational system that seeks to equip learners with those competencies deemed necessary for a world perceived to be unchanging, and regarding learning as a subjective process of apprehending the truths offered, Wendy's listening is correspondingly constrained. It is an evaluative listening that seeks to determine correctness, a largely passive attending to the verbal utterances of others of the sort that tends to forget its own responsibility in interactions (often blaming miscommunication on the speaker). It is a listening, in fact, that is a sort of telling . . . of exerting authority, of announcing who is responsible for learning, of tallying.

A concise description of Wendy's teaching, then, is that is seems to be a matter of telling—and this formulation was borne out in virtually all aspects of her lesson, from the telling of the homework answers, through the telling of the lesson, through the repeated telling of learners to stay on task, to the telling of what was to be done for the next day.

Enactment 2: Interpretive Listening ("Adding Integers" Lesson)
Wendy was more attentive in the second lesson—a point that is perhaps most clearly demonstrated through her manner of questioning. In contrast to the preceding episode, the questions posed in this lesson are more often information-seeking than response-seeking, requiring more elaborate answers and, very often, some sort of demonstration. In other words, these are questions whose answers cannot be fully anticipated by Wendy and so she is compelled to attend to them in very different ways.

Wendy's listening, then, is no longer a disguised form of telling—but that is not to say that the telling approach to mathematics teaching has been set aside. What is to be learned, what is to be done, and how one is to behave continue to be told, and listening enters as a complement to such telling. It is a means of assessing the effectiveness of what has been said, of interpreting the appropriateness of student interpretations. No longer subordinate to or subsumed in her explaining acts, Wendy's listening has become a vital component of her teaching action.

This being said, we might also note that, while this episode marks an important departure in the enacted conception of teaching, many of the principles that guided the interaction in the adding fractions lesson remain uninterrogated and unaltered. Teaching mathematics, for example, still seems to be about avoiding any sort of ambiguity: the goal of Wendy's instruction is to provide uncomplicated experiences that enable learners to progress toward more appropriate mathematical understandings. What is learned, while acknowledged to be outside the precise control of the teacher, is still thought to be manageable—Wendy seems to have defined her task in terms of converging on some sort of true or correct understandings of the concept at hand. Attempts have thus been made to identify in advance (and, again, in absence of learners) a set of precise steps that might be followed in order to achieve particular prespecified understandings (albeit with an awareness that individual understandings will be, at best, compatible and never shared).

As for the authority in the classroom, it remains with the teacher. Students' explanations, for example, are modeled on Wendy's explanation; the teacher decides which answers are adequate and which require elaboration. Nevertheless, while Wendy doesn't seem to be listening any *more* in this lesson than she did in the previous one, she is certainly listening *differently.* She is listening constructively: she is constructing the learners as they construct the mathematics. And, importantly, she is aware that she is doing so.

Enactment 3: Hermeneutic Listening ("All-at-Once Fractions" Lesson) One of the things that could be said about the first two teaching episodes is that, in each case, the teacher's project was different from the project of the students. In the first instance, Wendy's central task was cast in the simple and uncritical terms of "teaching math"—that is, to announce and to ensure the mastery of a cultural standard. The students' task was complementary: to internalize whatever concepts had been prespecified. In the second vignette, the teacher's primary task moved more toward making sense of or modeling each learner. Conversely, the learners' projects were to, individually, model the mathematics. And so, while the focus shifted from culturally sanctioned truths to student constructions, the roles and projects of teacher and learner remained distinct.

In the third classroom scene, however, a conflation of roles has occurred. No longer regarding her task as ensuring that learners converge onto some pregiven understanding, nor as honoring the subjective constructions of thirty ostensibly autonomous agents, Wendy has become a participant in the exploration of this piece of mathematics. That is, she has become complicit in the subject matter, in the project of formal education, in the understandings of those present. The authority is no longer exercised through formal assessment (evaluative listening) or preemptive interpretation (interpretive listening). There is, rather, a community established standard: a collective authority.

Through her listening, Wendy has opened up a space for the shared project, the conversation, in which the class is engaged. Her teaching, then, is participatory, transformative, concerned not merely with questions of knowing and doing, but with questions of personal and collective identity. Wendy is listening hermeneutically.

Re-Iteration

As noted earlier, the second part of this final section involves a re-iteration of some of the more important points and assertions of this text. It is developed around a retelling of the third classroom vignette.

That episode is presented in four separate pieces here, each part serving as a subheading for a brief discussion of one of the horizontal strands of this text (i.e., mathematics, formal education, cognition, and teaching). The principal headings for these discussions (i.e., "Listening *in*," "Listening *for*," "Listening *to*," and "Listening") are intended to draw attention to different aspects of listening by focusing on some of the linguistic markers that we use in our references to listening.

Through this re-iteration, my hope is that the manner in which the particular is embedded in the general, the way the general is enacted in the particular, the way we move back and forth between the appropriated (given) and the transformed (the interpreted) all become more audible, more present.

Listening *in*—Subject Matter

"Number one [writing $^1/_6 + ^3/_{12} + ^2/_{24}$]: one sixth plus three twelfths plus two twenty-fourths. How much is that . . . Elaine?"

"One half."

"Can you tell us how you got that?"

"I can draw it."

Wendy holds out the chalk and Elaine comes to the board to draw a picture of her arrangement of the pieces (see Figure 5.1). "It covers the same area as a half [piece]," she explains. "The sixth [piece] is as tall as a half [piece] and these three pieces [motioning across her diagram] are as wide as a half."

To the eye, there is not much new here. Progressive, perhaps, but not new. To the ear, however, this is not a typical classroom.

Consider for example, the sound of the mathematics. It does not have the tone of formal mechanized knowledge—there is no droning repetitive beat guiding the actions here. Instead of the sterile and neatly dissected facts and hermetically sealed concepts of the textbook, this mathematics is messy and tangled. It is an active mathematics that orders, arranges, reasons, and suggests. It is a participatory mathematics that both allows for and demands engaged action with one another and with the objects of one's world—in both cases, a reciprocal and a mutually specifying process is occurring. Words are knit together into a wider integrated knowing; actions prompt other actions as they alter the presented world.

The mathematics is a ground for exploration. There is some creation, some discovery—but the line between constructed and discovered is not clear in the conversation. That is to say, there is a rhythm to the movement in this classroom that passes beyond the merely coordinated actions of other modern school settings. The

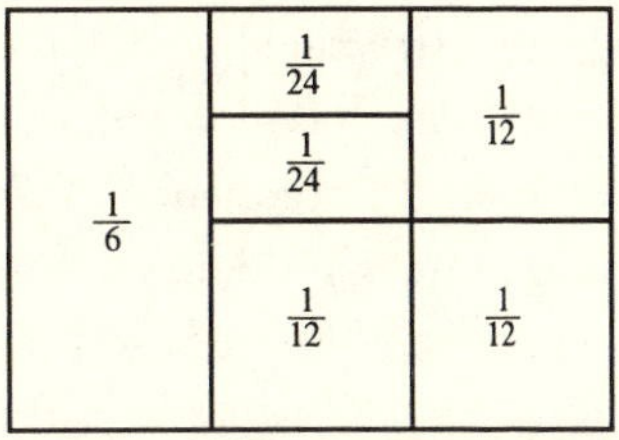

Figure 5.1. Elaine's diagram.

subject matter here is neither outside the learners nor in any one of them, but *about* them. It is a common text that flows about them; it tells about them.

Here we find the teacher positioned between the collective mathematics knowledge of the culture and the emergent mathematical knowings of the individual. The teacher is *listening in*—attuned—to both and, in this listening, is implicated as a full participant in both. In this way, she is enacting an ecological mathematics. It is a mathematics that is not held as distinct from nor thought to be superior to other disciplines and other modes of reasoning. These learners are not expected to leave behind (or suppress) experiences from other contexts—rather, they are offered a space to represent them and, in so doing, to reinterpret what was done and what is being done. And these learners are not held apart by a rigid seating pattern or by the irrelevance of an uninteresting or closed activity.

And so this teacher's *listening in* is not an attending that occurs at a distance. It is not an eavesdropping or a surveillance but an action that locates her in a complex web of existence—caught in intertwining and evolving lines of text from which one cannot extricate oneself. The teacher is not guiding a sight-seeing tour through a thoroughly mapped-out region, but is dwelling in, with, and through the complexity and ambiguity of emergent knowings. A full participant in the learning that is occurring, the teacher is part of the simultaneous transformation of knower and known, culture and mathematics.

What is the "curriculum" here? It is clearly not the narrow, instrumental, prescriptive program of studies that one finds represented in texts and enacted in most classrooms. And implementing the curriculum is not a matter of ensuring that learners achieve some set of predetermined technical competencies.

Rather, the static-ness of the curriculum has been dissolved into the fluidity of *currere*—from following a prestructured path to laying down a path in walking. The steps taken are thus more tentative and more explorative, for the attention is on the negotiation of the terrain rather than on the efficient passage through it. And so, there is no terminating point; no one says, "I'm done. What do I do now?"

But the mandated curriculum has not been cast aside in this dissolution. Reference to the relevant objectives or topics of study can easily be made (although it would be impossible to isolate a single concept as the textbooks and curriculum manuals do). The important point here is that *listening* does not imply an abandonment of the official program of study in a misguided attempt to pursue the richness of student action. Far from abdicating responsibility, in allowing for a more fluid curriculum, the listening teacher takes on a critical response-ability. It is not a listening that follows, but a listening that leads. In its attentiveness, it prompts and encourages—it shapes by questioning or by gesture. Put differently, the listener selects in the speaker what is said and what is not said through a differential attendance. It is thus that the criticism, "You're not listening," is more than an accusation of nonattendance. It is an accusation of nonparticipation.

But how does one plan for such teaching? An answer, I think, is revealed in the issue that has oriented this class's activity. It is not merely a questing for a single solution (as the orienting question would likely prompt in most conventional settings). It is an exploration of possibilities, and so the teaching and the setting are proscriptive rather than prescriptive, opening rather than defining possibilities for action. Contrasting it with the more traditional "lesson concept," this class is not focused on an isolated or fragmented idea. Rather, it is an occasion for learners to devise questions of their own, to add, subtract, multiply, compare—all at once and all at levels of complexity that, in this case, far surpass the recommendations of the mandated program of studies.

The setting is thus one that is not so much "planned" as it is "anticipated." What sorts of mathematical investigating *might* (versus *will*) students undertake, given their backgrounds and the materials at hand? What sorts of prior experiences are necessary for learners to be productive (versus reproductive) in this context? These are the types of questions involved in this anticipating. As such, it is a "planning" founded on a broad familiarity with, but far from a complete mastery of, the mathematics as well as an extensive knowledge of the learners.

Such anticipating is thus only possible through a history of *listening in*—further underscoring that *listening in* does not distance the teacher, nor does it exclude her from the action. Rather, even while standing apart from a group of busy learners, Wendy is an integral element in their activity through a *listening in* that enters in, that participates.

Listening *for*—Education

"So they're exactly the same size and shape as a half piece when you lay them out that way. Good. Did anybody get any other answers . . . Truong?"

"Six twelfths."

"Can you show us how you got that?"

"You can use that picture," Truong responds, pointing to Elaine's diagram. "You have three twelfths already; two twenty-fourths together is another twelfth, and the sixth can be cut into two twelfths. That's six twelfths altogether."

"Okay. Good answer. Any other answers? . . . Van?"

"Four eighths."

"Four eighths? How can you get four eighths using these pieces?"

Auditory perception is not a simple matter of recording the sounds that reach our ears and replaying them in our minds. In fact, in greater part, perception flows in the other direction. What we hear is primarily a matter of what we expect or anticipate—what we are *listening for*. As an awareness of this phenomenon and of its implications are developed, we open the possibility for a deeper listening—one that still *listens for*, since we can never step outside of our prejudices, but one that listens for possibilities and not for just actualities. It is a listening that questions and that entertains questions. It is a listening founded on the fluidity of our knowledge rather than on its rigidity. It is a listening that, in the words of Herbert Marcuse, is "not only the basis for the epistemological constitution of reality, but also for its transformation, its subversion in the interest of liberation."[3]

Consider Wendy's response to Van's answer, "How can you get four eighths with these pieces?" It is a question that announces surprise, some disbelief, perhaps even an accusation that Van has strayed off-topic—but it is a question that is posed out of a sincere desire to know. It is thus one that locates her, her students, and their mathematics in the tentative, inquisitive space of transformation. It is a space away from the surety of the right answer, but one that does not surrender to the insecurity of the unknowable. It is thus a space for thought and action, of appropriation and transformation, of *listening for* that which speaks to us here and now out of our traditions. It is the space of education.

"How can you get four eighths?" is a hermeneutic question. It is a stance in teaching. The essential quality here is not to know everything, but to be *listening for* those things that are not known. The teacher's task is not to transmit, not to manipulate learners into performing in desired ways by pretending to not have an answer. Rather, it is to seek out those spaces where *all* is not yet known. It is there that the mathematics can serve to open up the world. It can begin to educe and to present, moving beyond its current classroom functions of reducing and representing.

"How can you get four eighths?" is an invitation to explain, to negotiate, to hypothesize. It is a call not so much to do formal mathematics as it is to think and to act mathematically. It is a statement on the role of the student. Learning is about neither acquisition nor subjective construction. It is about joint exploration, interactive investigation—play-full conversation.

All of this has become possible because of the secure relational space of this classroom. The teacher's interest in these children extends far beyond a concern for their academic competence. Hers is a pedagogical concern for their well-being, and it is revealed in her every movement. She embodies the qualities of hope, trust, patience, and humor—and nowhere is this attitude more apparent than when she leans in to listen. It is a listening that moves outward to engulf the speaker, to bring the two of them together in an interactive unity.

The educative potential of her listening is revealed in Van's actions. In another classroom, Van might have finished the assigned exercises and moved on to free reading or some other activity. Here he is pushing out the bounds of his own understandings, looking for patterns inside patterns, patterns which connect.

Listening *to*—Cognition

"Easy," Van announces," rising to go to the chalkboard. "One fourth of a sixth plus one twenty-fourth plus a half of a twelfth is an eighth," drawing a dotted line across Elaine's diagram (see Figure 5.2).

"You do that twice, so you can trade that for two eighths. Then, across the bottom, you have one fourth of a sixth and two halves of twelfths, twice, so that's two more eighths," adding more dotted lines and then simplifying the diagram by erasing the unwanted marks.

It is clear in this instance that knowing has nothing to do with the computer-influenced notion of inputting, processing, and outputting data, for Van's actions are too playful, too creative, and too bound up in a web of events to explain through a mechanical, prescriptive metaphor. In this Fraction Kits setting, designed as an explorative and interactive space, one's knowing is inextricable from one's doing. Most importantly, it is a space that invites a range of mathematical actions—from less sophisticated (in formal mathematics terms) rearranging of paper pieces to more formal and abstract activities such as Van's. And so, in this setting, the measure of knowing is not the number of correct answers generated, but the appropriateness of one's actions.

As this attitude toward knowing is placed into the larger contexts of the classroom situation and Van's history with school mathematics, it moves from a "simple" issue of epistemology (of knowing) to one of ontology (of being). At the start of the unit, in Wendy's words, Van was a "typical," "average," "quiet" student who "did what he was told, and not much more." But now, he is "into it," "flying." His mathematics is no longer instrumental, but creative. In effect, his identity within this mathematics classroom has been completely reconfigured. He is not the same person. For him, learning—mathematizing—is an event of being.

Knowledge, then, is not something that is merely incorporated into one's cognitive structure; rather, each and every learning helps

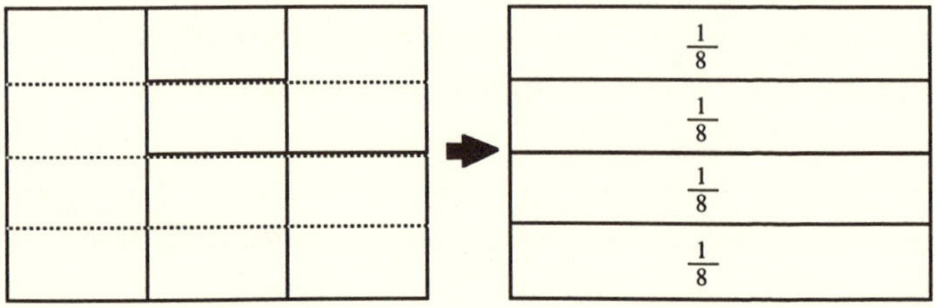

Figure 5.2. Van's diagram.

to re-shape what was learned earlier and, simultaneously, to determine what will next be noticed. Moreover, the effects of such learning can never be predetermined—and certainly cannot be thought of in the singular terms of one life. By teaching, as the account of Van illustrates, we are affecting, however subtly, the individual and collective identities of the learners and of ourselves. Van became a mathematizer. This claim is an important one because it is not merely a statement that his knowledge-base was broadened or that he became able to deal with more sophisticated ideas. Nor is it merely a statement of how he stood in relation to others; it is a statement about not just Van's understandings and meanings, but about the conflation of his and our knowledge, his and our actions, his and our identities.

Understanding and meaning, in this setting, are qualities that are inherent in student actions and which cannot be separated from their actions. They are thus diverse—and perhaps the most critical feature of understandings is the possibility for such diversity. Just as genetic diversity is an essential quality for the viability of a species, so conceptual diversity is a critical element in any learning situation. Much in contrast to a conventional classroom, where the desired goal might be described in terms of achieving uniform competencies and standard understandings, here the focus is on an openness to—a *listening to*—the possible. Wendy's request to Van that he explain his thinking was a prompt toward, or an occasion for, such diversity. What followed, in terms of both Van's action and the collective response, was unpredictable and unrepeatable—an instance of diversity, an enlarging of the space of possibilities.

This diversity places significant demands on the listening teacher who must constantly negotiate the tension between what was anticipated and what is happening. What it strongly points to is the need for a common repertoire of experience among learners on which to base actions and interpretations. Lacking such a foundation for shared meanings, one's interaction with another is severely constrained. This is the place of the Fraction Kits activity in this setting; it serves as a common text; a space for joint action, common language, and shared understandings; a space that not only demands, but facilitates, listening; a possible subject matter.

More importantly, perhaps, it is a space wherein the unformulated understandings that are enacted in every movement are not ignored. Rather, they are considered alongside those understandings that have been formally re-presented for inspection, confirmation, and revision. Formulated and unformulated knowings are thus understood not independently but in terms of their reciprocal (mutual) affect. The teacher listens to not just the words that are spoken, but to the actions that precede, accompany, and follow those actions.

Put differently, the Fraction Kit activity presents a space of play—of acting, of imagining, of moving. As Van's contribution illustrates, it is a space that allows room to negotiate the given task, to turn it over, to play with it. (Such play is almost impossible when questions for which the answers are predetermined form the basis of student action.) In a setting such as that occasioned by the Fraction Kits, there must also be play in the teacher's listening. Lacking such play, for example, it is easy to imagine the response of a nonlistening teacher to Van's answer: "Nice, but you're doing the wrong thing."

Play, as Gadamer has pointed out, opens the space of transformation. In that space, subjectivity is put aside and, as the self is remembered afterward, it is changed. It might be said, then, that play engages, embraces, and encompasses. In playing—in moving, in understanding—our beings come to form. The teacher, then, cannot be considered apart from the learner's play. She is not a director or a facilitator, but an important part of the interactive setting—caught up in the play—*listening to* whatever might be happening.

Listening—Teaching

The lesson continues with an exploration of other possibilities, and students present similar cases for other answers (which included $^{12}/_{24}$, $^{2}/_{4}$, and 1.5 thirds). More than half of the 45-minute time block is taken up in reviewing the homework "questions." The remainder of class time is spent in group work on another, similar set of addition exercises which are developed by the students themselves. Wendy gives the additional instruction that groups are to find several different answers for each question and to explain why those answers are correct.

As teachers, we are continually confronted with claims that this textbook is better, this method is more effective, these activities are the best. There is a perpetual search for the optimum—the fastest procedure, the surest approach, and, in a spirit of unrelenting competition, the highest score. As if it were possible to attain such goals.

The sort of teaching that emerges from a listening orientation might be described as "good enough." It makes no attempt at optimization. Instead, the listening teacher works with the contingencies of the particular classroom setting. It is founded on the realizations that no learning outcome can be prescribed, no active setting can be controlled. But neither must we forego attempts to influence (or fail to acknowledge our influence upon) what might come about. The key to teaching, in this conception, is to present a space for action and then to be present to participate in—and through this participation, to shape—the joint project that emerges.

In the vignette above, Wendy could in no way have foreseen the mathematics that would arise from a seemingly mundane question. What these learners did was not "caused" by what Wendy did; their actions were, rather, determined by their own structures. Wendy merely provided an occasion for them. While she may have anticipated what might occur (based on her familiarity with the learners and the situation), she could not have predicted or controlled (that is, caused) the outcome. It is precisely because the actions that the teacher occasions cannot be anticipated that one is compelled to listen: attuned to, in sync with, and following the rhythm of their actions. The teacher, in this conception, is not responsible for motivating learners. Rather, she takes advantage of their own (structurally determined) playful motivations.

The learning occasion described was a powerful one, especially when compared to more algorithmically-based settings, but it was one that cannot be considered in terms of optimization. Rather, it was one that worked. Similarly, the measure of the resulting understandings cannot be discussed in terms of perfection, but must be considered in terms of their localness and particularity to the occasion. They, like the understandings that help us to maintain our viability in any other context, were *good enough.*

That is to say, they *fitted.* This criterion of fitness, borrowed from a neo-Darwinian conception of evolutionary theory by which the logic of survival is proscriptive (requiring an adequate fit) rather than prescriptive (requiring an optimal fit), calls for a teaching orientation that is not just attuned to, but able to be shaped by, the learning setting. It must be able to maintain its fitness—that is, it must be listening to the events that are about it.

In listening, I am able to bring the insights that emerge from the mass of my experiences onto the developing conceptualizations of learners—not for the purposes of imposing "truth" or assessing performance, but to assist them in exploring and affecting (conversing with) the world. I need not downplay my wider experience, because it is precisely that experience that enables my listening. But, as I teach, I must be prepared to interrogate and to reformulate what I know, for, in order to listen, I am compelled to open my understandings and my self to transformation. If I do not, then I am keeping myself apart from—closing myself to—the very learning attitude that I am demanding of students. The listening teacher is thus the person who is able to forget the unified, coherent, self and to enter the conversation.

The role of the listening teacher is neither *telling* nor *orchestrating*—although proponents of both traditional and constructivist perspectives would likely see these elements to be woven into the teacher's actions. In Wendy's case, for example, the initial structuring of the activity and the selection of the orienting question was very directive. At the same time, the active and explorative setting might be described by some as "constructivist."

But her departure from these orientations is clear, first in her reluctance to rigidly predetermine what would be considered "appropriate" actions or understandings, and second in her refusal to privilege either the "voice" of the learner or that of established knowledge. Rather, a space was opened for their dialogue, and Wendy was an unabashed participant in the conversation that emerged. Her role was thus to provide occasions that would provoke and support ongoing actions, and to play it by ear from there. In effect, she was creating the conditions for ambiguity—pointing at the gaps in knowing—while providing a space to negotiate the play in one's understandings. It is thus that Wendy opened the possibility for and acted upon several *haps* (including, in the brief account provided, Elaine's diagram and Van's explanation) which, together, form a complex web of events that could never have been deliberately provoked. But, with the prodding of an attentive, attuned, and knowledgeable—that is, listening—teacher, an ever expanding sphere of possibilities was presented.

Of course, this does not preclude the possibility of effective teaching occurring in conventional mathematics lessons. Rather, it shifts the location of teaching toward the opportunity for thoughtful action that is occasioned by the lesson and away from the formal lesson presentation. Teaching, then, does not occur in the well-articulated 10-minute explanation nor in the carefully selected and thoughtfully structured set of exercises that follow. Rather, teaching takes place in mutually specifying dynamics of the teacher-student relationship. There the teacher participates in the play-full learning of the student; there the teacher, so-disposed, can listen.

In sum, then, an enacted curriculum is one that should be planned, but not predetermined. It involves a complex weaving of intended and chance happenings, of deliberate and accidental actions. At times the teaching is based on careful analysis and thoughtful decision; more often it is simply a consequence of the way the teacher stands in the world. It is a mathematics teaching that exists and consists in

a genuine curiosity in the mathematical subject matter of the setting (Chapter 2),
awarenesses of the place of education and where teaching takes place (Chapter 3),
a hermeneutic attitude toward the playful learning actions of students (Chapter 4).

In the example given, Wendy embodied mathematics, lived her pedagogy, and enacted her interest in learner understandings. Her teaching, then, was not merely informed by her listening; it was in itself an act of listening. In listening she positioned herself amid the dynamic interplay of evolving meanings and established understandings. In listening, she created a place for mathematics teaching to happen.

Back Word

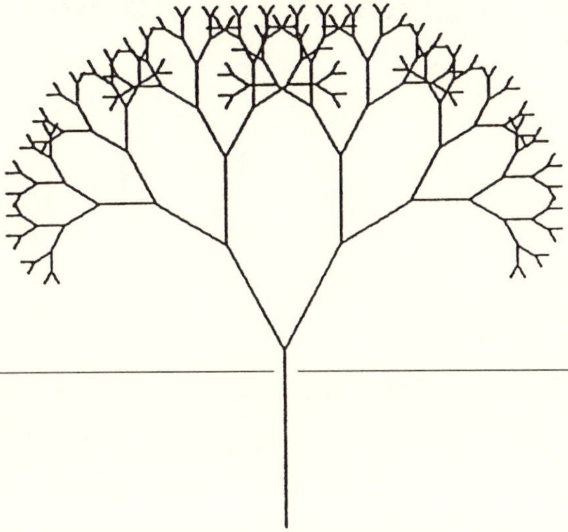

Listening to Reason

Closing Remarks

"If the protests of children were heard in kindergarten, if their questions were attended to, it would be enough to explode the entire educational system." Gilles Deleuze is right. Why do we not listen to children? Why do we not hear what they are telling us? Do we not need, all of us, to learn what it means to listen, really listen, to our children? If we practiced the art of listening, of welcoming their experience, we might learn something. And what if they can hear *our deafness?*

—David Levin[1]

If a tradition has become, implicitly, a dominating force because of the naiveté of our explicit objectification of it in historical study, then . . . a new attitude is called for. This new attitude would recognize the power of tradition for what it really is, treat it accordingly and in that way would attempt to destroy its artificial domination. Heidegger calls this new attitude a "destruction" of tradition. But this "destruction" is positive rather than violently negative. . . . The destruction of a tradition, which he characterizes as a conversation "with that which has been handed down to us," "is not a break with history, nor a repudiation of history, but is an appropriation . . . and transformation . . . of what has been handed down to us. . . . Destruction means—to open our ears, to make ourselves free from what speaks to us in the tradition as the being of being."

—Shaun Gallagher[2]

Listening to Reason

The drama of philosophy resides specifically in the frustrated straining of language to reconstruct the world, and the farce of ideology springs from the illusion that language has succeeded.

—*Robert Grudin*[3]

It is not merely a question here of confronting ideas but of incarnating them and making them live, and in this respect we cannot know what they are capable of except by trying them out. This attempt involves taking sides in a struggle.

—*Maurice Merleau-Ponty*[4]

Some time ago I heard a radio broadcast on the topic of irradiation as a means of food preservation. As debates go, I found this an interesting one, for it was far more than a mere academic exercise. The participants were passionate about their causes, and the goal of each team was not just to win, but to win over. Each sought to enlighten.

The substance of their arguments was fairly predictable—the affirmative drawing upon scientific evidence; the negative maintaining a more theoretical position founded on the premise that current knowledge might simply be inadequate. And, as also might be predicted, neither side made much headway in convincing the other. As the argument began to heat up, a member of the affirmative (scientific) team finally exclaimed in a fit of exasperation: "If you would only listen to reason!"

As though suddenly aware of the problem, the captain of the negative team responded, out of turn, "No, you're the one who needs to listen to reason."

Listening and Reason

Two interpretations of the phrase "listen to reason" were at play here: the first a demand to *acquiesce to scientific evidence*—in effect, to submit to an external source whose authority is founded on a mathematized rationality; the second a demand to *give serious consideration to the sane and rational argument*—to allow one's inner convictions to be appropriately swayed by a logical explanation. Yet, somehow the participants seemed to be neither listening nor reasonable. Both sides missed the import of their mutual invocation. Both sides were demanding the sort of listening that teachers demand of students—a listening that insists on receptivity and lacks reciprocity, a listening that seeks out precision and exorcises play. Both sides were demanding a reasonableness that stands in a determinate relation to "reality." And so, both senses of listening were passive, submissive, and divisive; both forms of reason were methodical, monological, and authoritarian.

In the preceding pages, I have attempted to describe a *listening* that is active and generative and a *reason* that moves beyond the constraining bounds of a mathematized rationality. The starting point for my investigation was not that our cultural emphasis on scientific and discursive knowing is wrong, but that, in the words of Morris Berman, it is "pathetically incomplete, and thus winds up projecting a fraudulent reality."[5] It is a reality against which we determine and justify our actions by calculation rather than sound judgment, a reality that we push beneath us as we claim a place at the top of the "evolutionary ladder."

The complicity of mathematics teachers in the modernist project of promoting this fraudulent reality is undeniable. In the classroom we endeavor to convince a captive audience that to be "rational is to be methodical: that is, to have criteria for success laid down in advance."[6] It is to define, to separate, to master—to ascend an imagined slope rather than to recognize our place in an ecological web. My premise has been that it is thus time to broaden our conception of rationality—an evolution that is inextricably bound to a broadening of our conception of listening. As Rorty explains:

Another meaning for "rational" is, in fact, available. In this sense, the word means something like "sane" . . . rather than "methodical." It names

> *a set of moral virtues: tolerance, respect for the opinions of those around one,* willingness to listen, *reliance on persuasion over force.*[7]

It is a rationality that is incommensurate with current incarnations of school mathematics, but one that need not be incompatible with a mathematics teaching that begins with listening rather than telling . . . a teaching that is concerned not just with knowledge, but with the manner in which that knowledge is held . . . a teaching that does not privilege listening over seeing, but which, in fact, opens our sight by listening more closely.

In Table 6.1, I have attempted to elaborate on the relationship between our understanding of rationality and our orientation to listening. On the left side is William Irwin Thompson's list of the "four mentalities" through which Western civilizations have passed or are passing. He describes these changes in basic mentality as shifting from one geometry to another.[8] In the right column is David Michael Levin's list of the "four stages" of listening through which the individual passes or might pass on his or her way to "becoming."

I am suggesting in this comparison that, just as there is a general movement toward complexification of our understanding of the universe, so must there be an evolution toward a more complex (and hence, more difficult) understanding of our relationships with one another. Put differently, the current shift in our cultural knowledge (that is, in our collective patterns of acting) away from the linear static and toward the complex dynamic corresponds to a movement in our conception of the self from the isolated subject/object (the hearer) to the participating and ever-becoming being (the listener). My thesis is that teachers can and must play an important role in this development—not primarily by teaching about a new world view, but by enacting it, by listening.

Thompson qualifies his elaboration by adding that most people, thoroughly enframed by modern, linear, and reductive ways of thinking, are incapable of making the sort of radical transformations required to move from the Third Mentality to the Fourth. Levin also points to the constraining effects on listening of the dominant modes of thinking and being. In effect, both authors are acknowledging the slow and uncontrollable processes of change that are implicit in the hermeneutic attitude. As Crusius explains:

Table 6.1. *An ontogeny of listening recapitulates a phylogeny of rationality.*

William Irwin Thompson's[9] Four Mentalities of Western Civilizations	**David Michael Levin's[10] Four Stages of Listening**
The first mentality was the arithmetic, the line of counting goods in space and generations in time.	In [the] first phase, our hearing may be said to inhere in, and be attuned by, the field of sonorous Being as a whole. . . . The infant's ears are the body as a whole. . . . [It] is an elementary hearing, deeply, symbiotically embedded in the elemental ecology of nature.
The second mentality is the geometric and it expresses the intellectual revolution wrought by Pythagoras and Plato. For these ancients, motion was imperfect and sinful, and only the unmoving geometry of perfect spheres in the ideal realm was a true expression of the Good.	Stage II culminates in a hearing that is personal, adequately skillful in meeting the normal demands of interpersonal living, and ruled over by the ego, which habitually structures all the auditory situations in which it finds itself in terms of subject and object.
The third mentality was the dynamic mentality of modernism, the mentality of Galileo, Newton, Descartes, in which motion and falling bodies became the focus of attention.	[In] the third stage of listening, we are essentially involved in developing our listening as a practice of compassion, increasing our capacity, as listeners, to be aware of, and responsive to, the interrelatedness and commonality of all sonorous beings.
Now we are moving out of this modernist science with its narratives of linear equations into a postmodernist science of which Chaos Dynamics is one important visual expression.	[In stage IV, listening] becomes *a gathering* of sonorous Being: a gathering mindful of its utterly open dimensionality, attentive to the primordial difference by grace of which all auditory structures are possible, and respectful of the incommensurability of the Being of sonorous beings, letting the inaudible be inaudible.

[Hermeneutics] does not maintain that change is impossible or undesirable, only that meaningful sustainable change is gradual, evolutionary, and cannot be effected by critique alone. In short, we can hope to make things better; we cannot hope for wholesale transformation on either the individual or collective level.[11]

This writing is thus not intended to contribute to a badly needed revolution in mathematics teaching, but to an inevitable evolution. What I hope has been offered here is a possible alternative for mathematics teaching—one that might help to reconnect us to one another, to our knowledge, to nature—but one that I acknowledge cannot be extracted from the modernist context of the school. Listening is difficult there, and it is thus that I am comforted by Heidegger's words:

What we can do in our present case, or anyway can learn, is to listen closely. To learn listening, too, is the common concern of student and teacher. No-one is to be blamed, then, if he is not yet capable of listening.[12]

Reason to Listen

As the correspondence between Thompson's and Levin's frameworks suggests, there is great potential in a fuller understanding of the sonorous realm. It is a place that does not permit the simple and lasting distinctions of our visual field. Instead of indisputable see-it-with-my-own-eyes facts, our ears present us with possibilities, complexities, connectings . . . if we are open to interpretations other than our own.

But an openness to other interpretations is only a start to listening. For each action and each word has a history. It carries an echo of humankind's past. The call to listen is thus a call to complexity, to relationality, to transformation, to fluidity. It is a quest for participatory fitness, rather than an adherence to pregiven boundaries.

Moreover, words are used by persons, and one's "choice of words" is a reflection of one's personal history, one's context, one's relationships. Each utterance is a chorus of one's dispersed identity—a structure that is "rooted in, and channeled through, the body of our experience. Thus we must not let these processes get cut off from our bodily nature."[13] We must rather listen to our bodies of knowledge, participating in the evolution of those bodies by being mindful of the way we speak.

And so, the call to listen is a call to interrupt what has come to be our "commonsense"—that is, of both the prevailing discourse and one's hearing of it. As Heidegger[14] more dramatically states it, we need to develop an attitude of "destruction." It is this attitude that I have attempted to bring to this investigation of mathematics teaching. This sort of positive destruction must be brought to bear against the negative destruction that our society is carrying out under the neutral-sounding labels of "instruction," "construction," "mathematics," and "education."

I have argued that current conceptions of mathematics, of education, of learning, and—perhaps most of all—of teaching are violent, where "violent" is intended to provoke a sense of thoughtless transgression in addition to its more familiar sense of furious destruction. It is a violence that is deaf to (and ultimately silencing of) the voices of its victims—ourselves. Moreover, mathematics teaching is, in my opinion—and I speak here as a teacher who has been complicit in the project—not amoral, as it claims, but indisputably immoral. In allowing itself to forget that its subject matter is a humanity, it has become an inhumanity. It is thus that we have created a system that values compliance over creativity, that spawns destructive behavior by destroying our experience, and that conditions learners to reach for the formulaic ahead of the imaginative.

I left the public school mathematics classroom because I could not abide what I was doing. Although I lacked a means of articulating the source of my dis-ease, I had reached a point that I could no longer ignore it. I think that I have now found a language to express those troubling intuitions, a language to support alternative patterns of acting, and a language that announces the sort of transformations that I have undergone through this project.

Has it been a success? I cannot be the final judge. In the end, this research was worth the effort *not* if it has convinced everyone to listen to reason, but if it has provided someone with a reason to listen.

Notes

Front Word: Setting the Tone—Introduction

1. Richard Rorty, *Contingency, irony, and solidarity* (New York: Cambridge University Press, 1989), 78.
2. Ibid., 74.
3. Joachim-Ernst Berendt, *The third ear: On listening to the world* (New York: Henry Holt, 1985), 56.
4. Mary Catherine Bateson, *Peripheral visions: Learning along the way* (New York: HarperCollins, 1994), 43.
5. Hubert Reeves, *Malicorne: Earthly reflections of an astrophysicist* (Toronto: Stoddart, 1993), 16.
6. Maurice L. Hartung, *Seeing through arithmetic, Grades 1–6* (Toronto: Gage, 1957).
7. This list is drawn from David Michael Levin's *The listening self: Personal growth, social change and the closure of metaphysics* (London: Routledge, 1989), 31. He uses these terms and others to describe what he calls a "metaphysics of vision"— a modern technocratic mind-set that he argues to be pervasive in Western cultures.
8. Both these terms are derived from words that had to do with seeing and vision.
9. It was not always thus. R. Murray Schafer, in *The soundscape: Our sonic environment and the tuning of the world* (Rochester, VT: Destiny Books, 1977), for example, suggests that, in the days of prophets and of oral epics, the sense of hearing may have been more vital than the sense of sight. In some parts of the world, such as rural Africa, it appears that the aural still predominates. In such places—that is, ones that have not been so drenched in unwanted sounds (noise) that their citizens have learned to ignore them—each auditory sensation is of direct personal significance for the hearer. Moreover, such settings are free of the dense overpopulation of sounds that we find in our mechanized world—sounds that distract and restrict as they prevent us from hearing anything but what is in our immediate vicinity, noises that may be contributing to our closing in on ourselves.
10. Erwin Straus, *Phenomenological psychology* (New York: Basic Books, 1966), 286 (emphasis in original).
11. Richard Rorty, *Objectivity, relativism, and truth: Philosophical papers, volume 1* (New York: Cambridge University Press, 1991), 13–14 (emphasis added).
12. See William H. Schubert, "Philosophical inquiry: The speculative essay," in *Forms of curriculum inquiry*, ed. Edmund Short (New York: SUNY Press, 1991).
13. See Norman K. Denzin and Yvonna S. Lincoln, "Entering the field of qualitative research," in *Handbook of qualitative research*, eds. Norman K. Denzin and Yvonna S. Lincoln (Thousand Oaks, CA: Sage, 1994).
14. Wendell Berry, *The unsettling of America: Culture and agriculture* (San Francisco: Sierra Club Books, 1977), 21.

15. This structure is borrowed and adapted from Kieren and Pirie's model of mathematical understanding. See Susan Pirie and Thomas Kieren, "Growth in mathematical understanding: How can we characterize it?" in *Educational Studies in Mathematics* 26, no. 2–3 (March 1994): 165–190.
16. For the purposes of illustration, the reader might compare the simple fork with the completed tree (i.e., "completed" in the sense that the capacity of the drawing program was extended to its limit), as presented on the title page of the bibliography. There, circles, spirals, webs, and polygons of all sorts emerge and contribute to a rather dense "foliage." (See p. 303.)

Chapter 1: Close Your Eyes and Listen—Conceptual Underpinnings

Section 1A: Enactivism

1. Maurice Merleau-Ponty, *Phenomenology of perception* (London: Routledge, 1962), 347.
2. Gretel Ehrlich, cited in Hannah Merker, *Listening: Ways of hearing in a silent world* (New York: HarperCollins, 1992), 179.
3. Francisco Varela, Evan Thompson, and Eleanor Rosch, *The embodied mind: Cognitive science and human experience* (Cambridge, MA: The MIT Press, 1991), 218.
4. Thomas Merton, *Raids on the unspeakable* (New York: New Directions, 1964).
5. Plato had already argued that the world is revealed to reason alone and not to ordinary sense perception. See Roger Scruton, *A short history of modern philosophy: From Descartes to Wittgenstein* (London: Routledge, 1981).
6. It is interesting to note that, at the time, mathematics was not highly regarded. In fact, it was neither seen as an independent discipline nor as a means of deducing unquestionable truths, and was as closely associated with mystical endeavors as with scientific. I return to this issue in the first section of the next chapter.
7. Richard E. Palmer, *Hermeneutics: Interpretation theory in Schleiermacher, Dilthey, Heidegger and Gadamer* (Evanston, IL: Northwestern University Press, 1969), 144 (original emphasis).
8. Explicit formulations of this mode of dualistic thinking extend back at least to the Pythagoreans of Ancient Greece. They identified ten fundamental opposites: odd/even, male/female, good/evil, wet/dry, right/left, rest/motion, hot/cold, light/dark, straight/curved, limited/unlimited. See John McLeish, *The story of numbers: How mathematics has shaped civilization* (New York: Fawcett Columbine, 1991) for a more detailed account of these notions.
9. Palmer, *Hermeneutics*, 144, 146.
10. For example: Merleau-Ponty, *Phenomenology of perception*; Rorty, *Objectivity, relativism, and truth, volume 1*; Hans-Georg Gadamer, *Truth and method* (New York: Continuum, 1990).
11. For example: Jean Piaget and Bärbel Inhelder, *The psychology of the child* (New York: Basic Books, 1969); L.S. Vygotsky, *Mind in society: The development of higher psychological processes* (Cambridge, MA: Harvard University Press, 1978); and Jerome Bruner, *Actual minds, possible worlds* (Cambridge, MA: Harvard University Press, 1986), Jerome Bruner, *Acts of meaning* (Cambridge, MA: Harvard University Press, 1990).
12. For example: Berry, *The unsettling of America*; Gregory Bateson, *Mind and nature: A necessary unity* (New York: E. P. Dutton, 1979); James Lovelock, *Gaia, a new look at life on Earth* (New York: Oxford University Press, 1979).
13. For example: Humberto Maturana and Francisco Varela, *The tree of knowledge: The biological roots of human understanding* (Boston: Shambhala, 1987); Varela et al., *The embodied mind*.
14. Following Varela et al., in *The embodied mind*, I will be using "enactivism" as a gathering term to refer to the related schools of thought.

15. Varela et al., *The embodied mind*, xvii.
16. Ibid., xv.
17. Lev S. Vygotsky, *Thought and language* (Cambridge, MA: The MIT Press, 1962).
18. Maturana and Varela, *The tree of knowledge*, 100.
19. The etymology of "person" is uncertain. Most etymological dictionaries do suggest a relationship to the sonorous realm.
20. Ibid., 96 (original emphasis).
21. Varela et al., *The embodied mind*, 174.
22. Ibid., 172.
23. Mark Johnson, *The body in the mind: The bodily basis of meaning, imagination, and reason* (Chicago: University of Chicago Press, 1987).
24. Varela et al., *The embodied mind*, 149.
25. Maturana and Varela, *The tree of knowledge*, 26.
26. Lovelock, *Gaia, a new look at life on earth.*
27. Maturana and Varela, *The tree of knowledge.*
28. M. Mitchell Waldrop, *Complexity: The emerging science at the edge of order and chaos* (New York: Simon and Schuster, 1992), 12.
29. See Jack Cohen and Ian Stewart, *The collapse of chaos: Discovering simplicity in a complex world* (New York: Penguin Books, 1994).

Section 1B: Hermeneutics

1. Merleau-Ponty, *Phenomenology of perception*, 393.
2. Berendt, *The third ear*, 44.
3. Joel Weinsheimer, *Gadamer's hermeneutics: A reading of "Truth and method"* (New Haven, CT: Yale University Press, 1985), 9.
4. See, for example, Palmer, *Hermeneutics*; Gadamer, *Truth and method*; Shaun Gallagher, *Hermeneutics and education* (Albany, NY: SUNY Press, 1992).
5. Timothy W. Crusius, *A teacher's introduction to philosophical hermeneutics* (Urbana, IL: National Council of Teachers of English, 1991), 5.
6. Ibid., 14.
7. Ibid.
8. Varela et al., *The embodied mind*, 3 (emphasis added).
9. David G. Smith, "Hermeneutic inquiry: The hermeneutic imagination and the pedagogic text," in *Forms of curriculum inquiry*, ed. Edmund Short (New York: SUNY Press, 1991), 190.
10. Quoted by Smith, ibid., 190.
11. The reference to the "social sciences" rather than the "hard sciences" is deliberate. Reporting on a paradoxical shift in the two broad areas, Margaret Donaldson, in *Human minds: An exploration* (New York: Allen Lane The Penguin Press, 1993), describes how, earlier in this century, social scientists endeavored to write themselves out of their research at the same time that physical scientists were compelled to write themselves in. In her words, "we see the strange state of affairs that, while prominent schools of psychology were trying to push consciousness out of their theorizing, physicists were finding they had to bring it in" (p. 187).
12. It is important to note, in the context of this discussion of research orientations, that hermeneutics moves well beyond the commonly drawn distinction between "qualitative" and "quantitative" studies. Very often, whether one is describing a phenomena or measuring it, the epistemological commitments of researchers do not vary much. Hermeneutics entails a very different approach to inquiry than those perspectives that seek to determine some measure of truthfulness—that is, where truth is understood in terms of some correspondence between one's theories and some independent reality. Founded on a recognition of our complicity in various social phenomena, hermeneutics rejects the positivist's goal of detached objectivity as unattainable and somewhat naive. This does not

mean that the hermeneut engages in some sort of subjective, idiosyncratic interpretive process, however. Centrally concerned with neither objectivity nor subjectivity, the hermeneut replaces conventional demands for validity, reliability, and generalizability with concerns for viability, reasonableness, and relevance.

13. Smith, "Hermeneutic inquiry," 191.
14. Ibid., 192.
15. Hugh J. Silverman, *Textualities: Between hermeneutics and deconstruction* (New York: Routledge, 1994), 12.
16. Gadamer, *Truth and method.*
17. Silverman, *Textualities*, 31 (original emphasis).
18. Gadamer, *Truth and method*, 366.
19. Ibid.
20. Crusius, *A teacher's introduction to philosophical hermeneutics*, 37–38.
21. Ibid., 37.
22. This point may require some elaboration. I am not attempting to argue here that we, in some way, forget who we are or what we are doing when we converse with one another. The point, rather, is that the focal point of the conversation is neither you nor me, but a topic of shared interest. If the focus shifts to subjective or self-ish concerns, the mode of interaction tends to become something other than a conversation.
23. An interesting side note is that there appears to be a physiological foundation to the suggestion that vision is more *fixing* or *stating* of phenomena than hearing. We are capable of distinguishing sounds that are separated by as little as 2 to 5 milliseconds, but flashes of light blur together if they are separated by less than 20 or 30 milliseconds. (It is this relatively slow response that makes it possible to "trick" our vision into seeing discrete images—such as the frames of a film—as continuous ones.) Hearing, then, is far more attuned to and capable of coping with the rapid flux of existence.
24. Walter Ong, *Orality and literacy: The technologizing of the word* (New York: Methuen, 1982), 72.
25. Merleau-Ponty, *Phenomenology of perception*, vii.
26. Max van Manen, *Researching lived experience* (Toronto: The Althouse Press, 1990), 184.
27. Merleau-Ponty, *Phenomenology of perception*, 430.
28. van Manen, *Researching lived experience*, 184.

Section 1C: Listening

1. Merker, *Listening*, 29.
2. Levin, *The listening self*, 223.
3. I am attempting to invoke Heidegger's sense of "dwelling" here—a formulation that is more toward a dynamic and affecting participation with one's e*cos* (home; living place). To *dwell in* is not simply to *live among.* The latter evokes senses of separate existences (ones that become associated only because of their proximity), whereas the former implicates all present in mutually-specifying and co-emergent processes. See Martin Heidegger, *Basic writings* (San Francisco: HarperCollins, 1977).
4. Ong, *Orality and literacy.*
5. Mary F. Belenky, Blythe M. Clinchy, Nancy R. Goldberger, and Jill M. Tarule, *Women's ways of knowing: The development of self, voice, and mind* (New York: Basic Books, 1986), 167.
6. Ibid., 18.
7. Berendt, *The third ear.*
8. See Diane Ackerman's *A natural history of the senses* (New York: Vintage Books, 1990).
9. At first hearing, the suggestion that listening can be *seen* may seem unsound.

But a quick trace of its etymology suggests that our forebears were aware of a visual dimension of listening. Related to the term "lust," listening has in its history a sense of active longing and directed focus—qualities that are normally considered very observable. (Listening is also related to "listless"—and a correspondence might be drawn between our obviously *listless* classroom and our *listening-less* classrooms.)

10. Here I am borrowing from Charles Taylor's "The dialogical self," in *The interpretive turn: Philosophy, science, culture*, eds. David Hiley, James Bohman, and Richard Shusterman (Ithaca, NY: Cornell University Press, 1991).
11. Ibid., 310.
12. This use of the term "subject matter" may seem somewhat ambiguous in the context of a piece of writing that is developed around a particular "subject area." Here the term is not intended to refer to the "subject matter of mathematics" or to any other discipline (although such a reference might be an interesting metaphorical extension of the current idea). Rather, the point being made is that the conversation is more than the sum of its parts; it has an integrity that exists in the joint action of its participants—an integrity that gives rise to actions and insights that would not otherwise have come about. To say that "the subject matter exists only in the conversation," then, is not intended to suggest that the subject matter lacks a history or that it dissipates when the conversation ends. It is to say, rather, that we are capable of engaging in joint action, and that action is itself the subject matter of the conversation.
13. Merleau-Ponty, *Phenomenology of perception*, 354.
14. Maurice Merleau-Ponty, *The primacy of perception* (Evanston, IL: Northwestern University Press, 1964), 118.
15. Ibid.
16. Ibid.
17. Maturana and Varela, *The tree of knowledge*.
18. Further to this point, Maturana and Varela also argue that our language is the analog of the physical substances that pass between other same-species organisms in a process referred to as *trophallaxis*. Trophallactic substances are constituent parts of the organisms and make possible their structural coupling.

    I believe this analogy may assist us in developing a deeper sense of the conversational relation. Consider, for example, the implications of the following sentence (from Gadamer, in *Truth and method*) if "trophallaxis" is substituted for "language": "Every conversation presupposes a common language, or better: it creates a common language" (p. 378). The implications for our capacities to hear and to listen are profound.
19. As will be elaborated in Chapter 4, *understanding* is understood herein in terms of our capacity for action. A "deepened understanding" is thus, in Maturana and Varela's terms, an expanded "sphere of behavioral possibilities." In colloquial terms, the point being made with regard to the conversation is that "two heads are better than one"—a notion that the enactivist might rephrase as, "two heads, in structural unity, have a far greater range of potential action than the two heads acting separately."
20. van Manen, *Researching lived experience*, 8.
21. Levin, *The listening self*, 181 (emphasis added).
22. Robert Pirsig, *Lila: An inquiry into morals* (New York: Bantam Books, 1991), 158.
23. Levin, *The listening self*, 17 (emphasis in original).
24. In the library system of the University of Alberta, the institution at which the first draft of this text was completed, there are literally hundreds of resources on the topic of improving listening skills. Some titles include: *"I hear you": How to use listening skills for profit*; *Listening made easy: How to improve listening on the job, at home, and in the community*; and *A manager's guide to speaking and listening*.

    Interestingly, *most* of the resources on listening are housed in the education library—and almost all of those focus on students' listening skills (i.e., on means of improving these skills or the correlation between listening abilities and academic achievement). Those few that deal with the teacher's listening focus on how one might listen to appraise and assess student articulations.

25. See Richard A. Leva, *Psychotherapy, the listening voice: Rogers and Erickson* (Muncie, IN: Accelerated Development, 1987).
26. Schafer, *The soundscape*, 11.
27. Erwin Straus, *The primary world of senses* (Glencoe, NY: The Free Press of Glencoe, 1963).
28. Taylor, "The dialogical self."
29. Merleau-Ponty, *Phenomenology of perception*, 234.
30. Further to this point, it is important to emphasize that, by describing listening in this manner, I am not suggesting that it is a "meta-awareness"—a perceptual capacity that can somehow move outside of itself and assume a detached, objectifying stance. Quite the contrary, such "meta"-notions are antithetical to listening. To use the relatively popular idea of *metacognition* as an illustrative comparison, the belief that we can somehow stand above our own cognitive processes and, in so doing, to enable them, has the effect of underscoring rather than erasing the dichotomous traditions in which much of educational discourse is mired. Alongside mind/body, thought/action, knowledge/knower, and self/other, we are urged to include thought/metathought.
31. Levin, *The listening self*, 111.
32. An illustrative example of this phenomenon occurred when a teacher was introducing himself to a new group of students. One student, named "Yoofi," was asked to repeat his name several times, and then to spell it, before the teacher was able to hear it. Lacking appropriate prejudgments (which could be found only in phonetic analysis), this teacher's listening was constrained.
33. Varela et al., *The embodied mind.*
34. Oliver Sacks, "A neurologist's notebook: To see and not see," *The New Yorker*, May 10, 1993, 59–73.
35. This account might also be used to further explicate how our perceptions of the world are *enacted.* Vision, for example, is clearly not the biological equivalent of using a camera to capture images and to re-present them in another context. Rather, the capacity to see (like each of the other senses) emerges as we live through and interact with the world. Another interesting point is that it might be more appropriate to speak of the development of vision as a process of learning how *not to see*, because far more is disregarded than is noticed in our seeing.
36. Levin, *The listening self*, 47.
37. Ibid.

Chapter 2: An Ear to the Ground—The Subject Matter

Section 2A: Mathematics

1. Quoted by John D. Barrow, *Pi in the sky: Counting, thinking, and being* (Oxford: Clarendon Press, 1992), 121.
2. Berendt, *The third ear*, 15 (emphasis in original).
3. Morris Kline, *Mathematics: The loss of certainty* (New York: Oxford University Press, 1980), 296.
4. Rorty, *Contingency, irony, and solidarity*, 5.
5. See, for example, Murray Bookchin, *The philosophy of social ecology: Essays on dialectical naturalism* (Montreal: Blackrose Books, 1990).
6. See, for example, Gregory Bateson, *Steps to an ecology of mind* (New York: Ballantine Books, 1972); Berry, *The unsettling of America*; David W. Orr, *Ecological literacy: Education and the transition to a postmodern world* (Albany, NY: SUNY Press, 1992).

7. Berry, *The unsettling of America*, 22 (emphasis in original).
8. See, for example, Berendt, *The third ear.*
9. Further to this point, although I do not align myself with this particular movement, the emerging discourses of spirituality and sacred relations rely heavily of the figurative language of harmonies (as the foundations of "things") and listening (as our mode of situating ourselves relative to those phenomena that we differentiate from ourselves). As W.I. Thompson, in *Imaginary landscape: Making worlds of myth and science* (New York: St. Martin's Press, 1989), suggests, whether we agree with "religious fanatics" or not, they seem to have remembered for us, through this modern age of analysis and disjuncture, that there is something beyond the solitary ego.
10. Philip J. Davis and Reuben Hersh, *Descartes' dream: The world according to mathematics* (Boston: Houghton Mifflin, 1986), 201.
11. I am using the word "mentality" rather than a temporally situated term (such as "era") because, as should become apparent in the reading, elements of each of the five categories continue to be enacted in some form. I must thus emphasize that the "mentalities" I describe are as much historical eras as they are different ways of thinking about mathematics.
12. With the exception of "Oral," these terms are similar to those used by Imre Lakatos in *Proofs and refutations* (Cambridge: Cambridge University Press, 1976), an insightful and influential analysis of various perspectives on mathematical knowledge. While there are some correspondences to his definitions of the terms, my uses are not intended to parallel his.
13. Ong, *Orality and literacy.*
14. I do not mean to imply that oral cultures have no "accumulated knowledge." Quite the contrary, to use a modern "containment" metaphor, their stories and songs serve as repositories of knowledge and wisdom. However, unlike the literate's conception of history and epic tales as essentially static objects (and hence things that are reread), the oral citizen's stories change with each telling as narrator and audience interact. Histories are not penned (i.e., *constrained*) because they are not penned (i.e., *written*). Put differently, knowledge is not *stored* in the narrative; rather, knowledge is collectively and actively *storied* in the (transformative) recitation of the narrative. It is immediate, negotiated, mutable; it demands the active participation of both teller and listener, implicating all.
15. To elaborate, we cannot hear a whole word all at once. In order to hear "word," for example, the "wo-" has to fade before the "-rd" arrives. By contrast, with written text, words are presented (and recognized) in their entirety.
16. Aleksandr Romanovich Luria, *Cognitive development: Its cultural and social foundations* (Cambridge, MA: Harvard University Press, 1976).
17. Ong, *Orality and literacy*, 55.
18. Edmund Carpenter, *Eskimo realities* (New York: Holt, Rinehart and Winston, 1973), 37.
19. George Gheverghese Joseph, *The crest of the peacock: Non-European roots of mathematics* (London: Penguin Books, 1991), 23.
20. Alfred North Whitehead, *Science and the modern world* (London: Free Association Books, 1926).
21. While this leap may seem mundane to our modern perceptions, the magnitude of this insight should not be underestimated. Donaldson, in *Human minds*, and Rudy Rucker, in *Mind tools: The five levels of mathematical reality* (Boston: Houghton Mifflin, 1987), discuss this intellectual milestone, both in terms of the difficulty children have in achieving it and in terms of the tremendous conceptual advance that it represents.
22. An interesting side note is provided by Mark Johnson in *Moral imagination: Implications of cognitive science for ethics* (Chicago: The University of Chicago Press, 1993). He suggests that the individual develops logical thinking when language

skills are sufficiently developed to allow that person to construct chains of causal thought. In his words, there "exists an intimate connection between life stories and the structures of rationality. These stories are our most basic contact with rational explanation" (p. 179). In other words, Johnson is suggesting that the individual's deductive thinking emerges in a similar manner to that in which our culture's deductive logic was developed.

23. Ong, *Orality and literacy*, 52.
24. Carl B. Boyer and Uta C. Merzbach, *A history of mathematics, second edition* (New York: John Wiley and Sons, 1991).
25. Ibid., 280.
26. "Idea" comes from the Greek *idein*, to see.
27. Kline, *Mathematics*, see especially p. 110.
28. Donaldson, *Human minds*.
29. Pythagoras is often given credit for coining the term "mathematics" ("that which is learned"), a word that he used to describe his intellectual activities. See Boyer and Merzbach, *A history of mathematics*.
30. George Steiner, *Language and silence* (New York: Atheneum, 1967).
31. Lest I be accused of labeling all premodern mathematics (other than that of the Greeks) as utilitarian, I would draw the reader's attention to the insightful work of Joseph who, in *The crest of the peacock*, convincingly argues that other civilizations (including Babylonian, Egyptian, Chinese, and Hindu) had other than pragmatic motivations in developing their rather sophisticated systems of mathematics. Further, Joseph points to the contributions of many of these civilizations to Greek thought, demonstrating that what tends to be considered an isolated contribution by one civilization was more likely a conflagration of ideas from many cultures.
32. Heidegger, *Basic writings*, 254.
33. Steiner, *Language and silence*.
34. Barrow, *Pi in the sky*, 127.
35. Davis and Hersh, *Descartes' dream*, 8.
36. René Descartes, *Discourse on method* and *Meditations on first philosophy* (Indianapolis: Hackett Publishing Company, 1993) (emphasis added).
37. Davis and Hersh, *Descartes' dream*, 12.
38. Accessible and insightful accounts of this "world mathematization" are offered by Davis and Hersh in *The mathematical experience* (Boston: Houghton Mifflin, 1981) and in *Descartes' dream*, and by Barrow, in *Pi in the sky*.
39. Gadamer, *Truth and method*, 276.
40. E.g., Jean-François Lyotard, *The postmodern condition: A report on knowledge* (Minneapolis: Minnesota Press, 1984).
41. See Alan J. Bishop, "Western mathematics: The secret weapon of cultural imperialism," in *Race and Class* 32, no. 2 (October–December 1990): 51–65.
42. See, for example, Ubiratan d'Ambrosio, "Ethnomathematics and its place in the history and pedagogy of mathematics," in *For the Learning of Mathematics* 5, no. 1 (February 1985): 44–47.
43. E.g., Bookchin, *The philosophy of social ecology*.
44. E.g., Valerie Walkerdine, *The mastery of reason: Cognitive development and the production of rationality* (London: Routledge, 1988).
45. Davis and Hersh, *Descartes' dream*.
46. Levin, *The listening self*, 33.
47. It is important to note that these mathematicians were not attempting to render mathematics *devoid* of meaning. Rather, their aim was to relieve mathematical principles of the excess weight of associated (meaningful) experience and, in so doing, to allow mathematics to become more powerful. At the same time, it was felt, the potential for new and more profound mathematical insight would be enabled since much of the obscuring—and, to the formalist perspective, irrelevant—details could be disregarded. Hilbert's goal, in fact, might be expressed in

terms of simplifying the process of proof. He sought a "meta-mathematics" of sorts: a means of checking a proof by stepping outside it, thus providing verification without having to return to first principles.

48. Reeves, *Malicorne*, 27.
49. Ibid.
50. Ibid., 27 (original emphasis).
51. Davis and Hersh, *Descartes' dream*, 16.
52. Karl Popper, *The logic of scientific discovery* (London: Hutchinson, 1959).
53. Thomas Kuhn, *The structure of scientific revolutions* (Chicago: University of Chicago Press, 1962).
54. Lakatos, *Proofs and refutations*.
55. Davis and Hersh, *The mathematical experience*.
56. It must be noted, however, that the formalist and hyper-formalist projects have hardly been set aside. On the contrary, as Paul Ernest elaborates in *The philosophy of mathematics education* (London: The Falmer Press, 1991), several different schools of thought have emerged in this century, all dedicated in one way or another to the reformulation of mathematics.
57. See John Horgan's "The death of proof," *Scientific American*, October 1993, 92–103.
58. The Four-Color Conjecture: "any planar map can be colored using at most 4 colors in such a way that no two adjacent areas are on the same color."—E.J. Borowski and J.M. Borwein, *HarperCollins dictionary of mathematics* (New York: HarperPerennial, 1991), 227.
59. A thorough account of the emergence of this branch of mathematics is given by James Gleick in *Chaos: Making a new science* (New York: Penguin Books, 1987).
60. Lynn Arthur Steen, "Pattern," in *On the shoulders of giants: New approaches to numeracy*, ed. Lynn Arthur Steen (Washington, DC: National Academy Press, 1990), 7.
61. Kline, *Mathematics*, 295.
62. Barrow, *Pi in the sky*, 267–268 (emphasis added).
63. Davis and Hersh, *Descartes' dream*, 86.
64. This is one of Gregory Bateson's provocative phrases.
65. Ernest, *The philosophy of mathematics education*.
66. For a more thorough articulation of this question, see Richard W. Hamming, "The unreasonable effectiveness of mathematics," *American Mathematical Monthly* 87 (February 1980): 81–90.
67. Kline, *Mathematics*, 332.
68. See Waldrop, *Complexity*; John L. Casti, *Complexification: Explaining a paradoxical world through the science of surprise* (New York: HarperCollins, 1994); Cohen and Stewart, *The collapse of chaos*.
69. This idea is borrowed from Gadamer's description of the work of art—an idea that I return to in the next chapter.
70. Adapted from Warren McCulloch's, "What is number that man may know it, and a man that he may know number?" in *Embodiments of mind* (Cambridge, MA: MIT Press, 1963), 1.
71. Varela et al., *The embodied mind*, 253.
72. Max Horkheimer, *Eclipse of reason* (New York: Continuum-Seabury, 1974), 176.
73. Davis and Hersh, *Descartes' dream*, 98.

Section 2B: Mathematics Curriculum

1. Susanne K. Langer, *Problems of art* (New York: Charles Scribner's Sons, 1957), 48 (emphasis in original).
2. Madeleine Grumet, *Bitter milk: Women and teaching* (Amherst, MA: The University of Massachusetts Press, 1988), 172.
3. A "Mad Minute" is a page of computation questions. Students are given one minute to complete as many of the questions as possible.

4. Louise Berman, "Perspectives and imperatives: Re-searching, rethinking, and reordering curriculum priorities," in *Journal of Curriculum and Supervision* 1, no. 1 (Fall 1985): 66–77, 66.
5. See William F. Pinar, William M. Reynolds, Patrick Slattery, and Peter M. Taubman, *Understanding curriculum* (New York: Peter Lang, 1995) for an up-to-date and comprehensive overview of the perspectives and personalities that have participated in shaping the field of curriculum studies.
6. Franklin Bobbitt, *The curriculum* (Boston: Houghton Mifflin, 1918); Franklin Bobbitt, *How to make a curriculum* (Boston: Houghton Mifflin, 1924).
7. William H. Schubert, *Curriculum: Perspective, paradigm, and possibility* (New York: Macmillan Publishing Company, 1986).
8. John Dewey, *The child and the curriculum* (Chicago: The University of Chicago Press, 1956 [1902]).
9. Bruner, *Actual minds, possible worlds*, 123.
10. Pinar et al., *Understanding curriculum*, 3. In making this statement, the authors are actually referring to the field of curriculum. Their book, in fact, is an effort to demonstrate how curriculum is comprised of actual living people, not disembodied ideas—a task that is consistent with the enactivist framework.
11. Walkerdine, *The mastery of reason*, 186.
12. Bookchin, *The philosophy of social ecology.*
13. Orr, *Ecological literacy.*
14. Some examples are in order here. With regard to "the gender issue," Elizabeth Fennema (see Elizabeth Fennema and M.J. Ayer, eds., *Women and education: Equity or equality?* Berkeley, CA: McCutchan, 1984) has written extensively and insightfully on societal traditions and educational practices that serve to militate against the success of females in mathematics schooling. Jean Anyon ("Social class and the hidden curriculum of work," in the *Journal of Education* 162, no. 1 (Winter 1980): 67–92) investigated different approaches to mathematics instruction and has provided us with a penetrating analysis of the relationships between social class and educational experience.
15. William F. Pinar, ed., *Curriculum theorizing: The reconceptualists* (Berkeley, CA: McCutchan, 1975).
16. The terms "epistemology" and "ontology" have been subject to a wide range of interpretations. In particular, the term "ontology" is often associated with a conception of the world as preexistent and accessible to the senses. I do not wish to conflate ontology with metaphysical conceptions of reality. The term is used in this context to call attention to issues of identity and existence—*being*—which tend to be disregarded in discussions of (particularly mathematics) curriculum.
17. William F. Pinar and Madeleine R. Grumet, *Toward a poor curriculum* (Dubuque, IA: Kendall/Hunt Publishing Company, 1976).
18. Ibid., 18.
19. Francisco Varela, "Laying down a path in walking," in *GAIA, a way of knowing*, ed. William Irwin Thompson (Hudson, NY: Lindisfarne, 1987).
20. Heidegger, *Basic writings.*
21. I am referring here to cultures that have developed some sort of writing or symbolization processes—a reference that is implicit in the phrase "human records." As argued in the preceding section, the technology of symbolization is likely necessary for the conception of the mathematical as articulated here.
22. Richard Courant, cited in Kline, *Mathematics*, 298.
23. National Council of Teachers of Mathematics, *Curriculum and evaluation standards for school mathematics* (Reston, VA: NCTM, 1989); NCTM, *Professional standards for teaching mathematics* (Reston, VA: NCTM, 1991); NCTM, *Assessment standards for school mathematics* (Reston, VA: NCTM, 1995).
24. Jerry P. King, *The art of mathematics* (New York: Fawcett Columbine, 1992), 34–35 (emphasis in original).
25. Richard Courant, cited in Kline, *Mathematics*, 298 (emphasis added).

26. Ibid., 126.
27. Ibid., 195.
28. Bishop, "Western mathematics."
29. I am indebted to Elaine Simmt for the idea of "variable-entry."
30. I am indebted to Susan Pirie and to Dennis Sumara for this notion.
31. For a more detailed description of the mathematical activity used, see Elaine Simmt and Brent Davis, "Fractal cards: A space for exploration in geometry and discrete mathematics" (forthcoming in *Mathematics Teacher*).
32. Ernest, in *The philosophy of mathematics education*, develops a theory to "explain" how subjective mathematical knowledge becomes "objective." His explanation is relevant to the current discussion—because it reveals how tightly we wish to cling to our modern ideal of objectivity. A consequence of Ernest's desire to retain a rigid subject-object dichotomy is that he is compelled to articulate a perspective on school mathematics that varies little from the structures he initially sets out to critique. It continues to focus on content- and goals-oriented curricula, standardized testing, streaming, etc.
33. Max van Manen, *The tone of teaching* (Richmond Hill, ON: Scholastic-TAB, 1986), 45 (original emphasis).

Section 2C: Mathematics Curriculum Anticipating

1. Max van Manen, *The tact of teaching* (Toronto: The Althouse Press, 1991), 103.
2. Levin, *The listening self*, 19 (emphasis added).
3. Rorty, *Contingency, irony, solidarity*.
4. Deborah Britzman, "The question of belief," in *International Journal of Qualitative Studies in Education* 8, no. 3 (1995): 229–238, 237.
5. E.g., Davis and Hersh, *Descartes' dream*; Barrow, *Pi in the sky*.
6. See Tom Kieren, Brent Davis and Ralph Mason, "Fraction flags: Learning from children to help children learn" (in press in *Mathematics Teaching in the Middle School*) for a fuller description of Fraction Kits.
7. Pausing for a moment to represent Van's actions in formal terms, the complexity and sophistication of his thinking become more apparent. Symbolically his action might be expressed as follows:

$$2[(^1/_4 \times {}^1/_6) + (^1/_2 \times {}^1/_{12}) + {}^1/_{24}] + 2[2(^1/_2 \times {}^1/_{12}) + {}^1/_{24}]$$
$$= 2(^3/_{24}) + 2(^3/_{24})$$
$$= 2(^1/_8) + 2(^1/_8)$$
$$= {}^4/_8.$$

8. Maturana and Varela, *The tree of knowledge*, 69.
9. Gleick, *Chaos*, 94.
10. Marjorie Senechal, "Shape," in *On the shoulders of giants: New approaches to numeracy*, ed. Lynn Arthur Steen (Washington, DC: National Academy Press, 1990), 175.
11. I might note here that the transcriptions of this meeting are essentially incomprehensible—partly because the objects of reference are unavailable to the reader, but mostly because much of our interaction was, simply put, coupled. Persons outside the interactive unity (like me, a year after the fact) simply cannot participate in the enacted meanings.
12. "F, C, Z, and X angles" are the (unconventional) names that Wendy and I used to refer to corresponding angles, co-interior angles, alternate interior angles, and opposite angles, respectively. The letter-names are descriptive of the patterns formed by each angle pair.
13. Grumet, *Bitter milk*, 172.

Chapter 3: Stood on One's Ear—The Educational Endeavor

Section 3A: Culture Making—The Place of Education

1. David Pimm, *Symbols and meanings in school mathematics* (London: Routledge, 1995), 183.
2. Merker, *Listening*, 194.
3. Cited in S. van Matre and B. Weiler, *The earth speaks* (Warrenville, IL: The Institute for Earth Education, 1983).
4. Michel Foucault, *Madness and civilization* (New York: Random House, 1965), vii–viii.
5. David Orr, *Earth in mind: On education, environment, and the human prospect* (Washington, DC: Island Press, 1994), 163.
6. Dennis Sumara discusses the educational implications of this notion in "Counterfeiting," in *Taboo* 1 (Spring 1995): 94–122. Clifford Geertz, in *Works and lives: The anthropologist as author* (Stanford, CA: Stanford University Press, 1988) develops a similar idea in the context of anthropological reporting.
7. Ernest, *The philosophy of mathematics education.*
8. It must be emphasized that Ernest's use of "Progressivism," a term that is often associated with the philosophy of John Dewey, is unrelated to Dewey's philosophy. Ernest's analysis of Progressivism is more toward the work of Rousseau.
9. See Mortimer J. Adler, *The paideia proposal: An educational manifesto* (New York: Macmillan, 1982).
10. See E.D. Hirsch, Jr., *Cultural literacy: What every American needs to know* (Boston: Houghton Mifflin, 1987).
11. See Paulo Freire, *Pedagogy of the oppressed* (New York: Seaview, 1971).
12. See Henry Giroux, *Teachers as intellectuals: Toward a critical pedagogy of learning* (Granby, MA: Bergin and Garvey, 1988).
13. Ibid., 172.
14. Peter McLaren, in ibid., xx.
15. Cleo Cherryholmes, *Power and criticism: Poststructural investigations in education* (New York: Teachers College Press, 1988), 186.
16. Derek Edwards and Neil Mercer, *Common knowledge: The development of understanding in the classroom* (London: Routledge, 1987), 167.
17. Walkerdine, *The mastery of reason*, 202.
18. Gallagher, in *Hermeneutics and education*, discusses the link between Critical Pedagogy and critical hermeneutics, pointing out that, while the former finds much of its inspiration in the latter, "few attempts have been made to consider or justify critical education theory in terms of critical hermeneutics" (p. 25). As such, the hermeneutical dimension has remained far in the background of the Critical Pedagogy movement—an unfortunate situation, given the open and conciliatory tone and intentions of hermeneutics.
19. Karl Jaspers, *Philosophy of existence* (Philadelphia: University of Pennsylvania Press, 1971).
20. Gadamer, *Truth and method*, 220.
21. Karl Deutsch, cited in Bateson, *Peripheral visions*, 75.
22. C.A. Bowers and David J. Flinders, *Responsive teaching: An ecological approach to classroom patterns of language, culture, and thought* (New York: Teachers College Press, 1990), 241.
23. Ibid.
24. David E. Denton, *Gaia's drum: Ancient voices and our children's future* (Hanover, MA: The Christopher Publishing House, 1991), 25.
25. Varela et al., *The embodied mind*, 196.
26. Orr, *Ecological literacy*, 84.
27. Berry, *The unsettling of America*, 4.

28. Robert Young, *Critical theory and classroom talk* (Clevedon, GB: Multilingual Matter Ltd., 1992).
29. James T. Fey, "Quantity," in *On the shoulders of giants: New approaches to numeracy*, ed. Lynn Arthur Steen (Washington, DC: National Academy Press, 1990), 91.
30. Alberta Education, *Junior high mathematics: Teacher resource manual* (Edmonton, AB: The Crown in Right of Alberta, 1988), 2.
31. National Research Council, *Everybody counts: A report to the nation on the future of mathematics education* (Washington, DC: National Academy Press, 1989), 21.
32. Nel Noddings, "Does everybody count? Reflections on reforms in school mathematics," in *Journal of Mathematical Behavior* 13, no. 1 (March 1994): 89–104, 91.
33. Grumet, *Bitter milk.*
34. Orr, *Ecological literacy*, 83.
35. E.g., Walkerdine, *The mastery of reason*; Nancy Shelley, *Mathematics is a language*, presented at the Seventh International Congress for Mathematics Education (Quebec City, PQ, August 1992).
36. E.g., Bookchin, T*he philosophy of social ecology*; Orr, *Ecological literacy.*
37. Gregory Bateson, *Steps to an ecology of mind*, 45.
38. My uses of the terms "moral" and "ethical" here are according to a cooperative rather than a competitive basis for human interaction. As Levin, in *The listening self*, elaborates:

    The two different ways of thinking about moral problems are (1) a competitive model, which gives primacy to the individual and relies on the supervenience of formal and abstract rules to achieve co-operation and consensus and, (2) a co-operative model which gives primacy to relationships and relies on contextual narratives and dialogue—communication—to resolve moral problems. The two different modes of describing the relationship between self and other are essentially two different ethics, the one an ethics of 'universal' rights and duties and 'universal' rational principles, the other an ethics of care, responsiveness, and responsibility. . . . The first ethics is represented mainly by images of opposing positions and hierarchical orderings, while the second is represented mainly by images of communicative and collaborative positions, and replaces images of hierarchy with images of webs, networks, and weavings. (p. 221)

    Johnson, in *Moral imagination*, elaborates on these contrasting orientations of morality through a linguistic analysis of various brands of moral argument.
39. Berry, *The unsettling of America*, 47.
40. Cohen and Stewart, *The collapse of chaos.*
41. Bruner, *Actual minds, possible worlds*, 123 (emphasis in original).
42. Martin Heidegger, *What is philosophy?* (New York: Twayne, 1958), 71.
43. Varela et al., *The embodied mind*, 253.
44. Charles Taylor, *The malaise of modernity* (Concord, ON: Anansi, 1991).

Section 3B: Artistry—The Place of the Teacher

1. Crusius, *A teacher's introduction to philosophical hermeneutics*, 74.
2. Mary Catherine Bateson, *Peripheral visions*, 87–88.
3. Gadamer, *Truth and method*, 151.
4. Langer, *Problems of art*, 26.
5. Grumet, *Bitter milk*, 79.
6. Ibid., 81.
7. Stanley Aronowitz and Henry Giroux, "Radical education and transformative intellectuals," in *Canadian Journal of Political and Social Theory* 9, no. 3 (Fall 1985): 48–63.
8. Berendt, *The third ear.*

9. Pirsig, *Lila*, 254.
10. Lynn Arthur Steen, ed., *Mathematics today* (New York: Springer Verlag, 1980), 10.
11. King, *The art of mathematics*, 4 (original emphasis).
12. Philip Davis, "Applied mathematics as a social contract," in *Math worlds: Philosophical and social studies of mathematics and mathematics education*, eds. Sal Restivo, Jean Paul Bendegem, and Roland Fischer (Albany, NY: SUNY Press, 1993), 82.
13. I, of course, am arguing the contrary point: that the exclusion of such considerations requires a deliberate ignorance. On this issue, it is worth mentioning, I part company with the Criticalmathematics Educators Group who, to my reading, appropriately call for an attendance to both the utilitarian qualities and the critical political implications of mathematics knowledge—but appear to regard the two elements as separable (or perhaps even separated) in the first place. A conflation of collective knowledge and individual cognition (see Chapter 4) renders this formulation untenable.
14. Specifically, his Law of Contradiction (*A* cannot be both *B* and *not-B*) and his Law of the Excluded Middle (*A* must be either *B* or *not-B*).
15. Numerous examples of the sorts of hostility that have greeted some of these areas of inquiry are presented in various popular accounts of their emergence. See, for example, Gleick's *Chaos*, Waldrop's *Complexity*, and Daniel McNeill and Paul Freiberger's *Fuzzy logic: The revolutionary computer technology that is changing our world* (New York: Simon and Schuster, 1994).

    It is interesting to note that fuzzy logic has not been well received in the Western world, either within academia or by business. Noting the rapid acceptance and widespread application of fuzzy logic in Japanese, Chinese, and other Eastern cultures, McNeill and Freiberger argue that the difference in attitudes toward the field has to do with a general reluctance of Westerners to loose their grip on Aristotle's axioms of logic. Eastern cultures, which do not share the tradition of drawing rigid distinctions, have thus had comparatively little difficulty recognizing and exploiting the power of fuzzy logic.
16. Hans Freudenthal, *Didactical phenomenology of mathematical structures* (Dordrecht, The Netherlands: D. Reidel Publishing Company, 1983), ix.
17. Ibid. (emphasis added).
18. Bruner, *Actual minds, possible worlds*, 126 (emphasis in original).
19. Ibid., 126.
20. Ibid.
21. Ibid., 127.
22. van Manen, *The tone of teaching*, 45 (original emphasis).
23. Alba G. Thompson, "The relationship of teachers' conceptions of mathematics and mathematics teaching to instructional practice," in *Educational Studies in Mathematics* 15, no. 2 (May 1984): 105–127.

Section 3C: Pedagogy—Where Teaching Takes Place

1. David E. Denton, "That mode of being called teaching," in *Existentialism and phenomenology in education*, ed. D. E. Denton (New York: Teachers College Press, 1974), 107.
2. van Manen, *The tone of teaching*, 45.
3. Not at all content with that response, the student quipped back, "But you're not my boss," suggesting that he had a different (and incompatible) sense of their relationship than the one enacted by Wendy.
4. Denton, "That mode of being called teaching," 101.
5. Dwayne Huebner, "The vocation of teaching," in *Teacher renewal: Professional issues, personal choices*, eds. F. S. Bolton and J. M. Falk (New York: Teachers College Press, 1984), 19.
6. Ibid., 29.

7. I am attempting here to practice what I announced in the preceding section: to use a mathematical idea, albeit metaphorically, to *present* some aspect of the world. To adapt Freudenthal's words, I am trying to show a place where we might step into the learning process of humankind.
8. Roger Penrose, *The emperor's new mind: Concerning computers, minds, and the laws of physics* (New York: Vintage, 1989), 160.
9. Ibid.
10. Ibid., 161.
11. Otto F. Bollnow, "The pedagogical atmosphere," in *Phenomenology + Pedagogy* 7 (1989): 5–11, 5.
12. I flag this word to signal my own discomfort in using it—a symptom, perhaps, of the pervasive technical/clinical orientation to adult-child relationships in the contemporary school setting. Nevertheless, encouraged by the examples of curriculum theorist Madeleine Grumet and scientists Maturana and Varela, I have elected to include it.
13. Heidegger, *Basic writings*, 332 (original emphasis).
14. van Manen, *The tact of teaching*, 18.
15. Levin, *The listening self*, 88.
16. Anthony Paul Kerby, *Narrative and the self* (Bloomington, IN: Indiana University Press, 1991), 34.
17. Michel Foucault, *Language, counter-memory, practice: Selected essays and interviews* (Ithaca, NY: Cornell University Press, 1981), 137.
18. Gadamer, *Truth and method.*
19. Ben Spiecker, "The pedagogical relationship," in *Oxford Review of Education* 10, no. 2 (1984): 203–209, 204.
20. van Manen, *The tone of teaching*, 52.
21. Spiecker, "The pedagogical relationship."
22. van Manen, *The tone of teaching*, 72–73.
23. Berry, *The unsettling of America*, 79.
24. I am indebted to Dennis Sumara for this anecdote.
25. Levin, *The listening self*, 154 (original emphasis).

Chapter 4: All Ears—Cognition

Section 4A: Knowing

1. Hannah Arendt, *The life of the mind* (New York: Harcourt, Brace, Jovanovich, 1978), 110–111 (emphasis in original).
2. Nick Herbert, *Elemental mind: Human consciousness and the new physics* (New York: Penguin Books, 1993), 74.
3. Gregory Bateson, *Mind and nature*, 93 (emphasis in original).
4. David Burrows, *Sound, speech and music* (Amherst, MA: University of Massachusetts Press, 1990).
5. Michael J. Reddy, "The conduit metaphor—A case of frame conflict in our language about language," in *Metaphor and thought*, ed. Andrew Ortony (New York: Cambridge University Press, 1979).
6. Bruner, *Actual minds, possible worlds*, 65 (emphasis in original).
7. Ernst von Glasersfeld, "An introduction to radical constructivism," in *The invented reality*, ed. P. Watzlawick (New York: Norton, 1984).
8. Ibid., 20.
9. Constructivism—like feminism, postmodernism, Marxism, and a plethora of other -isms—has been subject to a wide range of interpretations. Not wishing to get bogged down in the intricacies that separate these theories, I will be using the term to refer specifically to the theory of "radical constructivism" as elaborated upon by von Glasersfeld and others. Where a differing perspective is referenced, it will be flagged with an appropriate modifier.

10. Ibid., 39.
11. Denton, in *Gaia's drum*, points out that "fact" is not a modern concept; rather, our modern use of the term is a distortion of earlier uses. Originally a fact was a deed (or the doer of the deed), not a building block of reality. As such, the constructivist movement might be characterized as "a return to the facts," in the ancient sense of the phrase.
12. Elliot W. Eisner, "Forms of understanding and the future of educational research," in *Educational Researcher* 22, no. 7 (October 1993): 5–11, 6.
13. Piaget and Inhelder, *The psychology of the child*, 28–29.
14. Ernst von Glasersfeld, "Constructivism in education," in *The international encyclopedia of education, supplementary volume*, eds. T. Husen and T. N. Postlethwaithe (Oxford: Pergamon Press, 1989), 162.
15. Ernst von Glasersfeld, "An exposition of constructivism: Why some like it radical," in *Constructivist views on the teaching and learning of mathematics* (a monograph of the *Journal for Research in Mathematics Education*), eds. R. B. Davis, C. A. Maher, and N. Noddings (Reston, VA: National Council of Teachers of Mathematics, 1990).
16. This particular criticism is, perhaps, more appropriately leveled against more "trivial" versions of constructivism. As Les Steffe (personal correspondence) has pointed out, radical constructivism assumes that the individual is an interactive organism: "A construction only follows on from interaction—without interaction there is no construction."

    However, it remains the case that the issue of our tremendous interactive capacities is simply not one that is addressed by even radical versions of constructivism—not because the theoretical framework offers no insight into this phenomenon but because, with the particular focus of constructivism on how the individual comes to know, such issues as communication and collective knowledge are peripheral.
17. Taylor, "The dialogical self."
18. Vygotsky, *Mind in society*, 57 (original emphasis).
19. Levin, *The listening self*, 150.
20. See Jere Confrey, "A theory of intellectual development," in *For the Learning of Mathematics* (published in three parts) 14, no. 3 (November 1994): 2–8; 15, no. 1 (February 1995): 38–48; 15, no. 2 (June 1995): 36–45, for a more thorough treatment of the contextual and historical factors contributing to the two models.
21. See, for example, Walkerdine, *The mastery of reason;* Jean Lave, *Cognition in practice: Mind, mathematics and culture in everyday life* (New York: Cambridge University Press, 1988).
22. Paul Cobb, "Where is the mind? Constructivist and sociocultural perspectives on mathematical development," in *Educational Researcher* 23, no. 7 (October 1994): 13–20, 15 (emphasis in original).
23. Gregory Bateson, *Mind and nature.*
24. It might also be noted that this same argument enables enactivists to avoid the conception of cognizing agent as a puppet of social movement, a criticism that has been leveled against sociocultural accounts of individual agency.
25. Ernst von Glasersfeld, *Aspects of radical constructivism and its educational recommendations*, presented at the Seventh International Congress for Mathematics Education (Quebec City, PQ, August 1992), 2 (emphasis added).
26. Gallagher, *Hermeneutics and education*, 51.
27. Gadamer, *Truth and method*, 103.
28. Taylor, "The dialogical self."
29. Maturana and Varela, *The tree of knowledge*, 174.

Section 4B: Understanding and Meaning

1. Martin Heidegger, *The question concerning technology and other essays* (New York: Harper Torchbooks, 1977), 112.

2. Berendt, *The third ear*, 60 (original emphasis).
3. Ernst von Glasersfeld, "Learning as a constructive activity," in *Problems of representation in the teaching and learning of mathematics*, ed. Claude Janvier (Hillsdale, NJ: Lawrence Erlbaum Associates, Publishers, 1987).
4. To elaborate briefly on this point: in current discussions on the topic of mathematical understanding, a distinction tends to be drawn between "conceptual" and "procedural" understandings, to use the terms developed by James Hiebert in *Conceptual and procedural knowledge: The case for mathematics* (Hillsdale, NJ: Lawrence Erlbaum Associates, Publishers 1986). In similar veins, Richard Skemp, in *The psychology of learning mathematics* (Baltimore: Penguin Books, 1986), uses the terms "relational" and "instrumental" and Anna Sfard, in "On the dual nature of mathematical conceptions: Reflections on processes and objects as different sides of the same coin" (in *Educational Studies in Mathematics* 22, no. 1 (February 1991):1–36) talks about "structural" and "operational." These terms and categories have provided us with a means of talking about the tension between the abstract nature of mathematics and the algorithmic focus of many conventional classrooms. They thus represent valuable contributions to discussions of mathematics learning and teaching.

   However, all of these categories or forms of understanding focus on the formal and formulated dimensions of the phenomenon (i.e., both "relational" and "instrumental" understandings tend to be interpreted in terms of the stated or the observed). The enacted and unformulated dimensions of our knowing tend to be overlooked.
5. The phrase "shared understandings" should not be interpreted in terms of "sameness of internal (or subjective) formulation/construction/conceptualization/idea/representation." Rather, our (largely unformulated) shared understandings point to the possibility of (and are revealed through) our joint and harmonious actions. To suggest, for example, that we share an understanding of "dog" is not to say that we would, regardless of situation, agree on its meaning. Rather, it is intended to suggest that, in the specific context in which "dog" arises, our intersubjective action is not "de-railed."

   An interesting side-note is that the sorts of fluid interactions that emerge from our sea of shared understandings can also be the source of considerable unease and great mystery for persons who are unfamiliar with such patterns of behavior. Numerous accounts of autistic persons, for example, report on the difficulty that these individuals have in responding appropriately to the social cues (i.e., the shared understandings) that most of us take for granted. Many of these persons, in fact, attribute our capacity for such joint (coupled) action to extrasensory perception. (See Oliver Sacks, "A neurologist's notebook: An anthropologist on Mars," *The New Yorker*, December 27, 1993, 106–125.)
6. Vygotsky, *Mind in society*, 26.
7. Johnson, *The body in the mind.*
8. This idea has been developed by Wilhelm Reich. See Morris Berman, *The reenchantment of the world* (Ithaca, NY: Cornell University Press, 1981).
9. Again I emphasize that the term "constructivism" is being used strictly in reference to "radical constructivism."
10. Pirie and Kieren, "Growth in mathematical understanding: How can we characterize it?"
11. Reprinted with permission.
12. Not unlike the orientations to cognition that were introduced and critiqued in the first section of this chapter, such orientations to meaning (and to language) might be called "representationist." Words are thought to stand in for objects and concepts, and hence must themselves be considered as objects. The alternative offered by enactivism is that words are part of our complex patterns of interactive behavior.

13. Hilary Putnam, *Representation and reality* (Cambridge, MA: The MIT Press, 1989).
14. Walkerdine, *The mastery of reason.*
15. I do not mean to overstate the case here. Not everyone "suffers" in learning. There are those—myself included—whose experiences with mathematics are far more "friendly" and for whom the learning of mathematics is clarifying rather than obfuscating. The extreme example of this phenomenon might be those autistic persons who find comfort and respite from the incomprehensibility of human emotion in the reductive and consistent predictability of the mathematical. Oliver Sacks, in "A neurologist's notebook: An anthropologist on Mars," presents a case study of one such person.
16. Donaldson, *Human minds,* 141.
17. Antonio R. Damasio, *Descartes' error: Emotion, reason, and the human brain* (New York: G. P. Putnam's Sons, 1994).
18. Cited in Bruner, *Actual minds, possible worlds.*
19. Rorty, *Objectivity, relativism, and truth,* 123.

Section 4C: Play

1. Denton, *Gaia's drum,* 7.
2. Jim Unger, *The 1st treasury of Herman* (New York: Andrews and McMeel, 1979), 132.
3. John Dewey, *Democracy and education* (New York: The Free Press, 1966 [1916]), 180–181 (emphasis added).
4. Gadamer, *Truth and method,* 102. I might add here that the "repetition" of play should not be confused with the repetitiveness of certain activities—such as rote recitation or drillwork. Rather, within the repetition itself, there is movement (play), so that each act of repetition is indeed a new (informed and transformed) act. It is thus that play sustains itself.
5. Ibid., 106.
6. Ibid., 102.
7. Denton, *Gaia's drum,* 158.
8. Gallagher, *Hermeneutics and education,* 50 (emphasis added).
9. T.L. Good, D.A. Grouws, and H. Ebmeier, *Active mathematics teaching* (New York: Longman Inc., 1983).
10. Alan Lightman, *Einstein's dreams* (Toronto: Alfred A. Knopf Canada, 1993), 23.
11. Ibid., 24.
12. Etymologically, "to obey" (from the last line of the preceding paragraph) means "to listen from below."
13. Ibid., 27.
14. John Dewey, *Experience and education* (New York: Collier, 1963 [1938]).
15. Denton, *Gaia's drum,* 114.
16. In Chapter 2, I argued that Descartes' project has largely been realized. I continue to maintain that position, in that mathematics has achieved a pervasive presence in almost all aspects of modern life. The point being made in this chapter is that, in spite of this "success," the Rationalist project of Descartes, from the outset, was destined to failure. It bore the seeds of its own destruction.
17. Maturana and Varela, *The tree of knowledge.*
18. Cohen and Stewart, *The collapse of chaos.*
19. Pinar and Grumet, *Toward a poor curriculum,* 11.
20. van Manen, *The tone of teaching,* 44.

Chapter 5: Playing It by Ear—Teaching

Section 5A: The Nature of Teaching

1. Ackerman, *A natural history of the senses*, 204.
2. Varela, "Laying down a path in walking," 50.
3. Rorty, *Objectivity, relativism, and truth*, 16.
4. Robert Grudin, *The grace of great things: Creativity and innovation* (Boston: Ticknor and Fields, 1990), 146.
5. William Pinar and Madeleine Grumet, "Socratic *caesura* and the theory-practice relationship," in *Contemporary curriculum discourses*, ed. William Pinar (Scottsdale, AZ: Gorsuch Scarisbrick, 1988), 99.
6. Alexander Humez, Nicholas Humez, and Joseph Maguire, *Zero to lazy eight: The romance of numbers* (New York: Simon and Schuster, 1994), 141.
7. Madeline Hunter, *Mastery teaching* (El Segundo, CA: TIP, 1986), 3 (emphasis added).
8. This critique of constructivist teaching must not be interpreted as suggesting that the constructivist framework is wrong or that it has little to offer. Quite the contrary, it is clear that any insight into the processes of learning is valuable in discussions of teaching. To this end, considerable preliminary work into the possibilities for constructivist teaching has been done by persons in mathematics education—with notable contributions coming from Jere Confrey, Robert B. Davis, Les Steffe, and Paul Cobb. For a good introduction to some of this work, see Robert B. Davis, Carolyn A. Maher, and Nel Noddings, eds., *Constructivist views on teaching and learning of mathematics (Journal for Research in Mathematics Education, Monograph No. 4)* (Reston, VA: National Council of Teachers of Mathematics, 1990).

   The important point is that constructivism is not fundamentally concerned with teaching or with education. The particular domain of constructivism—that is, the individual's cognition—is an inadequate basis for redefining the socially, historically, and politically saturated realm of educational practice. As such, we need to move beyond constructivism in order to consider the interpersonal, intentional space of teaching.
9. As I explain later, while there are some powerful consequences of interpreting teaching as listening metaphorically, for the most part my use of the phrase is quite literal.
10. Ong, *Orality and literacy.*
11. Daiyo Sawada, "The converse structure of communicative classrooms," in *Math monograph no. 10*, ed. Daiyo Sawada (Edmonton, AB: Mathematics Council of the Alberta Teachers' Association, 1992).

Section 5B: Assessment

1. Heidegger, *Basic writings*, 252.
2. Mary Jane Drummond, *Learning to see: Assessment through observation* (London, ON: Pembroke, 1994), 134.
3. Personal communication.
4. Drummond, *Learning to see.*
5. Gadamer uses the phrase "pedagogical question" instead of "teacherly question." Because "pedagogical" is being used in quite another manner in this text, I have elected to make this nominal change.
6. Gadamer, *Truth and method*, 367.
7. Douglas R. Barnes, *From communication to curriculum* (Hammondworth, GB: Penguin Books, 1976), 179 (emphasis added).
8. Edwards and Mercer, *Common knowledge*, 30.

9. Gadamer, *Truth and method*, 363.
10. Alfred North Whitehead, *The aims of education and other essays* (London: Williams and Norgate, 1931), 7.
11. Michel Foucault, *Discipline and punish: The birth of prison* (New York: Pantheon Books, 1977), 183 (emphasis in original).
12. Gallagher, *Hermeneutics and education*, 298 (original emphasis).
13. Stephen Jay Gould, *The mismeasure of man* (New York: W. W. Norton, 1981).
14. Eisner, "Forms of understanding and the future of educational research," 7.
15. Thomas Carpenter and Elizabeth Fennema, "Cognitively guided instruction: Building on the knowledge of students and teachers," in *Researching educational reform: The case of school mathematics in the United States*, ed. W. Secada (a special issue of *International Journal of Educational Research*, 1992): 457–470, 467–468.
16. Gallagher, *Hermeneutics and education*, 343.
17. Weinsheimer, *Gadamer's hermeneutics*.

Section 5C: Pedagogy—Mathematics Teaching as Listening

1. Varela et al., *The embodied mind*, 123, 234.
2. Sylvia Ashton-Warner, *Teacher* (New York: Simon and Schuster, 1963), 58.
3. Herbert Marcuse, *Counter-revolution and revolt* (Boston: Beacon Press, 1972), 71.

Back Word: Listening to Reason—Closing Remarks

1. Levin, *The listening self*, 86 (original emphasis).
2. Gallagher, *Hermeneutics and education*, 86 (emphasis added).
3. Grudin, *The grace of great things, 181.*
4. Maurice Merleau-Ponty, *In praise of philosophy* (Evanston, IL: Northwestern University Press, 1963), 27.
5. Berman, *The reenchantment of the world*, 270.
6. Rorty, *Objectivity, relativism, and truth*, 37 (emphasis added).
7. Ibid., 37 (emphasis added).
8. Thompson's framework is quite similar to the five-level analysis that I developed in Chapter 2. A major difference is that his third mentality seems to encompass both my Formalist and my Hyper-Formalist categories.
9. Contents of the left column are quoted from Thompson, *Imaginary landscape*, xix.
10. Contents of the right column are quoted from Levin, *The listening self*, 45–49.
11. Crusius, *A teacher's introduction to philosophical hermeneutics*, 72.
12. Martin Heidegger, *What is called thinking?* (New York: Harper and Row, 1968), 25.
13. Levin, *The listening self*, 174.
14. Heidegger, *What is philosophy?* (See the epigram on the title page of this section.)

Bibliography

1. Trinh T. Minh-ha, *Framer framed* (New York: Routledge, 1992), 23.
2. Levin, *The listening self*, 206.

Bibliography

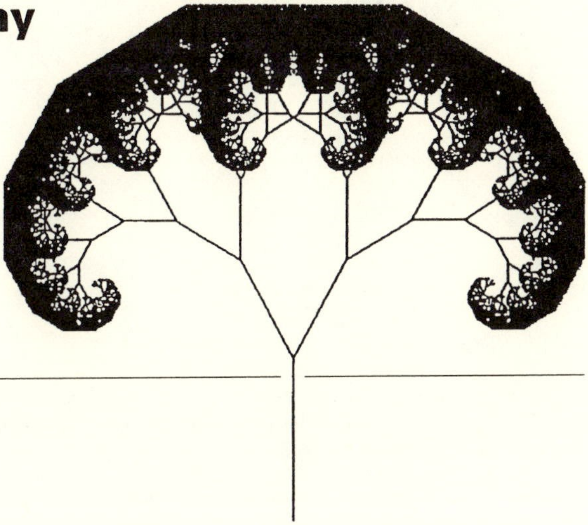

A music bound up with movement, dance and speech, one in which the listener becomes a co-performer, one that has no overall form except one of continually recurring sequences of notes and rhythms, one that plays endlessly . . . has been repeatedly called elemental or rudimentary. Is irritable to most Westerners' ears.

—Trinh T. Minh-ha[1]

If we should find ourselves appropriated by such an uncanny experience, hearing ourselves being heard by the field of sound and silence, we may encounter, and may in fact for the first time be hearing, the hollow ring to an entire history of modern philosophy, a discourse which has attempted again and again to ground the possibility of knowledge in the self-certainty of a monadic subjectivity—a subject-centered reason.

—David Levin[2]

Bibliography

Ackerman, Diane. *A natural history of the senses.* New York: Vintage Books, 1990.

Adler, Mortimer J. *The paideia proposal: An educational manifesto.* New York: Macmillan, 1982.

Alberta Education. *Junior high mathematics: Teacher resource manual.* Edmonton, AB: The Crown in Right of Alberta, 1988.

Anyon, Jean. "Social class and the hidden curriculum of work." *Journal of Education* 162, no. 1 (Winter 1980): 67–92.

Arendt, Hannah. *The life of the mind.* New York: Harcourt, Brace, Jovanovich, 1978.

Aronowitz, Stanley, and Henry Giroux, "Radical education and transformative intellectuals." *Canadian Journal of Political and Social Theory* 9, no. 3 (Fall 1985): 48–63.

Aston-Warner, Sylvia. *Teacher.* New York: Simon and Schuster, 1963.

Barnes, Douglas R. *From communication to curriculum.* Hammondworth, GB: Penguin Books, 1976.

Barrow, John D. *Pi in the sky: Counting, thinking, and being.* Oxford: Clarendon Press, 1992.

Bateson, Gregory. *Steps to an ecology of mind.* New York: Ballantine Books, 1972.

———. *Mind and nature: A necessary unity.* New York: E. P. Dutton, 1979.

Bateson, Mary Catherine. *Peripheral visions: Learning along the way.* New York: HarperCollins, 1994.

Belenky, Mary F., Blythe M. Clinchy, Nancy R. Goldberger, and Jill M. Tarule. *Women's ways of knowing: The development of self, voice, and mind.* New York: Basic Books, 1986.

Berendt, Joachim-Ernst. *The third ear: On listening to the world.* New York: Henry Holt, 1985.

Berman, Louise. "Perspectives and imperatives: Re-searching, rethinking, and reordering curriculum priorities." *Journal of Curriculum and Supervision* 1, no. 1 (Fall 1985): 66–77.

Berman, Morris. *The reenchantment of the world.* Ithaca, NY: Cornell University Press, 1981.

Berry, Wendell. *The unsettling of America: Culture and agriculture.* San Francisco: Sierra Club Books, 1977.

Bishop, Alan J. "Western mathematics: The secret weapon of cultural imperialism." *Race and Class* 32, no. 2 (October–December 1990): 51–65.

Bobbitt, Franklin. *The curriculum.* Boston: Houghton Mifflin, 1918.

———. *How to make a curriculum.* Boston: Houghton Mifflin, 1924.

Bollnow, Otto F. "The pedagogical atmosphere." *Phenomenology + Pedagogy* 7 (1989): 5–11.

Bookchin, Murray. *The philosophy of social ecology: Essays on dialectical naturalism.* Montreal: Blackrose Books, 1990.

Borowski, E.J. and J.M. Borwein. *HarperCollins dictionary of mathematics.* New York: HarperPerennial, 1991.

Bowers, C.A. and David J. Flinders. *Responsive teaching: An ecological approach to classroom patterns of language, culture, and thought.* New York: Teachers College Press, 1990.

Boyer, Carl B. and Uta C. Merzbach. *A history of mathematics, second edition.* New York: John Wiley and Sons, 1991.

Britzman, Deborah. "The question of belief: Writing poststructural ethnography." *International Journal of Qualitative Studies in Education* 8, no. 3 (1995): 229–238.

Bruner, Jerome. *Actual minds, possible worlds.* Cambridge, MA: Harvard University Press, 1986.

———. *Acts of meaning.* Cambridge, MA: Harvard University Press, 1990.

Burrows, David. *Sound, speech and music.* Amherst, MA: University of Massachusetts Press, 1990.

Carpenter, Edmund. *Eskimo realities.* New York: Holt, Rinehart and Winston, 1973.

Carpenter, Thomas and Elizabeth Fennema. "Cognitively guided instruction: Building on the knowledge of students and teachers." *Researching educational reform: The case of school mathematics in the United States,* edited by W. Secada (a special issue of *International Journal of Educational Research,* 1992): 457–470.

Casti, John L. *Complexification: Explaining a paradoxical world through the science of surprise.* New York: HarperCollins, 1994.

Cherryholmes, Cleo. *Power and criticism: Poststructural investigations in education.* New York: Teachers College Press, 1988.

Cobb, Paul. "Where is the mind? Constructivist and sociocultural perspectives on mathematical development." *Educational Researcher* 23, no. 7 (October 1994): 13–20.

Cohen, Jack and Ian Stewart. *The collapse of chaos: Discovering simplicity in a complex world.* New York: Penguin Books, 1994.

Confrey, Jere. "A theory of intellectual development, part I." *For the Learning of Mathematics* 14, no. 3 (November 1994): 2–8.

———. "A theory of intellectual development, part II." *For the Learning of Mathematics* 15, no. 1 (February 1995): 38–48.

———. "A theory of intellectual development, part III." *For the Learning of Mathematics* 15, no. 2 (June 1995): 36–45.

Crusius, Timothy W. *A teacher's introduction to philosophical hermeneutics.* Urbana, IL: National Council of Teachers of English, 1991.

Damasio, Antonio R. *Descartes' error: Emotion, reason, and the human brain.* New York: G. P. Putnam's Sons, 1994.

d'Ambrosio, Ubiratan. "Ethnomathematics and its place in the history and pedagogy of mathematics." *For the Learning of Mathematics* 5, no. 1 (February 1985): 44–47.

Davis, Brent. "Mathematics teaching: Moving from telling to listening." *Journal of Curriculum and Supervision* 9, no. 3 (Spring 1994): 267–283.

———. "Why teach mathematics? Mathematics education and enactivist theory." *For the Learning of Mathematics* 15, no. 2 (June 1995): 2–8.

———. "Thinking otherwise and hearing differently: An alternative enactment of mathematics teaching." *JCT: An Interdisciplinary Journal of Curriculum Studies,* 11, no. 4 (Winter 1995).

———. "Listening for differences: An evolving conception of mathematics teaching." In press in *Journal for Research in Mathematics Education.*

Davis, Philip J. "Applied mathematics as a social contract." *Math worlds: Philosophical and social studies of mathematics and mathematics education.* Edited by Sal Restivo, Jean Paul Bendegem, and Roland Fischer. Albany, NY: SUNY Press, 1993.

Davis, Philip J., and Reuben Hersh. *The mathematical experience.* Boston: Houghton Mifflin, 1981.

———. *Descartes' dream: The world according to mathematics.* Boston: Houghton Mifflin, 1986.

Davis, Robert B., Carolyn A. Maher, and Nel Noddings, editors. *Constructivist views on teaching and learning of mathematics (Journal for Research in Mathematics Education, Monograph No. 4).* Reston, VA: National Council of Teachers of Mathematics, 1990.

Denton, David E. "That mode of being called teaching." *Existentialism and phenomenology in education.* Edited by D. E. Denton. New York: Teachers College Press, 1974.

———. *Gaia's drum: Ancient voices and our children's future.* Hanover, MA: The Christopher Publishing House, 1991.

Denzin, Norman K. and Yvonna S. Lincoln. "Entering the field of qualitative research." *Handbook of qualitative research.* Edited by Norman K. Denzin, and Yvonna S. Lincoln. Thousand Oaks, CA: Sage, 1994.

Descartes, René. *Discourse on method* and *Meditations on first philosophy.* Indianapolis: Hackett Publishing Company, 1993.

Dewey, John. *The child and the curriculum.* Chicago: The University of Chicago Press, 1956 [1902].

———. *Experience and education.* New York: Collier, 1963 [1938].

———. *Democracy and education.* New York: The Free Press, 1966 [1916].

Donaldson, Margaret. *Human minds: An exploration.* New York: Allen Lane The Penguin Press, 1993.

Drummond, Mary Jane. *Learning to see: Assessment through observation.* Markham, ON: Pembroke, 1994.

Edwards, Derek and Neil Mercer. *Common knowledge: The development of understanding in the classroom.* London: Routledge, 1987.

Eisner, Elliot W. "Forms of understanding and the future of educational research." *Educational Researcher* 22, no. 7 (October 1993): 5–11.

Ernest, Paul. *The philosophy of mathematics education.* London: The Falmer Press, 1991.

Fennema, Elizabeth and M. J. Ayer, editors. *Women and education: Equity or equality?* Berkeley, CA: McCutchan, 1984.

Fey, James T. "Quantity." *On the shoulders of giants: New approaches to numeracy.* Edited by Lynn Arthur Steen. Washington, DC: National Academy Press, 1990.

Foucault, Michel. *Madness and civilization.* New York: Random House, 1965.

———. *Discipline and punish: The birth of prison.* New York: Pantheon Books, 1977.

———. *Language, counter-memory, practice: Selected essays and interviews.* Ithaca, NY: Cornell University Press, 1981.

Freire, Paulo. *Pedagogy of the oppressed.* New York: Seaview, 1971.

Freudenthal, Hans. *Didactical phenomenology of mathematical structures.* Dordrecht, The Netherlands: D. Reidel Publishing Company, 1983.

Gadamer, Hans-Georg. *Truth and method.* New York: Continuum, 1990.

Gallagher, Shaun. *Hermeneutics and education.* Albany, NY: SUNY Press, 1992.

Geertz, Clifford. *Works and lives: The anthropologist as author.* Stanford, CA: Stanford University Press, 1988.

Giroux, Henry. *Teachers as intellectuals: Toward a critical pedagogy of learning.* Granby, MA: Bergin and Garvey, 1988.

Gleick, James. *Chaos: Making a new science.* New York: Penguin Books, 1987.

Good, T. L., D. A. Grouws, and H. Ebmeier. *Active mathematics teaching.* New York: Longman Inc., 1983.

Gould, Stephen Jay. *The mismeasure of man.* New York: W. W. Norton, 1981.

Grudin, Robert. *The grace of great things: Creativity and innovation.* Boston: Ticknor and Fields, 1990.

Grumet, Madeleine. *Bitter milk: Women and teaching.* Amherst, MA: The University of Massachusetts Press, 1988.

Hamming, Richard W. "The unreasonable effectiveness of mathematics." *American Mathematical Monthly* 87 (February 1980): 81–90.

Hartung, Maurice L. *Seeing through arithmetic.* Toronto: Gage, 1957.

Heidegger, Martin. *What is philosophy?* New York: Twayne, 1958.

———. *What is called thinking?* New York: Harper and Row, 1968.

———. *Basic writings.* San Francisco: HarperCollins, 1977.
———. *The question concerning technology and other essays.* New York: Harper Torchbooks, 1977.
Herbert, Nick. *Elemental mind: Human consciousness and the new physics.* New York: Penguin Books, 1993.
Hiebert, James, editor. *Conceptual and procedural knowledge: The case for mathematics.* Hillsdale, NJ: Lawrence Erlbaum, 1986.
Hirsch, E. D., Jr. *Cultural literacy: What every American needs to know.* Boston: Houghton Mifflin, 1987.
Horgan, John. "The death of proof," *Scientific American*, October 1993: 92–103.
Horkheimer, Max. *Eclipse of reason.* New York: Continuum-Seabury, 1974.
Huebner, Dwayne. "The vocation of teaching." *Teacher renewal: Professional issues, personal choices.* Edited by F. S. Bolton, and J. M. Falk. New York: Teachers College Press, 1984.
Humez, Alexander, Nicholas Humez, and Joseph Maguire. *Zero to lazy eight: The romance of numbers.* New York: Simon and Schuster, 1993.
Hunter, Madeline. *Mastery teaching.* El Segundo, CA: TIP, 1986.
Jaspers, Karl. *Philosophy of existence.* Philadelphia: University of Pennsylvania Press, 1971.
Johnson, Mark. *The body in the mind: The bodily basis of meaning, imagination, and reason.* Chicago: The University of Chicago Press, 1987.
———. *Moral imagination: Implications of cognitive science for ethics.* Chicago: The University of Chicago Press, 1993.
Joseph, George Gheverghese. *The crest of the peacock: Non-European roots of mathematics.* London: Penguin Books, 1991.
Kerby, Anthony Paul. *Narrative and the self.* Bloomington, IN: Indiana University Press, 1991.
Kieren, Thomas E., Brent A. Davis, and Ralph T. Mason. "Fraction flags: Learning from children to help children learn." In press in *Mathematics Teaching in the Middle School.*
King, Jerry P. *The art of mathematics.* New York: Fawcett Columbine, 1992.
Kline, Morris. *Mathematics: The loss of certainty.* New York: Oxford University Press, 1980.
Kuhn, Thomas. *The structure of scientific revolutions.* Chicago: University of Chicago Press, 1962.
Lakatos, Imre, *Proofs and refutations.* Cambridge: Cambridge University Press, 1976.
Langer, Susanne K. *Problems of art.* New York: Charles Scribner's Sons, 1957.
Lave, Jean. *Cognition in practice: Mind, mathematics and culture in everyday life.* New York: Cambridge University Press, 1988.
Leva, Richard A. *Psychotherapy, the listening voice: Rogers and Erickson.* Muncie, IN: Accelerated Development, 1987.
Levin, David Michael. *The listening self: Personal growth, social change and the closure of metaphysics.* London: Routledge, 1989.
Lightman, Alan. *Einstein's dreams.* Toronto: Alfred A. Knopf Canada, 1993.
Lovelock, James. *Gaia, a new look at life on earth.* New York: Oxford University Press, 1979.
Luria, Aleksandr Romanovich. *Cognitive development: Its cultural and social foundations.* Cambridge, MA: Harvard University Press, 1976.
Lyotard, Jean-François. *The postmodern condition: A report on knowledge.* Minneapolis: Minnesota Press, 1984.
Marcuse, Herbert. *Counter-revolution and revolt.* Boston: Beacon Press, 1972.
Maturana, Humberto and Francisco Varela. *The tree of knowledge: The biological roots of human understanding.* Boston: Shambhala, 1987.
McCulloch, Warren. *Embodiments of mind.* Cambridge, MA: MIT Press, 1963.
McLeish, John. *The story of numbers: How mathematics has shaped civilization.* New York: Fawcett Columbine, 1991.

McNeill, Daniel, and Paul Freiberger. *Fuzzy logic: The revolutionary computer technology that is changing our world.* New York: Simon and Schuster, 1994.

Merker, Hannah. *Listening: Ways of hearing in a silent world.* New York: HarperCollins, 1992.

Merleau-Ponty, Maurice. *Phenomenology of perception.* London: Routledge, 1962.

———. *In praise of philosophy.* Evanston, IL: Northwestern University Press, 1963.

———. *The primacy of perception.* Evanston, IL: Northwestern University Press, 1964.

Merton, Thomas. *Raids on the unspeakable.* New York: New Directions, 1964.

National Council of Teachers of Mathematics. *Curriculum and evaluation standards for school mathematics.* Reston, VA: NCTM, 1989.

———. *Professional standards for teaching mathematics.* Reston, VA: NCTM, 1991.

———. *Assessment standards for school mathematics.* Reston, VA: NCTM, 1995.

National Research Council. *Everybody counts: A report to the nation on the future of mathematics education.* Washington, DC: National Academy Press, 1989.

Noddings, Nel. "Does everybody count? Reflections on reforms in school mathematics." *Journal of Mathematical Behavior* 13, no. 1 (March 1994): 89–104.

Ong, Walter. *Orality and literacy: The technologizing of the word.* New York: Methuen, 1982.

Orr, David W. *Ecological literacy: Education and the transition to a postmodern world* Albany, NY: SUNY Press, 1992.

———. *Earth in mind: On education, environment, and the human prospect.* Washington, DC: Island Press, 1994.

Palmer, Richard E. *Hermeneutics: Interpretation theory in Schleiermacher, Dilthey, Heidegger and Gadamer.* Evanston, IL: Northwestern University Press, 1969.

Penrose, Roger. *The emperor's new mind: Concerning computers, minds, and the laws of physics.* New York: Vintage, 1989.

Piaget, Jean, and Bärbel Inhelder. *The psychology of the child.* New York: Basic Books, 1969.

Pimm, David. *Symbols and meanings in school mathematics.* London: Routledge, 1995.

Pinar, William F., editor. *Curriculum theorizing: The reconceptualists.* Berkeley, CA: McCutchan, 1975.

Pinar, William F., and Madeleine R. Grumet. *Toward a poor curriculum.* Dubuque, IA: Kendall/Hunt Publishing Company, 1976.

———. "Socratic *caesura* and the theory-practice relationship." *Contemporary curriculum discourses.* Edited by William F. Pinar. Scottsdale, AZ: Gorsuch Scarisbrick, 1988.

Pinar, William F., William M. Reynolds, Patrick Slattery, and Peter M. Taubman. *Understanding curriculum.* New York: Peter Lang, 1995.

Pirie, Susan, and Thomas Kieren. "Growth in mathematical understanding: How can we characterize it?" *Educational Studies in Mathematics* 26, no. 2–3 (March 1994): 165–190.

Pirsig, Robert. *Lila: An inquiry into morals.* New York: Bantam Books, 1991.

Popper, Karl. *The logic of scientific discovery.* London: Hutchinson, 1959.

Putnam, Hilary. *Representation and reality.* Cambridge, MA: The MIT Press, 1989.

Reddy, Michael J. "The conduit metaphor—A case of frame conflict in our language about language." *Metaphor and thought.* Edited by Andrew Ortony. New York: Cambridge University Press, 1979.

Reeves, Hubert. *Malicorne: Earthly reflections of an astrophysicist.* Toronto: Stoddart, 1993.

Rorty, Richard. *Contingency, irony, and solidarity.* New York: Cambridge University Press, 1989.

———. *Objectivity, relativism, and truth: Philosophical papers, volume 1.* New York: Cambridge University Press, 1991.

Rucker, Rudy. *Mind tools: The five levels of mathematical reality.* Boston: Houghton Mifflin, 1987.

Sacks, Oliver. "A neurologist's notebook: To see and not see." *The New Yorker,* May 10, 1993, 59–73.

———. "A neurologist's notebook: An anthropologist on Mars." *The New Yorker*, December 27, 1993, 106–125.

Sawada, Daiyo. "The converse structure of communicative classrooms." *Math monograph no. 10*. Edited by Daiyo Sawada. Edmonton, AB: Mathematics Council of the Alberta Teachers' Association, 1992.

Schafer, R. Murray. *The soundscape: Our sonic environment and the tuning of the world*. Rochester, VT: Destiny Books, 1977.

Schubert, William H. *Curriculum: Perspective, paradigm, and possibility*. New York: Macmillan Publishing Company, 1986.

———. "Philosophical inquiry: The speculative essay." *Forms of curriculum inquiry*. Edited by Edmund Short. New York: SUNY Press, 1991.

Scruton, Roger. *A short history of modern philosophy: From Descartes to Wittgenstein*. London: Routledge, 1981.

Senechal, Marjorie. "Shape." *On the shoulders of giants: New approaches to numeracy*. Edited by Lynn Arthur Steen. Washington, DC: National Academy Press, 1990.

Sfard, Anna. "On the dual nature of mathematical conceptions: Reflections on processes and objects as different sides of the same coin." *Educational Studies in Mathematics* 22, no. 1 (February 1991): 1–36.

Shelley, Nancy. *Mathematics is a language*. Paper presented at the Seventh International Congress for Mathematics Education, Quebec City, PQ, August, 1992.

Silverman, Hugh J. *Textualities: Between hermeneutics and deconstruction*. New York: Routledge, 1994.

Simmt, Elaine, and Brent Davis. "Fractal cards: A space for exploration in geometry and discrete mathematics." Forthcoming in *Mathematics Teacher*.

Skemp, Richard. *The psychology of learning mathematics*. Baltimore: Penguin Books, 1986.

Smith, David G. "Hermeneutic inquiry: The hermeneutic imagination and the pedagogic text." *Forms of curriculum inquiry*. Edited by Edmund Short. New York: SUNY Press, 1991.

Spiecker, Ben. "The pedagogical relationship." *Oxford Review of Education* 10, no. 2 (1984): 203–209.

Steen, Lynn Arthur, editor. *Mathematics today*. New York: Springer Verlag, 1980.

———. "Pattern." *On the shoulders of giants: New approaches to numeracy*. Edited by Lynn Arthur Steen. Washington, DC: National Academy Press, 1990.

Steiner, George. *Language and silence*. New York: Atheneum, 1967.

Straus, Erwin. *The primary world of senses*. Glencoe, NY: The Free Press of Glencoe, 1963.

———. *Phenomenological psychology*. New York: Basic Books, 1966.

Sumara, Dennis. "Counterfeiting." *Taboo* 1, no. 1 (Spring 1995): 94–122.

———. *Private readings in public: Schooling the literary imagination*. New York: Peter Lang, 1996.

Taylor, Charles. "The dialogical self." *The interpretive turn: Philosophy, science, culture*. Edited by David Hiley, James Bohman, and Richard Shusterman. Ithaca, NY: Cornell University Press, 1991.

———. *The malaise of modernity*. Concord, ON: Anansi, 1991.

Thompson, Alba G. "The relationship of teachers' conceptions of mathematics and mathematics teaching to instructional practice." *Educational Studies in Mathematics* 15, no. 2 (May 1984): 105–127.

Thompson, William Irwin. *Imaginary landscape: Making worlds of myth and science*. New York: St. Martin's Press, 1989.

Trinh T. Minh-ha. *Framer framed*. New York: Routledge, 1992.

Unger, Jim. *The 1st treasury of Herman*. New York: Andrews and McMeel, 1979.

van Manen, Max. *The tone of teaching*. Richmond Hill, ON: Scholastic-TAB, 1986.

———. *Researching lived experience*. Toronto: The Althouse Press, 1990.

———. *The tact of teaching*. Toronto: The Althouse Press, 1991.

van Matre, S., and B. Weiler. *The earth speaks*. Warrenville, IL: The Institute for Earth Education, 1983.

Varela, Francisco. "Laying down a path in walking." *GAIA, a way of knowing.* Edited by William Irwin Thompson. Hudson, NY: Lindisfarne, 1987.

Varela, Francisco, Evan Thompson, and Eleanor Rosch. *The embodied mind: Cognitive science and human experience.* Cambridge, MA: The MIT Press, 1991.

von Glasersfeld, Ernst. "An introduction to radical constructivism." *The invented reality.* Edited by P. Watzlawick. New York: Norton, 1984.

———. "Learning as a constructive activity." *Problems of representation in the teaching and learning of mathematics.* Edited by Claude Janvier. Hillsdale, NJ: Lawrence Erlbaum Associates, Publishers, 1987.

———. "Constructivism in education." *The international encyclopedia of education, supplementary volume.* Edited by T. Husen and T. N. Postlethwaithe. Oxford: Pergamon Press, 1989.

———. "An exposition of constructivism: Why some like it radical." *Constructivist views on the teaching and learning of mathematics* (a monograph of the *Journal for Research in Mathematics Education*). Edited by R. B. Davis, C. A. Maher, and N. Noddings. Reston, VA: National Council of Teachers of Mathematics, 1990.

———. *Aspects of radical constructivism and its educational recommendations.* Paper presented at the Seventh International Congress for Mathematics Education, Quebec City, PQ, August, 1992.

Vygotsky, Lev S. *Thought and language.* Cambridge, MA: The MIT Press, 1962.

———. *Mind in society: The development of higher psychological processes.* Cambridge, MA: Harvard University Press, 1978.

Waldrop, M. Mitchell. *Complexity: The emerging science at the edge of order and chaos.* New York: Simon and Schuster, 1992.

Walkerdine, Valerie. *The mastery of reason: Cognitive development and the production of rationality.* London: Routledge, 1988.

Weinsheimer, Joel. *Gadamer's hermeneutics: A reading of "Truth and method."* New Haven, CT: Yale University Press, 1985.

Whitehead, Alfred North. *Science and the modern world.* London: Free Association Books, 1926.

———. *The aims of education and other essays.* London: Williams and Norgate, 1932.

Young, Robert. *Critical theory and classroom talk.* Clevedon, GB: Multilingual Matter Ltd., 1992.

Index

DATE DUE
